TRAJECTORIES AND THEMES IN WORLD POPULAR MUSIC

TRAJECTORIES AND THEMES IN WORLD POPULAR MUSIC

GLOBALIZATION, CAPITALISM, IDENTITY

SIMONE KRÜGER BRIDGE

SHEFFIELD UK   BRISTOL CT

Published by Equinox Publishing Ltd.

UK: Office 415, The Workstation, 15 Paternoster Row, Sheffield, South Yorkshire S1 2BX
USA: ISD, 70 Enterprise Drive, Bristol, CT 06010

www.equinoxpub.com

First published 2018.

© Simone Krüger Bridge 2018

All rights reserved. No part of this publication may be reproduced or transmitted in any form or by any means, electronic or mechanical, including photocopying, recording or any information storage or retrieval system, without prior permission in writing from the publishers.

British Library Cataloguing-in-Publication Data
A catalogue record for this book is available from the British Library.

Library of Congress Cataloging-in-Publication Data
Names: Krüger Bridge, Simone, author.
Title: Trajectories and themes in world popular music : globalization, capitalism, identity / Simone Krüger Bridge.
Description: Bristol : Equinox Publishing Ltd, 2018. | Includes bibliographical references and index.
Identifiers: LCCN 2017040438 (print) | LCCN 2017042506 (ebook) | ISBN 9781781796238 (ePDF) | ISBN 9781781796214 (hb) | ISBN 9781781796221 (pb)
Subjects: LCSH: Popular music--Social aspects. | Popular music--Political aspects. | Music and globalization. | Popular music--History and criticism. | Dissemination of music.
Classification: LCC ML3918.P67 (ebook) | LCC ML3918.P67 B76 2018 (print) | DDC 781.63--dc23
LC record available at https://lccn.loc.gov/2017040438

ISBN: 978 1 78179 621 4 (hardback)
      978 1 78179 622 1 (paperback)
      978 1 78179 623 8 (ePDF)

Typeset by CA Typesetting Ltd, www.publisherservices.co.uk
Printed and bound in the UK by Lightning Source UK Ltd., Milton Keynes and Lightning Source Inc., La Vergne, TN

To Sheila Whiteley
(1941–2015)

Contents

Companion Website	ix
Acknowledgements	x

	Introduction	1
	A Brief History of Modern Globalization	4
	Trajectories and Themes in World Popular Music	7
1	**Popular Music before Neoliberalism**	15
	The "Birth" of Popular Music under Liberal Capitalism	16
	Popular Music during the Golden Age of (Organized) Capitalism	41
	The Other in Popular Music	59
2	**Neoliberalism and the Global Music Industry**	84
	The Cultural Logic of Neoliberalism	86
	The Global Music Industry	91
	Musical Transnationalism	125
3	**Globalization and World Music**	150
	The Birth of World Music in Britain	151
	Authentic Hybridity	158
4	**The Cool Culture of Neoliberal Capitalism**	174
	The Origins of Cool	175
	Neoliberal Capitalism as Cool Capitalism	178
	Patriarchy and Resilience in Neoliberalism	188
	Cool Masculinities	191
	Postfeminism as an Ideology of Cool	208
	Technologies of Cool	221
5	**Popular Music in Postdemocracy**	228
	Citizenship	229
	World Music and Democracy	233
	Feminism, Resistance, and Popular Music	240
	Black Nationalism and Resistance in Political Hip Hop	251

Resistance to Global Capitalism, White Nationalism,
and Popular Music   255

After Globalization   262

Bibliography   268
Index   292

Companion Website

Trajectories and Themes in World Popular Music will be of interest to the specialist market of undergraduate and postgraduate students of popular music, including those studying on courses in ethnomusicology, musicology, sociology, cultural studies, and media and communication. The companion website that accompanies this book provides students and instructors with ready-to-use teaching and learning materials, including PowerPoint slides and instructor's manuals; essay and discussion questions, including sample essays; web links to related readings, listening examples, and music videos; videography of relevant documentaries; and hands-on learning activities. These resources are free of charge and designed to maximize the learning experience. The book's companion website is available at https://www.equinoxpub.com/home/instructor-resources-trajectories-themes-world-popular-music/.

Acknowledgements

This book represents to me an important culmination of my professional and academic work to date. As a banking operations manager and university student of business economics and marketing in the early 1990s, I had to reflect on the impact of economic globalization on the transnational corporate landscape that shaped the world post-1989 (myself stemming from the former Communist bloc). Subsequently during 2000, I became increasingly interested in the role played by cultural and musical globalization, specifically intercultural music education seen from an anthropological perspective, while drawing on theoretical foundations and music-cultural insights from ethnomusicology. In 2009, I hosted an international conference for the British Forum for Ethnomusicology under the theme "Music, Culture and Globalization", which led to a co-edited book exploring the current themes of tourism and migration in the study of musics under globalizing conditions, followed by ethnographic research exploring the impact of cultural globalization in two geographical contexts, and the conception and editorial leadership of the *Journal of World Popular Music*. This book brings together these themes, experiences, and trajectories in a concise introduction to modern popular music studies, and is the culmination of fifteen years of teaching modules on world music cultures, World Music, gender and sexuality, race and ethnicity, music censorship, and musical globalization. I am indebted to a vast number of people throughout this time, whose support and advice have shaped and continue to contribute to my engagement with and teaching of popular music in world perspective. I am indebted to all my former and current academic colleagues at Liverpool John Moores University, research collaborators and editorial colleagues, and in particular Britta Sweers and Janet Joyce, for providing useful comments on the final draft. Over the years, my students have been a great source of musical inspiration and pleasure that had an effect on the final manuscript. Thanks also to the anonymous reviewers for their valuable feedback and comments, as well as to everyone at Equinox Publishing for believing in this book and handling it so efficiently through its revision. My sincere gratitude goes to copy-editor Sarah Norman, who attended to the most meticulous details during the manuscript preparation process. Personally, I am greatly indebted to my husband and son, David and Lorcan Pío, who continue to enrich my life in unexpected ways.

In 2008, I had the great privilege to personally meet feminist musicologist, researcher, and writer Sheila Whiteley, who over the years became an inspiring role model and critical friend to me. As external examiner, Sheila became very familiar with my approaches to teaching popular music in world perspective, which have greatly informed the final text. In gratitude, I would like to dedicate this book to Sheila Whiteley.

Introduction

This book offers a way to study world popular music from the perspective of critical social theory. It is about understanding popular music within the context of modern globalization and as a result of globalization since the modern era. The different processes and issues inherent in modern globalization have been variously labelled westernization, modernization, urbanization, secularization, industrialization, commercialization, commodification, homogenization, hybridization, and democratization before it became a buzzword in the 1980s.[1] Modern globalization goes hand in hand with European expansionism and colonialism, industrialization and modernization, capitalism, shifts in technology and production, the movement of populations, the sudden extensions in the circulation of commodities, and the worldwide spread of representations of hegemonic beliefs. It is a term that has been applied to global culture, global economy, global trade, global capital, global migration and movement of people, global society, global ideas and beliefs, global warming, global governance, and so on. Clearly, then, globalization is a messy concept, yet some things have come to be associated with it: the end of the nation-state, brought about by shifts in economic systems and technological innovation; new technological forms that made the world faster and smaller, and have shaped and play a key role in the new economic system, including air travel, computer technologies, and new media forms like the internet and mobile phones; and changes in economic practices like just-in-time manufacturing, global production chains, and international labor outsourcing. Yet rather than a system, globalization is better understood as a powerful *discourse* that helps to conceptualize globalizing processes and effects, and that it was used to obscure and disguise "capitalism" since the Cold War (Cazdyn and Szeman 2011: 20). So while modern globalization described the transformations in economics, culture, politics, and ideology since the nineteenth and twentieth centuries, *capitalism* has reappeared in the early twenty-first century in narratives of the globalized "system" in attempts to describe the circumstances now faced by people around the world.

The discourse of globalization captures transformations in politics, technologies, and economy, which, combined, brought about a historical phase-change. It captures the meetings of cultures, collaborations, and conflicting ambitions that resonate with the divided viewpoints about and attitudes toward globalization, and whether it should be celebrated, or not. On the one hand, globalization was an effective concept in extending US hegemony after the Cold War, while on the other, it also offered possibility and promise: Globalization was, on the whole, greeted positively, pointing to new possibilities for human communities and the overcoming of the nation-state system and the promise of cosmopolitanism. Its discourse captured the possibility of real, imagined, and fantasized travel and movements across borders, and new forms of communication and human interrelations, leading to new hybrid or post-national identities. It offered the promise of a global rise in living standards, and novel experiences with new, innovative technologies. In short, "the 'one world' narrative of globalization generated energies for an economics and politics other than the status quo of capitalism and liberal democracy" (Cazdyn and Szeman 2011: 28). The circuit of cultural globalization involves at least three theoretical approaches: first, it has been linked to the idea of cultural imperialism and a resultant world monoculture marked by cultural homogenization; second, it is characteristic of transnational, multi-directional cultural flows, including counter-hegemonic ones; and third, it has shaped the emergence of truly global communities and cultural networks. Popular music is inextricably linked to modern globalization. Globalization is mirrored by developments in the music industry, which has developed from a local grassroots business to a global industry with rapid expansion of both the recording and aligned entertainment industries. It is true that globalization has led to the homogenization of popular music, and yet there is also strong demand for musical hybridization, cross-fertilization, syncretism, and/or the preservation of local music practices. While transnational music corporations may control the circulation of music culturally, world popular music is not simply the product of a dominant western culture.

One of the key drivers and effects of globalization has been the global movement of people, including migrant underclasses, a vital element in the creation and transmission of globalized, hybrid cultural products like popular music, which in turn resonates with, reflects, and models the new sociocultural identities that have emerged as a result of the global movement of people. Thus, alongside an interest in unpacking the impact of global capitalism on world popular music, the book seeks to illustrate notions of identity, power, and inequality as these are reflected, represented, and challenged in contemporary musical expressions around the world. It explores the juxtaposition of phenomena like the commodification of the other, authenticity, and capitalism versus social citizenship, advocacy, and responsibility. Identity is a powerful concept to understand social difference and belonging. Identity creates communality, belonging, sameness, continuity, and thus inclusion in one collective, as well as separation and exclusion from another. It is socially constructed and discursively defined in order to categorize self vs. others. Categorization highlights difference, marked by the politics of othering, which implies a necessary other who is not "us" and unlike "us".

Since identity creates classifications of inclusion and exclusion, sameness and difference, the concepts of power and inequality are hugely relevant in popular music studies, and raise questions as to where power is situated and how inequality is experienced in the contemporary world, answers to which can be found by looking at the historical, social, and cultural factors that have shaped these notions. This book seeks to illustrate this by contextualizing these shaping factors historically, economically, socially, and culturally. Historically and economically, the book explores the development of a global culture marked by the birth, growth, and global expansion of capitalism and, in turn, a highly concentrated, commercialized global music industry. Culturally and socially, it discusses the ways in which hegemonic concepts have assumed constructed meanings that are applied to identity characteristics of others, highlighting the ways in which inequality and prejudice are constructed in the representations of world popular music. It illustrates forms of democratization and resistance to the spread of western culture, beliefs, practices, and norms through the lenses of citizenship, democracy, and global civility, while considering audiences animated by social justice and cosmopolitan imagination, who challenge global capitalism's commodification of the gendered, sexualized, racialized other. Showing how both individual and group identities do away with "traditional" understandings of core and periphery, the book challenges issues of social stratification, used to order society into hierarchies of people for the purpose of privileges, and seeks to understand social injustices, such as discrimination, stereotyping, and disadvantage.

We are living through a new period since the early noughties, an interregnum in the age of postdemocracy, in which neoliberalism is fading and the new period, an "after globalization", is just beginning to be born among uncertainty. The book deconstructs established and newer critical social theories and contributes to emerging debates on culture, identity, power, and inequality seen through the lens of musical globalization as it is manifested, expressed, and represented in popular music across a number of continents and musical styles. It seeks to provide a powerful contemporary framework for contemporary popular music studies with a distinctive global and interdisciplinary awareness, covering empirical research from across the world in addition to well-established and newer theory from the music disciplines, social sciences, and humanities. In doing so, the book offers fresh conceptualizations about world popular music seen within the context of cultural, economic, technological, and historical globalization.

A Brief History of Modern Globalization

Globalization is an important catchword for both proponents and opponents of today's globalized world. Although often represented as a coherent system, since the early 2000s globalization has come to be understood as a discourse, and as a "set of processes or effects across widely different spheres of social life, tossed together for a specific end and effect" (Cazdyn and Szeman 2011: 20). As a discourse, "globalization" helped to conceptualize globalizing processes and effects, and to disguise the spread of global capitalism since the 1940s. The consequences of globalization thus remain a subject of significant contention, particularly in regards to whether globalization results in positive or negative outcomes for individuals, cultures, and societies in the contemporary world. As Philip Bohlman suggests, there is a "paradox in the rhetoric and reality of globalisation ... both good and bad, a worldview to be celebrated and vilified ... and most people ally themselves with one or the other" (2002: i–ii).

Globalization can be regarded as a phenomenon with a long history, given that social, cultural, and market integration and exchange is as old as humanity (see also Steger 2017). In music studies, however, the beginnings of globalization are often located in the modern era (Stokes 2004). Modern globalization has its roots in the colonization of the Americas, Africa, and Asia by the dominant economic powers of Europe from ca. 1500 to 1850. This time was marked by European expansionism during the colonization of large parts of America and Oceania by the Spanish, British, French, and Portuguese. Globalization is seen as the consequence of imperialism and, with it, the spread of European culture, institutions, and Christianity. Europe's relationship to the rest of the world was marked by domination and abuse, exploration and discovery of the Americas and Australasia; the repressive policies against and extermination of colonized people; the colonization and colonialism in Africa, Middle East, India, Pakistan, and parts of the Asia-Pacific region (among others), which involved control and domination of indigenous people through European laws; the exploitation of the natural resources of colonized lands and the labor of indigenous people; imperialism and the emergence of European empires (e.g. Dutch, French, German, and British); and the integration of ethnic groups or minorities into the dominant or colonizing culture while eradicating difference and rendering it invisible. It was specifically the British Empire that provided the framework for present-day globalization, which grew out of the economic style (based on imperial trade) of the British Empire, rather than the strategies deployed by the Dutch, Spanish, Portuguese, or French, and formed the foundations of a global economic system based on capitalism, whereby profits were reinvested in Jamaican real estate, rather than spent recklessly, and the cultivation of sugar saw Britain thrive from what once was a mere agricultural economy (Ferguson 2003). The British Empire united the world under a single capitalist economy since the seventeenth century and, as a result, became the world's first mass-consumer society. The subsequent historical event of colonialism in the eighteenth and nineteenth centuries impacted on the major current ideas of western culture, while shaping the West's ideas about itself and others. Eurocentric ideology has been profoundly shaped by the nineteenth-century belief in European racial superiority as a means to justify Europe's colonialism, supported first by religious, then by anthropological, and later by scientific discourses, which aimed at demonstrating that whites were more advanced, civilized, and moral than the colonized people. Europeans were discursively constructed as more fully evolved, more civilized than other racialized groups; other races needed "civilizing", a "burdensome task" of maintaining order and control and establishing right and wrong bestowed upon Europeans—"the white man's burden".

Modern globalization points toward the 1940s as the beginnings of globalizing tendencies when globalization became inextricably linked to the evolution of capitalism in major industrial economies (e.g. North America, Western Europe) (Lash and Urry 1994; Giddens 1990). Unlike market capitalism (ca. 1700–1850) and modernism's monopoly capitalism (ca. 1850–1945), the new phase since the 1940s is marked by "organized capitalism" (Lash and Urry 1987) and "late capitalism" (Jameson 1991), the latter being the dominant term in the 1980s and 1990s and later replaced by the term "neoliberal capitalism".[2] The shift toward neoliberal capitalism involved a shift in economic practice. From the 1940s, the western economies adhered to Fordism as an economic practice, characterized by large-scale production of standardized goods for mass consumption, and accompanied by a developing culture of promotion and advertising. However, in the 1970s, saturated western markets and overproduction, combined with competition from Japan and newly industrialized countries (e.g. Taiwan, Korea, Singapore), led to a restructuring of the economies toward post-Fordism. Instead of uniformity and standardization, post-Fordism began to involve flexible, variable production for niche markets (e.g. customized specialization) and internationalization in search for new markets, made possible by new communication technologies emerging in the 1980s, such as satellite and cable. The shift toward neoliberal capitalism also involved a shift from a Keynesian theory of the relationship between the government and the economy, whereby the economy and social well-being programs are regulated by the government, toward a post-Keynesian ("neoliberal") theory, whereby the government is not expected to play a role in regulating the economy and in sustaining social programs for general well-being (Ortner 2011).

In the economic context, the emergence of modern globalization is often associated with Marshall McLuhan's invocation of the "global village" in the 1960s (1964: 3) and his predictions of what social theorist David Harvey later termed "time-space compression" (Harvey 1989: 284), the acceleration of instantaneous global communication that would benefit transnational corporations. Consequently, globalization has resulted from the ascension of powerful, transnational corporations (TNCs) in search for new markets beyond national borders. The TNC is characterized by its transnational perspective in terms of production, operation, and investment, maintaining facilities across countries to reduce costs and maximize capital profits. Meanwhile, the collapse of the Eastern bloc in the late 1980s led to further TNC cross-border expansion in former communist countries. Satellite services, such as CNN (Cable News Network), MTV (Music Television), and ESPN (Entertainment and Sports Network) grew into truly global enterprises, with transnational corporations crossing and undermining sovereign national states "with varying prospects of power, orientations, identities and networks" (Beck 2000: 11). Today, the major economies, sometimes referred to as the OECD countries (Organization of Economic Cooperation and Development), are globally oriented and integrated, and dominated by transnational trade. Globalization is thus a consequence of the development of modern capitalist societies, marked by digitization and the accumulation of capital on transnational markets. Its fundamental principles are commodification, commercialization, and consumerism on a supranational level. In this way, the term "globalization" assumes a western-centric position to describe the worldwide domination of western (notably American) concepts, beliefs, and practices.

This book adopts two fundamental contexts for modern globalization: the economic and the non-economic context, the latter to include socio-cultural, historical, and political dimensions (see also Sengupta 2001: 3138), while both contexts are interdependent from one another. Globalization is therefore viewed differently, depending on which context is privileged. The economist perspective usually concentrates on the hardcore economics and the global economic disparity between the richest fifth of the world's population and the poorest fifth since the 1960s (Kurien 1999: 3654), even though this perspective tells us nothing about the quality of life or state of culture. Nevertheless, it is generally accepted today that the history of early capitalism has been one borne out of racism and sexism, with the means of production and distribution firmly placed in the hands of white (European) men. The subsequent evolution of capitalism in the name of economic globalization has led to "imperialist white supremacist capitalist patriarchy" (hooks 2004: 17) and "multi-racial white supremacist patriarchy" (James 2015: 12), terms for twentieth and early twenty-first-century globalized western race/gender/sexuality/capitalist hegemony. These forms of hegemony have in turn impacted on the trajectories and themes surrounding much world popular music.

Trajectories and Themes in World Popular Music

In most parts of the world, the boundaries between popular music, art music, and traditional music are fictive. Popular music in modern capitalist societies is generally of primarily urban origin that is intended for secular entertainment, whose production and consumption are not intrinsically associated with "traditional" life-cycle functions or rituals (see also Manuel 1988: 1–3; Langlois 2011: xiv–xvi).[3] Popular music often has its "official" beginnings in the 1950s (Bennett 2001; British Music Experience 2016; Moore 2011: ix; Regev 2013),[4] and its discourses have been preoccupied with a canonical focus on American and British white and "black" popular music since the 1950s (Langlois 2011: xiii) (see also Longhurst 2007). Discussions of popular music outside the West are also often the domain of ethnomusicologists,[5] who have since the 1980s began to focus their attention on world popular music due to the dissolution of the holistic concept of culture, the emergence of popular music studies in the 1980s, and the globalizing trends and processes that impacted on the traditional music they were typically studying (e.g. Langlois 2011; Marre and Charlton 1985a; Manuel 1988). The history of popular music, here, often begins in the late nineteenth century with the mass production opportunities provided by early sound recording technologies. Historically, cultures were assumed to be historically more or less stable, principally closed systems, and as relatively consistent and corresponding to a geographical space. In the 1980s, this holistic concept of culture was increasingly brought into question, and ethnic and other social groups became understood as "imagined communities" (Anderson 1983). Consequently, ethnomusicologists began to incorporate insights from popular music studies and shifted their attention to music cultures "created out of contact histories and colonial legacies, out of diaspora and hybridity, out of migration, urbanization and mass media", and expanded their focus of research beyond live performance to include musical recordings as objects of their study (Feld 2000: 10–11). Since then, studies of world popular music have surfaced in academic writings (see, for instance, the *Journal of World Popular Music*, the first journal dedicated to the study of world popular music), as well as in commercial circles with the lucrative breakthrough of World Music.

Much focus in popular music studies has been placed on understanding popular music as a commodity or to critique the global music industry, often based on an assumption that musical production is capitalist, while viewing capitalism as an economic system. The economic context is clearly important in discussions on musical globalization, yet this has led to a mythical, widespread belief in the 1950s as the birth year of popular music in the US. In reality, the long-term event of musical globalization has lasted, historically, from sometime in the nineteenth century and reached its peak during the 1990s with the emergence of satellite, cable, and digital technologies. This book works accordingly and adopts the three phases in the history of capitalist hegemony since the nineteenth century—liberal, organized, and neoliberal capitalism—to consider world popular music in each of these cultural contexts. It regards capitalism as a cultural system that has since its earliest beginnings profoundly shaped the production, distribution, and consumption of world popular music, as well as people's social relations, experiences, and perceptions.

The book considers the historical dimensions of musical globalization, conceptualized here through terms like modernization and industrialism, globalization, neoliberalism, postdemocracy, and the period after globalization. While the book is laid out chronologically, it does not strictly adhere to the timeline so as to allow explorations of consequential threads and themes, many of which are parallel, concurrent, or overlapping across periods. Indeed, like organic growth in nature, the trajectories of world popular music are non-linear. Concepts, issues, and themes are explored interpretatively and interspersed with musical examples and facts throughout the book. The detail of explanations across them is not entirely nuanced and there are untold musical contributors who are not honored here, which does not imply any meaning about their worth or importance. Famous and not-so-famous individuals are used primarily to exemplify examples of a style, period, shift, or concept and not because their contributions are more important than others. The organization of content historically and according to the evolution of capitalist hegemony since the nineteenth century helps to define and understand world popular music with a more inclusive and distinctive global awareness, while bringing together pertinent themes and issues that span across historical, economic, technological, social, and cultural dimensions.

Chapter 1 considers world popular music before neoliberalism. The chapter is divided into three parts that discuss musical modernization under the influence of liberal capitalism (in the first section) and organized capitalism (in the second section), exploring the early/subsequent trajectories and themes related to modern globalization from the late nineteenth century through the mid-twentieth century and until the 1970s. This is followed (in section three) by considering the othering processes rooted within capitalism and, by default, musical globalization.

Under the influence of liberal capitalism (nineteenth century–1940s), musical modernization meant to balance the advantages of western advancements, including the adoption and integration of western sound recording and broadcasting technology and other products of western culture, alongside an insistence that the core of cultural values remains unchanged and different to the West. In this way, compatible but non-central elements of the music could be adopted, coupled with the changing of aspects of the old system in order to save its essence. Across the globe, musical modernization went hand in hand with urbanization—the development of vast urban centers as a result of industrialization. The new urban societies were a fertile breeding ground for new syncretic music, which around the world often were (and still are) created in such a way as to syncretize and reinterpret "old" and "new" elements of culture. Many musicians aimed to modernize their music for economic reasons, but also for reasons associated with personal, social, and cultural values. The emergent syncretic popular music embodied and expressed the hybrid social identities of the new urban classes in the US, Europe, and elsewhere. New technologies and mass media since the nineteenth century have aided the wide dissemination of popular music and its commodification for profit. The media, in particular, have played a crucial role in bringing foreign styles to countries around the world, expediting musical fusions, and contributing to global cross-fertilizations, with popular styles emerging with the growth of urban centers that became melting pots for interethnic and interracial contact and conflict. The emerging popular music blended many characteristics of its local and traditional forms with imported, usually western, forms alongside a desire for musical modernization. The phase of musical modernization has transformed indigenous and national cultural formations under the impact of the spread of western culture on musical practices since the nineteenth century.

During the subsequent phase in the history of capitalist hegemony, the Golden Age of Capitalism (1945 until mid-1970s), the US was able to build a successful economy, including a dominating music recording industry, which became driven by the logic of organized capitalism and Fordism as an economic practice, and led toward a "democratic moment" in Western Europe and the US. Since the 1960s, nations in Western Europe and Asia adopted similar economic models and witnessed a huge economic rise. This time marked the beginnings of an increasingly integrated and concentrated music recording industry, while "youth" emerged as a new social class and became a new target market for youth-oriented popular music. The post-war era marked the enormous success of rock 'n' roll in the 1950s and of rock in the 1960s, while electric instruments transformed the sound of popular music. The electronic musical revolution, along with western pop-rock music, spread globally and has affected music cultures all over the world. The structure and workings of the US-based music recording industry became replicated in the local music industries of countries around the world, so that international music industries became similarly marked by the standardization of production patterns and the pop-rock aesthetic. Western pop-rock music spread worldwide, initially via covers of Anglo-American stars and hits and subsequently via more localized versions of pop-rock music within a national context. The creative practices by musicians around the world have led to the emergence of "hybrid" musical forms by merging and fusing ethno-national heritage and pop-rock music.

In considering the economic and technological dimensions of globalization and their impact upon society and culture, Chapter 1 is also concerned with the politics of othering in popular music under liberal and organized capitalism, as these have been born out of historical, economic, social, and cultural manifestations of globalization. Representations in modern popular culture help us understand the way that popular music functions in constructing difference and otherness through racialized and gendered discourses within the hegemonic order of the global music business and wider society, as these are shaped by imperialist white supremacist capitalist patriarchy. Critical discussions of othering processes help us understand the construction and negotiation of race and gender/sexuality in everyday social practices, cultural encounters, and popular discourses, and that terms like race and gender are ambiguous, contested concepts that have no relation to biological differences between groups of humans, but are socioculturally constructed in different places and at different times. The chapter illustrates this by focusing on politics of othering through racialized and gendered representations in popular music since its beginnings in the late nineteenth century.

Chapter 2 moves on to the phase of neoliberalism that began in the 1970s (even though it only become a dominant term since about 2000). Neoliberalism emerged as a result of the rise of free-market ideas, policies, and institutions, and led literally to the collapse of the modernist project in many parts of the world, while acquiring a different and more consistently dark meaning. For many poor communities within rich nations, as well as for many poor nations in an increasingly unbalanced world, the neoliberal world order has led to gross injustices, and has meant that the rich become richer and the poor are staying poor or becoming poorer. The 1980s marked a new era, "the most recent regime of globalization" (Taylor 2014: 193), which was driven by the emergence of new technologies, such as satellite and cable, the collapse of the Eastern communist bloc and "truly" global reach of TNCs, and the evolution of neoliberal capitalism.[6] This was a period marked by more intense globalizing tendencies, intensified musical commodification and cultural homogenization, and the consolidation of neoliberal capitalism in major industrial economies. The structures and workings of the global music industry illustrate this, dominated by the growth of transnational music corporations and their expansionist strategy in the name of corporate capitalism. Much academic thinking during the 1970s and 1980s was dominated by the idea of cultural imperialism, which was believed to lead to a global capitalist monoculture. In popular music discourses, analyses of the structure and workings of the global music industry often drew neo-Gramscian conclusions about the resultant musical diversity, or lack thereof. The 1980s also marked a shift toward a global preoccupation with "image" (notably on MTV) and the sexualized female form that serves to objectify women. Concepts in feminist media analyses like the "male gaze" and "controlling images" became powerful tools for analyzing and critiquing traditional white supremacist patriarchy, including the representation of black women and femininities. In considering the politics of othering in neoliberal culture, it is equally critical to highlight that the remnants of racist identity constructions still reverberated throughout this phase. While obvious racist stereotypes in mediated representations became rare, more subtle and hidden racialized narratives continued to be expressed in popular music. Since the early 1990s, academic thinking gradually moved away from the theory of cultural imperialism and toward explanations of globalizing trends through the lens of hybridization, conceptualized through the idea of "expressive isomorphism", a term to describe the way that cultural globalization has led to the growing connectivity, proximity, and overlap between popular music cultures around the world. Aesthetic cosmopolitanism is a useful concept to understand world culture as "one complexly interconnected entity" (Regev 2013: 3). We now live in a world marked by global cultural interconnectedness, cultural hybridization, and musical participation, through which the global becomes received in new and different ways in different locales.

Chapter 3 is rooted in the 1980s when many music consumers in the West yearned for new, more authentic and meaningful music as rock and punk's appeal began to wane and popular culture was dominated by a glitzy, artificial world of chart-friendly pop. The "new" soundtrack of globalization was the commercial pseudo-genre of World Music, which was constructed on notions surrounding authenticity, difference, and otherness. Using the notion of genre as a sociocultural framework, the World Music genre is seen here as a subfield referring to specific musical and extra-musical conventions that pertain primarily to the sphere of production. The branding of World Music illustrates the way that popular music is organized and maintained in the form of genres as a means for music industries to streamline production, and as a source of pleasure or identification for audiences and consumers. The commodification practices surrounding World Music discourses are shaped by concepts of authenticity, difference, and otherness. Genre is thereby a constructed, flux concept, and this is well illustrated by how and why musicians become constructed and (in some cases) successful as World Music stars within the World Music brand. Commercial interests in World Music are characterized by a certain academicism among consumers coupled with a "serious" educational interest in the music cultures they encounter, thereby distinguishing themselves from others through their specialized musical knowledge and cultural interests in more "authentic" musics. Yet World Music is characteristic of both hybridity and authenticity, which resembles some kind of paradox between the mixing of musical styles, on the one hand, and a desire to leave a musical "tradition" intact, on the other. Artists who "make it" as World Music stars must therefore navigate carefully between hybridity and authenticity, and western consumers' ideas and expectations of "authentic hybridity".

Chapter 4 moves on to explore the way that popular music consumption in the noughties became influenced by a new cultural logic—the cool and the hip. In the age of neoliberal capitalism, the ideology of cool determines cultural production and consumption, and has thereby become the focal point of popular culture globally, influencing a diverse range of contemporary trends and fields from food, music, and fashion, to technology and cinema. The hip and the cool are examples of non-economic forms of value created through branding practices. Coolness has become an incredibly powerful concept within business and marketing. It is a universal motivator for teens and youths, as well as for a large range of other age groups. Coolness excites consumers, adds symbolic value to products, and drives consumer trends. Coolness and consumption are intrinsically linked. Consumption in postmodern popular culture is central to identity formation and acquisition of status, triggering in consumers the desire to achieve a cool lifestyle through consumption. The cool culture of neoliberal capitalism is clearly evident in the branding processes surrounding the "cool celebrity personae", relevant to which is artists' resilience to contemporary forms of (gendered, racist) patriarchy presented in much contemporary world popular music. Chapter 4 illustrates the way that coolness is gendered, exploring cool masculinities and cool postfeminism in world popular music, while showing "our" cultural complicities with patriarchy and the persistence of racism and sexism in cool popular culture globally. Moreover, cool technologies have further contributed to the veritable explosion of commodity fetishism and cool seduction under cool capitalism. Cool (neoliberal) popular culture extols celebrity and success, and promotes and celebrates values of the public self and possessive individualism.

Chapter 5 focuses on the postdemocratic conditions of today's neoliberal culture and asks important questions about the role of social democratic citizenship, conceptualized here through the role of popular music in democracy and resistance. Real World (music label), The Elders (governance collective), and Witness (charity) are all examples of social democratic citizenship which show that a more optimistic, moral stance toward globalization is possible. Democracy and resistance are also at play through the role played by feminism and the civil rights and anti-racism movements in popular music within the hegemonic order of the global music business and wider society. Popular music can indeed function in opposition to the cultural hegemonic norm. Unequal power structures and stereotypical and oppressive role models have been revealed, challenged, and resisted by feminist and postcolonial musical practices, a reminder of the way that race, gender, and class have assumed constructed meanings that are applied to identity characteristics of others, and highlighting the ways in which inequality and prejudice are constructed in the representations of popular music. This chapter highlights local forms of resistance to the spread of western culture, beliefs, practices, and norms through the lenses of hybridity, democracy, and global civility, considering audiences animated by social justice and cosmopolitan imagination, who challenge global capitalism's commodification of the gendered, exotic, and racialized other. Yet, troubling as it may seem, neoliberalism has also led to periodic outbreaks of conservative, nationalist, right-wing socialism, and some popular music has served as a powerful means to negotiate, express, and model ethnocentric political identities. When aligned politically with the "Right", such popular music is often most directly concerned with right-wing socialism and white nationalism. Some of these movements do, of course, raise concerns and questions regards their compatibility with democracy. Yet they do share with the anti-globalization movement a discontent with postdemocracy, internationalism, and the consequences of uncontrolled global capitalism.

Notes

1. According to the Oxford dictionary, the word globalization was first employed in the 1930s and entered the Merriam-Webster dictionary in 1951. It was used by economists and social scientists by the 1960s, but became widely accepted as a term with the publication of Theodore Levitt's paper "The Globalization of Markets" in 1983.

2. There is no clear-cut distinction between late capitalism and neoliberalism; neoliberalism is "simply late capitalism made conscious, carried to extremes, and having more visible effects" (Ortner 2011: n.p.).

3. Popular music also involves a "star system", "wherein the media promote personality cults around the musician's life-style, fashions, or private life, which aims to distance

the artist from the public [in order] to weave an aura of fantasy and glamour about him" (Manuel 1988: 3). Popular music is characterized by a high turnover of repertoire, with the aim "to promote continual interest in the most recent releases of an artist" (Manuel 1988: 3).

4. It is important to note here that popular music existed well before the mass media came into existence, but it is difficult, in the period before the twentieth century in Europe and America, to distinguish meaningfully between classical, folk, and popular music, which in turn explains the fact that journalistic and academic discourses on popular music history either began in the late nineteenth century or in the 1950s.

5. Even before the emergence of ethnomusicology in the 1950s, Europeans have long collected traditional music from the countryside and from exotic, faraway places outside their homelands in the belief that the "real" traditional music was dying out (Nettl 2005). What they did not realize at the time was that music is never static and is constantly changing due to inside and outside pressures.

6. This development coincided with a political move in some countries, including Britain and the US, toward the celebration of multiculturalism.

1 Popular Music before Neoliberalism

Beginning in the late nineteenth century and lasting into the 1930s, the transition from tradition to modernity (in the Weberian sense) swept across Europe, the US, and other parts of the world when new sound recording and broadcasting technologies revolutionized the way that music could be objectified and commodified. Modernization coincided with processes of urbanization and early industrialization, early capitalism and westernization around the world, and the spread of institutionalized forms of education. It meant a gradual development from "traditional" to "modern" societies in many parts of the world. Musical modernization similarly meant a gradual development toward modernizing "traditional" music and, with it, the emergence of so-called "popular traditions": "a shift from active musical production to passive pop consumption, the decline of folk or community or subcultural traditions, and a general loss of musical skill" (Frith 1988: 11). New sound recording and broadcasting technologies were a major source of this change in many parts of the world, as people responded to the new technologies. Across the world, music changed under the impact of modernization and commodification in a number of ways, ranging from people's desire to leave traditional culture intact (resistance), modernization of traditional culture, or complete westernization and assimilation into western cultural systems (Nettl 1983, 2005).

Resistance, modernization, and westernization have variously dominated academic discussions. The complete westernization of music by changing a traditional music culture in the direction of the western, and thereby total loss or abandonment of the musical tradition, seems rarely to have happened. The arrival of western music may have reduced traditional practices, musical instruments, or traditional technology, but traditional music has continued to exist in some (altered, recast) form. The most dominant response therefore occurred in the realm of musical modernization, brought on largely by economic reasons, but also for reasons associated with personal, social, and cultural values, including "the quest for status, participation, and parity in modern world culture" (Regev 2013: 10). Musical modernization meant the spread of western influence to many parts of the world, and it succeeded due to western music's perceived complexity, specifically classical and art music, its accompanying technology, and economic power. Cultural idioms like music became absorbed, indigenized, and domesticated at the collective, institutional, and individual level as vehicles for modernizing national culture. The term musical modernization is thereby a useful theme to understand the dramatic social, industrial, and economic changes in Europe, the US, and elsewhere. Under the influence of modernism's capitalism, music, like other cultural expressions, gradually became a commodity, and, linked to an overarching process of rationalization with heightened importance of the individual, individual musicians, specifically within the European high art tradition, were elevated to the status of "genius".

The "Birth" of Popular Music under Liberal Capitalism

Since the mid-nineteenth century, the historical event of "our" globalization meant the Europeanization of parts of the world, characterized at the time by an acceleration of global networks and cultural flows, and mass migrations of Europeans to the New World and (later) Australia and New Zealand, which transformed the continents technologically, culturally, socially, and otherwise. Industrialization, concepts of European "high" culture and taste, and explorations of other, exotic cultures intensified European influence around the world. Old forms of market capitalism (ca. 1700–1850) became gradually replaced by modernism's monopoly capitalism (ca. 1850–1930). The latter phase of capitalist development is often labelled *liberal* capitalism, which emerged nationally and soon spread, through international trade, internationally. Under liberal capitalism, principles of trade with legal arrangements to facilitate business and mass production were put into practice by the British bourgeoisie, backed up by capitalist exploitation and class domination by military force (McGuigan 2016: 120). Slavery was abolished and child labor curtailed. World history was now written in such a way to valorize Europe, and its advances in technology and science, literature and art, and to spread concepts of rationality and creativity as superior over the rest of the world. Geographical knowledge placed Europe at the center of the then unknown world, conceiving the rest of the world as an accessible entity that could be explored and exploited. Many countries willingly adopted European culture, institutions, Christianity, and other European standards, including the Gregorian calendar and Greenwich meridian. In other parts of the world, meanwhile, music changed under the impact of westernization and commodification in a number of ways, ranging from people's desire to leave traditional culture intact, modernization of traditional culture, or complete westernization and assimilation into western cultural systems.

Technologies of Musical Industrialism
Beginning in the late nineteenth century, new technologies of sound recording emerged that paved a new, even revolutionary way for music to be objectified and commodified. Prior to sound recordings and beginning in the late fifteenth century, music was already objectified in the form of published scores. Since the seventeenth century, music became commodified for profit as live sound at public concerts, which coincided with the emergence of concert halls and theaters in urban centers. However, new technologies of sound recording like the player piano and phonograph that emerged in the late nineteenth century and radio broadcasting in the 1920s, coupled with the influence of liberal capitalism, meant that music, like other cultural expressions, gradually became a different kind of mass commodity. During the 1920s and 1930s, new music professions developed, including the professional pop singer, session musician, A&R person, record producer, disc jockey, studio engineer, and critic. The industrialization of sheet music and recorded music production and broadcasting led to a shift in people's perception of music as a commodity that has exchange value and profoundly transformed musical experience per se. At the same time, individual musicians, specifically within the European high art tradition, were elevated to the status of "genius", a concept that spread to and became similarly important as a signifier of musical quality, artistry, and creativity in other parts of the world. Records and radio not only impacted on new national and, later, international tastes, but also "set up new social divisions between 'classical' and 'pop' audiences" (Frith 1988: 13). The period of musical modernization was thus marked more generally by the production of cultural commodities, the changing nature of music as a commodity, the rise of the ideology of exchangeability, the rise of the individual artist and concept of genius, and the rise of social class and, with it, differences in cultural production and consumption (Burgess 2014; Gronow and Saunio 1998).

The close relationship between popular music with the mass media is its most important distinguishing feature (Manuel 1988: 4–7). By 1900, the phonograph and its successor, the gramophone, became the first mass-recording devices, followed later by the LP, cassette and CD, MD and MP3 recording format, as well as video and DVD as a widespread medium for the dissemination of popular music. The invention of sound recording began as early as 1877, and its development coincided with the creation of huge industrial enterprises in fashion, photography, telephony, telegraphy, and moving pictures at the end of the nineteenth century. Phonograph recordings from the 1890s included banjo and cornet solos, humorous and sentimental songs, and brass band selections were sold, and jukeboxes installed, in public entertainment venues. The recording industry was born. The phonograph wrought a revolution in people's relationship to recorded music, as for the first time music became characterized by its increased sonic transportability, enabling people to listen to and buy music many miles away from its creator. The Deutsche Grammophon Company (est. 1898) and the US-based Victor Talking Machine Company (est. 1901) marketed this new sound reproduction technology by using "local" sounds from around the world and distributing them "translocally". The newly established record companies shared out territories around the world: Victor "got" North and South America, and Eastern Asia; Grammophon got Europe, the rest of Asia, Africa, and Australia (Gronow and Saunio 1998: 11). They also established local subsidiaries in more important countries. In the early twentieth century, the companies' recording technologists embarked on recording trips to Europe, Russia, and more exotic places, including Georgia, India, Burma, Thailand, China, and Japan to record music for the local markets (Gronow and Saunio 1998: 12). American recording technicians also toured the musical centers of South America, recording popular styles like Mexican *corrido*, Trinidadian *calypso*, Cuban *son* and *rumba*, Argentinian *tango*, and Hawaiian music for distribution in local, European, and American markets (Gronow and Saunio 1998: 30–32). Tourism, romantic Hollywood movies, and touring orchestras from, say, Cuba and Mexico, contributed to the spread of Latin popular music around the world. The talent scouts of Victor and Columbia also recorded the music of immigrant artists in New York to cater for their "foreign-speaking" local customers, notably Irish-Americans. They sold thousands of records of traditional music from Europe and the Near East to the American immigrant market at a time when little traditional music was commercially recorded in Europe, the latter also becoming an important market for these records. The flourishing new industry soon attracted entrepreneurs, and local record industries emerged in England, Germany, France, and Russia in the early twentieth century, with the more successful ones later consolidating and merging. In Greece, the first records—Orfean records—of Turkish, Greek, and Armenian music featuring traditional instruments like *oud*, *kanun*, and *sanduri* were made locally in the early twentieth century, making way gradually for the evolving proletarian *rebetika*, which remained popular until the 1950s and subsequently shaped newer forms of Greek popular music. In Japan, meanwhile, record companies emerged at the turn of the century, growing into six significant record companies, which by the 1930s had licensing agreements with major German and US firms.

By the 1920s, records had been made in nearly every country, with the exception of small and poor countries that were of little interest to record manufacturers (e.g. Trinidad), while most of the more "exotic" recordings were sold in local markets. This time also marked the "official" beginnings of the industrialization of recorded music production and broadcasting. The American record industry was concentrated in New York where the nature of American popular music changed dramatically. Recorded music was superseded by dance band orchestras, reflective of a new trend in the US that led to a wave of new dance crazes. Millions of dance music records of foxtrots, waltzes, tangos, and so on, were sold in the US and Europe in the mid-1920s, and new companies had emerged, although Victor was still the undisputed market leader, followed by Columbia. Dance music of the late 1920s increasingly featured solo singers over dance band accompaniment, made possible by the invention of the microphone, which formed the basis of the modern pop song. American dance music spread around the world and shaped the pattern of modern dance music everywhere.

By the beginning of the 1920s, black musicians began to be recorded on a larger scale in Chicago, which, with musicians from New Orleans increasingly moving to the city, became an important musical center. Pianists developed a new rhythmical style—ragtime, which had by 1917 evolved into jazz. New York became the center of jazz since the 1920s, where the best musicians settled and the new trends started. The first jazz records were made by white musicians, as American record companies were reluctant to record black bands. Jazz records were issued as "race records" solely for the black population in the US, and thus produced for one minority group. Yet this changed in the 1930s when jazz became part of the popular music of the era. Ragtime also spread to Europe and created a basis for new dance music after World War I, and soon after there were jazz bands in all major European cities. The spread of jazz to Europe and elsewhere since the 1920s "was the first great trend in musical history to occur mainly through the medium of recordings" (Gronow and Saunio 1998: 73). Jazz enthusiasts' clubs, like the Hot Club of Berlin, arose in the big cities of Europe in the 1930s.

The 1920s also saw the first recordings of the Southern white folk tradition, initially marketed and aimed at rural customers as "old time tunes" or "hillbilly", eventually growing into the colossal country music industry. The Texan singer Vernon Dalhart's 'Prisoner's Song' from 1924 was one of the first songs, with over one million sales (Gronow and Saunio 1998: 51). The popularity of country music meant that, alongside black and immigrant music, it established itself as a leading branch in the American record industry, with Nashville becoming its primary center. As a uniquely American genre, country was initially confined to American markets, but found great response in the early 1930s in Australia and New Zealand. The latter 1920s also saw the first recordings made in sub-Saharan Africa and the emergence of a local music industry in Australia (Gronow and Saunio 1998: 41).

Australia had mainly imported American and British music records, with Sydney-based EMI (a merger between Columbia and HMV in 1931) being the headquarters, but by the 1930s local artists of American hillbilly began to emerge, who successfully absorbed the idiom into a uniquely Australian context, while adopting the imagery of the Australian outback (Gronow and Saunio 1998: 80).

Radio played a significant role in disseminating more recorded music to more people than other media, which caused record sales to slump in the 1920s. Radio broadcasting (non-commercial state-directed and commercial broadcasting systems) emerged around 1920 with the establishment of stations on the medium wavelengths, which became truly global with the development of the shortwave band in the late 1920s, providing an inexpensive means to broadcast globally from within the borders of a single nation. The earliest purpose of what became radio broadcasting was military and imperial in order to aid the conduct of war and colonial administration. The possibilities of a broadcast medium (as opposed to a narrowcast medium) were explored subsequently. Early radio broadcasting was mainly a domestic medium of reception, which was pioneered in the US and Britain in connection with the emergence of mass popular culture, consumerism, and privatized experience of the nuclear family. While recording technology was in its infancy in the 1920s and phonographs were still expensive for the average person, most people still relied on the radio to listen to music. More radio stations emerged, playing music instead of news, which gave musicians more opportunities for exposure. In its early days, almost all music broadcasting was live, and music was listened to recorded or live in people's homes. Moreover, with the aid of microphones and electric amplifiers, radio technology provided new opportunities for recording and reproducing sound, and the first attempts at recording with microphones were made as early as 1919, leading toward a growth in the record industry that was accelerated by the economic boom, while electrical recording quickly spread all over the world.

The Wall Street stock market crash in 1929 impacted the economic life, including record production, of the US and other industrialized countries. Throughout the 1930s, radio was the primary source of entertainment that included stories, poetry, news, live music, variety shows, and more. At the time, the big radio stations had their own musicians and did not play recorded music. Many established record companies went bankrupt or merged, such as Grammophon and Columbia which became EMI, a trend of concentration that also occurred in the US. The emphasis was now on "hits", while classical and minority music gradually vanished from catalogues. A new type of recording artist emerged, as singers no longer needed a full-throated, operatic voice, enabling artists with a soft, almost whispering style to be recorded, such as Bing Crosby. European record production followed the American pattern, and brought about a new type of singer whose voice was small, but charismatic, and with emotional appeal and photogenic appearance, such as Al Bowlly, Tino Rossi and Tauno Palo (Gronow and Saunio 1998: 74). Musical films became popular and were soon mass-produced in the US, which also spread to the Middle East and India, giving rise to completely new forms of musical entertainment. Radio's popularity helped to keep the record industry alive, as, gradually, the music industry made particular use of the potential reach offered by radio broadcasting when it became a potent medium for advertising. Advertising developed as an industry in its own right in the late nineteenth and early twentieth centuries, along with the various industries that are now collectively known as "culture industry" (Adorno and Horkheimer 1944; Adorno 2001), "cultural industries" (Miege 1989; Hesmondhalgh 2013), and "creative industries" (Creative Industries Task Force 1998) in academic and policy discourse, terms that reflect the move away from culture and toward economy in contemporary thought, as today the purpose of the cultural and creative industries is to commercialize expressive value (McGuigan 2009: 160). In the US of the mid-1930s, concerts of jazz and classical music flourished, Hollywood featured singers who attained international popularity, large radio companies offered new opportunities for renowned artists (many of whom had emigrated from Socialist Russia and Nazi Germany), extremes of technical performance and volcanic interpretations reasserted themselves, and jukeboxes appeared in bars and restaurants (Gronow and Saunio 1998: 63–69). For instance, 1935 saw the first broadcast in radio history of popular records, presented by Martin Block on the New York station WNEW, and similar programs soon appeared in many European stations. Consequently, record sales rose in the mid-thirties, also driven by the growing popularity of the new dance music of swing, which, through the media of film and records, quickly spread to Europe.

The Commodification and Spread of European Classical Music
Since the 1920s, the leading centers of the early record industry were based in the US (New York) and Europe, with Berlin ranking alongside cities like London, Paris, and Vienna. German record companies, specifically, played a significant role in producing classical recordings. Since the late nineteenth century, European art music became increasingly regarded as a commodity to be consumed, which coincided with the rise of the notion of the unique, autonomous individual that was part of a larger shift in historical capitalism.

Many Europeans learnt to believe that they are unique individuals rather than parts of a collective. Early music recording industry executives and advertisers understood that connections exist between class structure and musical taste, namely that elite groups display univore tastes for high culture and fine arts, and therefore targeted so-called highbrow music to higher-income groups. Thus, while a wide range of "local" popular music now appeared on record, it was the opera singers who provided the key to success for record companies at the turn of the century. And Europe was at the monopolizing forefront for the recording of opera (Gronow and Saunio 1998: 148). The concept of artist-as-genius, born in the early nineteenth century, became firmly established in the commodification of European art music. The arrival of the gramophone record also meant that the old generation of violin virtuosi was now captured and sold on record, including the leading violinists Joseph Joachim and Pablo Sarasate, the latter being a virtuoso of the Paganini school. The recording of piano performances posed a challenge technologically, yet the earliest important pianist on record was Camille Saint-Saëns, followed by dozens of renowned pianists from the last century, including Johannes Brahms' wax cylinder recordings from 1889 (Gronow and Saunio 1998: 20–22). The instrumental virtuosi had for a short time displaced the opera singers who used to dominate the record market.

Early instrumental recordings paved the way for the recording of orchestral music in Europe in 1905, particularly by Grammophon. Between 1915 and 1925, most major orchestras and conductors in Germany and Great Britain made recordings, leading toward an impressive range of recordings of orchestral music, yet often in shortened form due to the limitations of acoustic recordings. The success in Europe meant that American record companies also became interested in symphonic works. Meanwhile, the success of record production increasingly depended on performances by renowned performers, with the Italian opera singer Enrico Caruso (1873–1921) becoming known in the United States as "the world's greatest singer" and best-selling artist in the early years of recording (Gronow and Saunio 1998: 17). Indeed, the Italian record industry was predominantly foreign-owned, even though many opera stars in the early years of recording were Italians. With practically all opera singers in the US making records by the 1920s, American opera lovers were thus offered a vast catalogue of thousands of records. The turn of the century is regarded as the Golden Age of opera.

Another type of recording to emerge in Britain was the music-hall record, followed by the cabaret record in the 1920s, given the upsurge of cabaret as a form of mass entertainment all over Europe. As a result of the rise of the ideology of exchangeability and rapid urbanization, classical composers and artists also began to regard "other" music as something to be appropriated and imported into their own music. Thus, with the rise of modern consumer cultures in Europe and the emergence of new sound recording technologies, "cultural forms stylistically and generically foreign to the artists' own could be appropriated, imported into the artists' own work... And such appropriations became commonplace in the late nineteenth and early twentieth centuries, in the music of Igor Stravinsky, Claude Debussy, Béla Bartók, Charles Ives, and others" (Taylor 2016: 30). The invention of the microphone in the mid-1920s led to the rise of great conductors and a flood of symphonic recordings. Entire operas were now recorded, given the new technology's dramatic impact on vocal music by great singing personalities. The use of the microphone also brought recordings of chamber music.

Popular Art Music in Latin America. The rise of the notion of genius and interests in the "other" to be explored and appropriated in European-inspired art music culture was a trend that also emerged in other parts of the world, notably Latin America, often as part of nationalist tendencies. An interesting example is provided by the Paraguayan classical composer and guitarist Agustín Barrios Mangoré, who is generally regarded as one of the first gramophone-recorded classical guitarists, with recordings made as early as 1909. As a composer, Barrios appropriated folk songs from South and Central America, while during his later concert career (1930–34) appropriated the native Guaraní culture in his concert persona, in which he literally adopted the figure of the sixteenth-century Guaraní warrior Mangoré and called himself "Chief Nitsuga Mangoré". Barrios would enter the stage in full "Indian" dress, including headdress with feathers, surrounded by palm leaves and bamboo to evoke ideas of the "jungle". Concert advertisements depicted Barrios as the exotic figure of Mangoré and described him as "the messenger of the Guaraní race ... the Paganini of the guitar from the jungles of Paraguay" (Regan 2010: 74; Stover 2012: 153; see also Szarán 1999: 266). As Mangoré, Barrios expressed a strong sense of musical nationalism that aligned with the prevailing political movements towards independence—politically, culturally, and so on—from colonial Spain, and with it an assertion of the culture of the New World against the Old World (McKenna Ward 2010: 7–8). As the "Paganini of the guitar", a title Barrios earned both as a performer and composer of western classical music, he also epitomized the concept of "heroic individualism" or "artist as hero" that emerged in the Romanticism of late nineteenth-century Europe, beginning with Beethoven in the late eighteenth century and followed in the nineteenth century by the emergence of the performing virtuoso with Paganini and Liszt (McKenna Ward 2010: 10). More specifically,

> The reason why we habitually think of conception as an individual matter is the enduring legacy of Romanticism in aesthetics. European Romanticism of the early nineteenth century represented a reaction against the nascent industrial civilization and its dehumanizing aspects ... The main tenets of Romanticism [was] its extreme individualism. Romanticism not only raised the flag of "culture" against the abominations of "civilization", it also revered the solitary artist as the source of fine sensibility and even ... as "an unacknowledged legislator" (McGuigan 2016: 154).

It was specifically "Barrios' conception of left hand [guitar] technique ... [that] position[ed] him as a virtuoso in the tradition of Paganini and Liszt, who, like these figures, extended the possibilities of instrumental performance beyond what had previously been imagined" (McKenna Ward 2010: 120). With the rise of consumer culture, Barrios embraced and epitomized the European ideology of the unique, autonomous individual while appropriating the other into his own work, both as a recording and live artist. Meanwhile, the commodification of classical music since the nineteenth century also occurred in the Arab Middle East, notably Lebanon and Egypt.

Popular Art Music in the Arab Middle East. Recordings of indigenous classical music became released more extensively on LP records in urbanized countries, including Egypt, Iran, India, Korea, Japan, and others, which were aimed at the concert-going public in their own countries. In the Arab world, for instance, music has a long history and includes diverse regional folk and religious musics, and classical music with a sophisticated music theory originally formulated between the ninth and thirteenth centuries. Instrumental improvisation (*taqsim*) is one of the most important aspects of Arab musical culture, but historically, vocal music (sung poetry) occupied a more prominent place (Danielson 1988: 141). Classifications into folk, popular, classical, or religious are somewhat difficult to make, given that much religious, folk, classical, and western music has become widely disseminated by the media and consumed by large populations across the Arab world. Arab popular music has been produced as well as enjoyed in virtually all Arab countries that span seventeen independent states and over one hundred million people (Danielson 1988: 157–60). Beirut (Lebanon) and Cairo (Egypt) were the two main centers for the production of commercial recordings, and therefore less is known about popular music of Iraq and the Arabian peninsula. In the late nineteenth century, Beirut was the cosmopolitan center of modern Arab culture, including music. Much popular music in Lebanon has been shaped by cultural and historical conditions distinct to that country, including folk and rural influences from the mountainous regions of central and northern Lebanon, and the growing impact of modernization and westernization in Beirut when it became a highly cosmopolitan community with non-rural, non-Lebanese, and non-Arabic populations. The eclectic social and ethnic make-up, combined with the extensive role of the emerging entertainment media—radio, television, concert halls, public theater—were conducive to the rise of an urban mass popular culture, which is particularly manifested in Fayrouz' songs. Fayrouz (b. 1935; her real name is Nouhad Wadie' Haddad) has been regarded since the 1950s as one of the most favorite singers of modern Arabic music (Stone 2007). Among her vast repertoire are performances of stylized harmonizations of Lebanese folk songs, classical *mawashshahat*, and hybrid songs blending various western, Russian, Balkan, and other elements, while making extensive use of European instrumentation, harmony, polyphonic melodies, and major and minor tonalities. Many of her songs in the 1960s were originally performed in musical plays and films that combined Lebanese traditions with orchestral suites of European, Russian, and Arab inspirations. Fayrouz has become an emblem of modernity, given that her classical renditions exemplify a neo-classicism that has constituted a trend in popular Arabic music throughout the twentieth century. Although these pieces only constitute a small percentage of popular music, they have been extremely popular and marketed on commercial recordings and broadcasts along with film songs, folk songs, and indigenous jazz. Popular music throughout the Arab Middle East has thereby tended to assimilate new musical styles from both neighboring peoples and the West, and been disseminated through the mass media. At the same time, musicians have strived to maintain their own authentic musical identity, and place high value on what they believe is indigenously theirs. The emergent new syncretic music is therefore at once eclectic and distinctively Arabic.

Egyptian music constitutes a special case of Arab musical influence, given that Egypt has been the prime center from which culture radiated throughout the Arab world (see also Danielson 1988: 141–50). There are two key reasons: Egypt's eminent Islamic University al-Azhar, its scholars, and its reformers; and its popular artists and writers. Indeed, Egypt has been a principal center for the development and dissemination of Arab popular music during the nineteenth and twentieth centuries (ibid.: 142). It was prompt to take advantage of the new media, notably gramophone, radio, film, and later television (see also Armbrust 2002). Its forte was popular music, which absorbed influences from the West and the Arab world, and passed them on to other Arabic countries. The urban center of Cairo gained early ascendancy in the development of the mass media and the musics associated with them. Modern Egyptian music has become well-known and influential throughout the Arab world and "has developed as a product of the complex relationships among musicians, audiences, and those who owned and controlled the various media" (Danielson 1988: 142). The nineteenth century marked a turning point in Arab music due to the French conquest of Egypt and subsequent military and cultural contacts with the West. Egypt's rulers made systematic attempts at westernization, which brought European-style brass bands, western theory and notation, musical instruments, hymns, conservatories, and musical theater and opera. The late nineteenth century is often regarded as the Golden Age of Arabic modern music when the music recording industry enjoyed early success in Egypt. By 1904, recordings were made of Egyptian music, which first included cylinder phonograph records, and later the flat 78rpm disk promoted by companies such as Grammophon, Odeon, Pathé, Columbia, and Bardophone (ibid.: 145). These recordings were exported across Egypt and other Arabic countries, enabling people throughout the Arab world to hear the voices of celebrities such as the Egyptians Shaykh Yusuf al-Manyalawi, Abd al-Hayy Hilmi, Shaykh Abu al-Ula Muhammad, Munira al-Mahdiyya, and Umm Kulthum. Meanwhile, the number of Arabic music recordings made in Europe and US grew substantially in popularity by the 1920s, with the spread of the phonograph among all classes of people, and public phonographs emerging in coffee houses and among mobile disc jockeys throughout the Middle East. The music recording industry at the time "was profit-oriented, generally conservative, and unlikely to take risks by recording unknown performers" (ibid.: 146).

Early in the twentieth century, the most pervasive type of musical performance was recorded by singers of religious and classical texts, the *mashayikh* (singular: *shayikh*), who typically performed at weddings and saints' days, for community gatherings and in coffee houses (Danielson 1988: 143). *Mashayik* had to pass a high degree of learning, initially to recite the Q'uran, and usually studied and performed religious and secular classical poetry (e.g. *qasidah*, *muwashshah*, and *mawwal*), mastery of which provided the singer with well-developed skills in composition and improvisation based on the *maqamant*. They came to be regarded as important custodians of Egyptian Arabic culture. For instance, Darwish al-Hariri (1881–1957) was one of Egypt's most popular composers of musical plays, films, and commercially recorded songs, while his contemporary Ali Mahmud (1881–1946) recorded and performed many religious songs on the radio. During this time, musical theater became extremely popular among the middle- and upper-middle classes in Egypt, where religious songs were skillfully and sensitively integrated into the plots of plays. Musical theater and music halls also served to disseminate solo song performances, with singers (both male and female) usually performing modern popular songs from musical plays, light-hearted *taqatiq*, and *qasidah* accompanied by a small ensemble of

Arabic instruments, including *ud*, *qanun*, violin, and *riqq*. The recording industry became extremely attractive to musicians due to the potentially high financial rewards and broad public exposure (ibid.: 147). However, commercial sound recording was a factor in the transformation of traditional Arab music because record companies favored pre-composed, short, self-contained songs over long, improvised, interactive live performances, which did not fit the limited duration of early phonograph disks. This meant that the 5 to 6-minute time limit per recording restricted improvisation, which was essential to certain genres like the *qasidah*, and consequently the recording industry promoted the *taqtuqah*, which could be easily composed, learnt, and tailored to the 5-minute limit.

For popular artists who successfully negotiated recording contracts, the music recording business was extremely lucrative. One of the most noteworthy performers and recording artists to emerge at the time was Umm Kulthum (1904–1975), a female *mashayik* singer and superstar of Arab music in the twentieth century (see further Danielson 2002). However, with the Great Depression and the establishment of a strong Egyptian national radio station, the economic success of the recording industry and its artists declined after the 1920s. Where communications are generally inadequate, the radio is an important means of propagating the notion of national identity, since radio is often listened to in public spaces, as in the Arab world. Radio became extremely popular throughout the Arab world, easily replacing the phonograph as the predominant medium of popular culture, and a principal "patron" for musicians (Danielson 1988: 147). Established stars like Umm Kulthum and Abd al-Wahhab were offered first choice in scheduling and regularly performed live. Umm Kulthum, for instance, negotiated the best contract that Egyptian radio offered to any star, and by 1937 she arranged for her legendary performances to be broadcast live from the concert hall every first Thursday night of every month, thereby putting full-length performances on air. "'Umm Kulthum night' became an institutionalized media and social event" (ibid.: 148). At the same time, this scheduling left much broadcasting time for other singers and attracted musicians from other parts of the Arab world who believed their careers would advance through broadcasting. With continued government support, radio's facilities were continuously expanded, particularly during the 1950s. Radio retained its popularity well into the 1960s until the event of the cassette player.

Like Indian film music, popular music in many other cultures has similarly evolved in close connection with its use in musical theater and cinema, including modern Egyptian urban music. In the early 1930s, the music recording industry promoted the development of film song when musical film became a popular medium, replacing theater and featuring artists such as the renowned singer, film actor, and composer Muhammad Abd al-Wahhab. At that time, it was the aim of every commercial singer to star in a musical film, given that cinema offered great financial reward and publicity. Arrangements of film songs further altered more traditional conceptions of proper performance, with songs shortened and accompanied by large orchestras modelled on those of Hollywood, sung once through without improvisation, and background music borrowed from western sources, ranging from nineteenth-century symphonic works to contemporary western dance tunes. The 1950s saw an increased influence of electronics, mass media, and westernization, combined with an outlook that favored western classical music. By the 1960s, television became increasingly popular with broadcasts that included live concerts by Umm Kulthum and other stars. Muhammad Abd al-Wahhab wrote songs for Umm Kulthum that moved toward a more vernacular or popular style, marked by short meters, popular-sounding melodies, and a highly structured, heavily orchestrated format with little room for flexible interpretations. These and other songs performed in variety shows on TV often combined elements from folk dance and short electric guitar motifs intended to evoke American popular music. Since the early 1980s, Arab music has departed further from the modernized traditional models, and new popular musical forms have been developed across the Arab world. As we shall see in subsequent chapters, Arabpop is highly eclectic and strongly influenced by the media in its conception, content, and distribution. It has modern and postmodern features, and is increasingly detached from earlier mainstream practices and the traditionalist-modernist rhetoric of the preceding decades. Traditional musical practices and aesthetic criteria tend to remain recognizable, although mostly in sacred and secular contexts that may have become specialized or even marginalized.

Vernacular Popular Music in Europe
While classical music, notably European art music, was the focus of early commodification in Europe and elsewhere, the rise of modern consumer cultures in Europe since the mid-nineteenth century also witnessed the emergence of local vernacular styles and genres of popular music, such as *rebetika* and *bouzouki* music (Greece), *arabesk* (Turkey), *fado* (Portugal), *flamenco* (Spain), Neopolitan rock (Italy), and many others (Sorce Keller 2000). These styles were often regarded as minority music, blending western with vernacular styles, and usually remained more localized and largely unknown outside of their country of origin. However, some minority styles have become more widely accepted and recognized as a symbol of national identity by a larger social group, even a nation, notably Spanish *flamenco*, which, once popular, were entered into modern consumer culture as objected and commodified music recordings.

Spanish Flamenco. The development of flamenco from the rural song of Andalusia to the most urbanized, professionalized form of traditional Spanish music clearly reflects and symbolizes the modernization and urbanization of Spanish culture since the nineteenth century (see also Manuel 1988: 121–26; Miles and Chuse 2000: 596–600). Musically, flamenco art form was shaped by the emerging global economy and became "a manifestation of romantic orientalism and its preference for the exotic" (Aoyama 2007: 105). Flamenco's popularity is closely associated with the rise of tourism, starting with the early (mainly French and British) international tourism of the nineteenth century, which marketed flamenco as an exotic product of Oriental mysticism with a distinct Andalusian identity. The meanings attached to older and newer forms of flamenco have shifted with commercialization, one rooted in the "rougher" vocal gypsy styles and community participation, the other associated with staged performances, glamour, and attractiveness (Marre and Charlton 1985d). While there exist no written or recorded records of older styles of flamenco prior to the nineteenth century, flamenco initially had a distinct local character, and is often described as a popular art that was created bottom-up as the music of a desperately poor and exploited rural underclass, the Roma (Silverman 2000). These were, for example, the gypsy communities in the caves of Sacro Monte on the hills adjacent to the city of Granada who have a rich musical heritage. The traditional flamenco style associated with the social minority of the *gitanos* of southern Spain is an emotional, deeply expressive art form.[1] Historically, its most important aspect was the song (*cante*), originally performed with rhythmic accompaniment from a stick (*palo seco*) or sometimes claps (*palmas*). *Cante jondo* (deep song) is usually considered the oldest, most serious group; *cante intermedio* (intermediate song), also known as *cante flamenco*, is regarded as a hybrid form from the fusion of *cante jondo* and forms from Spanish folk and popular musical styles, in particular the *fandango* (a dance of Arab origin); and *cante chico* (light song) is rhythmically less complex, except the *bulerias*. The texts consist traditionally of "couplets" (*coplas*), three- to five-line stanzas, and are sung in the Andalusian dialect. Themes usually communicate personal suffering in personal vignettes with directness, simplicity, and lyricism, and evoke a deep sense of fatalism and nihilism. Death is a principal theme, as are conflicts between hope and despair, love and the pains of love, guilt and atonement, and evil and divine protection. Flamenco was nurtured during the last two centuries by assimilated, settled gypsies in the cities and large towns off Seville and Cadiz provinces. In the early nineteenth century, flamenco was popular at parties in *gitano* homes, jam sessions (*juergas*), in tavern bars, and brothels, and was patronized by members of the wealthy, *senorito* class of the Andalusian landed gentry.

Flamenco gradually began to unite song (*cante*), guitar (*toque*), and dance (*baile*), the fusion of *gitano* musical traits and stylings, with popular forms of Spanish music. As a vocal form (*cante*), flamenco was not appealing to international tourists who did not possess Spanish proficiency, which provided a growing market for dance (*baile*). Another important development was the addition of the guitar as accompaniment, played through strumming (*rasguado*) alternating with plucked melodic phrases (*falsetas*). The playing technique was soon expanded to include complex arpeggios, the four-finger tremolo, and more difficult left-hand work. Onlookers played important roles through their active participation in the *jaleos* (a chorus of shouts of encouragement and hand-clapping) by encouraging and admiring shouts from the audience. Aficionados participate with claps (*palmas*), playing rhythmic patterns based on the rhythmic structures of the *cante* and finger snaps (*pitos*), and performing complex counter rhythms in the *compass* (rhythm), complementing the guitar's rhythms and the dancer's footwork (*zapateo*). With increasing professionalization and commercialization during the period of musical modernization (1850–1940s), flamenco art was frequently performed in cabarets called cafés-cantates in the cities and larger towns of Seville and Cádiz provinces, which offered gypsy musicians regular contracts with fixed salaries (Manuel 1988: 121). Since then, flamenco was shaped and reshaped through the consumers and the market in the light of exoticism and artistic orientalism of the gypsy culture.

Since the 1920s, flamenco was taken to the theatrical stage and became known as flamenco opera (*operismo*). This development transformed more "authentic" styles into the commercialized forms. At the same time, flamenco ceased to be an exclusively gypsy art, as several Andalusian *payos* (non-gypsies) had become recognized as leading performers. They started to incorporate non-gypsy folk musics (especially the regional varieties of *fandango*) and Latin American (especially Cuban) influences alongside the basic gypsy *cantes* (*soleares, bulerias, tientos, tangos, siguiriyas,* etc.) (Manuel 1988: 122). Spanish dance companies' touring resulted in international interest, and the number of nightclubs (*tablaos*), small flamenco clubs (*penas*), regional flamenco festivals, contests (*concursos*) of *cante* and *toque* grew. By the 1960s, flamenco had moved from the intimate setting of the *juerga* to *cafes cantantes*, contemporary professional *tablaos*, festival circuits, and concert stages, and became increasingly professionalized and commercialized. The informal gypsy *juerga* (session) remained an ideal and archetypical flamenco performance context, and during 1920–60, there was a declining public interest in flamenco due to the perceived "bastardization" of the genre in the context of theatrical flamenco opera (ibid.: 122). Aiming to expand into the larger music market, flamenco became subject to a degree of homogenization (through universal "exoticizing" musical tendencies).

In the 1950s/60s, there occurred a renaissance of older, more serious styles, and *operismo* came under attack by intellectuals led by the composer Manuel de Falla and poet Frederico García Lorca to counteract the consequences of commercialization. They developed a romanticized, mythic, spiritual interpretation of flamenco as the "soul of Andalusia", in which they developed the concept of transcendent emotion (*duende*) as the inspiration of flamenco. During this time, dictator Franco promoted flamenco along with tourism in the otherwise depressed Spanish economy. This led to flamenco becoming a "quasi-national performance symbol" for the entire nation (Aoyama 2007: 106). Besides tourism, international tours of major flamenco artists—often with Spanish government support—further disseminated flamenco as a commodity. This, combined with performances in nightclubs (*tablaos*), small flamenco clubs (*penas*), regional flamenco festivals, and contests resulted in heightened international interest. Flamenco moved increasingly to festival circuits and concert stages. National recording studios and multinational firms too were actively involved in disseminating the flamenco genre worldwide. With increased professionalization, flamenco's association with the gypsy culture became increasingly ambiguous, triggered by the fact that many artists (dancers, singers, guitarists) were non-gypsies (*payos*). At the same time, flamenco was undergoing a tension between public interests and commercialism versus private interests and anti-commercialism. Public consumption promoted the faster-paced, festive rhythms of certain types of flamenco, such as *tangos* and *bulerias*, and faced criticisms to become increasingly superficial, debased, and deceptive. By contrast, deep song (*cante jundo*) with themes of oppression and suffering, such as *siguriyas* and *soleas*, were increasingly de-emphasized. Marketed as an "exotic" product to tourists and consumers, various elements in flamenco have been emphasized or de-emphasized, including Spanishness, Andalusian characteristics and identity, and gypsy influence. The latter was constructed through associations with subcultural, marginalized, bohemian, or even post-conventional cultural values and resistance to authority and the mainstream. Flamenco became appealing to those who prefer the Romantic, the alternative, the uniquely transcultural, and the marginal.

Increased urbanization and modernization in Spain from the late 1960s dramatically altered the demography of southern Spanish society through mass migration to cities in France and Germany, as well as to Spanish cities like Madrid and Barcelona, where an entire population sub-culture consisting of first- and second-generation transplanted Andalusians emerged, engendering a new musical and cultural aesthetic that reflected their new social environment (Manuel 1988: 123). Here, commercialized flamenco has, like most popular music, emerged out of people's geographic mobility, particularly large-scale labor migration, mostly from the periphery to the core of centers of economic activity. These new hybrid societies were fertile breeding grounds for flamenco-pop and other fusions, driven by a new generation of brilliant young musicians, many of whom experimented freely with eclectic fusions, and absorbed foreign musical influences on flamenco-pop, including Cuban *rumba* (or *son*), rock music, jazz, Arab music, R&B, rap, and other world popular music. The most foremost musicians were Paco de Lucia and star vocalist Camaron de la Isla, who recorded and performed both traditional and modernized flamenco, together with tasteful pop-flavored hits like the tango 'Como el agua' (1985). By the mid-1970s, Paco de Lucia was already becoming recognized as the leading flamenco guitarist, and as the most outstanding genius in the recorded history of the genre (Manuel 1988: 124). Besides "pure" flamenco concerts and recordings, de Lucia also experimented with a number of eclectic innovations, including an instrumental rumba 'Entre dos aguas' (1974), combining virtuoso guitar improvisations over a lively percussion background. Paco de Lucia also engaged in collaborations with foreign musicians like John McLaughlin and Ali de Meola.

Processes of such musical transculturation and hybridization are further reflected by the subsequent emergence of *nuevo flamenco*, which expresses people's (newly emerging) regional socio-political consciousness. The lyrics typically address issues of Andalusia's underdevelopment, unemployment, and consequent migration in an attempt to raise socio-political consciousness. The genre addresses a unique kind of audience and fanship, namely a relatively small group of students and activists. Its unique style is reflected in a distinctive Andalusian flavor in its musical characteristics (such as harmony, guitar style, etc.). In many ways, the music reflects people's search for identity that is rooted in the particularity of place, which—in the globalized world, where the confluence of global culture with local and national culture leads to the fragmentation of local identities and the construction of new, hybrid identities—is becoming increasingly pivotal in people's lives. An example of *nuevo flamenco* is provided by Ojos de Brujo, a group of musicians who use flamenco as the foundation for cross-genre experimentation, incorporating elements of hip hop, funk, salsa, and reggae. The group was formed by members of Fabrica de Colores, a loose-knit group of artists in Barcelona. Their musical creations sound distinctively Spanish, with flamenco being at the heart of their hybrid sound, even though they are borrowing from a variety of styles and traditions. In their lyrics, they often tackle a paradox: the philosophy of life versus the difficulties of the present moment. The new hybrid flamenco styles that have emerged since are the product and expression of a new regional socio-political consciousness, with lyrics often addressing Andalusia's underdevelopment, unemployment, and consequent migration in an attempt to raise socio-political consciousness.

Musical Modernization in Africa and Latin America
The rise of modern consumer cultures in other parts of the world in the nineteenth and twentieth centuries led to the development of modern, industrialized music industries, although the exact timing of the industrialization of music recording production and broadcasting differs profoundly between different countries, shaped by each country's own historical, political, and cultural contexts. Under the influence of western forms of capitalism, music became increasingly produced and commodified for the purpose of exchange, influencing musical production significantly. This trend paved the way for musical appropriations and importations in many countries, using western cultural idioms, styles, and expressions for musical inspiration. Musical modernization was brought on largely by economic, personal, social, and cultural reasons. All cultures have historically displayed openness and curiosity to other forms of culture, and have assigned worth and importance to those cultural idioms "that convey creative innovation, of 'the new and exciting' in art and culture, that do not lag behind recent stylistic trends" (Regev 2013: 4), and "especially to those forms and idioms that gain global institutionalized status as the frontiers of creativity" (ibid.: 8). Musical modernization into the direction of the dominant (western) culture thereby works to heighten worth and importance, specifically when these cultural forms have global institutionalized status as beacons of creativity. People's hierarchical perceptions of musical value and creativity, in turn, "relegate to a lower status on the scale of modernity those individuals and collective actors whose tastes hardly consist of works from the creative frontiers, actors whose sense of distinction and uniqueness is based on forms of art and on styles that lag behind recent stylistic trends" (Regev 2013: 11).

While European art music became objectified and commodified and marketed for the tastes of social elites, popular music is historically associated with a socially marginalized class (Manuel 1988: 18–19). The rise of popular music in many parts of the world is a reflection and a product of the emergence of vast new urban societies, "which have undergone socio-economic transformations unprecedented in their rapidity and profundity" (ibid.: 16). The evolution of popular music thereby usually parallels the evolution of new societies brought on by modernization, urbanization, and industrialization. Popular music embodied and expressed the new social identities that emerged as products of these. To many oppressed, marginalized peoples among the new urban classes, popular music serves "as a powerful and meaningful symbol of identity" (ibid.: 16), functioning as an avenue of expression and mediation of conflict. Identity creates communality, belonging, sameness, continuity, and thus inclusion in one collective, as well as separation and exclusion from another. Popular music has helped to create shared spaces of common meanings and cultural ideologies among the new urban classes. Much popular music has therefore become a term to distinguish music of "the people".

Musical modernization meant the spread of western influence in many parts of the world, and it succeeded due to western music's perceived value, creativity, and complexity, specifically classical and art music, its accompanying technology, and economic power. And yet, while European art music influenced musical commodification in the early period, the dominant force, both quantitatively and qualitatively, in world popular music has subsequently been the spread of the "pop-rock aesthetic" (Regev 2013)—pop-rock music that originates from the US and the UK. Both western classical and pop-rock music has become consumed, absorbed, indigenized, and domesticated at the individual, structural, and collective level. Since the 1960s, aesthetic cultures of western pop-rock music have thus been present in countries all over the world. Yet, instead of seeing musical modernization as imperial imposition, cultural idioms like western music have selectively been absorbed, indigenized, and domesticated as vehicles for modernizing national culture.

Afropop. Africa has historically been an economically deprived continent with a low share in world trade, and so record companies had fairly little interest in sub-Saharan music for a long time. The first records were made by Grammophon in 1912 in South Africa, followed by Nigeria in 1914. In the 1920s, European companies from Britain, France, and Germany also recorded music in Madagascar, the Gold Coast, Kenya, and others. The companies' interest waned with the Depression, and production continued only in South Africa during the 1930s when the growing urban black population triggered demand for black South African popular music. At that time, a new musical style called *highlife* developed in West Africa (Nigeria, Sierra Leone, Ghana), blending swing and African drums (Waterman 1990). Post-1945, urban populations grew across the continent. With the arrival of new recording technology, both international companies arrived and new local record companies sprung up. In West Africa, for instance, Decca and EMI, and later also Philips, were the leading record companies in the 1950s and 1960s. Although a large portion of the record industry was controlled by a few multinationals, copyright protection had been minimal with rampant piracy and copying. During the 1960s, new trends emerged in Nigeria, such as Fela Kuti's Afro-pop and Sunny Adé's *juju*, blending African drums and electric guitars. New popular music genres emerged and gained popularity within regional and national music markets all over the African continent during the twentieth century, including genres like the Senegalese *mbalax* (Brunner 2010), Zimbabwean *chimurenga* (Turino 2000), Ivory Coast's *zouglou* (Schumann 2010), and Cameroonian *makossa* and *bikutsi* (Brunner in press), among others, all of which became important markers of "national uniqueness" (Regev 2003: 98). The fastest growth in popular music, though, occurred in South Africa under the auspices of the Gallotone company and EMI, producing music for the rapidly expanding population of the black slums of Johannesburg and Cape Town. This was the birthplace of successful new genres like *kwela*, a youth music movement from the street that featured the (cheap) penny whistle, and *mbaqanga*, an electrically amplified popular music. African popular music was released on 78rpm records into the 1960s, which were sold on local markets, as well as in the capitals of former colonial powers, like London and Paris, with considerable African communities (Gronow and Saunio 1998: 131–33).

The radio played a crucial role in the development of African popular music (Impey 2000). Radio stations promoted local music, which, along with the weakness of foreign competition, led to the emergence of an unusually buoyant live music scene marked by a variety and widespread popularity of African popular music. The advent of the mass media created a new awareness of foreign musical styles, with three major sources of external influences: European music, including Christian (missionary) hymns and brass band music; Afro-American and Afro-Latin musics, particularly from Cuba and Jamaica; and regional styles within Africa itself, especially the Congolese rumba and its living legends.[2] Many current Afropop styles are fusions of traditional characteristics with heavy rock rhythms and instrumentation, which reflects the more general trend that popular music around the world is often created in such a way as to syncretize and reinterpret old and new elements of culture (see also Manuel 1988: 84–89).

Although it is difficult and essentialist to generalize the musical characteristics of sub-Saharan "traditional" music, there is a general consensus that much African music south of the Sahara shares similar features, including short ostinato patterns and steady tempi; the arrangement of voices or instruments in overlapping pairs of call and response; successive entries of new instruments and voices; simultaneous use of contrasting rhythmic patterns (polyrhythm); and an expanded sound world (e.g. buzzing membranes, vibrating attachments). African pop usually differs from its traditional predecessor, including oral traditions, folklore, and/or classical music, particularly in instrumentation (e.g. using electric guitar and keyboard, computer, recording equipment), styles and forms (pop song format), and dance accompaniment. African pop is also characterized by the simplification of the rhythm section as compared to traditional music, whereby in Afropop a simple, unvarying quadratic pulse is far more common over which relatively straightforward, albeit syncopated lines are added. Afropop demonstrates hybridity and syncretism in musical form, style, harmony, and rhythm. It is very different from traditional folk music, because many African musicians are adept at borrowing instruments and styles from different cultures, both from the West and from other parts of Africa. The many styles and forms making up the genre of Afropop reflect and resonate with the many diverse local circumstances and particularities of musicians, performers, and listeners across the African continent. In these musics, the local and the particular are revalidated and revitalized, emphasizing a sense of identity rooted in the particularity of place and locality. There are many ways of making music in everyday life, often shaped by people's desire for expressing their local identities.

South Africa. Afropop with political commentary has become an important category of modern popular music. In South Africa, for instance, political songs have reflected the complex contradictions and interactions between different classes of Africans involved in the liberation struggle (see also Coplan 2002; Marre and Charlton 1985b). Here, popular musical forms developed within colonialist contexts. White settlers (Afrikaans and English) were more numerous than in other African countries and exerted enormous influence on the native population. South African pop music is therefore quite distinct stylistically from that of the rest of Africa, having evolved under a unique set of socio-historical conditions (Manuel 1988: 106–111). Traditional music in South Africa was shaped by European styles brought by white settlers and missionaries, characterized by choral singing in complex, overlapping responsorial patterns, while instrumental music was less developed, partly also due to the scarcity of trees from which drums and other instruments could be made. During the 1920s and 1930s, recordings and radio played a crucial role in bringing Afro-American music to South Africa, but popular styles emerged as early as the 1860s with the growth of urban centers, for instance the early syncretic genre of *makwaya*, followed by *marabi* in the 1920s, township jazz in the 1930s, *kwela* in the 1940s and 50s, *mbube* and *isicathamiya* in the 1940s, *jive* and *mbaqanga* in the 1950s. With the growth of cities by imported workers and members of native tribes, which were melting pots for interethnic and interracial contact alongside racial segregation, black South Africans began to absorb musical influences from Afro-American styles. South African popular music has therefore little in common with percussive, polyrhythmic instrumental styles, as in West Africa, and absorbed the rhythmically simpler Afro-American popular styles, such as swing-era jazz. Afro-American music like minstrel songs and ragtime were compatible with their vocal traditional music. Moreover, South African blacks identified with their black brothers and sisters in the US who fought a similar struggle against discrimination, and this ideological affinity enhanced their interest in Afro-American musics (Manuel 1988: 106).

Since 1948, South Africa was ruled by the National Party, which instituted the repressive apartheid system of severe racial inequality and enforced racial separateness. During the 1950s, Johannesburg's culturally and musically most thriving suburb Sophiatown became replaced by the prison-like barracks of Soweto, and censored much public musical and theatrical life. Since the early 1960s, the South African Broadcasting Corporation, which controlled the airwaves, tended to promote apolitical pop, rock, jive, and *mbaqanga* styles and western popular music, and exercised censorship, banning, torture, and imprisonment over performances and recordings of socio-political songs within an extreme legal-political system. Both the Directorate of Publications (the official government censor) and the SABC (South African Broadcasting Corporation) decided on which songs to ban. Commercial aspects of popular music in South Africa have been characterized by white domination, exploitation, and corruption. In the early 1960s, while the rest of Africa gained independence, South Africa moved in the opposite direction, intensifying apartheid with draconian pass laws, artificial homelands, and massacres of protestors. The only overt musical expressions of African solidarity operated entirely outside the commercial South African media. Amidst apartheid and censorship, black South African musical life continued to develop, and many musicians opposed the dominant system through their music in support of the anti-apartheid political cause. For instance, musicians of different "races" like Johnny Clegg and Sipho Mchunu continued to play together when it was illegal; others continued to record overtly resistant songs (e.g. Roger Lucey who was "monitored" by policeman Paul Erasmus), or used camouflaged messages and disguised tunes. South African pop music became a powerful tool in the liberation and anti-apartheid struggle. South Africans have all suffered the disruptions caused by the colonization of South Africa and apartheid. Urbanization, proletarianization, racial segregation, cultural syncretism, and harsh white political segregation all governed the socio-cultural evolution of South African popular music, which led to the black-consciousness movement in an attempt to recapture and stress African roots and origins.

In the early stages of the black resistance movement during the late nineteenth/early twentieth centuries, the assimilationist black petty bourgeoisie with its profound ambivalence toward the dominant white culture tended to promote westernized musical expressions and new syncretic forms like *makwaya* choral music, since the use of traditional tribal styles posed problems for the leaders' goals in transcending ethnicity and forming a pan-tribal, modernist solidarity movement. *Makwaya*, a vocal style variously integrating hymn-derived European harmonies or ragtime elements with traditional (predominantly Xhosa) rhythms and overlapping choral formats, emerged in the late nineteenth century among the more acculturated, middle-class Africans and came to be associated with the African nationalist movement. A well-known example of the *makwaya* style is the national anthem of South Africa 'Nkosi Sikelel'I Afrika' ("Lord Bless Africa"), which originated from the reworking of white gospel hymns and features four-part western harmony.[3] The song has been sung in several different South African languages, and it was spread internationally in the 1980s by the South African choral group Ladysmith Black Mambazo, who gained international success through their collaboration with Paul Simon. By 1912, 'Nkosi Sikelel'I Afrika' was sung at meetings of the pre-African National Congress (ANC), who led the fight against apartheid and whose leader during the second half of the twentieth century was Nelson Mandela (Shelemay 2001: 285–90). It transformed into a musical emblem of political resistance against apartheid, and in the 1990s became a respected national anthem and international symbol of victory in the fight for racial equality. 'Nkosi Sikelel'I Afrika' continues to be transmitted as an anthem of freedom and independence throughout Africa, and it even became the official anthem of Tanzania and Zambia. Beyond the importance of this song within South Africa's new political order, the song has also been used as a worldwide anthem of human rights. The liberation movement continued to use hybrid and imported musical forms like ragtime, reggae, and Zulu jazz-rock.

Latin Pop. As has been shown so far, the world was blanketed by mass media and electronic communications during the twentieth century, and populations worldwide experienced intense social and cultural changes, variously labelled westernization, modernization, urbanization, secularization, industrialization, commercialization, commodification, and globalization. New popular music evolved in response to this, which arose from and was marketed to a mass audience of consumers. Most popular music blended local and traditional forms with imported, usually Western, norms. Its classification under the rubric "popular" emphasized the mass appeal and mass mediation, and distinguished it from pre-existing conceptual categories, such as folk and art music. Popular music typically functions as entertainment in urban environments, and usually shares several traits, such as being "mass-mediated, commodified (reproduced and commercially marketed), syncretic, rapidly obsolescent (though hits may be nostalgically preserved as markers of certain periods), and accessible (not overly demanding of listeners)" (Averill

1998: 92). In Latin America, specifically, popular movements have sometimes connected popular music to national or ethnic identity, for instance in the case of Jamaican *ska* and Trinidad's steelband music.

Latin America encompasses a huge landmass containing South America, Mexico, Central America, and the Caribbean. Its colonial demography, marked by the bringing together of African, European, and indigenous populations since the late fifteenth century,[4] has shaped musical fusions in popular music, which was bred primarily from fusions of European and African-derived musical elements, with the indigenous contribution rather low, given the relative absence and social marginality of indigenous populations in urban areas (Manuel 1988: 24-83). Diverse European elements came from the national musical styles of Spain and Portugal, while African elements came particularly from Angola and the Congo (Portuguese colonies), West African Fanti and Ashanti (British colonies), and the Yoruba people (Spanish colonies). For example, Spanish-American popular music (such as in Cuba) is hybrid, syncretic music, which developed in response to the encounter of European, Amerindian, and African cultures. The emergence of the mass media greatly expedited such cross-fertilizations and exportations, particularly in the case of Cuban popular styles, which have interchanged with the US, Africa, and elsewhere. Indeed, Latin American pop returned to Europe and Africa in the nineteenth and twentieth centuries where it was stylized and modified, and re-exported to the New World. Moreover, recording, broadcasting, and film have played important roles in expanding musical activity, particularly in Cuba and Mexico, which have been important exporters of popular music styles. These musics, like the *son* associated with Cuba, which is still performed in traditional and modern forms, are recorded and disseminated through the mass media on the basis of record sales. Besides Cuba, the most influential sources of popular music have been Brazil and Argentina.

As Latin America's largest country, Brazil is an important center of popular music where practically every form of popular music is influenced by traditional music. The country's recording industry is well-developed, and its market ranks among the top seven worldwide with the big multinationals dominating the field (Perrone 1998). The *samba, bossa nova, tropicalia,* and their nineteenth-century precursors, the *lundu, modinha,* and *maxixe,* have exerted considerable influence in the US, Portugal, and Africa (Manuel 1988: 64–68). The evolution of Brazilian popular music was influenced by several factors, including a rich heritage of neo-African music that emerged as a result of the importation of large numbers of African slaves, including the Yoruba-derived *candomble* cult, as well as European genteel light-classical music, which was in turn exported to Portugal. In the twentieth century, urbanization and the mass media further influenced the emergence of new syncretic genres, such as *samba*, which blended European (notably Portuguese) and African elements in such a way as to acquire the status of national music.

The samba was originally street music and a dance genre, and consequently there exist several types of samba throughout Brazil, the most influential of which is the one that emerged in association with the pre-Lenten Carnival festivities of Rio de Janeiro (see also Marre and Charlton 1985c). In the nineteenth century, carnival was celebrated by revelers throwing water-filled balls of wax at passers-by and by groups of costumed dancers marching to brass band music. By the early twentieth century, the event became a popular annual diversion, whose musical accompaniment included an assortment of marches, *maxixes*, *choroes*, and others. At this time, these genres were replaced by the urban (commercial) samba, marked by the 1917 recording of Ernesto "Donga" dos Santos' 'Pelo Telefone', which featured strong influences from the *maxixe* and *modinha*. By 1928, the more sentimental, slow-tempo *samba cancao* (samba song) emerged, which became the most popular national urban dance due to wide radio and record promotion. In the late 1950s, a reaction against the increasingly "sweet" ballroom samba led toward a greater diversity for performance styles, including samba styles heavily influenced by American rock, and the emergence of *bossa nova*. This continuum of samba styles thereby ranged from pieces identical to street sambas to more sentimental and "sweet" songs with heavy orchestration, muted percussion, and a softer, more intimate vocal style.

The street samba, specifically, is intimately associated with the proletarian *favelas* (hillside slums in Rio de Janeiro), and some samba composers have attempted to confront social issues and the nation's opulent wealth and abject poverty.[5] The carnival samba became a focal activity for favela residents and is performed throughout the year at various formal and informal occasions, reaching its climax at Carnival in Rio de Janeiro. Since 1928, the processional Carnival samba groups were formally organized into "schools" that competed for prizes awarded by a selected jury. Samba processions became increasingly extravagant, combining elaborate floats, sumptuous costumes, narrative or topical themes (in the case of *sambas de enredo*), intricate group choreography, and samba music. Musically, the samba comprises a choral melody with instrumental accompaniment; the vocal part consists of verses sung by a solo male, alternating with refrains rendered (generally in unison) by a female or mixed chorus. The arched, quadratic, diatonic melodies are wholly European in character. The lyrics occasionally deal with contemporary topical or sociopolitical events, but more often, they concern unrequited love, Carnival, or the samba itself. The musical accompaniment of the street samba is dominated by the *bateria* of percussion instruments, which perform intricate syncopated ostinati over the steady binary pulse of the *surdo* bass drums. Chordophones (especially the ukulele-like *cavaquinho*) are also present but often inaudible alongside brass instruments and the *bateria* of percussion instruments, and samba ensembles range widely in size, from informal groups of around a dozen musicians to massive and accordingly cacophonous entourages of over several hundred. The commercial samba was exploited by the government and the dominant classes as a vehicle for propaganda, and it became subject to censorship under Brazil's harsh right-wing military rule. Since the early 1980s, under partial civilian rule, a more open and free ambience has led to greater socio-politicization of song texts, as well as new levels of banality and pornography in lyrics and performance acts.

The evolution of popular music in Latin America can be seen as the result of the blending of European and African musical elements into new, syncretic music conditioned by urbanization and the mass media, and, with it, intense social and cultural changes labelled under the broad umbrella term of globalization (see also Manuel 1988: 24–26). These music styles, including calypso, mambo, reggae, salsa, samba, steelband, tango, *balada*, and others, have all competed with markets around the world (Averill 1998: 93), and numerous crazes for Latin American popular music, such as for the *balada* sung by Cuban singer Ibrahim Ferrer, figure prominently in the popularity of international music marketed as World Music (see, e.g., my interview with World Circuit owner Nick Gold, who produced the multi-million-selling album *Buena Vista Social Club*; Krüger 2015). Since the 1980s, the *balada* (commercially called Latin pop)—romantic music often sung by males interpreting modern romance while clearly appealing to women—has become the most widely consumed and commercially successful music. The growing interest in World Music reflects and explains the growth of music labels and production and distribution companies that release or rerelease original recordings to new markets. Spanish-American music with success on international markets has often been disseminated indirectly through others' interpretations, rather than through original versions by Latin American musicians, such as in *Buena Vista Social Club*. Musical pieces are also often transformed to conform to fit stereotypes of Latin American people and cultures; possibly Ibrahim Ferrer is such a Cuban stereotype, depicted by the media in a particular way to reflect Cuban people and life.

Popular Music during the Golden Age of (Organized) Capitalism

The 1940s are often regarded as the beginnings of more intense globalizing tendencies, linked to the evolution of capitalism in major industrial economies. Often called the Golden Age of capitalism, which lasted until the mid-

1970s, this time marked the take-off phase of globalization and the boom of "organized capitalism" (Lash and Urry 1987) in major (western) industrial economies. As the "winner" of the Cold War, the United States established hegemonic control over the international economic system, which led the US to play a dominating role in the last decades and Europe to play a subordinate role to the US. The US was able to build a successful economy, with little economic competition from western countries like Germany, France, Britain, or Japan, which all struggled to recover from the devastation caused during World War II. The US economy became driven by the logic of organized capitalism and Fordism as an economic practice, characterized by large-scale production of standardized goods for mass consumption, and accompanied by a developing culture of promotion and advertising, and internationalization in search for new markets. The societal formation of organized capitalism in the West resulted from governmental intervention to save capitalism "from a near-terminal crisis" that resulted from "the excesses of an earlier, 'liberal' phase" (McGuigan 2016: 66), as well as the challenges posed by the counter-system of socialism/communism to capitalist civilization since the early twentieth century. The organized phase thrived on the successes of Keynesian economic policies in generating rapid growth with high employment (Marglin and Schor 1992). It was a period of considerable equalization in the capitalist world, including enhanced access to and participation in the arts, with the state playing a greatly extended role in the cultural field. Modern forms of public-sector cultural policy were established in arts councils, broadcasting corporations, and cultural ministries. The incorporation of socialist elements became a notable feature of western organized capitalism until the late twentieth century, including, for example, extensive state intervention and economic planning, strong representation of labor and reward systems, welfare states, strong trade unionism, and nationalization of health services (McGuigan 2016: 34). The mid-point of the twentieth century is thus defined by its democratic moment in Western Europe and the US:

> For the first time in the history of capitalism, the general health of the economy was seen as depending on the prosperity of the mass of wage-earning people. This was clearly expressed in the economic policies associated with Keynesianism, but also in the logic of the cycle of mass production and mass consumption embodied in so-called 'Fordist' production methods. In those industrial societies, which did not become communist, a certain social compromise was reached between capitalist business interests and working people ... [whereby] business interests learned to accept certain limitations on their capacity to use their power. And democratic political capacity concentrated at the level of the nation state was able

to guarantee those limitations, as firms were largely subordinate to the authority of national states ... The basic democratic imperatives of an economy dependent on the cycle of mass production and mass consumption sustained by public spending remained the main policy impetus of the mid-century moment until the mid-1970s (Crouch 2004: 8).

Social democracy thus transformed capitalism in the US, Western Europe, and satellite territories. Since the 1960s, nations in Western Europe, Asia, and elsewhere adopted similar economic models and witnessed a huge economic rise, even though the US remained the largest international investor and dominant military power well into the late 1990s.[6]

The Golden Age of capitalism coincided with the "official" beginnings of popular music in many historical studies of popular music (e.g. Bennett 2001; Moore 2011: ix; Regev 2013; see also the British Music Experience 2016). The post-war era marked the enormous success of rock 'n' roll in the 1950s and of rock in the 1960s. While the phonograph was the first mass-recording device, it was now followed by the LP as a widespread medium for the dissemination of popular music. The first half of the twentieth century also saw the emergence of the film industry, which coincided with "the formation of a mass entertainment market and the sociality of theatre in an urban-industrial society" (McGuigan 2016: 98). Dominated by only few, very large studios of which almost all were American based in Hollywood, cinema was the first media industry to serve a truly global market and has undoubtedly contributed to the importance of the movie as a way of mass disseminating popular music. The most dramatic and important media technology to emerge was television, which has gradually replaced the global dissemination of popular music via cinema, notably MTV since the 1980s. While early broadcasting, both radio and television, was mainly a domestic medium of reception, broadcasting gradually developed into a global phenomenon. In the US, radio and television have since their beginnings been vehicles for advertising and sponsorship, and thus exclusively commercial media, a trend that has also been imported into other countries where hitherto public service broadcasting has been privatized. In terms of technologies, electric instruments (electric pedal-steel guitars and basses, pianos) transformed the sound of popular music in Europe and the US during the 1950s. This electronic musical revolution, along with Anglo-American pop-rock music, spread globally and has affected music cultures all over the world.

From the 1940s onwards, "youth" emerged as a new social class during this phase, which became a new target market for youth-oriented popular music and for new markets more generally. Youth in both the US and Europe, as well as elsewhere, became increasingly preoccupied with exploring the self, their identity, sexuality, ethnicity, and race. Musical consumption became a means for "self-definition, of self-construction, of making fantasies, experiencing nostalgia" (Taylor 2016: 41). This was followed in the 1960s by the rise of social movements led by the youth counterculture, contributing toward a new "ideology of freedom" that included freedoms of expression, sexual relationships, consumer choice, lifestyles, and artistic expression. The 1960s were regarded as a period when popular music became completely revolutionized, whether it was due to experimentation with drugs, anger over the Vietnam War, or the civil rights and women's movements. For the first time in modern history, humans journeyed into space and completed an orbit of the Earth in 1961 (Yuri Gagarin), followed in 1969 by Neil Armstrong who became the first human to walk on the moon, which completely changed the way that the world became perceived—as one global entity. The civil rights and feminist movements achieved significant success, eventually culminating in the passage of the Civil Rights Act in 1964, which made it illegal to discriminate on the basis of race, color, religion, sex, or national origin. Commodified music thereby became a means by which (young) people construct, express, and shape identities. And yet these freedoms, including the belief in one's individuality, has led to a rise in social incoherence. And some social groupings have sought to combat this social incoherence by reviving older forms of fascism and nationalism, evident by the rise in popularity in Nazi rock and, later, white power music, which revived culturally deep-rooted racialized ideas and narratives. Identity is important for self-fashioning through the consumption of particular goods, which enables entry into a particular social group and finding a sense of social stability. By the 1970s, music had thus become not only an object of consumption but an important means for self-definition and identity-making.

The Music Recording Industry
In the 1940s, the recording industry in Europe was almost destroyed and suffered from a post-war shortage of materials. London-based Columbia and Berlin's Deutsche Grammophon offices were destroyed, and the public did not have the means to buy records. This was also true for Japan, whose record industry was devastated and only slowly recovered during the 1950s. Across the ocean, record production in the US was about to peak. The US recording industry witnessed a dramatic boom during the 1940s, with more than half of the world's total records sold in the US. Consumer demand now grew for popular music, including country, and "race records" (e.g. rhythm 'n' blues (R&B)). This was the decade of the crooner with such household names as Bing Crosby, Frank Sinatra, and Perry Como, while the jazz scene was dominated by Ella Fitzgerald and Louis Armstrong. The distribution network of "black

music" increasingly expanded, with black popular music developing separately from theater, dance halls, and tours of black artists. The emergence of originally black-oriented but mostly white-owned labels led gradually to the widespread popularity of black music in the North. Yet the boom in record sales also enabled the production of more obscure classical repertoires, including lute music, ancient music, and ultra-modern experimental music. By the late 1940s, a wide range of 78rpm records was available in the US. American "hits" of the 1940s and 1950s included songs in a simple catchy melody and tunes from Broadway shows.

Postwar culture saw significant technological changes, including tape recording and the LP record, which, together with the widespread use of radio equipment, meant that the history of the music industry became the history of the American record industry. Bing Crosby, for example, began to record on tape his hugely popular radio programs in 1947, and other radio stations, recording studios, and film companies soon utilized the new technology. The new technology improved the sound production of records considerably, most evident in recordings of classical music. Classical music and jazz were recorded on LP records by big companies like CBS, while RCA introduced in 1949 both the single (for popular hits) and EP (extended play; for larger-scale works) record in individual cardboard sleeves, issuing its first LP record in 1950. The quality of domestic equipment improved too, including sound reproduction equipment, amplifiers, and speakers. The recording of popular music on LP record became common in the late 1960s (Gronow and Saunio 1998: 98). The new technology spread to Europe in the 1960s where the rising standard of living and growing competition between record companies provided new opportunities for artists, conductors, and entrepreneurs.

The new record speeds of 33 and 45 signaled the power of the big American companies. Indeed, the 1940s saw the beginnings of an increasingly integrated and concentrated music recording industry, dominated by an oligopoly of US-based major record companies and their take-overs of/tie-ins with more wide-ranging music interests and other entertainment industries like film and radio. Integration and concentration occurred along vertical lines, connecting companies up and down the production-consumption chain. By 1938,

> the music business [in the US] was now part of film and radio corporations of a sort that did not yet exist in Britain ... As radios replaced record players in people's homes ... the source of music profits shifted ... to rights and royalties [which] marked a fusion of interests between the radio, cinema and record industries (Frith 1988: 17).

By the mid-1940s, there were three giants, Columbia, RCA Victor, and Decca, with competition from three smaller competitors, Capitol, MGM, and Mercury, which, with their own factories and effective sales organization, imitated the operations of the Big Three and produced a wide range of music aimed at music consumers all over the US (Gronow and Saunio 1998: 99). As demand for records grew, people working at the fringes of the music industry, including record salesmen, radio shop owners, managers, and the like, began to set up their own record companies, and within a few years hundreds of smaller independents specializing in one particular kind of music had sprung up all over the country, some of which had considerable influence on the future development of the record industry and recorded music (ibid.: 100). By the 1950s, the music recording industry was clearly divided into the major companies and the smaller independents, some of which became very successful indeed.

Successful Independents. The film *Cadillac Records* (2008) provides an insight into the rise of the record label Chess Records in 1940s Chicago. Directed by Darnell Martin, the film depicts the evolution of popular music through the eyes of Leonard Chess, who started Chess Records in Chicago in 1947 and recorded some of the most influential musicians of blues, R&B, gospel and rock 'n' roll. It shows how the label began recording blues music with Muddy Waters and Little Walter in 1947, and eventually gave birth to rock 'n' roll in 1955 with Chuck Berry. The record label was established in Chicago in 1947 by the Polish-Jewish brothers Leonard and Phil Chess. As nightclub owners on the South Side of Chicago, they had heard the electrified blues played by immigrants from the south. The Chess brothers recorded singers and players who played the blues from the Mississippi delta, some of whom had learnt the blues from the likes of Charley Patton, Robert Johnson, and others, including Muddy Waters and Howling Wolf. The brothers quickly signed up younger talent in the mid-1950s when a lighter and faster-paced blues developed in Chicago, including Chuck Berry and Bo Diddley, who soon became the leading figures of rock. Since then, Chess Records has sold in the millions (Gronow and Saunio 1998: 101).

Meanwhile, Moses Asch, a Polish-Jewish immigrant from Warsaw, set up a new company, Folkways, in 1947 that specialized in American folk music (Gronow and Saunio 1998: 117). The label also featured field recordings by early ethnomusicologists from many parts of the world. The catalogue featured more than 2000 LPs and represented every country in the world. The catalogue constitutes the only available collection of the bygone music by particular tribes or regions. While the label did not attract the "big" stars of folk from the 1960s like Pete Seeger, Bob Dylan, and Joan Baez (reflexive of the emerging "personality cult in folk music"), Folkways became the world's leading specialist folk music label. In 1987, the label archives passed to the national museum of the US, the Smithsonian Institution.

The 1950s. In the 1950s, the audience for commercial music grew substantially, also marked by a noticeable broadening of the taste of concertgoers. Even so, there was a continued separation between popularized classical music, and blues, swing, and jazz. Black entrepreneurs entered the lucrative recording industry of black music, but with varying success. There have been many black-owned companies since the 1940s, but most have been short-lived. The label Motown was an exception. Established by black businessman Berry Gordy Jr in 1959, Motown Records scored its first hit in 1961 with 'Shop Around', the best-selling record and number one in the R&B charts in the US at the time, followed by a string of hits throughout the 1960s with names like Martha Reeves, Stevie Wonder, Marvin Gaye, the Supremes, and the Jackson Five in its catalogue, which meant that by the early 1970s Motown was the largest black-owned label in the US and became renowned for its distinctive Motown sound (Gronow and Saunio 1998: 158–60).

During the 1950s, R&B records were played more regularly by radio stations in the North with predominantly young and white listeners, and black musicians played concerts increasingly for white audiences. Records by white singers increasingly imitated or even copied the R&B style. The emerging popular music became rock 'n' roll, starting a new musical wave whose global influence began to be felt within a few years (Gronow and Saunio 1998: 102). While rock 'n' roll was just in its infancy, there was a huge outburst of musical activity around this newly evolving style. Most popular hit rock 'n' roll records in the 1950s were about innocent love stories and adhered to familiar popular and folk music styles from the last century (ibid.: 161). Rock 'n' roll became youth-oriented music, quite separate from other popular music, and introduced influences from black music. Rock 'n' roll led to big changes in the record industry, as previously small local companies, like Chess or Atlantic, now acquired national significance. While classical music, jazz, and other local music still generated significant sales, it was rock 'n' roll that triggered an economic boom in the American record industry, a trend that followed in Europe only in the 1960s.

With increased competition for record sales at the time, new sales tactics had to be developed, leading to the emergence of aggressive advertising and promotional campaigns in newspapers and on billboards that could only be afforded by major companies. Another key to success was radio, which had the potential to trigger big hits of completely unknown records through promotion by the radio announcer. Record companies regularly began to bribe radio announcers, forged request letters to radio stations, bought their own records to increase sale statistics, offered an artist to play for free, or credited a radio announcer as co-composer. This way of promotion by way of bribery by the record companies, which amounted to thousands of dollars, became known as "payola" (Gronow and Saunio 1998: 106). An often-cited, more current example is when Interscope Records paid KUFO-FM (101.1), a Portland, Oregon radio station US$5000 to play the Limp Bizkit song 'Counterfeit' regularly during a five-week period (Jackson *et al.* 2013: 126). The new marketing logic coincided with the realization that "huge sales of one title are much more profitable than tidy sales of lots of titles" (Frith 1988: 17), which impacted on sale strategies of rock music in the 1960s that depended on a "star" system of performers who could guarantee financial profits to cover such upfront promotional costs. (Even so, the industry also supported some musicians who turned out to be moderately profitable—stars, "who shone less brightly" (Taylor 2016: 51)). Under the motto "sex sells", sexual exploitation and objectification of women, as well as gendered stereotyping, developed as core advertising strategies to achieve profitable music record sales at the time (Goffman 1979). Many small companies discontinued, as the Big Few, with their superior organized distribution networks, advertising departments, and famous artists won back their dominance over the US music market. In the 1950s, overall record sales in the world were dominated by the US record market (Gronow and Saunio 1998: 118).

While the US record industry had exploded into rapid growth immediately after the war, Europe experienced an era defined by the decline of the old great powers. As two new superpowers emerged, the Soviet Union and the US, Europe became divided into a US-led Western Bloc, which was rebuilt through the American Marshall Plan, and a Soviet-led Eastern Bloc, which fell in the Soviet sphere of influence. While Western Europe slowly recovered from the economic downturn of the war, the record industry began to flourish again in the 1960s, with West European record sales doubling between 1955 and 1960 (Gronow and Saunio 1998: 118–20). A large proportion of records sold here were of American origin, pressed locally under license agreements, and so West European record companies sought close ties with their American colleagues. The newly emerging singing stars in the US thus became famous in Western Europe too. Meanwhile, vernacular popular music, or popular music in national idioms, from across Europe was still being produced. Most of this music was sold nationally, with some exceptions like Evelyn Kuenneke (German comedienne), Eddie Calvert (British trumpeter), Edith Piaf (French chanteuse), Olavi Virta (Finnish tango singer), or Italian *canzone*, who became fairly successful European-wide (Gronow and Saunio 1998: 129). Yet popular music suffered a serious identity crisis in Europe, and the younger postwar generation yearned for different music, and so the best-selling records were dominated by American singers of the 1950s and 1960s. West European record companies thus began to record domestic rock 'n' roll stars, but their American counterparts were still more successful. Meanwhile, sales of classical music recordings recovered more quickly and the role of the record producer became more demanding. Thus besides EMI, Decca, Grammophon, and Philips became significant again in the recording of classical music, including previously unknown Baroque music and older music from the Middle Ages, large-scale classical productions of Romantic music, and Italian and German opera, alongside newly appearing small enterprises devoted to classical music (ibid.: 122–24). Yet the conservativeness of classical music culture and relative unpopularity of local vernacular popular music may explain the rapid subsequent breakthrough of American rock 'n' roll in Western Europe.

In Eastern Europe and the Soviet Union, the record industry developed differently and remained largely unknown to the West. In the Soviet Union, the record companies that existed before the revolution became nationalized under socialism, with its first products featuring speeches by Lenin and reissues of selected old recordings, followed in the 1930s by more concentrated efforts to record "the entire gamut of music ... from the soloists of the Bolshoi to the latest accomplishments in Soviet jazz ... [and] the country's minority Asiatic nationalities" (Gronow and Saunio 1998: 127). The record industry in the communist bloc was typically concentrated in the hands of one state-owned company: Melodiya (Soviet Union), AMIGA (GDR), Polskie Nagranie (Poland), Supraphon (Czechoslovakia), Hungaroton (Hungary), Electrecord (Romania), and Balkanton (Bulgaria). Educational and cultural-political goals tended to dominate record production in these countries, and recording artists and their recordings had to be wedded to socialist realism promoted by their communist states. Since the 1960s, socialist labels like the newly established Melodiya company in the Soviet Union began marketing their artists' recordings on a larger scale abroad, and with annual sales of nearly 200 million during the 1970s, Melodiya became one of the six largest record companies worldwide (see further Gronow and Saunio 1998: 179–81).

The East German label AMIGA, for example, has become legendary for its turbulent success in both East and West Germany, both musically and economically (Sittner 2017). The monopoly label of the GDR belonged to the state-owned Volkseigener Betrieb Deutsche Schallplatten, and besides economic objectives also adhered to the objectives of the Kulturministerium (Cultural Ministry). With its profits, the label subsidized the entire cultural sector of the GDR. For fifty years, AMIGA recorded the complete repertoire of contemporary GDR music, with more than 2000 records and 5000 singles, ranging from rock and pop, via jazz, to Schlager and folk, with hits like Silly's 'Bataillon d'Amour', 'Kleine weiße Friedenstaube' (Little White Dove of Peace), and Depeche Mode's classic 'Enjoy the Silence'. AMIGA also brought out records by artists from Western Europe, including hits by The Beatles, Bob Dylan, and Roger Whitaker. Limited edition AMIGA records were quickly sold and known in colloquial circles as "Bückware" (goods "hidden" behind a sales desk, only in reach for a "befriended" sales person willing to bend down to get that limited edition record in promise for a favour returned by the buyer). AMIGA coined the new music genre of Ostrock (East Rock) with bands like City, Puhdys, Karat, Silly, and others, branding it as the "sound of the GDR" and exported Ostrock successfully to West Germany. The most successful album by Karat, *Der Blaue Planet* (The Blue Planet), sold nearly 480,000 records in West Germany until the fall of the Berlin Wall in 1989. The recordings are renowned for their superior quality. With musical and technological perfection, producers, musicians, and technicians produced the records superbly under conditions of real socialism. Up to the present day, Ostrock is hugely popular among German rock music fans.

In Asia, Japan slowly recovered from the devastation of World War II, and with the introduction of the LP, the number of record companies grew. While there was a growing number of smaller local companies, the most significant companies were joint ventures between electronics companies and the largest record corporations: Sony-CBS, Matsushita-PolyGram, Toshiba-EMI, JVC-RCA (Gronow and Saunio 1998: 209). During the 1950s and 1960s, there was a growing demand for western popular music, notably rock, but also for other genres like jazz, classical music, and other styles. This trend turned around during the 1970s when demand for domestic products grew and outsold musical imports, although modern Japanese music has been moving closer toward rock in style. Since the 1980s, Japan has grown into the second largest record market worldwide, with Japanese-owned CBS Records (acquired by Sony in 1988) becoming one of the world's largest record companies. During the 1980s and following Japan's lead, other Asian countries such as South Korea, China, Taiwan, Singapore, Indonesia, and the Philippines have witnessed growing record sales.

The 1960s and 1970s. From the early 1960s until 1978, the recording industry witnessed considerable growth worldwide due to the gradual decline of international trade barriers, the increasing standard of living and spending power of consumers, and the arrival of cheap cassette recorders (Gronow and Saunio 1998: 135–38). The US was still the leader in the recording industry in the 1960s, and CBS was one of the biggest record companies worldwide (ibid.: 140). The big corporations like Victor and CBS (US) and EMI and Decca (Europe) grew in size as they extended their operations into all continents, and smaller companies continuously emerged, which either disappeared, or merged with the big corporations. By the 1970s, Decca declined and the giants PolyGram (Europe) and Warner (US) rose to TNC size, with operations in electronics and entertainment. By the 1970s, there were five giants dominating the recording industry, CBS, EMI, PolyGram, Warner, and RCA, who were all part of larger conglomerates and controlled around half of all record sales worldwide. The other half was shared between mid- and smaller-sized companies all over the world, which produced records in smaller numbers and were able to follow new trends more quickly, to nurture local traditions, and to produce music for minorities, while continuously interacting with the large corporations "in a sort of symbiosis, with each needing the other" (ibid.: 143). Growth in record production itself was thereby steepest in developing countries, where large populations could now afford records, and where local subsidiaries of large corporations operated alongside small local companies to produce records for the local market. In the socialist bloc, meanwhile, the Soviet Union became the second biggest record manufacturer by 1970. The American practice of playing records on radio began to spread to Europe, adopted first by Radio Luxembourg and Radio Monte Carlo, and later by numerous "pirate" radio stations. The record content of radio programming increased considerably, and so did record content and jukeboxes in restaurants, dance halls, and shopping centers. Two-thirds of the most popular records were of European or American origin in the 1960s (ibid.: 164), yet as the record industry grew, pirate production, made possible by the cassette player, reached gigantic proportions in the US, Italy, and many developing countries in the Arab region, Asia, Africa, and parts of South America. By 1976, there were six giants, EMI, CBS, PolyGram, Warner, RCA, and Decca, which experienced a decline in overall sales, possibly due to the prevailing economic slump in England, the lack of new superstars, normal fluctuations in the economy, and, most likely, widespread bootlegging worldwide.

In the late 1950s/early 1960s, sound reproduction moved to stereophony, which marked an important technological development. Simultaneously, studio recording began to make use of the new multi-track technique. One of the great landmarks in recording history exploiting the possibilities offered by recording tape and stereophony to enhance a performance and create a perfect interpretation was Richard Wagner's *Ring of the Nibelung*, made for

Decca between 1958 and 1965 by John Culshaw (Gronow and Saunio 1998: 148–50). In the early 1960s, multi-track recording became more common for popular music, soon developing from 4-track to 8-, 24-, and 32-track recording and an attitude shift toward "layered thinking". Recording possibilities further expanded with newly emerging electronic devices, including the noise reduction system, equalizer, compressor, and limiter, which meant that rock music could now be recorded at full volume. Synthesized sound emerged on new electric instruments such as improved electric organs (e.g. Hammond electric organ) or the Moog synthesizer, while drum machines could keep the beat perfectly, leading to experimental outbursts by some rock groups. The Vocorder device enabled experimentation with vocal production. The electric guitar too was subjected to unprecedented experimentation; its sound altering through a sound breaker, an echo or phasing device, or a pitch changer, as demonstrated by Jimi Hendrix, through whom the electric guitar became a new instrument (ibid.: 158).

During the 1960s, jazz received a surge in popularity in the US with adolescents and young adults, and spread elsewhere, including Germany (e.g. Berlin Jazz Festival), France, and some Scandinavian countries, as well as Japan where jazz artists like Duke Ellington, Gerry Mulligan, and Harry James became popular among young people. The new generation of jazz musicians was shaped by the LP age, some conceiving of jazz as art music, yet others like John Coltrane or Miles Davis seeking complete freedom in improvisation, which meant only modest record sales. Meanwhile, records by big stars in both classical and popular music now enjoyed success worldwide, while country remained successful for its loyal US audience, a genre that is steeped in tradition. The folk music industry flourished in Europe, particularly in German-speaking Alpine regions of Switzerland, Bavaria, and Austria, producing popular records of yodelers, brass bands, and accordion groups in a pure oompah style sung in local dialects about topics drawn from Catholic mythology. German labels have since produced thousands of records of *Volksmusik*, promoted by television programs like *Feste der Volksmusik* solely dedicated to this genre, all of which producing up to the present day its own immensely successful stars like Heino, Andrea Berg, Florian Silbereisen, and others.

By the 1960s, rock music had replaced the Broadway tunes and had become the prevailing style in the international record industry. This youth-oriented, modernized rock 'n' roll music became the music of the US baby-boom generation of the hippie culture, with its opposition to the Vietnam War and nuclear weapons, the advocacy of world peace, and hostility to the authority of government and big business. It meant a new roster of artists and a transformation of the whole economy of record production, including rising artists' fees. The blues from the 1920s became increasingly recognized again, and new groups in the US and England such as the Butterfield Blues Band and Fleetwood Mac started to play blues borrowed from old blues records to growing audiences, signing contracts with the big corporations as their popularity grew. Blues-derived music became influenced by artists' political, religious, and societal views. This was a period of great intellectual ferment in the US, as

> successful rock musicians began to think of themselves as artists, who had important things to say ... [and] took on board influences from electronic music, eastern music, blues, and jazz. Song lyrics no longer told of love, but took a stand on the Vietnam War, politics, feminism, ecology, religion, drugs and everything that was being publicly debated (Gronow and Saunio 1998: 161).

Rock accounted for over half the record sales in the US in the early 1970s and was internationalized with great success. More localized versions of rock music, sung in native languages, began to emerge in different parts of the world when Anglo-American hits were translated into the vernacular and the rhythms impacted on the indigenous sounds. The rapidly growing music industry had spread rock everywhere. In Europe, for instance, it was in the 1960s when rock's influence became noticeable. In England, new songs were sung in English, yet this was not so in France, Italy, Finland, Sweden, and (to a lesser extent) the Netherlands and West Germany (Gronow and Saunio 1998: 164), and many other countries or regions in Europe. (National) folk rock was born, which was released by small national labels in small batches, and marketed to an enthusiastic following. Meanwhile, hundreds of instrumental groups, consisting of a solo singer, electric guitar, bass, and drums, sprung up in the early 1960s, particularly in England, whose music was initially influenced from American rock 'n' roll, with some increasingly composing their own material. 1964 became known as the "Year of The Beatles", the first Boy Band phenomenon to achieve global hyper-success. Great emphasis was placed on the perfection of sound through studio production in Europe. Live performances at ear-splitting volumes, made possible by the new technologies, rendered bands like Led Zeppelin to be "the kings of stadium rock", while new studio technology captured "the illusion of colossal power" on record (ibid.: 161). Music festivals became increasingly popular and were dwarfed by the immensity of the famous Woodstock music festival. While many successful rock groups got louder, the latter half of the sixties also saw the rise in popularity of softer pop music for "easier listening".

In the 1970s, the pioneering efforts of musicians and producers from the 1960s meant that jazz and rock musicians began to explore collaborations, both in the West and elsewhere. Meanwhile, synthesized sounds began to shape pop music, and radio stations gave increased air time to pop music produced with new-fangled electronic synthesizers. Gradually, electronic instruments like electronic keyboards and drum machines became standardized and mass-produced. Social progressive values from the 1960s continued to grow in the 1970s, even though the hippie culture faded towards the middle part of the decade. Music styles and genres seemingly exploded in variety, which were all consumed via affordable vinyl records. Improved mixing desks paved the way for musical experimentation beyond the technical capabilities of the 1960s and led to the rise in popularity of electronic music. By 1977, punk rock developed with bands like the Sex Pistols and the Ramones thrashing their way to success, marked by outrageous stage behavior and offbeat arrangements that drew both praise and discouragement. Punk was about simplicity, loudness, aggressiveness, and irritation, and its subcultural style aimed at "a surrealistically ragged look, with ripped garments, safety pins, and carefully planned clashes of style ... clothing found in a rubbish bin" (Gronow and Saunio 1998: 163). Along with other trends, punk represented youth's general suspicion with capitalism, class, politics, and the record companies' partiality for superstars. It spread elsewhere in the world, leading to the production of self-financed rock records by local punk labels across Europe, the US, Iceland, New Zealand, Finland, and others, including socialist states, and their distribution by hand and mail order, and through fanzines. By the 1980s, independent labels had shaped public consciousness to such an extent that "indie" rock became a concept or musical genre in itself. Yet, encouraged by their success, the most successful punk or rock groups agreed to recording contracts with the big corporations, who could buy out any label that had nurtured promising artists. Thus, the ultimate winners were the big giants by the 1980s.

As punk waned, smooth disco dance music began to dominate the late 1970s when the "avant-garde-ness" of experimental rock of the 1960s gradually became a prominent ingredient in dance and popular music. The discothèque first emerged in the 1960s and became popular with people when disco music gained growing popularity and was played increasingly on the radio in the late 1970s. The Bee Gees exploded into the music world as the ushers for the disco era, which was in full swing in 1978, selling more records than anyone thought possible. For instance, the soundtrack for the film *Saturday Night Fever*, whose subject was fanatical disco dancers and which became an international phenomenon, sold nearly thirty million copies. The film was produced by Paramount and songs released by PolyGram, which shows the combined power of the record and film industries.

The Global Spread of Pop-Rock Music
The period from 1945 until the mid-1970s is regarded as the early historical phase (1950s and 1960s) and a period of consecrated beginnings (late 1960s and 1970s) in the spread and influence of western pop-rock music globally (Regev 2013: 105). With the evolution of production and dissemination technologies, western pop-rock music spread worldwide, with the initial effect that many musicians began to cover Anglo-American stars and hits, and performed imitations of American pop-rock. The late 1960s saw the beginnings of more localized versions of pop-rock music and paved the way for musical adaptations within a national context, marked by the emergence of national rock in many countries. Many musicians around the world self-mobilized into membership of pop-rock music and embraced the new western musical styles and instruments, while at the same time moving within the field of national culture, "where they were propelled to create works whose form, content, and meaning arguably represent some variants of ethnic singularity or national uniqueness" (ibid.: 98). Their creative possibilities came to consist of both western pop-rock music and their own ethno-national heritage, thereby transposing schemes from the global to the national field by, for instance, singing in native languages about topics concerning local issues, experiences, and situations, and/or incorporating stylistic elements and creative techniques from their own tradition, such as native musical instruments, indigenous vocal techniques, and traditional rhythmic or melodic patterns, or recording cover versions of traditional music. The term hybridization is often used in this context to explain the creative practices of merging and fusing elements of ethno-national heritage with pop-rock music.

Thomas Mapfumo's Afropop. In Zimbabwe, a unique political and national popular musical style emerged by the mid-1970s under the impact of urbanization and Africanization, even though Zimbabwe was not immune to Congolese, South African, and Afro-American musical influences (see also Manuel 1988: 104–106). Urbanization meant that young workers adapted and reoriented their cultural values brought with them from traditional village life, which was often accompanied by considerable poverty, exploitation, insecurity, alienation, and impoverishment brought on by wage labor, money economy, work patterns, nationalism, the individual or nuclear family as the predominant socio-economic unit, new bureaucracies, and the mass media (Manuel 1988: 16). In this context, artistic creation helped in adapting to the new urban environment. Thomas Mapfumo ("Lion of Zimbabwe") is perhaps one of the most foremost Zimbabwean musicians, whose popular music style is characterized as electric *mbira* music. While his early musical engagements were influenced by western rock and other well-established styles, he began creating his own music since the 1970s when Zimbabwe experienced the phase of Africanization that swept the continent. So while Thomas Mapfumo is a musician who has absorbed "pop-rock music ... [as] a signifier of universal modernity" (Regev 2013: 4), he later transformed his music into "an expression of late modern musical nationalism" (ibid.: 23).

The emphasis on identifiable African musical features is significant, which reflects the Africanization process that occurred in the 1970s, marked by a strongly nationalist post-independence period in Africa (Murphy 2007: 45). During this time, scholars and artists across the continent sought to revive older rural forms, or searched for new, distinctive national modes of cultural expression by incorporating so-called ethnic traditions. The cultural project sought to break with the colonial period by asserting an authentic African identity (ibid.: 46). The desire to adopt local culture for popular music grew significantly. Rather than looking outside for cultural influences, Africans were increasingly turning toward their own, local cultures for inspiration. Consequently, Afropop is popular music that expresses and resonates with people's hybrid, complex, and urban identities in contemporary Africa. It is "not simply a bi-product of Western culture: it is the product of African, national, ethnic and regional cultures, and it is given specific meaning within these contexts" (ibid.: 57). As such, it is aimed at Africans in local markets, and it bears little resemblance to the traditional music found in rural contexts, or the music marketed as World Music to consumers and audiences in the West. The creation and production of Afropop is thus defined by urbanity, secularism, entertainment, and a star system, and its styles depend significantly on where and whom it is aimed at: the local market, the global market, both, or those situated between and beyond them. Afropop is genuinely the product of regional, ethnic, national, and African cultures in different markets. It is given different meanings by different consumers, which illustrates the complex nature of intercultural relations in the modern world, and the crucial role played by economic factors.

Mapfumo's Africanized music became unique through his experimentation with traditional sounds and beats that he derived from the traditional musics of the Shona tribe, and his adopting of the mbira by bringing mbira players into his band and translating the rhythms and sounds into guitar riffs. For the vocals, he drew on traditional songs and chants and began to use Shona lyrics, which could not be understood by whites. Some of Mapfumo's lyrics were overtly political, including his sharp criticism of the government of President Robert Mugabe. His *chimurenga* songs ("songs of struggle") had considerable political influence and soon became a valuable means of communication and tool for the liberation movement. His modern music differed considerably from traditional styles in its instrumentation, with the use of electric guitars, keyboards, computers, and recording equipment, as well as in its pop song styles and forms, and in terms of the social contexts, which in traditional music in sub-Saharan Africa usually involves communication with ancestors, and the use of musical instruments (like the mbira) by specialist musicians for a specific deity or ancestral spirit while utilizing an expanded soundworld. Indeed, many traditional African beliefs are based on the idea that the ancestors watch over their communities, and so music is often played to "talk" to the ancestors. By comparison, Zimbabwean pop is an archetypal example of secular entertainment music, whose production and consumption are not associated with rituals or religion, and instead involves a star system and modernized musical sound, while still absorbing and adapting many characteristics of traditional sub-Saharan African music.

Other Afropop styles have been similarly shaped by the pop-rock aesthetic. For example, highlife, a West African style of dance music, developed in Ghana in the 1950s by merging influences from brass bands, traditional dance rhythms, palm-wine guitar music, and western dance music, and was soon taken up by newer electric bands who used western instruments and adopted a sound related to western pop music. The social context for music making differs too, as popular styles like West African *juju* are typically played for recreation and entertainment, rather than used in traditional functional contexts like births, weddings, funerals, and the like. In Senegal, Baaba Maal developed a playing technique on the acoustic guitar that echoes traditional *kora* music, while also having a blues feel from the guitar sound. He has made both more traditional and popular music based on *griot* traditions, evident in his first international album, *Bayyo* (Orphan) (1991) with arrangements in the Fulani style (a nationality within Senegal) and percussion that draws on Wolof, Mandinka, and Casamance traditions, while being produced to western recording standards. Meanwhile, Youssou N'Dour epitomizes the new generation of West African pop performers. While adopting western instrumentation and recording techniques, N'Dour continued to sing in the Wolof language and used traditional songs and rhythms. The basis of much of his percussion is the *tama* armpit drum, which is traditionally played at Wolof weddings, baptisms, and other ceremonies, and is the drum that calls everyone to dance. With his Star Band, he developed a new style of dance music that he called *mbalax* (rhythm), which also contains reggae and jazz. The traditional Senegalese elements in his music are still strong today. These Afropop styles all share a very different rhythm to western popular music, alongside influences from the West, which makes them simultaneously unique and the same (Manuel 1988: 89–95).

Rock Music in Paraguay. In Paraguay, rock music is often termed *rock nacional* or *rock paraguayo* to describe rock music that originates in Paraguay, as well as rock music created and performed by Paraguayans residing abroad. Rock music became popular in Paraguay during the 1960s under the influence of American rock music culture and the introduction of electronic instruments, and gave rise to rock music festivals and rock bands in Asunción.[7] Early rock bands from the 1960s, such as Blue Caps, which was founded in Asunción in 1965, were inspired by American and Argentinian rock music and sang (in Spanish) about daily personal experiences, including the political system and oppression under the fierce dictatorship of former President Alfredo Stroessner (ruled 1954–1989). They usually performed music of their own compositions alongside covers of songs by international bands from the US, Europe, and Latin America, specifically Argentine rock. Wearing long hair and clad in leather as a sign of rebellion, this underground rock movement (also known as *música progresiva*) was targeted by the state and branded as a bad influence and suffered political censorship. The Blue Caps therefore settled in Argentina where they spent nearly a decade, while recording three EPs (1968, 1969 and 1971). Professional recordings of Paraguayan rock music during this time are extremely rare, given the political context, and mostly survive in the form of home-made tape recordings. In this political climate, the first significant event in the emergence of *rock paraguayo* was the Primer Festival Beat de la Canción (First Beat of the Song Festival) held in the Estadio Comuneros in 1968. The 1970s were less tense for Paraguayan rock music culture and witnessed the emergence of new rock bands, such as Aftermads, Hobbies, and Tommys Superstars, as well as another rock music event, the Festival de Música Progresiva (Festival of Progressive Music) in 1974. Rock bands of the 1970s were less engaged in original and rebellious musical material, but primarily copied American rock songs, while imitating their style of vocal delivery and instrumental line-up.

The year 1980 marked the official beginning of (recorded) Paraguayan rock music with the emergence of the band Pro Rock Ensamble. The band is regarded as the pioneer of rock music and debuted with the release of a single in 1980, a vinyl record containing two songs, 'Ego Kid y Joe el Justiciero' and 'En los campos del amor'. This was followed with the release of their LP *Música Para Los Perros* on 23 November 1983,[8] the first full-length LP ever recorded in Paraguay that earned the group—after three years of intense activity—the reputation of "el mejor conjunto de rock del país" (the major rock band of the country) (Szarán 2009). Indeed, the album represents the realization of the rock underground movement that had begun more than ten years ago, even though the band were unaware at the time that they were making the first rock music album.[9] For the first time, a song from the rock movement, 'Los Junior's Beat' from the album *Música Para Los Perros*, was played by radio stations, while *Billboard* magazine commented, "The anticipated release of the LP by Pro Rock Ensamble meets all expectations and reveals even more unsuspected possibilities of this band."[10]

In 1996, the album *Música Para Los Perros* was re-released on CD, containing all songs in remastered format together with one bonus track of an unreleased live recording.

Although Pro Rock Ensamble split up in 1983, given the low profitability of rock music at the time, their work led to a gradual increase during the 1980s in recordings of *rock paraguayo*, notably on demo tapes for radio broadcasts and cassettes for hand-to-hand distribution. Rock began to assert itself with the appearance of new rock bands that engaged in a variety of musical sub-styles, including hard rock/heavy metal and thrash metal. Moreover, there was a trend among some rock bands (e.g. Krhizya, Dos Tribus, Corrosión, Taperã) to explore the roots of Paraguayan traditional and popular (folklore) music, notably the *polca paraguaya*, *guaranía*, and songs in the Guaraní language. For instance, Taperã, a Paraguayan band who had emigrated to Argentina, released a cassette in 1989, which was marked by Socialist ideology and the use of the Guaraní language. Paraguayan rock bands have since continued to develop new rock and metal sub-genres, including experimental and fusion rock music. Rock paraguayo clearly reflects the cultural influence of the West in spreading pop-rock music worldwide as it becomes blended with national and local styles and sensibilities.

To conclude, beginning in the nineteenth century, musical modernization meant to balance advantages of old and new, and adopt western sound recording and broadcasting technology and other products of western culture. Across the globe, musical modernization went hand in hand with the evolution of new urban societies, which were a fertile breeding ground for new syncretic music, which expressed the hybrid social identities of the new urban classes in the US, Europe, and elsewhere. The US-dominated music recording industry grew into an increasingly integrated and concentrated music recording industry that became replicated in the local music industries of countries around the world. Rock 'n' roll and rock music, electric instruments, mass media, and new recording and dissemination technologies transformed the sound of popular music globally. Yet economic globalization, that is, expanding global capitalism, also has an "ugly" side to it, conceptualized through the politics of othering in popular music. Representations in much world popular music function in the construction of difference and otherness through racialized and gendered discourses within the hegemonic order of the global music business and wider society.

The Other in Popular Music

Notions of identity, power, and inequality are critical in discussions on the globalization of popular music. The institutionalization of sexist, racist, and other othering sentiments, coupled with commercial opportunism, has shaped the stereotypes and narratives around much commercialized popular culture. Such categorizations highlight difference, marked by the politics of othering, which implies a necessary "other" who is not "us" and unlike "us". Since identity creates classifications of inclusion and exclusion, sameness and difference, the concepts of power and inequality are hugely relevant here, and raise questions as to where power is situated and how inequality is experienced in the contemporary world, answers to which can be found by looking at the historical, social, and cultural factors that have shaped notions of identity, power, and inequality. Indeed, identity has often been used by people in power positions to categorize "self" alongside and/or versus "others". A deeply connected theme here concerns the politics of racialization, which has persisted well into present-day popular culture. Race is steeped in the engineered histories of modern Europe and their particular political and ideological agendas, which sought to construct white definitions of whiteness in terms of their differences from non-whites. European expansionism and colonialism have shaped early globalizing trends and provided the conditions for western forms of racialization in much popular commodified culture. Since the early beginnings of the US-based music industry, popular music entrepreneurs promoted a "negro market" of "race records", which included genres like blues and jazz, and later soul. Deep-rooted racialized ideas have similarly impacted on much commercialized popular culture, given that (musical) globalization is deeply entrenched in racialization since Europeans first arrived in the New World. The discussions that follow here offer explanations about the racialized narratives expressed through and experienced in expressions of racialization in popular culture and explore more outwardly racist expressions in fascist popular music.

Race Music, Race Records in the US
While American record companies had made records for every immigrant community by the 1920s, black music (except "refined" versions for white audiences) had not yet been included in the record companies' catalogues due to a long history of racial segregation. The business of early American popular entertainment was Southern-based, which shaped the plantation-derived stereotypes of black entertainers. Blacks replaced whites as entertainers in blackface minstrelsy in the 1870s, which portrayed stereotyped characters of African Americans, including the smiling "Sambo", the Jim Crow, the Zip Coon, the black muck, Mammy, Uncle Tom, etc., and depicted "African-Americans as happy-go-lucky slaves fit only for the hard work and dependence of plantation life" (Dinerstein 2017: 43). Yet minstrelsy was a means through which whites

saw blacks, believing real African Americans were similar to those portrayed in the shows, and these social contradictions continue to confound race relations today. Jazz gradually helped to combat the Southern plantation images in popular entertainment, yet to have spoken out against racism directly would have been suicide. Jazz musicians instead used language that sublimated violence, such as the horn as ax, "cutting" and "carving", and "ofays" (foes) to describe whites. Black jazz musicians were excluded from Hollywood as composers, musicians, and in studio orchestras (ibid.: 3). Southern jazz venues of the 1920s with names like Cotton Club, Plantation Club, Kentucky Club, or Club Alabam, and jazz bands like McKinney's Cotton Pickers, the Dixies Syncopators, or the Chocolate Dandies are remnants of the racist history of popular entertainment for whites within predictable plantation-derived tableaux, while "most Americans believed in the reality of these racial types as co-invented by Northern minstrels and Southern slave owners to emphasize black inferiority, and perpetuated both by pseudo-scientific theories of social hierarchy and Hollywood imagery" (ibid.: 43–44). Classical music recordings featuring large orchestras, opera companies, and smaller ensembles still enjoyed the most success, and racially-based musical censorship by radio stations and a general disinterest in black audiences by early radio stations had the consequence that jazz and blues recording developed into a separate music category (Frith 1988: 17).

The remnants of racism were well alive in the US-based music recording industry in the early twentieth century. Music record production and broadcasting were outwardly racist and quite literally split into "white" and "black" along the lines of racial segregation. Its industry promoted a "negro market" maintained mainly by small American, independent music companies on a regional level. The recording and promotion of "black music" began in the early twentieth century as a result of a growing demand for classic blues recordings (Garofalo 1993: 238). The new recording sub-industry claimed its own "race market", given that the still legally segregated, established white venues and radio stations usually barred black artists from performing live. For instance, Otto Heinemann, a German immigrant and manager of the OKeh company in New York, suspected that the large black minority would make for a potential music market, and so he recorded the popular black singer Mamie Smith and regularly issued records for the black clientele under the umbrella of "race records", 78rpm phonograph records that were marketed predominantly to African Americans since the 1920s. Other companies soon followed. Ownership of "race music" was thereby firmly in the hands of white entrepreneurs and their record labels, including OKeh, Emerson, Vocalion, Victor, Paramount, and several others. Since the mid-1920s, jazz records also increasingly featured, besides the small jazz band, guitar-playing singers, and jazz grew in popularity with growing demand for famous bands and soloists, with sales peaking between 1927 and 1930 (Gronow and Saunio 1998: 48). Initially recording in New York, the record companies began to discover talent in Chicago, Atlanta, Memphis, New Orleans, and other southern cities. "Race records" included genres like blues and jazz, and later soul, thereby constructing a "black" canon around particular styles and genres. Only a few African American artists were marketed to white audiences; however white Americans gradually began to like and purchase "race records". Between 1945 and 1949, *Billboard* published a Race Records chart, initially covering jukebox plays and from 1948 also covering sales.

The success of some "race records", such as Mamie Smith's recording of 'Crazy Blues' (1920), prompted early record labels to market particular musical styles to distinct markets of African Americans, Italian Americans, Jewish Americans, and others, assuming that their specific musical tastes would in some way be connected to their racial identities, even though in reality listening habits traversed racial boundaries during the jazz age and swing era of the 1920s and 1930s (Ramsey 2003). Record company executives nonetheless continued to assume a homology between race and music consumption, and this assumption reinforced deep-rooted racial essentialism and transplanted it to modern sound recordings. This was compounded by the fact that until 1964, many American states still had racial segregation laws. During the 1940s, thousands of R&B records aimed at black audiences were sold by labels such as Atlantic (New York), King (Cincinnati), Chess (Chicago), Peacock (Houston), and Modern (LA), yet nearly all the turnover was pocketed by the white company owners. By the 1950s, white rock 'n' roll evolved from black R&B. Yet, while African American music became America's popular music, assumptions about racial identity and musical meaning continued to shape the way that African American music was portrayed in American popular culture. The pervasive race consciousness in modern consumer cultures was partly shaped and informed by the conditions of modernity, which "had racism coursing through its development" (Levenson 2011: 99). Modernist literature of the twentieth century bore racist tendencies and institutionalized racism in cultural discourses that were circulating at the time. Social stratification based on race was blatantly visible and officially sanctioned. One contentious case of social stratification was the exhibition of human beings in "human zoos" in European cities like Paris, Hamburg, Antwerp, Barcelona, London, Milan, Warsaw, and Oslo, as well as in New York throughout the eighteenth and nineteenth centuries, which lasted well into the 1950s (David 2013; Mwesigire 2014).

The Politics of Racialization. Race has a long history of shifting meanings and has been associated with different referents like religion, class, culture, and ethnicity at different times. Race is not a universal or absolute concept; rather it is temporarily stabilized by social practice. According to Stuart Hall, race is "a discursive construct ... a sliding signifier" (1997a: 5), which is discursively constructed. This is illustrated in the historical shift of the meaning of the word "race". *La raza* was first used to define Christian aristocratic bloodlines during the Reconquista in the early modern Iberian Peninsula. It became transformed by modern European colonialism and the slave trade, during which "race" was used to justify slavery and colonial hierarchies. The European racially classifying system emerged when peoples from different cultures first encountered another, for example the Old World encountering the New World, and had to make sense of peoples who were significantly different from them (Hall 1997a: 11). The church supported the construction of human subordination and domination in order to justify slavery and exploitation of the indigenous population by Spanish and Portuguese colonialists in the New World. During the European Enlightenment, which celebrated human equality on the basis that everybody is one species, religious discourses were replaced by anthropological ones in order to "mark the difference *inside* the species [and] how, why one bit of the species is different—more barbarous, more backwards, more civilized—than another part" (Hall 1997a: 12). Anthropology now forged the "Truth" about human difference and social human classification, which was based in the biological discourses of Social Darwinism. (Darwin's *On the Origin of Species* (1859) introduced the idea that race might be inscribed within an evolutionary framework.[11]) Most of the racial studies from anthropology have influenced scientific racism. In more recent years, science has sought to utilize higher genetics in the laboratory in order to explain "why these people do not belong in the same camp, why they are very different from one another, why they really are a different species" (Hall 1997a: 12). Anthropology and science thus sought to define race on the basis of alleged biological and physical characteristics, such as skin pigmentation, hair, etc. ("color, bone, and hair") in order to draw divisions between human groups and rank "racialized" groups hierarchically. In Britain, America, and Australia, the historical construction of race is therefore one of power and subordination where "colored" people have been disadvantaged in social, political, and cultural life, such as in the labor and housing market, the education system, as well as in media representations.

The institutionalization of racist sentiments and implications has shaped the stereotypes and narratives around much commercialized popular culture. The most racist stereotypes often echoed colonial and slave histories, even though the stereotype attached to blacks has shifted to coincide with the political and social mood (Hall 1997a). Prior to the American Civil War, slaves were depicted as benign and happy with their position; however, during the Reconstruction when there was pressure on resources, this image was replaced by "the black brute whose sole aim was raping white women" (Rhodes 1993: 187), a trend that continued in the early twentieth century. Colonialism and slave history shaped the most obvious racist stereotyped representations in both Britain and America, evident in early Hollywood films (Bogle 2001; Hall 1995), which normalized the practice of slavery and black subjugation. Since the late 1950s and 60s, representations have often centered on the idea that there was something intrinsically criminal about black culture, leading increasingly toward imagery of black youth as muggers, urban rioters, and criminals. Media racism in the West became tainted by images of hedonism, evasion of work, and criminality, and by the late 1990s and early 2000s toward representations of potentially gun-toting members of drug-crazed gangs. There is thus a clear continuity in the representation of this particular group as a criminal threat to the social order.

The Remnants of Fascism in Rock Music in Europe
During the 1930s, the US-based music recording industry slowly recovered from the economic blow of 1929 and grew into the powerhouses as we know them today. Across the ocean, by contrast, the Nazis were consolidating their power in Germany and Fascism was advancing in Europe. Fascism was originally the name of a political movement founded in Italy in 1919 as the Fascio di Combattimento (Combat Group), which became the Fascist Party under the leadership of Benito Mussolini (1922–1945). During the 1930s, Fascism witnessed a triumphal progress in Europe. Fascism became an umbrella term for all extreme nationalistic and dictator-led anti-liberal, anti-Jewish, and anti-Marxist movements that opposed parliamentary democracy. Such movements were fairly widespread in Europe in the 1920s and 30s as a reaction to the social and political turmoils of the time (Wicke 2005: 228). The ranks of entertainers were thinned out by the Nazis, and many artists fled to the US and Britain, while the Nazi-controlled record companies only released Aryan music. From 1933, the German record industry was thereby forced to adopt the National Socialist ideology. Music played by Jews, blacks, or politically suspect persons was removed from the catalogues, and the music records from enemy-countries were also banned (Gronow and Saunio 1998: 91–94). Fascist music provided a powerful means to attempt to appeal to the masses and create groups of followers submissively dependent on their leaders (Wicke 2005). Songs, especially, could be used to serve these ends: people could sing them together, march to them in a show of physical uniformity, and receive

a clear ideological message promoting the goals of the movement. The Nazi record labels produced nostalgic and escapist songs, as well as martial music as the war advanced. Typical was, and still today is, the transformation of existing musical material (workers' songs, folk songs, military songs) with an already established mass appeal into aggressive right-wing combat songs by using new nationalistic lyrics and/or changes in the musical arrangements. This approach is characteristic of all fascist movements.

In post-war Europe, explicitly neo-fascist parties became marginal in most European countries. Ultra-rightist parties that do well are those that have shed that rhetoric, and instead have embraced the democratic "game" along with very extreme free market, law-and-order, and xenophobic policies. Even so, for some young people, Nazi symbols' shock value still constitutes their key attraction. In the late 1960s, some rock music started to contain racist ideologies, instigated by the British skinhead scene (Schmidt 2002), which aligned itself with fascism. Their music shared ideological positions on racism and antisemitism, abortion policies and gender issues, homophobia, anti-labor and anti-welfare politics, and had in common with Fascism a commitment to racist violence (Downing and Husband 2005: 62). More recently punk and heavy metal rock have been used for spreading nationalistic and fascist propaganda.

Nazi Rock. During the 1960s, rock music in the British skinhead scene started to contain racist ideologies. As relatives of the mods, skinheads belonged to the working classes of British society, visible through Dr Marten's boots, shortened jeans, and braces. While in the early days, skinheads listened to ska and reggae (the music of black youth) and were organized around fashion and music (Brown 2004), they began soon to be noticed due to their aggressive behavior toward minorities, including homosexuals and foreigners. In the early 1970s, and with the decreasing popularity of the skinhead movement, some skinheads joined neo-Nazi organizations like the National Front and the British Movement, and so in the mid-1970s the skinhead scene flourished again and with it the number of supporters of the National Front. This second skinhead generation listened to punk music, also known as Oi! music, while discarding ska and reggae. Instead, "white" music by bands like Sham 69 became available, through which racist and extreme right ideologies were disseminated. Oi! music is still synonymous with right rock, yet it is really only a description for fast punk rock, which is accessible to anyone due to its relatively simple structure and melodies (and therefore also listened to by punks). The band Cockney Rejects gave the scene its name with their song 'Oi!, Oi!, Oi!'. In their lyrics, Oi! music expresses political opinions in regards to right or left world views, while right Oi! music entices violence in nearly all songs. Concerts thus often resulted in violent clashes, leading to a ban of Oi! concerts and decreasing deals with record labels.

This boycott of Oi! music by the music industry led to the emergence of private, illegal concerts and the foundation (by the National Front) of the first nationalist label called White Noise Records, which signed Screwdriver as its main band, who later founded its own record label, Blood and Honour. In the early 1980s, meanwhile, skinheads were still a large part of the British neo-Nazi movement with leaders like Nick Cane of the British Movement and Screwdriver frontman Ian Stuart Donaldson of the National Front. The album covers by bands like Screwdriver resonate closely with the signifiers of German national-socialism, depicting slogans like "Hail the New Dawn", "Blood and Honour", and "White Rider", while depicting the mythological figure of a rider on a clothed horse synonymous with the extremist-racist Ku-Klux-Klan. This symbolism is further reflected in Screwdriver's album titles, such as *Tomorrow Belongs to Me* (1984), *Blood and Honour* (1985), and *Pride of a Nation* (1987). During the early 80s, the British right-wing skinhead scene arrived in Germany (Schmidt 2002) when right-wing organizations and neo-Nazi parties like the NPD became interested in the growing youth scene, while trying to use neo-Nazi music for their own gains. The music scene at that time consisted of only a few right bands like the Böhse Onkelz (from Frankfurt) and Kraft durch Froide (from Berlin). As the 1980s progressed, fewer and fewer bands played "pure" Oi! music, as a new form of right rock developed from a blend of Oi! and heavy metal. The sound of heavy metal was particularly suitable for right rock due to its clear structure and the lyrical possibilities of the ballad. The music thus turned away from fun punk and toward serious "message rock", which is often spoken or screamed, with fast tempo and aggressive lyrics, and often played at an extremely loud volume (Meyer 1995). Rarely do people listen to right rock for its musical quality, which is often based on a DIY aesthetic, but rather for its lyrics. The aim of right rock is to convey a central message, rather than a perfect lyric, often celebrating violence and adoring German national-socialism under the Nazi Party. Qualities such as commitment and pride are central to the lyrics, which often also discuss enemies of the right scene, including foreigners, "lefties", the state, and Christianity. The messages in these lyrics are communicated directly and without irony or ambiguity. The music's aggressiveness reflects the aggression of the message. The musicians often convey the shared sentiment that they feel "pushed out of society" and oppose this with calls for change toward and fight for a "better world". At the center is the situation of the social group, rather than the individual, so that I-songs are rare and the subject is the "we" of the community or another person ("you"). The songs thus often celebrate the solidarity between men. Through this, ideals are being explicitly propagated that are worth fighting for, thus enticing violence for a "better cause". The lyrics are most often racist and reactionary nationalist (Meyer 1995; Schmidt 2002).

The racialized narratives expressed through and experienced in popular music during the 1960s and 1970s draw on the idea of race circulating in the European imaginary since European expansionism, and thus the histories of racialization in western culture since the dawn of globalization. Nazi rock is an example of this. Racialization is based on an ideology that has grown out of the desire of white Europeans to rule in order to achieve and maintain dominance. Race, therefore, is a discursive construct applied to non-whites, who are being raced and othered and labelled as such in order to subordinate them. Racialization is inherently racist, which is "one of the most profoundly 'naturalised' of existing ideologies" (Hall 2010: 272), evident in depictions in mediated forms—representations in art, literature, scientific writing, photography, and popular music. Mediated representations thereby engage in the politics of othering through racist discourses, which have their historical roots in European expansionism and colonialism that have in turn shaped the West's ideas about (it)self and others. I will return to representations and discourses of racisms as manifested in contemporary popular music in subsequent chapters.

Masculine Hegemony in the Music Industry
In considering the politics of othering, a second theme concerns the sexist nature of the post-war music recording industry, which has spread gendered values, beliefs, and behaviors via representations in popular music on a global level. The social identities of women and men in music, and specifically their gendered and sexual lives, are constructed in popular culture through visual language and spoken discourse. And yet the popular entertainment media most often convey only few and particular ways of doing femininity and masculinity, thereby reinforcing and contributing to particular attitudes, beliefs, and behaviors surrounding gender. Since the 1940s, then, much world popular music has functioned in constructing difference and otherness through gendered discourses and representations.

In her recent acceptance speech at *Billboard* Women in Music 2016, Madonna addressed in deeply emotional ways the sexism, misogyny, and feminism she has experienced during her career spanning three decades in the music industry:

> Thank you for acknowledging my ability to continue my career for 34 years in the face of blatant misogyny, sexism, constant bullying, and relentless abuse. When I started, there was no Internet so people had to say it to my face. There were very few people I had

to clad back at because life was simpler then ... I am receiving an award for being Woman of the Year, so I asked myself "What can I say about being a woman in the music business? What can I say about being a woman?" When I first started writing songs, I didn't think in a gender-specific way. I didn't think about feminism. I just wanted to be an artist ... My real muse was David Bowie. He embodied male and female spirit, and that suited me just fine. He made me think there were no rules. But I was wrong. There are no rules if you are a boy. If you are a girl, you have to play the game. What is that game? You are allowed to be pretty and cute and sexy. But don't act too smart! Don't have an opinion! Don't have an opinion that is out of line with the status quo, at least. You are allowed to be objectified by men and dressed like a slut. But don't own your sluttiness, and do not, I repeat, do not share your own sexual fantasies with the world! Be what men want you to be, but more importantly be what women feel comfortable with you being around other men! And finally, do not age! Because to age is a sin. You will be criticized, you will be vilified, and you will definitely not be played on the radio! When I first became famous, there were nude photos of me in the *Playboy* and *Penthouse* magazine ... [and] I was expected to feel ashamed when these photos came out, and I was not, and this puzzled people. Eventually I was left alone because I married Sean Penn ... I was taken off the market, so for a while, I was not considered a threat ... Years later, divorced and single ... I made my *Erotica* album and my sex book was released. I remember being the headline of every newspaper and magazine, and everything I read about myself was damning. I was called a whore and a witch. One headline compared me to Satan ... This was the first time I truly understood that women really did not have the same freedom as men ... I remember wishing that I had a female peer that I could look to for support ... So I said, Fuck it! I'm a different kind of feminist. I'm a bad feminist. People say that I am so controversial, but I think the most controversial thing I have ever done is to stick around ... Women have been so oppressed for so long, they believe what men have to say about them, and they believe they have to back a man to get the job done. And there are some very good men worth backing. But not because they are men. Because they are worthy (Madonna 2016).

Throughout the short history of the music industry, musical and extra-musical behaviors and norms have shown the ways in which normative, and often oppressive, conceptions of gender and sexuality have been reinforced and regarded as natural. The naturalizing of gendered stereotypes in the global music industry has meant that women were, and still often are, the other in popular music. Historically, popular music has been created, produced, and promoted from a fundamentally sexist, misogynistic, and ageist position, maintained through the construction of the popular music canon. The belief that popular music and its industry is male-dominated is widely accepted by academics, journalists, and music industry insiders alike (Chapple and Garofalo 1977; Frith and McRobbie 1978; Reynolds and Press 1995; Whiteley 2000; Leonard 2007; Krüger 2016).

The music industry has grown out of a capitalist market economy, which itself is a traditionally masculine world (Wilson 1995: 114). The music business is male run. Men held and still hold the majority of leading roles in record companies, and men dominate production and consumption since the beginnings of the industry. Musicians, writers, and creators, producers, engineers, and technicians are mostly men. Throughout the music industry, women professionals have typically been underrepresented. Sexism has permeated the whole structure of the music industry during the 1950s, 1960s, and 1970s, including its business workings (and particularly senior executive positions), the creative processes surrounding songwriting and production, musical performance, and music journalism (Chapple and Garofalo 1977: 289). With its sexual division of labor, the music industry has been criticized as a chauvinistic business. The situation resonates with the major hierarchical divisions in the current employment statistics more generally. Indeed,

> in general, and of course with exceptions, the lower down a hierarchy, the lower the pay, and the lower the educational level, the more likely a non-manual worker is to be female. The gender divide provides at least as sharp a cultural cleavage within the non-manual hierarchy of the office or shop as the manual/non-manual one within the factory (Crouch 2004: 59; with specific reference to the cultural industries, see Oakley and O'Brien 2016; O'Brien et al. 2016).

Much literature available on the music industry frequently refers to A&R people, vice-presidents, managers, managing directors, and marketing directors as being "he" rather than "she" (Negus 1992; O'Brien 1995). While some women have moved into positions of managing director, women's progress across the music industry remains markedly slow. The first female managing director for BMG, Lisa Anderson, describes the industry as "inward-looking, gender-conservative ... in which 'older gender values' hold sway" (O'Brien 1995: 411). There is thus still a noticeable absence of women who hold executive positions. Since the 1990s, there has been a shift in gender relations in the music industry, whereby two typical areas of employment for women include PR-related and secretarial roles. In these supportive roles of press/public relations officer, women represented the public face of record companies, carrying out the long-established work convention of supporting men in positions above them, including male journalists, reflecting the notion of a "sexualised vocation" (Negus 1992: 115). In secretarial and assistant positions, women are equally subordinate and subservient to (predominantly male) superiors in their decision-making positions. The myth of the "attractive secretary" has been exploited in all areas of the industry to entice business dealings between men. In their assistant positions as personal assistants, executive assistants, and administrative assistants, women have often been little more than secretaries (Hesmondhalgh and Baker 2000). Meanwhile, men have continued to dominate roles in A&R and music journalism. Those women who do work as journalists often find themselves involved in menial journalistic tasks. By contrast, more "serious" and longer articles tend to be written by male music journalists, while senior editorial teams in the popular music press tend to be dominated by men.

Men have written, performed, and recorded music, and have been the critics and radio DJs. Hence rock music, the first type of mainstream popular music from the 1950s onwards, has become principally created for a male audience (Leonard 2007). Rock music has also been gendered masculine. It is essentially sexist (Chapple and Garofalo 1977: 269) by expressing masculine sexuality and superiority, as well as offering only limited representations of women, either as caring mother figures or as sex objects. The gendering of rock music and its discourses has been facilitated by the construction of a rock music canon. Canons work both commercially by establishing "classic" albums that people "need" to own, and ideologically by assigning aesthetic value to certain genres and musicians. And historically it has been men (e.g. journalists, biographers) who made these judgments, prioritized male performers, and thereby assigned more value to "masculine" traits in popular music. Once masculinity became favored and ascribed with authenticity, and male performers entered into a historically established tradition of "classics", a certain "circularity" in the canonizing process occurred that made it problematic for women and "femininity" to break into (Leonard 2007: 29). Indeed, "the gender of rock may appear stable, but it is 'stabilized' through a constant process of reiteration and the performance of 'masculinity', which act to keep that which is unrepresentable within it firmly outside" (ibid.: 27). In the early years of rock music, women thus had little control over their music, images, and performances, and instead had to fit into "male grooves", which is evident in the production, consumption, and structure of rock music.

Consequently, female creative roles were generally limited. Women's roles within the music industry were instead determined by male notions of female ability (Frith and McRobbie 1978). Women musicians who "made it" were almost always singers, while women in the wider business usually worked in publicity. In both roles, however, women's success depended on a male-made female image. Women's internalization of the other stems from the constant absorption of men's self-perpetuating cultural representations that consistently place women as other. Therefore the oppressed woman complies with expectations of femininity in terms of fashion items and beauty products that are "subject to the established order" (DeBeavoir 2010: 189). Self-acknowledged feminist musicians, on the other hand, often make conscious political decisions to reject items of clothing, such as "skirts, low neckline, high heels, and cosmetics" (ibid.: 181). Narcissism is a condition of the othered woman in that she becomes obsessed with her own image due to her desire to retain her "self" in situations where she is constantly placed as an object without function. Thus highly sexualized female clothing can be seen as a narcissistic means to create the illusion of "self", worth in the face of patriarchy, while remaining dependent on men's approval of her image.

The undervaluing of female authenticity and creativity is not limited to rock music, but has occurred in western societies since the Romantic era when distinctions between low and high culture were first established. In other words, the aesthetic ideologies prevalent today have their roots in the Romantic era when European culture established itself as superior to that of other cultures (Battersby 1989; Huyssen 1986; Mayhew 2004). At that time, European intellectuals constructed the idea of the Romantic "genius" in order to distinguish between art vs. craft, civilized vs. primitive cultures, while "genius" became associated as being inherently "male". Moreover, the notion of genius also functioned to deter female ambition in the arts and hinder the position of creative women (Battersby 1989: 5). Moreover, "in western culture, men have dominated the music profession and occupied positions of power and privilege. Before the 1850s, most orchestras refused to employ women, and it was thought 'improper' for a woman to perform in public" (O'Neill 2002: 133). The cultural discourse rooted in European romanticism thus constructed and naturalized masculine hegemony in western societies. Consequently, the concept of "man" is seen in western society as belonging to the symbolic order, while the concept of "woman" is seen as the "other" through the dynamics of signification and meaning attribution.

Sexism is not only confined to the western music industry, but can also be found in other parts of the world, as is illustrated in an interview with two female rappers from Senegal who describe their experiences and perspectives from within the Senegalese music industry (Funkeson 2005). Here, roles in production, managing, and sound engineering are similarly occupied by men, which puts female artists in a vulnerable position, as they are often abused and sexually harassed by men. Women's musical careers in Senegal often come to an end as they end up being pregnant with male rappers, or get married to their manager or producer. Myriam, one of the founding members of ALIF in Dakar (Attaque Libératoire de l'Infanterie Féministe), the Feminists' Infantry Liberation Army, explains that "one thing is for sure and that is that it'll never be easy if you are a woman and all alone without a man to support you in this business" (Funkeson 2005). It is also common for women's bodies to be taken advantage of, both by men in the music industry and women themselves, turning themselves into "pin-ups in video-clips, magazines, and on stage and exploiting their own bodies to get more publicity and sell music" (ibid.), an issue that is very much debated within the context of religion (e.g. Islam) and tradition in Senegal. The music industry is thus the key reason for women's fixation with beauty and body: "You have to bring photos before signing with a record label and for a woman musician it's very important to be good looking", says Myriam. There are also certain taboos that cannot be addressed by women in lyrics, specifically those concerning religion and politics. For instance, a highly taboo subject in Senegal is polygamy: "You cannot say that you're against polygamy ... because that would be the same thing as criticizing our religion" (interview with Myriam, in Funkeson 2005).

Rock Music. In the western world, masculine hegemony has shaped the music industry from its earliest beginnings, but it was specifically the start of rock 'n' roll in the 1950s, the decade known for rebellion against conformity, that marked the beginnings of misogyny and sexism in rock music. In suburban America at the time, women were not seen to be victims of domesticity but as responsible for forcing their husbands into mundane jobs and failing to raise their defiant teenage boys, a discourse that lived on well into the 1960s counterculture movement (Reynolds and Press 1995). Moreover, the "sexual liberation" movement in the 1960s, marked by the introduction of the contraceptive pill and the popular idea of "bodily self-determination" for women (Humm 2003: 2), failed to extend to female control of women's own sexuality and to liberate women from their roles as objects. Instead it proved to be a way for men to objectify women in rock music under the pretense of liberation, which "was really only the freedom for men to fuck women more easily" (Chapple and Garofalo 1977: 279). Similarly, the counterculture of the 1960s did not offer much freedom to women, as it did not acknowledge women as being oppressed and in need of freedom and change, but failed to include progress toward the independence of women and female liberation (ibid.: 280; Frith and McRobbie 1978; Reynolds and Press 1995: 231; Whiteley 2000: 28).[12] Some have argued that the overlooking of female oppression in the 1960s is largely due to women's historical existence in relation to men and their shared class status. For instance, Betty Friedan (1963) claimed that many women in the US at the time regarded themselves as an extension of their husbands and sought to construct an identity through family life and household lifestyle, expressive of the "plight" of the married white suburban mother and shaped by the media's bombardment of images that shaped perceptions of gender roles.

The common view of "rebel masculinity" versus "conformist femininity" meant that women were seen as signifiers of conventional lives and hence threatening to male creativity. By objectifying women in rock music lyrics and videos, masculinity thus became connoted with sexual aggression and control. As a result, the majority of music in the 1960s represented women as "either sexually aggressive and therefore doomed and unhappy, or else sexually repressed and therefore in need of male servicing" (Frith and McRobbie 1990 [1978]: 374). Rock is indeed the popular music genre that is most explicitly concerned with sexual representation. The conventions of sexual representation are most noticeable in rock's musical elements (e.g. sound and rhythm), while its lyrics often follow the rules of romance. Rock is essentially a male form of commercialized musical expression that refers to a specifically young and white audience, while rendering a specific artistic ideology, namely that rock has a creative "integrity" that pop lacks. Its most significant impact on audiences is the construction of sexuality: rock is a male form presenting and marketing masculine styles.

Since the 1950s and 60s, many rock musicians such as Elvis Presley, Mick Jagger, Roger Daltrey, Robert Plant, and bands like Mötley Crue and Thin Lizzy, became known under the substyle of cock rock. Thin Lizzy's performances were characterized by an "explicit, crude, and often aggressive expression of male sexuality" (Campbell 2013). An interesting and often cited example is Mötley Crue's success hit 'Girls, Girls, Girls' (1987), which depicts the band's rough lifestyle, while riding Harley motorcycles, drinking whiskey, using drugs, and spending their nights at striptease clubs.

> Cock-rock performers are aggressive, boastful, constantly drawing audience attention to their prowess and control. Their bodies are on display ... mikes and guitars are phallic symbols (or else caressed like female bodies), the music is loud, rhythmically insistent, built around techniques of arousal and release. Lyrics are assertive and arrogant, but the exact words are less significant than the vocal styles involved, the shrill shouting and screaming (Frith 1981: 227).

Their voices are usually rough and loud, vocal lines delivered with tension and experiential repression. Philip Tagg (1990) linked rock voices to the soundworld of the city: to make himself understood, valid as an individual, the rock singer has to shout above the din of the city. He suggested that rock's "broadband" noises reflect modern urban environment's "broadband" noises (car engines, air conditioning, fridge noise, etc.). Together with reverb, which enhances a sense of space and distance, the sound as a whole becomes "crowded" and "homogenized". The singers must then scream to be heard. Visually, rock musicians connoted the rampant destructive male traveler, smashing hotels and groupies alike, while performing crude male physicality (e.g. hardness, control, virtuosity). Rockers' musical skills often became synonymous with their sexual prowess, while constructing male sexuality as animalistic and superficial. Masculinity (or this particular kind) was thereby expressed in terms of (negative) stereotypes. And it was mostly male consumers who identified with these images, reminiscent of male, sexually exclusive, camaraderie.

Masculinity was also enacted through the "exscription" of the feminine (Walser 1993: 110) and misogyny. By constructing fantastic worlds without women, exscription has been a way for metal musicians and fans to stress the value of male bonding, while excluding the threat of the feminine. Most metal videos typically present the spectacle of live performance by using actual concert footage or by imitating the spectacle of an arena. Its main purpose is to evoke the concert experience of collectivity and participation, while presenting the performers "in all their glory, as larger-than-life figures" (ibid.: 114). Even if metal videos do not feature live performance settings, the objective is to "represent and reproduce spectacles that depend for their appeal on the exscription of women" (ibid.: 115). An example of this is Judas Priest's 'Heading Out to the Highway' (2001), which celebrates specifically a male kind of freedom without women. Exscription and male bonding are crucial in the enactment of male power and control, further signified through actual displays of metal on album sleeves, such as Black Sabbath's *Iron Man* (1970), evoking images of armored, metalized male bodies. The exscription of women and metallic hardening of the male body thereby represent a defense against culturally produced anxieties about gender. Where music videos include women more overtly, such representations are often "managed" through misogynistic display, for example the brutal stage shows and song lyrics by W.A.S.P. (e.g. 'F*** Like a Beast' (1997)), or the forthrightly misogynistic lyrics in some Guns N' Roses songs, notably 'Welcome to the Jungle' (1987). Yet few heavy metal videos have approached blatant narcissistic misogyny, and instead portray nonviolent fantasies of dominance, control, and repression of women

(Walser 1993), which may occur in the representation of women as the "femme fatale" and symbolic male victimization, often representing the male as entrapped, betrayed, or destroyed by the female. Examples include Mötley Crüe's 'Looks that Kill', Whitesnake's 'Still of the Night', or Dokken's 'Heaven Scent', among others. In these videos, women are represented as threats to male control, even male survival, constructing the mysterious woman as the dangerous other.

Women in Rock Music. At the time when female-led rock groups were a rare occurrence, some female musicians did succeed. A noticeable example is Stevie Nicks, who joined Fleetwood Mac in 1974 with her (then) partner Lindsey Buckingham. Nicks confidently assumed the position of a central, if not lead, figure in the band. Her singing style is often raunchy and even aggressive, similar to that of Janis Joplin, yet what makes Nicks unique is that she embraces her feminine identity, while working within the constraints of a male-dominated music industry (e.g. Lindsey Buckingham as the male songwriting partner and producer of many of her musical outputs in Fleetwood Mac). During this time, music journalism continued to represent female artists as sex symbols, despite feminist advancements and the bold female musicians of the 1970s punk movement. In press articles at the time, one can find a recurrent theme that focuses on the physical depiction of Nicks and positions her appearance as sexual, symbolically feminine, and "trivial" (to denote immaturity and indecisiveness), and as submissive and dependent in relation to men and to her fellow members in Fleetwood Mac (Van Zoonen 1994a: 17). Indeed women musicians have often been considered to be of lesser talent than men, whereby musical authorship and production were regarded to be male domains; this stems from the fact that the division of labor in the music production process often meant that the songs were written by someone other than the female artist. As a result, male musicians were usually considered to be authentic "authors" of the music (Lewis 1990: 63), with creativity being a male characteristic. Women who "make it" have often been associated with the ideology of sexual favors provided to their male superiors.

Within this sexist setting, Nicks' lyrics at the time reflect feminist themes, for example 'Rhiannon' (1975) is about a free-spirited woman who gains the love of men only to disappear, a theme that at first sight may seem similar to the popular mythologies constructed through representations of women in rock music at the time, which classified "woman" as "etherealized and inscribed within a dreamlike and unreal world ... defined by the male as a fantasy escape *from* reality" (Whiteley 2000: 35, original emphasis). Yet the difference is that "Rhiannon" can be regarded as a fantasy constructed by a *female* author, rather than as an account of male submission within the realms of male sexual fantasy, and so as empowering over men within the context of female pleasure and liberation. The woman is the agent; her behavior is dominant within the lyrics. As in many of her songs, Nicks uses metaphorical language to expand the narrative: *Rhiannon rings like a bell through the night ... takes to the sky like a bird in flight ... she is like a cat in the dark ... rules her life like a bird in flight.* While metaphors may evoke stereotypes, and metaphors involving women as birds, in particular, may evoke assumptions about women as weak and sensual (Mills 1995: 54), a feminist reading may also regard "bird in flight" as connoting freedom and free will, specifically freedom from patriarchal constraints and thus female empowerment. Similar examples of female agency and emancipated female sexuality can be found in other songs, for instance 'Gold Dust Woman' (1976), which once again foregrounds a female protagonist and accommodates the notion of women as agents (*Did she make you cry, make you break down...?*), in which the ideology of romantic love has little space (Mills 1995: 155). Nicks thus challenges gendered representations of agency within the standard formula of the love song, which gains added potency when used in conjunction with metaphoric language: *oooh pale shadow of a woman, black widow ... ooh pale shadow of a woman, she's a dragon ... gold dust woman.* The "gold dust woman" of which Nicks writes is not remorseful of her actions; she is empowered by them. In some lyrics, Nicks tends to focus entirely on the female perspective, for instance in 'Sisters of the Moon' (1979), which conjures the presence of a mysterious female: *Those black moons in those eyes of hers made more sense to me ... heavy persuasion, it was hard to breathe*, but Nicks is not threatened by her presence, *and so I followed as friends often do.* The woman is once again a site of agency, and the frequent use of "she" encourages self-identification by female listeners: *she walked in the room ... she was dark at the top of the stairs ... she called to me ... she asked me be my sister, sister of the moon.* The metaphor "sisters of the moon" can be read within the feminist concept of sisterhood, which was "central to the women's movement [and] places stress on female solidarity and co-operation" (Gamble 2001b: 315), while "moon" similarly evokes female solidarity due to the supposed connection between female menstruation and the lunar cycle. From a feminist perspective, the song 'Sisters of the Moon' thus celebrates the unity of women through their social and indeed biological similarities.

During her subsequent solo career and without the company of the male members of Fleetwood Mac, Nicks became referred to as "flaky", "witchy", and in some cases mad, commenting on her stage costumes, drug addiction, and mental instability, instead of concentrating on her musical outputs. Published articles and interviews often position Nicks as a victim who is not in control of her personal and professional life, and mentally unstable. While the label "madness" is used at times to highlight "an artist's creativity", in Nicks' case it acts as "a powerful label of exclusion" (Leonard 2007: 69), reflected in her acting out the "devalued female role" (Chesler 1972: 56) and outpouring emotional vulnerability, alongside the "total or partial rejection of one's sex-role stereotype" (ibid.). Indeed, Nicks' choice of clothing during performances which was described as irregular and "other" in many media articles, combined with the media's focus on the idea that Nicks is indeed a practicing witch, stemmed from her interests in mythical and spiritual culture that informed her music and choice in clothing. The identification of a woman as witch has its basis in historical misogyny where women exuding power and confidence were labelled as mad for breaking out of patriarchal constraints (Ussher 1991: 56–57). The popular representations of Nicks as witch similarly illustrate the ways in which male patriarchy defined women as "other" in order to retain male privilege and hegemony. Even so, Nicks was and still is very much in control of her own public image, herself designing and creating her own outfits and "look", and thus constructing a self-created individuality that she maintained through decades of fashion style changes. Nicks represents female empowerment through the celebration of feminine difference within the hegemonic order, subverting patriarchy by adopting an exaggerated femininity instead of adopting masculine identity markers, and by finding empowerment in "spiritual feminism" by altering perceptions of "witch" from hysterical, seductive, and capricious to "sensitive, sensuous, and adaptable" (Oakes 2006: 52). Even though she is attributed the most negative connotations in the patriarchal media in order to restrict the possibilities of such connotations being regarded as empowering, Nicks managed to create—through her clothing style, lyrics and performance style, and responses to the media—an image that strikes a balance between the positive and negative signifiers of spiritual feminism. Clearly, Stevie Nicks provides a striking example of a female artist within a patriarchal media world that has continually focused on her image and undermined the significance of her creative output, and thus rendered Nicks a victim of sexist evaluations.

The Female Singer-Songwriter. An alternative success route outside the rock music canon for women at the time was that of the singer-songwriter or "folkie lady", often being "long-haired, pure-voiced [and] self-accompanied on acoustic guitar" (Frith and McRobbie 1990 [1978]: 377), including musicians like Joan Baez and Joni Mitchell. A number of reasons explain why this genre proved successful for women in the 1960s and early 1970s, namely the change of the lyrical content in folk rock at the end of the 1960s from socio-political issues to more individual biographical writings, which appealed particularly to women who historically due to lack of education have had a strong oral storytelling tradition (Whiteley 2000). Moreover, due to domesticity women had less disposable income than men, which forced them to use cheap means to express themselves creatively, namely guitars and pens. The key factor that contributed to the acceptance of female participation, however, was that the singer-songwriter genre did not challenge patriarchal notions of femininity, as the genre allows for a sensitive, vulnerable, fragile, and essentially passive musician, characteristics widely accepted as "feminine" in patriarchal society. Female singer-songwriters' musical appeal and image, and the way they were sold, "reinforced in rock the qualities traditionally linked with female singers—sensitivity, passivity, and sweetness" (Frith and McRobbie 1990 [1978]: 377). High-pitched sounds, both in the western world and elsewhere where western ideas have been absorbed, signify "smallness" and "innocence", and female singer-songwriters were often stereotyped as innocent and vulnerable, seducing the listener with a high, childish voice. The female singer-songwriter style—soft, warm, hollow voice with an open throat and relatively low pitch, using the resonating chambers of the chest, connoting that the voice comes from the "heart" (van Leeuwen 1999)—constructs "woman" as emotional nurturer and reinforces the binary concept of the "feminine heart" versus the "masculine head" (Shepherd 1991). In this music genre, particularly, women are personified through their ability over men "to articulate emotion because femininity is defined in emotional terms" (Frith 1988: 155).

While the popularity in folk and singer-songwriter music of the early 1970s worked positively to include female participation within the rock music industry, by working within a "gentle" and "passive" music genre, female singer-songwriters were marketed as passive and easily controlled by the male gaze, thereby ascribing to patriarchal characteristics of femininity. The discourses produced by record companies and journalists surrounding these women are markedly different to those surrounding their male counterparts, and work actively to discredit the authenticity of female musicians. Joni Mitchell, for instance, was often referenced in relation to the men in her life, which popularized the idea of Mitchell being promiscuous (Moy 2007: 7). The media representations surrounding her relationships with famous men was thus a powerful way to diminish her status as a musician and punish her for sexual activity, as well as restoring patriarchal order. The most famous example of how Mitchell's private life was scrutinized was in the *Rolling Stone* magazine in 1972, which awarded her with the title "Old Lady of the Year" and included a family tree-style diagram of her supposed broken-hearted lovers (O'Brien 2001: 8). Such tactics can be seen as punishment for her sexual deviance and demonstrate that the sexual liberation of the 1960s did not change or challenge how female sexuality was perceived. Even today, journalists seek to establish which particular songs are about which famous musician with whom she was supposedly romantically involved. For example, her 1971 album *Blue* was released when she has had one failed marriage and some high-profile relationships with famous musicians; songs like 'Blue', 'My Old Man', and 'All I Want' are often claimed by journalists, fans, biographers, and academics to be about different men, for example Graham Nash, Steven Stills, Leonard Cohen, or James Taylor. Johnston (2003), for instance, claims that the entire album was written about her break-up with Graham Nash, while McDonald stressed that "the relationship that left the most marks on the singer and her songs was the one with James Taylor" (McDonald 1974; see also Hoskyns 1994, 2005, and Hinton 2000). The effect of these and other discourses, notably those describing Mitchell as "a freelance romantic, searching for permanent love" (Crouse 1971), thus a heartbroken woman desperately looking for love, is to discredit her creativity, so that her ambition as a serious creative songwriter becomes less threatening for a patriarchal status quo. Indeed, female ambition and achievement, if moving beyond maternity, have historically been associated with deviance, so by discursively representing *Blue* in this manner, namely as an album that expresses her loneliness, fragility, and sadness in the absence of men and romantic love (O'Brien 2001: 126), Mitchell's ambition is "cured" and her "career abandoned for marriage" (Dubois 2001: 298).

Meanwhile, the marketing strategies adopted to promote her albums adhered to gendered stereotypes. For instance, preceding the release of her second album *Clouds* (1969), record label Warner produced an advert published in *Rolling Stone* on 26 July 1969, at the center of which was the self-portrait of Mitchell,[13] which also served as the cover for the album, surrounded by slogans like "Joni Mitchell is 90% Virgin", "Joni Mitchell Takes Forever", and "Joni Mitchell Finally Comes Across". About the image, the record company wrote, "Joni painted her own portrait for the cover of the album. It's pretty." The language is deliberately childlike and innocent, with an effectively patronizing undertone, connoting no true artistic talent, but an ability of craftsmanship, which is historically associated with women. The advert is constructed for the male gaze by objectifying and controlling the image of the singer, even extending to ownership if wanted. Although there is no actual image of a man in the advert, the authoritative narrator of the advert represents not only the men running Warner, but the whole male music industry for the spectator to identify with. The text of the advert also reads:

> *After lo these 14 months – it has happened.*
> *On our part, it's taken blood, sweat, tears, and greed.*
> *Coaxing and cajoling.*
> *Even – yes – chicanery.*
> *But the blonde lady who only recently was subject of a Reprise ad head-lined "Joni Mitchell takes forever" has finally, at long last, come across*
> (Full-page ad for the album *Clouds*, 1969).

The language signifies an obvious play on sex, and the more likely meaning is the suggestion of an orgasm, providing the audience with narcissistic pleasure due to the idealized identification with the narrator, while indirectly feeling satisfied with his sexual ability. Meanwhile, when Joni Mitchell did not accept the passive role that was negotiated for her (she was famously described by David Crosby as being "about as humble as Mussolini" (O'Brien 2001: 5)), she was "punished" for her activity. Indeed, in order to keep up the hierarchical differences between men and women in rock music's value system, Mitchell could not be represented in similar ways to her male colleagues. Journalistic discourses thus often focused on her apparently arrogant stance, as being incredibly "inmodest ... because she routinely compares herself to Picasso and Bob Dylan" (Truss 2008: 8). And once a female object rejects her position as passive and tries to actively lead the narrative in popular culture, she has to be punished as a method of "restoring patriarchal order" (Dubois 2001: 298; see also Williams 1984; Modleski 1988). Mitchell is thus punished for not accepting the place in popular music presented to her, for comparing herself to male counterparts, and believing in her ability as a songwriter and musician, through which is crossed the invisible line that divides the "real" music canon from that of women.

Since the birth of rock music in the 1950s, women were positioned as the other in the male-dominated music industry which sought to diminish female creativity. Female participation in rock music since its beginnings has never been allowed a coherent history, also evident in much of the creative arts, which works to exclude future female musicians. The "masculinity" of the music industry shows how the canonization of rock music works in a circular way that excludes and devalues women, an ideology that has its roots in the Romantic era. Not only did fewer women work as professional musicians and attempt a musical career at the time due to the gendering of rock music, but women who were creating music were discursively represented differently to men in order to devalue female creativity and construct "woman" as the other. In order to understand the masculinization of rock music, one cannot disagree with a hegemonic construct that promotes male creativity, but constantly works to exclude women, if one does not initially explain the different ways in which this has become taken for granted, or naturalized. Representations of female artists show how female identity is actively constructed and manipulated by the media industry, which illustrates how patriarchy works, and that femininity is socially constructed. Cynically put, "what makes a woman special is not her biology, but the way society categorises and treats her because she is a woman" (Battersby 1989: 154). Societies around the world, not only in the West, have long histories of patriarchy, which view the qualities that connote value as the ones strongly connected to masculinity, so that men have been constructed as superior to women. Yet it is important to acknowledge that masculine traits of assertiveness and rationality do not always come naturally to men either, which are instead the results of preconceived and stereotyped beliefs that essentialize male-gendered norms and behaviors as hyper-masculine and tough (Katz and Earp 1999). All of these discussions make clear how women have come to be seen as the other in popular music by being represented in carefully constructed ways to emphasize their subordination: as sex objects within the control of the male gaze, as girlfriends of famous men, as in need of rescue by men, as femme fatales to be controlled by men, and as naturally quiet, delicate, and sensitive. Popular music readily embodies the gendered stereotypes that are openly reinforced in much popular culture, and they are being punished discursively for deviant attitudes by male patriarchal standards. Women are thereby sexualized and marginalized within the industry, a gendered other in popular music.

The birth of world popular music is linked to the evolution of western forms of capitalism. It mirrors the establishment of a global music market and economy where the focus of activity is on music as commodity. The globalization of music is thereby often understood in terms of the emergence and cultural domination of a global music recording industry and the mass production opportunities provided by early sound recording technologies in capitalist societies since the late nineteenth century. Under the influence of capitalism, music became gradually a commodity and linked to heightened expressions of individualism. The cultural systems of liberal capitalism and organized capitalism have shaped the production, distribution, and consumption of much world popular music, first in the West and later worldwide. Industrialization, modernization, and westernization have impacted upon world culture most notably by the cementing of western capitalist hegemony and its divisive ideological system based on race, sexuality, gender, age, ethnicity, and so forth, and the spread of western (capitalist) influence into most parts of the world. European colonialist ideas have shaped the globalizing trends during this period, and provided the conditions for the politics of othering in commodified culture, conditions that have also persisted in neoliberal culture.

Notes

1. The *gitanos* remained the only significant social minority in Spain after the expulsion of the Jews, and their early flamenco's ambiguous status reflected the societal distrust of the *gitanos* and international admiration of their music.
2. Antoine Moundana was one of the creators of the rumba and founding fathers of all of modern Zaire-Congolese music, which became widely popular and influential throughout much of the continent.
3. Enoch Mankayi Sontonga (1873–1905), a choirmaster of Xhosa descent who was a teacher at a Methodist mission school near Johannesburg, composed it in 1897 as a hymn, and it was first performed at the ordination of a minister in 1899. Sontonga composed only the melody, the first verse, and chorus; seven additional verses were later added by the South African poet S. E. K. Mqhayi, and the full English text was published in 1927. In 1996, Sontonga's grave in Johannesburg was declared a national monument, and a memorial was unveiled on the site by President Nelson Mandela (see also Taylor 1997: 72–73).
4. Under European colonization, new populations emerged: the "Mestizos" (part Spanish, part Native American), "Mulattos" (part Spanish, part African), and "Cafusos" (part Native American, part African). A powerful Creole aristocracy (native-born people of "pure" Spanish blood) continued to rule and control the predominantly Mestizo workforce. The nineteenth-century Civil Wars between royalists and republicans meant the legitimizing of Creole hegemony and the destruction of the Spanish administrative apparatus, when the continent emerged devastated with its internal political boundaries redefined in new nation states. Today, there exist six distinct groups of states in Latin America: Mexico and the countries of the isthmus (influenced by the US); the Caribbean islands (West Indies), Guyana, Surinam, French Guinea (former Eastern Brazil) (with differing European backgrounds, and a majority of African and Mulatto peoples); Venezuela and Colombia (to the North) (with a mixed population divided between mountain and coastland); Peru, Bolivia, Ecuador (the most "Indian" states); Brazil (to the East, with Portuguese inheritance and a predominance of Africans and Mulattos); Paraguay, Argentina, Uruguay, and Chile (Gaucho countries, and the most European states).
5. Brazil abolished slavery in 1888, which meant that many ex-slaves, who had migrated south from the northeastern colonial sugar plantations (due to the decline of the sugar trade and the outlaw of the slave trade in 1830) as forced laborers in the gold mines of Minais Gerais and coffee plantations in and around Rio de Janeiro, were free to settle in Rio de Janeiro. Samba now began to evolve in various forms as a music genre among Rio's poor blacks, who had been forced to flee to the outlying districts of Rio in the 1920s and settled in their isolated communities on the *morros* (hills), which became known as the hillside favelas or shantytowns. Here the musicians were persecuted by the police, and considered part of a marginal underworld.
6. It is impossible to generalize the development of capitalism, but Colin Crouch provides a useful (shortened) overview of capitalist developments in Scandinavia, the Neth-

erlands, UK, US, France, Italy, Spain, Portugal, and Greece (2004: 7-11). Jim McGuigan, meanwhile, suggests that the Golden Age of capitalism began in the US and spread to Japan, Western Europe, other parts of the First World, newly industrializing countries, and some cities and enclaves in the Third World (2009: 113).

7. As the economic center of Paraguay, Asunción is the capital and home to 10 percent (ca. 500,000) of the country's total estimated population of 6.5 million, and it is consequently the main center for the creation and performance of contemporary music genres and styles, such as rock.

8. Recorded at Estudios Tayî, Asunción, Paraguay. Manufactured by Gravaçôes Elétricas S.A. R.J., Brazil. Sleeve printed at Imprenta Modelo S.A., Asunción, Paraguay. C.G.C. 61.186.300/0003-63.

9. "Creo que no éramos conscientes que estábamos lanzando el primer disco del rock nacional. Simplemente queríamos hacer un disco. Particularmente, recién con los años, me di cuenta de la importancia histórica que para el rock nacional tenía este disco." [I think that we were not aware that we were releasing the first rock album. We simply wanted to make an album. Only over the years, I realized the historical importance that this album had for rock"] (Saol Ganoa, see http://www.myaclais.blogspot.co.uk/2013/11/30-anos-del-primer-disco-del-rock-en.html, accessed 23 September 2014).

10. "La esperada aparición del LP de Pro Rock Ensamble cumple todas las expectativas y revela aún más insospechadas posibilidades de este grupo". http://www.myaclais.blogspot.co.uk/2013/11/30-anos-del-primer-disco-del-rock-en.html (accessed 23 September 2014).

11. Along similar social Darwinist lines, French naturalist and zoologist Baron Georges Cuvier's *History of the Natural Sciences* (2012 [1890]) portrays the "Human Race" as divided into three categories (e.g. Caucasian, Mongol, and Negro), while Swedish biologist Linnaeus's *General System of Nature* (1758) established four basic color types in descending order (e.g. White Europeans, Red Americans, Yellow Asians, and Black Africans).

12. The counterculture in the US in the 1960s was a left-wing generation of young people (intellectual students, bohemian musicians, civil rights activists, etc.) who shared values of freedom, opposed the Vietnam War, and challenged traditional suburban living. As a movement, the counterculture focused on personal freedom, a society free from inequalities, corruption, exploitation and oppression, and viewed conventionality, capitalism, political institutions, consumerism, and war as the principal problems in society (Whiteley 2000).

13. The full-page advert can be seen on Joni Mitchell's website by following this link: http://jonimitchell.com/library/view.cfm?id=293 (accessed 11 December 2015).

2 Neoliberalism and the Global Music Industry

Popular music is one of the great globalizers. It exists because of globalization, which, in its most recent form—a comprehensive globalization in the latest phase of capitalism's global hegemony—and combined with digital technologies, has shaped and been shaped by neoliberal capitalism. Neoliberalism is thus the current phase of globalization, which is a product and producer of neoliberal capitalism. Neoliberalism encompasses ideology, governance, and policy (Taylor 2016: 4) and is of total and controversial significance globally (McGuigan 2016: 10–11). Neoliberalism has risen to hegemonic dominance in the world as a whole since the 1970s. Coinciding with the collapse of European communism, it has triggered economic transformation around the entire world, while shaping political, ideological, and cultural structures and processes. Thus, neoliberalism is more than an economic system: it is an ideological system that has become deeply embedded in cultures around the world, but with local variants.[1] Social leadership, or hegemony (in the Gramscian sense), became established on a global scale, serving the interests and representing "the ways of thinking and feeling of 'the transnational capitalist class' … within civil society" (McGuigan 2016: 20).

Historically, the neoliberal project aimed to revive *laissez-faire* economics of nineteenth-century liberal capitalism, and to turn back the socialist advances made during the Golden Age of organized capitalism in the West. Saturated western markets and overproduction during the 1970s led to economic crisis, which, together with the collapse of actual socialism in the late 1980s and the Chinese turn to capitalism, led to a restructuring of the economies toward post-Fordism (or neo-Fordism) even though standardization and uniformity have not disappeared entirely as an economic practice in the West. Post-Fordism means that vertical integration is disaggregated in industrial organization, and replaced by complex networking and outsourcing through a continued program of corporate consolidation and mergers. Post-Fordism involves flexible, variable production for niche markets (customized specialization) and thus greater consumer choice and faster response to consumer trends, disaggregation of vertically integrated major corporations, outsourcing, reduction in the social wage, and internationalization in search of new markets, made possible and facilitated by new communication technologies emerging since the 1980s, including satellite, cable, and computerized information systems. Many large corporations have since the 1980s developed a "whole company" approach as a result of the overwhelming demand for flexibility, given the uncertain markets and the centrality of stock exchanges that followed global financial deregulation. This full flexibility meant to "outsource and sub-contract more or less everything except a strategic headquarters' financial decision-making capacity" (Crouch 2004: 37).

Information technology, notably the internet, has been crucial to run the complex organization tasks that this involves. Since the 1980s, communication technologies have advanced significantly, including satellite and cable communication, followed in the 1990s by the advance of digital technologies, which are all part of the information revolution, a twentieth-century phenomenon as important as the industrial revolution in the nineteenth century. The arrival of continually upgraded and more sophisticated modes of dissemination, such as cable and satellite television, cassette recorders, CD players/recorders, computer audio-file players, and internet connections and facilities gradually established full-fledged participation in western music cultures around the world (Regev 2013: 133). The globalization of culture is thus facilitated in the network society by information and communication technologies and instantaneous communications. The mediation by technologies has, simultaneously, impacted on and led to new forms of (individualized, privatized) sociality. The US actively pursued and promoted economic "freedoms" in search for new markets, including open markets without capital controls and reduced tariff barriers, open-door policies, free flow of information, and free press, thereby ensuring minimal intervention by states as democratic principles for a democratic world order, and pushing other nations toward free trade agreements and liberalization of the telecommunication industry (e.g. through the US Telecommunication Act of 1996, a law that removed barriers to entries and consolidation, among other strategies). Consequently, international governance (e.g. WTO, OECD, IMF, and EU) is guided by corporate freedom, and this trade liberalization with complete absence of regulation serves the interests of the biggest corporations with oligopolizing effects (Crouch 2004: 106).

Global Hollywood provides an example of vertical disintegration and globalization that occurred between the 1950s and 1980s, which moved to a new international division of labor with manufacturing transferred from expensive to cheap cultural labor markets around the world. Indeed, post-Fordization was pioneered by Hollywood in 1948 when the big five studios discontinued the studio-factory system of production (modelled on Ford's assembly-line production of motorcars) and increasingly passed on production to cost-cutting independents who would take the risk and henceforth supply the distributive majors. The vertically integrated corporation evolved into a complex network system of production and circulation in the audio-visual industries, while the majors remained the nodal point of power in the system as a whole by retaining control over distribution, transmission, and overseas sales (McGuigan 2016: 157–59). In the 1980s, post-Fordism impacted on the television industry in Britain and broadcasting across the world, which corresponded with a shift from a public-service model to today's deregulated, free-market model. Since the 1980s, the surge to cut costs and emergence of digital technologies meant the closing of studio music departments. In order to keep production costs low, composers nowadays do everything themselves with electronics or (less expensive) musicians from elsewhere, an entrepreneurialism necessitated by neoliberalism that has become the current norm in film and television.

The salient features of globalized neoliberal hegemony today are excessive market orientation, and transnationalism combined with the decline of the social welfare state, free entrepreneurship, and "a generalised faith in the magic of market forces" (McGuigan 2016: 66). The logic of neoliberal capitalism is based on *free* market ideology, including individual liberty and limited/no government intervention. As a theory of political economic practices, neoliberalism is marked by its financialized nature, an era of global financialization, increasing commodification, obsessive consumerism and consumption (Steger and Roy 2010). Neoliberalism means thoroughgoing economism. It means strong private property rights, free markets and trade, privatization of public services and assets, and deregulation. State intervention is kept to a bare minimum. Represented especially by free-market policy, neoliberalism is said to be more aligned with right-wing politics. During neoliberalization, exploitation and inequality at a global level have increased hugely, with the rich becoming richer and the poor remaining poor or becoming much poorer. In the early twenty-first century, exploitation and inequality are astounding at a global level and "would have shocked Marx and Engels" (McGuigan 2016: 132).

The Cultural Logic of Neoliberalism

Neoliberal doctrines have been extended to cultural products. Today most cultural products—film, music, literature, painting, sculpture—are sold as a commodity, which has led to a stifling of creativity. Contemporary culture is neoliberal capitalist culture. Neoliberalism thereby opened a window to the emergence of the creative industries, notably in Britain. While the home of neoliberal globalization—economically and politically—is the US where "market reasoning and neoliberal norms of conduct have been cultivated most fully, including acquisitive individualism, ruthless competition, hypocritical distrust of democracy, and indifference to inequality at home and abroad, while, at the same time, paying lip service to democratic egalitarianism" (McGuigan 2016: 111), Britain has wholeheartedly embraced neoliberal privatization and marketization and thoroughly absorbed these American values into English common sense.[2] A particular manifestation of the transition to neoliberal capitalism spreading across the world since the 1970s has thus been the financialization and privatization of the public arts sector resulting from immense financial and ideological pressures (McGuigan 2016: 66). The neoliberal cultural industries' rhetoric meant that "culture" "has come to be seen as a magical elixir for economic growth [and] social problems as well as bringing wealth back to cities that have been in decline due to de-industrialisation" (ibid.: 19), which has also been influential in post-industrial societies throughout the world. Under neoliberalism, culture has become economized, and state-owned institutions increasingly individualized and managed by capitalist transnationals. Neoliberalism reduces the autonomous and aesthetic value of culture to economic value. A neoliberal conception of culture is thoroughly economistic. Neoliberalism "reduces art to money and distorts culture with commercial sponsorship, and philanthropic foundations take the place of a democratically accountable public sector in the endless struggle for hegemony" (ibid.: 5). The most obvious feature of neoliberalism is the privatization of the public sector, including public-owned industries and public-sector bodies.

Neoliberalism has thus gone beyond a mere economic project or political economy, since "it also entailed a battle for hearts and minds, a discursive and ideological campaign to legitimize a different set of hegemonic arrangements" (McGuigan 2016: 66). It is the hegemonic ideology today, and a civilizational structure in dominance ("neoliberal civilization") currently around the whole world that shapes the sociocultural makeup of people through socialization. There is today "a neoliberal structure of feeling" or *Zeitgeist* that encompasses people's ideas, emotions, habitual modes of conduct, and routine practices. While the "market" is the neoliberal Zeitgeist, at its heart is the sovereign consumer, an all-knowing subject who (apparently) has the power to make completely free choices in the marketplace. Consequently, neoliberalism constructs an "ideal type of a preferred neoliberal self" (ibid.: 27)—successful entrepreneur, sovereign consumer, hard-working taxpayer. The neoliberal self today "is a competitive individual who is exceptionally self-reliant and rather indifferent to the fact that his or her predicament is shared with others ... Such a person must be 'cool' in the circumstances, selfishly resourceful and fit in order to survive under social-Darwinian conditions" (ibid.: 132). The neoliberal self is a new type of economic person whose thoughts, practices, and self-conceptions are shaped by neoliberalism as an economic system and organizing ideology. Socialized into a cool-capitalist presentation of self, the neoliberal(ized) individual is thereby viewed in exclusively market terms. Neoliberalism connects human freedom to the actions of the rational, self-interested actor in the marketplace. In the ideological battle for hearts and minds, neoliberalism influences the very language used colloquially. The newly emerging "NewLiberalSpeak [is] an everyday, vernacular speech, which has been Americanised by the discourse of branding, consumerism and managerial 'science'" (ibid.: 25). Aided by celebrity role models, demotic neoliberalism influences people's behaviors, practices, and conduct, and "distorts ordinary human social relations" (ibid.: 21), particularly among the vulnerable young. According to the most pessimistic critiques, the neoliberal organization of society has led to the "generation me" of American and American-influenced youth.

Branding
During the 1980s, neoliberal capitalism was shaped by increasing cultural abstraction, and the emergence of a new wave of consumption based on an image industry in fashion, lifestyle, and popular culture. Music and fashion have been linked inextricably, considering examples like the partnerships between Igor Stravinsky and Coco Chanel, The Velvet Underground and Nico, Justin Timberlake and William Rast's denim line, Gwen Stefani and L.A.M.B., and Lady Gaga's fashion influence. The period since the 1980s marked a new aesthetic of modern life, in which *visible* brands and branding have become ubiquitous and accepted. The image industry is built on advertising, a defining feature of neoliberal capitalism, and a primary symptom of today's capitalism, in which the brand is its principal concept. Advertising was pioneered in the 1940s by US advertising agencies and became a defining feature of neoliberal capitalism. The US advertising industry was boosted particularly with the development of commercial television, and "the persuasion business was born as a profession" (Crouch 2004: 25). Indeed, "advertising is not a form of rational dialogue. It does not build up a case based on evidence, but associates its products with a particular imagery. You cannot answer it back. Its aim is not to engage in discussion but to persuade to buy" (ibid.: 26). MTV, owned by media giant Viacom, became established as a 24-hour commercial channel that promotes the products, lifestyle, and fashion of its owning corporation and its paying advertisers (Arsenault and Castells 2008: 721). Indeed, movies, radio, television, and the internet act as advertisers for music, with the latter becoming possibly the most powerful advertising and marketing tool. Simi-

larly, TV commercials for products like cars, perfume, clothing, burgers, and so forth, have increasingly been used to sell music records and break new acts. In this hyper-commercialized market, fashion and lifestyle choices are marketed over genuine needs.

> Thanks to advertising, music media and Hollywood movies, young adults are seen to be cool, laid-back and endlessly partying. We are also shown constantly how their lives are blessed by the fun-filled and fabulous use of newer, continually updated and improved communications technologies, especially Apple products—iPods, iPhones and iPads—with all their great and proliferating apps (McGuigan 2016: 133).

Marketing and branding serve to promote goods not for their use value, but for what they signify, such as social value, status, and power. Branding has also been extended to artists by the ideology of the star ("star-as-brand"),[3] which has replaced the Romantic ideology of the genius (Taylor 2016: 17). Branding is crucial due to the profound effects of the digitization of music, as the former recording music industry has been supplanted by new industries. The challenge for artists today is to stand out or to navigate some form of musical career, and branding to enhance an artist's social value, status, and power is formidable (Hughes et al. 2016). Important in this context is P. David Marshall's "celebrity persona pandemic" (2016), which has grown out of the increasing fetishization of the constructed public persona in contemporary culture. Marshall describes how consumer culture has increasingly focused on the individualized production of the self, while acknowledging the role of the intersecting media and entertainment system of communication in celebrating the construction of the public self, personalization, and individuality (ibid.: 2). It is thus branded celebrities who have become our most visible human brands. Online culture in particular, including Instagram, MySpace, and Facebook, has been instrumental to an increasingly greater focus on the production of the self through "a parallel world of mediatization of the self" (ibid.: 3). Online culture thus pushes people to construct a public image that resembles the same approach adopted by celebrities for the last century. Meanwhile, celebrities-as-brands have become entities that serve the interests of the entertainment industries in personalizing value via consumer culture, and are thereby part of a system of transferring value in a culture (see, for instance, Raphael and Lam 2017). Celebrity thereby elevates a kind of possessive individualism. The hyperindividual model of celebrity represents very directly the normalization and naturalization of the current obsession with the production of the public self—or self-branding, which has intrinsic dimensions with a focus on self-improvement through cosmetic surgery, fitness, and so forth, and extrinsic dimensions with a focus on the outwardly, public presentation of the self, for instance through "technologies of the social" (Instagram, television, Facebook, Twitter, and so forth).

The current era is marked by "the politics of recognition" (Marshall 2016: 40), which marks a significant shift from previous celebrity culture when "the fabricated identity of persona was seen as a disguise and the mask of performance, a lie" (ibid.: 11). Today, central to contemporary experience is persona formation. Personas are complex projections and masks—fabricated and strategic presentations of the self—in a consumer culture, in which the consumption of signs penetrates all spheres of life, famously termed "hypercommodification" (Crook *et al.* 1992) and "simulacra" (Baudrillard 1983). Baudrillard emphasized the heightened importance of imagery—the synergy between sound and vision—where signs and symbols become the "true" influential components in the world, as they "dissimilate the fact that there is nothing behind them" (1994: 5). Indeed,

> Our urban spaces are saturated with advertisements, not just on billboards but on our bodies and in our dreams. Every crack is filled with slogans, every piece of available space is occupied like enemy territory. Likewise, time is also saturated, every second filled with jingles and naked bodies, and more slogans—even slogans imploring us to stop looking at slogans (Cazdyn and Szeman 2011: 58).

The current visual obsession reflects the fact that since the Renaissance, the eye is seen as the predominant sensory organ over the ear in western culture, as also demonstrated in the (visual) interpretation of God in the form of portraiture (Schafer 2004: 31). This is a new era that marks a qualitative change in human experience (Castells 2000: 508). It is the era of postmodernism, which (to some critics) is no more than a meaningless consumer culture according to old, exploitative ways of capitalism.

Consequently, neoliberal forms of global capitalism have gradually replaced Europe's "high" culture with a new aesthetic based on an image industry in fashion, lifestyle, and popular culture. In the neoliberal era, identity-making is accomplished through the consumption and display of cultural goods like music and consumer goods, including the device one listens to music with, while the ideology of cool has been extended to certain consumer and cultural goods. Globalization, the product and producer of neoliberal capitalism, has thus led to the redefinition of cultural capital (in the Bourdieuan sense) or cultural resource in society. Thus, while cultural capital in the 1960s and 1970s was expressed through knowledge of the fine arts and conferred prestige upon the knower (Bourdieu (1984 [1979]), today's cultural capital confers "knowledge of the hip and the cool, the trendy [which] are becoming increasingly common around the world" (Taylor 2014: 195). Works of "high" art, meanwhile, are no longer valued primarily for aesthetic reasons but increasingly for their monetized worth and exchange value, which "represents a general process in a notably spectacular instance of the reduction of aesthetic value to economic value in the world of High Art ... [which is] secured by the mystifications of branding" (McGuigan 2016: 79). This shift marks a historic moment, as "this is the first time in history that the cheapest commodities are seen as chic" (Taylor 2016: 65). Internalizing the "artistic critique" of capitalism in the 1960s, the creative and cultural industries and increasingly every other industry have thus appropriated "whatever is thought to be cool, even manufacture what is thought to be cool, in order to sell ever more goods" (ibid.: 42), with advertising being the most important mediator of the hip and the cool, "the conquest of cool" (Frank 1997).

Culturally, neoliberalism is marked by postmodernism as "the cultural logic of late capitalism" (Jameson 1991) and the end of "grand narratives" and universal categorization. Postmodernism is thereby "not just a set of ideas but, instead, a framing of emotionality and everyday practice that is dialectically related to transnational, high-tech capitalism, whereby the human subject is disoriented and in desperate need of cartographical guidance" (McGuigan 2016: 91). The emergence of identity politics meant a shift in focus away from universalism ("the Truth") and toward relativism and differences (truths), away from ideology and toward representation. It marks the great divide in social theory between modern and postmodern theory: The project of modernity, broadly, sought to classify and establish truths about the physical and social worlds. Postmodernism recognizes the impossibility of an absolute set of values, ideologies, or truths, and denies the concept of an essentialist view of culture. Characterized by pastiche and irony, postmodernism describes the collapsing of boundaries between cultural forms. It regards culture as a construction, as fluid and negotiated. Postmodern ideology has also deconstructed engineered histories of hegemony. The postmodern turn toward representation is hugely important to deconstruct constructions, images, and discourses of difference, including inclusion and exclusion, stereotyping and othering, in popular culture.

The Global Music Industry

Following the economic downturn and decline of record sales since the late 1970s, the turn toward neoliberalism has meant intensified musical commodification and truly globalizing tendencies, alongside unprecedented musical changes. Popular music in the 1980s became heavily produced, marked by reverb-heavy snare drums, delay on the vocals, electronic rhythms, and the digital synthesizer (replacing the analog synth in the early 1980s). Madonna, Michael Jackson, Def Leppard are just some of the iconic celebrity names who set new standards for (economic) success in the global music industry. Classical music recordings, notably quality-improved releases of historical recordings, flourished once again. Mainstream rock, particularly heavy metal, thrived, while dance music grew musically and commercially. Music engineers, producers, and songwriters had more tools at their disposal than ever before, while technological advancements in audio and video recordings, including CD, MD, DCC, and DAT players, led to an economic boost for the record industry that continued well into the 1990s (Gronow and Saunio 1998: 192–93). Artists and producers increasingly blended musical styles, aided by the affordability of digital recording equipment that could now operate in artists' homes, and the ability to cut and paste sound files, which gave artists entirely new ways of looping and constructing recorded music. The musical soundscape was dominated by pop, country, rap and hip hop, industrial, and electronic music. The 1990s saw the birth of grunge and gangsta rap, both setting new trends for fashion, taste, and lifestyle, while hip hop and rap gained unprecedented popularity globally.

Given the huge appeal of rock music in the 1960s, the US-based music recording industry evolved into global business powerhouses, facilitated by continuous vertical and horizontal mergers and consolidations, connecting companies up and down the production-consumption chain (vertically), and aligning recording technologies with related entertainment and publication media (horizontally). The structure and workings of the US-based music recording industry and its production values, organizational structures, and managerial practices with the manufacturing, production, and marketing of western pop and rock became replicated in the local music industries of countries around the world (Regev 2013: 104). Since the 1970s, the international music industries became similarly marked by the standardization of production patterns and the pop-rock aesthetic, "because they were perceived by them as the model of sheer professionalism" (ibid.). This meant that local music industries either mimicked major music corporations, or implemented professional conventions and complied with norms by the majors with whom they collaborated.

The music industry has since become the most concentrated global media market. The music companies have gradually developed into large multi-business corporations, which have from the beginning been oriented to the interests of wealthy, revenue-providing nations. By 2012, there existed only four dominant TNCs, the "Big Four", after which the British EMI Group was acquired by Universal. Currently there are three large music corporations (The Big Three): Universal Music Group (US-based; part of French media giant Vivendi); Sony Music Entertainment (part of media giant Sony, both US and Japan; includes BMG, part of German Bertelsmann); and Warner Music Group (US-based; separated from Time Warner in 2004). They proudly promote themselves as global behemoths on their websites, displaying their power and dominance over a saturated marketplace with images of signed artists and lists of subsidiaries under their corporate control. For instance, Universal's market for album artists has grown from 40.5 percent in 2012 (*Music Week*, 20 April 2012) to 54.7 percent in 2013 (*Music Week* 2014), which signifies a substantial growth in market share due to Universal's acquisition of EMI. Each corporation consists of smaller companies and labels, making enormous profit and dominating the music market by over 90 percent in some countries (Shuker 2016: 19). The music recording industry is situated in the most developed countries (US, UK, Japan, Germany, France) that dominate the music market, representing around 75–80 percent of the total global market share (IFPI 2005). More specifically, Universal Music Group is the largest corporation controlling ca. 39 percent (now including EMI, which controls ca. 13 percent); Sony Music controlling ca. 25 percent; and Warner Music controlling ca. 14 percent of the global music market, although figures tend to vary across the literatures (Howard 2009).

In terms of their structure, two of the Big Three (Universal Music and Sony Music) are subsidiaries of larger media conglomerates, characterized by cross-border ownership, trade, and global concentration (Arsenault and Castells 2008). (Warner Music Group is independent, but similarly a conglomerate corporation.) The structure of the media conglomerates, to which Universal and Sony belong, is thus underpinned by acquisitions of sub-companies, as well as mergers across larger corporations (horizontal integration). Thus, while there existed 50 media companies in 1983, in the early twenty-first century it is six giant media corporations (GE, News-Corp, Disney, Viacom, Time Warner, and CBS) that control 90 percent of media outputs (Lutz 2012). For instance, the merger between Sony and BMG in 2004, a 50/50 joint venture between the two media giants, is a good example of horizontal integration (BBC 2004). The large media corporations that have absorbed music record corporations operate "in a variety of fields beyond recorded music, incorporating publishing, television, electronics, and telecommunications, thus extending their influence to cover more markets within the global entertainment industry" (Frontline 2014). Through vertical mergers, meanwhile, corporations can connect smaller companies further up and down the production/consumption chain, such as for music touring and retail. Both horizontal and vertical mergers enable corporations to create *synergy* with related entertainment industries by successfully aligning recording technologies with the dissemination capacities of other entertainment media, including radio, cinema, television, and the internet. Big corporations continuously buy up smaller companies to help sell products across markets, so that business is fed to companies within the same corporation. This networked structure works in favor of both corporations and smaller companies, which creates a system of mutual interdependence:

> Majors would scout and eventually purchase from the innovative work of small companies. And those companies live inter-dependently with the majors, sometimes doing deals with them, sometimes being taken over by them. It is a case of symbiotic relationship which calls into question the degree and nature of independence (Burton 2005: 157).

For example, two of the majors, Universal and Sony, have closed deals with the online music video company VEVO (with around 13 million users) in 2014 in order to market their artists online to a global music audience. The synergy is mutually beneficial, as the majors are able to target audiences across the world simultaneously by uploading a video by one of their artists, while VEVO benefits from the amount of views that they receive from audiences. How powerful this synergy is has been demonstrated by the fact that during the first week in 2014, the two most viewed music videos on VEVO were by artists signed to the majors, namely Miley Cyrus (signed to RCA, a sub-company of Sony Music) and Katy Perry (signed to Virgin, a sub-company of Universal). Thus synergy functions as a kind of "multi-platform storytelling" (Edwards 2012: 1) as a principal example of corporate synergy in media conglomerates. Multi-platform storytelling describes how texts are distributed "in a coordinated way" by these media corporations, often comprised of production units trying to generate transmedia content across film, games, TV, the Web, and mobile phones. This structure of media conglomerates in effect separates the production, distribution, and promotion of popular music in different locations, made possible via advanced communication systems.

The process of creating synergy horizontally is called *cross-media marketing*, where the artist is plugged into other entertainment media to create synergy between his/her song(s) and a movie, TV show, product (car, perfume, makeup), game, magazine, musical, or another outlet. Through cross-marketing, celebrities' value moves across different fields, and they are "used—and paid—to create events, sell magazines, and construct our world of entertainment value" (Marshall 2016: 80). Synergy can happen within one large corporation, as well as across large corporations, whereby artists and their music are plugged in such a way that it becomes beneficial to all companies involved. A good example of successful cross-media marketing is the 2008 chart-topping film *Mamma Mia!* (Universal Pictures), which was adopted from the 1999 West End musical *Mamma Mia* and is based on the songs of the pop band ABBA (among others). The buzz surrounding the film was further boosted through creating a sing-a-long version, which was shown in UK cinemas and is included as a bonus feature on the DVD (released by Universal Studios). This meant that people went to see the film again, doubling the ticket sales, while also buying the DVD, and appealing to the subsequent karaoke craze with the release of the soundtrack CD (Polydor, owned by Universal Music), karaoke CD (Stage Star), and games like Sony's *SingStar*. In 2005, Universal Music even brought out a soundtrack CD of *Mamma Mia!* in Spanish. In turn, the same pop songs were listened to, watched, sung, and lived everywhere. Meanwhile, *Pop Stars*, a youth music program from the early noughties, provides another interesting example:

> With *Pop Stars*, you have synergy through all of the AOL Time Warner machine. The show is on WB, which is obviously part of Time Warner Bros. Their album came out on Sire London, which is an affiliate of the Warner Music Group, which is also owned by Warner Bros. After they did all of that, and after the show aired, their strategic alliances really came into play when they offered the single exclusively on AOL, prior to its release. When that single was offered, it brought it 66,000 downloads on one day. They also launched a 'win and Eden Crush's makeover contest' which was offered exclusively on AOL. In addition, they plugged stories in all of AOL Time Warner's magazines, which include *Teen People, Entertainment Weekly* and *Time*. So you really see the synergy in play with a show like *Pop Stars* where it's fabricated, but in the end, it becomes the real deal (Shirley Halperin, in Jhally *et al.* 2005b).

Another successful example of cross-media marketing is demonstrated by the innovative artist Katy Perry. Perry encapsulates the western beauty ideal by evoking images of a Barbie Doll (Deliovsky 2008: 49), and often plays on this concept with her styling, which ranges from 1920s flapper to 1950s vintage swing skirts. Her "star" stance in the music industry is immediately apparent by having released four "top five" albums while signed to Capitol Records (Acharts 2013), which in turn helped to build a successful brand reaching into music, retail, television, film, and gaming. For instance, Katy Perry released three perfumes called Purr, Meow, and Killer Queen, the latter of which was accompanied by a one-minute-long advertisement, which also debuted on national television (Hollywood Life 2013). Meanwhile, the film industry used brand "Katy Perry" in 2012 when she released her debut film *Part of Me in 3D* based on her Teenage Dream tour, and in the gaming industry she released her own extension pack as part of the popular gaming range called *The Sims 3: Sweet Treats* (EA Games 2012). Synergy is thus clearly apparent within Perry's musical work: the artist is signed by Capitol Records, which is owned by Universal Music Group; her perfumes are manufactured and promoted by Coty Beauty (Billboard 2012); *Part of Me in 3D* was produced by MTV films, which is owned by Viacom, so her music videos and songs are frequently played on MTV channels (Frontline 2014); lastly, her personalized video game was created by Electronic Arts, a gaming company notorious for being the third successful gaming company in the world (Software Top 100 2010).

Further down the record music corporations are the imprint record labels. For example, Warner Music Group owns imprints like Elektra, Atlantic, Rhino, Kinetic, Maverick, and Warner Brothers Records; Universal Music Group has imprints like Def Jam, Island and MCA Records; Sony owns imprints like the Columbia and Epic label group; EMI, which used to be the smallest of the former Big Four and is now part of Universal, has imprints such as Hemisphere, Parlophone, Capitol, and Virgin Records (Knopper 2009). As corporations have become increasingly concentrated, they own growing portfolios of record labels in different territories globally. They also own many well-known smaller labels, which, while often started by entrepreneurs, have been absorbed into the corporations, specifically when the signed artists promise high degrees of corporate success. For example, Island Records, which was started in 1959 in Jamaica by entrepreneur Chris Blackwell out of his car with small investment, signed artists like Bob Marley, Grace Jones, Tom Waits, and U2. With promising record sales and rising popularity of its artists, the label was bought up by Polygram in 1989, which itself was bought up by Seagram, and then was merged into Universal Music Group in 1999 (Knopper 2009: 47).[4] Another example is the buy-up of independent labels like Tommy Boy (bought out 50 percent by Warner Brothers) and Def Jam (bought by Columbia Records), who began releasing grassroots, street-level hip hop from the south Bronx. Meanwhile, the band The Coral, a Scouse-centric band that signed with Deltasonic Records who dominate the Liverpool niche market, gained more national blanket success through internationalized distribution channels via Universal Music Group. Similarly, the Seattle-centric band Nirvana, who first achieved niche success with the independent Sub-Pop Records, were bought up by Geffen Records (a subsidiary of MCA) and later absorbed into Universal Music Group. In doing so, the majors are able to monitor independent labels who engage in innovative practices, while avoiding the risks involved in signing artists before they have reached some popularity and, at the same time, independent and smaller record labels are often easily influenced by corporate capitalist thinking. Small labels will continue to exist, yet their growth may be hampered without becoming part of one of the major corporations. If absorbed into a major corporation, independent labels contribute toward increased diversification and satisfy local niche markets as musically hybrid and diverse musics become available in different geographical musical markets. Even so, however, it is ultimately the Big Three who hold near-total control over musical production and consumption, as their complex production, distribution, and promotional networks make it difficult for alternative, independent companies to succeed.

Cultural Imperialism
During the mid-1970s, the circuit of cultural globalization became conceptualized by the dominant theory of cultural imperialism, when much popular music research focused on the linkage between musical diversity and the structures of the music industry. It was believed that cultural globalization leads to cultural homogenization (Tomlinson 1991; 1999: 71–105), or a "world monoculture" (Regev 2013: 5). Informed by leftist critiques of the ethical and sociological consequences of capitalist dealings by western mass media and multi/transnational corporations, the concept was influenced by Marxist understandings of "the need of a constantly expanding market for its products [which] chases the bourgeoisie over the whole surface of the globe" (Lamb 2015: 12). From these largely economic criticisms arose the image of the barbarous and bigoted westerner bent only on appropriation and exploitation without any concern for the cultures and practices of the proletarian strata of the global population. The impetus for this image came partially from the Italian theorist Antonio Gramsci and his notion of "cultural hegemony" (Forgacs 2000). In other words, the old colonialist forms of appropriation-by-brute-strength had been replaced by a more insidious pervasion of "discourse" via the mass media and large-scale institutions. Discourse must be understood in the context of Michel Foucault's "discursive formation" (Foucault 1970), that is, knowledge emerging from discourses in journalism, academia, education, and so forth, which are "constructive representations" of the world (Hall 1997b). The deluge of western cultures and ideologies emanating from the West would come to saturate the rest of the world, resulting in homogenized cultural and political practices, universal across the globe. Globalization, it was believed, consequently leads to the demise of local culture, which becomes overwhelmed by the symbols and icons of western (popular) culture.

The conceptual foundations were laid by cultural theorist Theodor Adorno (1903–69) in his critiques of the capitalist-driven "culture industry". He suggested that the carefully constructed imagery is thought to manipulate a desire in consumers to be incorporated *into*, as well as a desire *for* a capitalist economy. The public, who passively consume the images and meanings of the capitalist culture industry, thus absorb the ethos and philosophy of the industrialized, capitalist system (Longhurst 2007: 2–11). Adorno also argued that popular culture, including music, is depthless and little more than glossy appearance and superficial illusion. Since the culture industry and media had become excessively commercialized, the mass of people would no longer be passionately interested in really important matters, but were now distracted by consumer culture and trivializing entertainment. More current scholars similarly believed that the world is becoming culturally similar and

> subsumed by a shallow, inauthentic and synthetic global culture based on the economic domination of the West and the products of the gigantically powerful, transnational media operators... The most pessimistic version of cultural imperialism sees local culture being eradicated and surviving only in museums and heritage centres (Beynon and Dunkerley 2000: 23).

Cultural imperialism suggests that economic globalization is eroding local, indigenous culture and traditions, which become replaced by the icons of western, and particularly American, popular culture, accelerated through its drive for new global markets, which "will dissolve all cultural differences in a dull and colorless homogeneity throughout the world" (Lechner and Boli 2004: 287). The cultural imperialism thesis is preoccupied with the market, and suggests a cultural movement from the center to the periphery, from the West to the rest. Cultural imperialism is seen by many critics as a form of western neo-colonialist domination, one based on symbolic and psychological means of control. In their critiques of the music recording industry, critics seek to uncover the exploitative methods through means of cross-media marketing and consolidated corporate structures. According to this view, postmodern culture, including music, is regarded as nothing more than superficial gloss, as music everywhere begins to sound and feel the same. Artistic expression becomes a standardized commodity, while consumers are sucked into the manipulative and alienating ideologies of consumerist capitalism. A range of musical examples from the western and non-western world has shown that in many instances, this theory is true, as economic pressures mean that musicians do alter their music in style beyond recognition and devoid of local meaning and distinctiveness.

Rammstein's 'Amerika' (2004), and the Commodification of Christmas Culture. This criticism was taken up by the rock band Rammstein when conceiving their song 'Amerika' from their album *Reise Reise* (2004). The band adopts a cynical standpoint toward globalization. For instance, the lyrics and video make reference to various globally commodified goods of popular culture, including Mickey Mouse, Lucky Strike cigarettes, Nike trainers, Coca Cola, Wonderbra, pizza, television, and Santa Claus. The music video shows these icons of commodified culture in short sequences, while the image depicting Santa Claus delivering presents to children in a seemingly rural African setting may be read as the band's deliberate mockery of the American image of Santa Claus as the "God of Materialism". The lyrics also criticize the spread of English as the global language and American foreign policies of interventionism in foreign countries. In the music video, the band even mocks the spread of American culture to the moon, during which the band members are depicted as astronauts, walking on the moon, playing *Star Trek* games on a slot machine, and pitching the American flag as a symbolic gesture of victory. Toward the end of the video, the camera pans out to reveal an artificial setting, a film studio, thereby addressing the moon landing conspiracy theories, which claim that the moon landings were falsifications staged by NASA and other US organizations.

The critique of the image of Santa Claus is noteworthy here, since the globalization of (western) Christmas culture has led to the reform of Christmas imagery and music as a catalytic tool in the marketing of commodities, a process also termed "aggressive advertising" (Hirschman and LaBarbera 1989; see also Whiteley 2008 for a collection of essays on the theme of Christmas in popular culture). The criticism goes that the commodification of Christmas culture has in fact cannibalized the popularity of traditional religious carols just as cultural imperialism has allowed Christmas, as a concept, to be culturally rewritten and exploited as an event in which dominating corporations can battle for profit (Negus 1996: 172) by encouraging different cultures to consume Christmas culture, including music, without an understanding of what the particular songs are proposing. For instance, the Christmas-themed feature film *The Snowman* (Jackson 1982) and its title song 'Walking in the Air' have suffered similar fates, as Japan has become the leading market for the film's rebranding as *The Snowman and the Snowdog*, while selling an array of products that have little significance to the original film and recycling the festive imagery on hundreds of unrelated goods, one example being the 'Walking in the Air' song, which was shown on a TV commercial for "The Snowman chicken nuggets" (*Making of The Snowman* 2002). What makes *The Snowman* such a significant example is that it demonstrates how corporations may take advantage of a visual or aural motif by linking the success of its creativity to a principle that is operated by esteem. Put simply, marketing will fool us into believing that if an advertisement contains the right music and a successful imagery, then we must need the product in order to be fulfilled. In the context of Christmas culture, the image of Santa Claus can thus be read as the "God of Materialism", for he is a figure into which American society has had its deepest values ingrained (Hirschman and LaBarbera 1989).

The example of the commodification of Christmas culture highlights the worrying aspect of globalization, namely the standardization of beliefs and the ways in which these beliefs are dressed up in a traditional manner, since they themselves have now become a tradition, just as the way in which various religious fables had formed the concept of Christmas itself. Consumerism is now something that can "reach our hearts" and is occurring ever more powerfully through exposure to music (Clancy 2008: 13). According to this view, economic globalization leads to "cultural imperialism" (Tomlinson 1991), which refers to the hegemonic cultural, economic, and political role of the United States. We thus often find terms like Americanization, Westernization, and McDonaldization (Ritzer 2011) in discussions of cultural imperialism. All these terms imply a neocolonialist form of domination, based not so much on military control (as under European imperial rule during colonization), but on symbolic and psychological means of control. The cultural imperialism thesis is preoccupied with the market, which implies that the center (West) impacts on the periphery (the rest) through relentless cultural domination and influence.

Katy Perry's 'Chained to the Rhythm' (2017). In January 2017, Katy Perry delivered a more contemporary critical "take" on Americanized culture in a track from her fourth album, which Perry delayed in the wake of Donald Trump's US election victory, as she wanted to address the political upheaval in her music. In her video for 'Chained to the Rhythm', Perry indulges in the delights and distractions offered by a retro-futuristic theme park, "Oblivia", as the epitome of neoliberal culture. The theme park guests are dressed in 1950s fashion, an era of great optimism for American capitalism. People are exaggeratedly happy to get away from reality, eating giant cotton candy shaped in the form of atomic bomb clouds and crowding around an advert for "the greatest ride in the universe". The line *"so comfortable we're living in a bubble, so comfortable we cannot see the trouble"* is accompanied by girls taking selfies on their smartphones, referring to today's social media obsession. The song's lyrics depict a world of repetition and ignorance, where technology renders us oblivious to people's real problems. In the background, there are signs, icons, and statues of a hamster, signifying the monotony that drives neoliberal society and that makes the rich richer and poor poorer. Katy gets pricked by a rose thorn causing her to bleed, just as in the fairy tale of the "Sleeping Beauty", which leads to a short moment of awakening to realize that she is human, self-conscious, but still she follows the "rhythm" of the masses. Katy joins a rollercoaster named "Love me", with seats containing blue hearts (for men) and pink hearts (for women) with guests being divided into heterosexual pairs, making obvious references to outdated gendered norms that exclude LGBTs. As the rollercoaster speeds through a tunnel, the viewer cannot help but notice social media emojis, once again referencing today's social media obsession. As the camera pans around the theme park, another ride named "The Great American Dream Drop" can be seen, which hoists tiny suburban houses towards the sky and suddenly malfunctions, a metaphor for the US housing crisis where reckless lending left thousands of people homeless. Toward the end of the ride, each person receives reward points, drawing on critiques of gender inequality in that the guy collects around 9000 votes and the girl (Katy) around 20. The guests then follow red signs directing them where to go, dancing in synchronization, joyfully happy. A sign indicating the year 1984 could be a reference to a book about dystopian society, *Nineteen Eighty-Four*, by George Orwell, which conjured up the nightmare prospect of a Stalinist state in Britain. The camera then pans to a "Safe Trip Home" wall, which signifies the US-Mexican border and US immigration policies under Trump, which coheres with an attraction named "No Place Like Home". Another ride, "Bombs Away", is accompanied by Katy's lyrics, "*thought we could do better than that*". The petrol station, "Inferno H2O", supplies "inferno water", a reference to the West's dependency on oil and Trump's decision to support fossil-fuel production, albeit with significant environmental consequences, but also to the looming crisis over the world's water supply. Meanwhile, the oblivious, social media-obsessed crowds walk in unison and wait in long queues to run on the hamster wheel (Savage 2017).

The next scene sees Katy watching a 3D movie in the cinema, "A Nuclear Family", depicting an ordinary patriarchal family with the woman ironing clothes, the father figure reading a newspaper, and the child drawing on the floor. Katy notices a disturbing homogeneity among her fellow park guests who are by now moving entirely in unison, and she sees Skip Marley singing "*The truth they feed is feeble*", referencing the control exercised by corporations and governments over mediated representations. Gradually Perry begins to realize something is terribly wrong with the "American dream". The guests around Katy watch a big event and continue to be in a trance-like state, unable to notice what is happening around them. Katy, however, "awakens" and screams the lyrics to the other people to make them conscious. In the hamster treadmill, a Caucasian guy continues to run successfully, but those who fail and fall down on their way are an Asian girl and an Afro-American man, making critical references to sexism and racism in the world of oblivion. Katy, too, gets on the treadmill and starts running only to realize that she does not go anywhere, and that guests are not there to have fun but to be assets, cogs in the machine, literally hamsters on a wheel. Her realization is complete when Bob Marley's grandson, Skip Marley, raps *"Break down the walls to connect, inspire / Up in your high place, liars / Time is ticking for the empire / And we're about to riot / they woke up, they woke up the lions"*.

Musical Homogenization

The theory of cultural imperialism has been conceptualized in popular music discourses by analyzing the structure and workings of the global music industry as part of the larger cultural industries, and drawing conclusions about the resultant musical diversity, or lack thereof, often echoing the neo-Gramscian perspective with a focus on the theme of independence versus large corporate control. This body of discourse conveys the general agreement that by the 1980s and 1990s, the varying cycles of increased or decreased musical diversity exist under the auspices of the major transnational music corporations (Regev 2013: 80). It was suggested that musicians faced a serious crisis because of the concentrated ownership of music by three large corporations (Jhally *et al.* 2005b). These have had enormous control over what kind of music gets produced, and have been the reason why some musicians became huge stars heard by millions, while others did not. The success of musicians was not determined by their musical talent and ambition. Instead, the decision of who gets promoted was made on the basis of sales figures and profitability. Since the large corporations have become tied up financially in the global stock market, the emphasis of their activity has since been on financial stability and quick sales. Generally, they seek to avoid risks that can arise from musical innovation and development, and instead shifted their focus on selling sensation and spectacle, fashion, and lifestyle surrounding a few "big" artists:

> The music industry is now taking its cue from the success of *Thriller*, and the reasoning goes something like this: If I can sell forty million units of a single artist and consolidate all of the promotion, etc., all that promotional machinery into a single artist, why in the world do I want to deal with eighty artists who sell half a million each? The simplest thing to do so is to shop around until I find that one artist who can sell forty million, and the heck with the rest of the eighty. And so they are trimming their rosters in the hope of finding the next Michael Jackson (Reebee Garofalo, in Jhally *et al.* 2005b).

The only artist to beat Michael Jackson's top 10 US singles record is pop star Rihanna with her song 'Love on the Brain' (2017), which is also her 30th single to get into the top of the Billboard chart (Madonna is eight ahead on 38) (BBC Newsbeat 2017). Stars like Ed Sheeran, Rihanna, Drake, Madonna, Mariah Carey, Jackson, The Beatles, and others mean "safe" profits, and to the music corporations, there is little incentive to diversify their roster. This same trend is also noticeable in other parts of the world. In China, for instance, Hong Kong pop star G.E.M. is hailed as "China's Taylor Swift" with millions of fans across China. Singing in Mandarin and writing songs about love, G.E.M. has been compared to one of the world's biggest pop stars (Liu 2017). Meanwhile, New Zealand-born Parris Goebel has become established as a global dance and style icon, while Singaporean singer-songwriter Joel Tan, aka Gentle Bones, has been described as Singapore's Ed Sheeran.

Yet it is also the promotion of artists and their music that has been influenced and controlled by the centralized music industry. The Big Three corporations have connected smaller companies further up and down the production/consumption chain, such as for music touring and retail, while through horizontal mergers, they aimed to create synergy with related entertainment industries, including radio and television. As a result, the companies who controlled radio, TV, touring, and retail could serve the interests of the dominant corporations, and vice versa. Radio broadcasting has historically been a powerful medium to break new acts, and the major labels have tended to work closely with radio stations by buying commercial time to advertise their artists on air, thereby determining the playlists played by radio DJs.

The near-monopoly situation in radio in the US resulted in streamlining and standardizing of playlists for carefully selected profitable artists, a working practice that has spread around the world. For instance, Limp Bizkit is said to have gained success through this "pay for play" commercial system. At the same time, the increased move toward the privatization of radio broadcasting has meant that companies were able to buy unlimited numbers of radio stations. In the US, for instance, Clear Channel Communications owned more than 1000 radio stations, which meant that radio DJs "play the same songs in the same order by the same artists" (Jhally et al. 2005b), which clearly results in uniformity in the music played across these stations. Meanwhile, MTV, owned by media giant Viacom, became a 24-hour commercial channel created to promote the products, lifestyle, and fashion of its owning corporation and its paying advertisers. To this end, MTV has been created as an infomercial that sells music for a label or clothing product, fashion and lifestyle. Critics of globalization have thus regarded MTV as a centralized national marketing system controlled by advertising. MTV, now a global channel that reaches over 320 million households in ninety countries on five continents, twenty-four hours a day is vital to the marketing of music. And again, the major record labels have extremely close links with MTV (Thurston Moore, in Jhally *et al.* 2005b).

The power of the Big Three went further into touring. Large venues have been owned by promotion companies that were in turn owned by one of the large record labels, which in turn exercised enormous control over which artists play in these venues. Even in instances where a large venue was/is run independently, it was commonly only artists who have the corporate backing that play in these venues. For the record companies, it was obviously only "safe" acts who get corporate backing for touring, as they did not pose financial risks for the stifling costs and expensive venues involved in touring, simply because:

> Tours these days are outrageously big. They require eighty-something trucks, hundreds of local crew people and travelling crew people. They have pyro, they have special effects, they have video—they're just massive, massive endeavors these days. They require massive corporate backing—sponsorships—just to put on the show (Shirley Halperin, in Jhally *et al.* 2005b).

Retail was another important gatekeeper for the record companies to reach their customers, through which musical homogenization was reinforced and perpetuated. Large national and transnational chains have accounted for significant numbers of album sales. For instance, the HMV group, which is linked to EMI, exercised significant influence over the kinds of music to be sold, based on criteria of marketability. Big box stores (e.g. Best Buy, Target, Walmart in the US; HMV, Tesco, ASDA in the UK) have largely destroyed smaller, independent record shops, since they control what music they sell and at what cost, which has greatly changed the landscape of music retailing before the impact of the Internet. Retail has gradually declined due to the disappearance of the independent record store and the growth of digital piracy.

A further driver of musical standardization is the fact that movies, radio, television, and the internet have increasingly acted as advertisers for music. TV commercials for products like cars, perfume, and clothing have frequently been used to sell music records and break new acts for the major record labels. Well-known examples of pop songs used in advertisements have included Michael Jackson's 'Billy Jean' for a Pepsi commercial, The Beatles' 'Revolution' used for a Nike advert, Ray Charles' 'You Got the Right One, Baby!' for a Diet Pepsi advert, Nick Drake's 'Pink Moon' used in a Volkswagen Cabriolet commercial, and many others (PRS for Music 2010). The resultant celebrity culture marked by hyper-commercialization and cross-marketing is shaping much of today's neoliberal culture. The celebrity, larger-than-life figure, is admired and celebrated and, at times, even emulated. Exemplary role models and their characteristic patterns of conduct in the celebrity culture of business illustrate "the preferred self of neoliberal culture [which] can be understood as an ideal type in the Weberian sense" (McGuigan 2016: 4). This is a culture said to be characterized by standardization and homogenization. For instance, the phenomenon of teen pop that emerged in the late 1980s reflects this to a certain extent, as there are concrete similarities between the various acts, such as Britney Spears, Kylie Minogue, Christina Aguilera, or Justin Timberlake: the narratives are often romantically or sexually involved; the artist is often stereotypically seen as either the half-naked singer, a product of the male gaze and the male-dominated industry, or the edgy-yet-pretty male star; a slight growl is used by the soloist to signify sexual emotion; several voices are used in unison, while connoting sensitivity and tenderness. Across mainstream popular music, there is indeed a tendency for songs to be marketed through the construction of personalities and their individual performance quirks and rhetorical gestures, and these songs often share similar lyrics, structures, chord progression, and drum patterns.

The power of advertising and branding is so great that it can break new acts or inject new life into old ones, while exposing them to a whole new audience. It is one of the main reasons why so few artists actually "make it" at the level that is deemed successful by the corporations in their search for fashion and lifestyle brands. To many critics, this hyper-commodification of popular music reflects "the bankruptcy of our culture ... and with that, it mocks the music, it demeans it, it demeans the culture" (Robert McChesney, in Jhally *et al.* 2005b). This is a consumer culture, in which artists are valued for their potential tie-ins across the entire creative industries. And since advertising is the key driver in neoliberal market structures, huge amounts of money are spent on the promotion and branding of artists. Yet it is not the record companies, but the artists themselves who usually underwrite the upfront costs for the promotion of their latest record. Prior to the release of an album, for instance, an artist can owe the record company between $300,000 and $800,000 (Michael Franti, in Jhally *et al.* 2005b), a debt that will be deducted directly from his or her royalties. Often artists are not even aware that this is happening to them:

> If you're an artist and you're dealing with a major label you just can't tell what's going on. A lot of the time you don't know that a hundred thousand dollars is being spent on your video and it's going to come

> out of your end of it. And unless you have twenty-four hours a day to be on top of every single aspect of what you're doing, then you're going to be losing money in all different pockets without knowing (Kathleen Hanna, in Jhally et al. 2005b).

Marketing and promotion are the biggest expense in introducing a musician to the public. As consumers have increasingly accessed music digitally, marketing efforts have shifted substantially online. A major international signing costs between $500,000 and $2 million to break in a major market, of which between US$200,000–700,000 is spent on marketing and promotion. For example, "with Justin Bieber's album, Purpose, his record company harnessed its global reach in coordination with local teams around the world. In total around 1,500 marketing experts were involved in launching it to his fans, helping to make it a huge global success" (IFPI 2016: 12).

The capitalist market structure that underpins the workings of the Big Three thus favors few, but safe artists, as they can guarantee financial security to underwrite the huge costs afforded for promotion and advertising. Meanwhile, musical diversity is said to be under threat, as the corporate workings of the music industry homogenizes music. Music begins to sound and feel the same the world around. This view resonates closely with Theodor Adorno's critique of the capitalist culture industry, whose exploitation and manipulation have the power to enslave artists and consumers within the ideology of capitalism. Through means of limitations of choice for the consumer, there is thus a determining standardization pervading the entirety of popular culture. Today's oligopoly of major record labels that comprise much of the global recording industry can be interpreted as major exponents of this philosophy:

> The production of a mass cultural form like popular music is similar to the production of any mass produced product, such as an automobile or a bar of soap. Recordings generally sound the same with some variation due to the handicraft nature of music production, because record companies seek to maximise profits by limiting the cost of production, and the risks involved in innovation. Artistic expression and cultural significance have no place within the assembly line (Fenster and Swiss 1999: 235).

Musicians thus often face a critical dilemma: while many are drawn to music to do something special, they quickly realize that they are merely one of many commodities that the corporation is trying to pitch. It forces musicians to orient themselves toward the interests of wealthy, revenue-providing markets, and to pitch their music and image according to (mostly) western musical tastes. Musicians often comply in their desperate desire to secure a record deal with one of the majors. In other words, musicians willingly self-censor their music and image, as the music industry has the power to decide what to release, usually with an imagined market in mind.

Music Television and the Male Gaze
The power of the concentrated music industry is further illustrated by the shift in the 1980s toward a *global* preoccupation with "image" and the sexualized female form that serves to objectify women. The post-war music recording industry was characterized by sexist divisions in its industrial practices, and creativity was judged within the boundaries of stereotyped gendered values, beliefs, and behaviors. Since the 1980s, music television further enhanced masculine hegemony and the objectification of women. The deregulation of broadcasting by market force governments in the US and the development of cable and satellite services have resulted in the introduction of 24-hour music channels. For instance, motivated by commercial imperatives, "Warner Communications MTV opened for business on 1 August 1981, and within two years the first American cable music channel Music TeleVision became second in importance to radio as a music industry promotional vehicle" (O'Brien 1995: 215). Driven by the need to attract a large audience, MTV used the emergence of rock as the "music of the youth" to develop demographics-inspired media products, thereby developing niche music programming and moving away from the prior mass audience approach by bringing together demographic categories of age (12–34 year olds) and geographic location, as well as class, race, and gender. MTV's success was determined by getting record companies to supply videos using playlists, which essentially acted as advertisements. Musicians would appear on the videos, while the chosen songs would promote single releases. By 1986, MTV was available in 28 million homes (Gronow and Saunio 1998: 201).

With its commercial viability secured, a specific system of representation, to be constructed and naturalized in music videos, had yet to be formulated, which became underpinned by the ideological assumptions surrounding the specified target audience—youth—which were shaped by stereotypical biases. Gender, specifically, became a marketing variable that reproduced socially constructed gender ideologies. Consequently, rock was elevated above pop, and made to represent art and artfulness, artistic superiority and the "struggling genius", authenticity and sincerity. Pop, by contrast, became a sign of industrial manipulation and commercial exploitation, devoid of any significant and authentic meaning. By creating this difference, rock music became useful to MTV's goal of "elevating white-male musicianship and creating an idealized vision of white-male spectatorship" (Lewis 1990: 32), while oppressing female musicians and their audiences who were devalued as artists by relegating their music to pop music categories. Gender became a limiting parameter to establish difference through the representation of male youth privilege and male ideology. Pop images thus became crucial mass-marketing tools, creating desire for "slick sexual presentation", which ranged from alluring clothing (or lack of clothing) to sexual innuendo, such as the crotch grab made famous by Michael Jackson to simulate sexual acts (Andsager and Roe 2003: 79–80). It was usually the female artists and women in pop videos who were overtly sexualized and subjected to the "male gaze", which in turn normalized patriarchal ideologies that placed women as sex objects in a position of male subordination. The practice of looking—the gaze—meant "to look" or "to stare", often with eagerness or desire.

Laura Mulvey (1975) made an important contribution to the understanding of media constructions of woman as spectacle, the gender of the gaze, and voyeuristic pleasure, which applies primarily to representations of white women and femininities (James 2015: 95). Mulvey took a psychoanalytic feminist approach to film study, while drawing on Freudian and Lacanian psychoanalyses to examine the pleasures of scopophilia and narcissistic identification, and conceptualized the patriarchal definition of "looking as a male activity" and "being looked at as a female 'passivity'", "women as objects of the male gaze", ideas that have also been extended and applied to the study of other forms of visual culture, including music video. Mulvey argued that mainstream films confirm patriarchal gender perceptions of women as passive and men as active, by constructing films for a male viewer who takes pleasure in watching films, in two different ways: using the Freudian term scopophilia, she argued that films are made to objectify the female body and allow for a controlling male gaze, while drawing on Lacan's notion of a person's ego and identifying a narcissistic element in film spectatorship that allows male viewers to identify with the idealized male hero on screen (1975: 164).

Psychoanalysis as a feminist tool was taken up by second-wave feminists and became hugely influential in the late 1970s. Freud's theory was initially heavily criticized by feminists for its phallo-centricity, but was later re-evaluated, particularly by French feminists and film studies scholars. The appeal of psychoanalysis for feminists is twofold: firstly, as a means to "advance our understanding of the status quo, of the patriarchal order in which we are caught" (Mulvey 1975: 159), and secondly, because Freud acknowledged that the physical differences alone between men and women are insufficient to understand why men and women are given different characteristics: "I shall conclude that you have decided in your own minds to make 'active' coincide with 'masculine' and 'passive' with 'feminine'" (Freud 1964: 115). And these gendered beliefs "of men as aggressor/initiator/definer and women as passive-object/follower/defined" were reinforced in representations of men and women in popular culture and music (Chapple and Garofalo 1977: 269). Consequently, the problem "is not the act of looking itself, but the viewing relationship characteristic of a particular set of social circumstances" (Sturken and Cartwright 2001: 76). The gaze is thus critical in terms of race, class, disability, and age, but most significantly gender. In terms of the latter, feminist thinkers believe that "a core element of western patriarchal culture is the display of woman as spectacle to be looked at, subjected to the gaze of the (male) audience" (Van Zoonen 1994b: 87).

> In western society, to be looked at is the fate of women, while the act of looking is reserved to men ... Men act and women appear. Men look at women. Women watch themselves being looked at. This determines not only most relations between men and women but also the relation of women to themselves. The surveyor of woman in herself is male: the surveyed female. Thus she turns herself into an object—and most particularly an object of vision: a sight (Van Zoonen 1994b: 88).

This "to-be-looked-at-ness" has the effect that the culture industries prescribe women to be beautiful and slender, a pleasure to be looked at. Across many popular music genres, the emphasis is directed at women's image: how they look and how they dress, and this relates directly to patriarchy in music culture: "Women are mere beauties in men's culture so that culture can be kept male" (Wolf 1991: 59). The constructing of femininity as spectacle for male voyeuristic pleasure has been evident across the media: in adverts, TV shows, photography, Hollywood cinema, art, pornography, and music videos, all of which build on the representations of women's bodies as objects of sexual desire and fantasy, and at times even violence and misogyny.

The male gaze is a powerful tool for analyzing and critiquing traditional white supremacist patriarchy. Another important concept to feminist analyses of media is Patricia Hill Collins' notion of "controlling images" (2000), which analyzes the representation of black women and femininities in US pop culture. The images are stereotypes like the mammy, welfare queen, black lady, breeder, and hoochie that function to mediate the gaze directed at black women. The white patriarchal gaze sees black women only in these stereotyped terms, which, similarly to Mulvey's concept, are based on the binaries of black/white, women/men, using them to mark race/gender differences and assigning relative value to these differences. Objectification is central to the construction of otherness through racial/gendered difference. "Black woman" is thereby viewed as a passive object to be manipulated and controlled, and to assert one's authority over. The theory of "controlling images" and objectification has been applied to theorize political and economic exploitation of black women and femininities in US pop culture. Combined with Mulvey's theory surrounding fragmentation, these are techniques with which the male gaze and controlling images regulate and exclude femininity. Gazing and objectification thereby produce a particular kind of aesthetic pleasure around controlling images.

Since its inception in 1981, MTV has been predominantly used for the production and distribution of male-address video where the image of "the street" became a predominant symbol to represent male adventure and rebellion, relationships with women and sexual encounter, all of which emphasized a sense of male privilege. Most videos at the time positioned images of girls' and women's bodies as objects for male voyeurism, which included both images of female peer (the adolescent girl) and the more mythical image of the adult woman (for boys) (Lewis 1990). In turn, music videos not only reflected dominant societal values surrounding inequality and sexism, but they also became a source for the general reproduction of patriarchal relations (see, e.g., Fenton 2001) and the "symbolic annihilation" of women (Tuchman 1978: 172). Consequently, many female artists have had to adopt similar visual conventions used in music videos by male artists in order to gain success in the music industry. Many successful artists in the West and elsewhere seductively perform for the camera, touch and undress themselves, with the camera roaming their bodies and zooming in on disconnected body parts. Female artists, who have actively sought to convey a powerful, independent persona, have used their sexuality in order to express power in music video. Other artists' images like Gwen Stefani, Miley Cyrus, Janet Jackson, Jewel, Britney Spears, Mariah Carey, Jessica Simpson, and Christina Aguilera have all changed gradually from a more innocent adolescent feminine image to one defined by conventional sexualized and hyper-sexualized imagery. Indeed, "to be accepted in the mainstream of the culture, female artists find that they must embrace the vision of the pornographic imagination and enact the fantasies of male video producers and viewers" (Jhally *et al.* 2007).

Within the neoliberal capitalist music industry, the image of woman was simplified into little else than a sexual being. "MTV is orgasm", asserted John Fiske, "when signifiers explode in pleasure in the body in an excess of the physical" (Fiske 1986: 75). Women have been used to simulate sexual arousal, and their highly sexualized form in music videos legitimized this as their predominant use. Numerous studies surrounding the content of MTV have shown that

2 Neoliberalism and the Global Music Industry 111

"female roles were generally grounded in sexuality, as prostitutes, nightclub performers, goddesses and servants" (Aufderheide 1986: 69). In much popular music of the neoliberal era, the connections made between the music, visuals and imagery, lyrics and language clearly establish, construct, and emphasize a narrative of eroticism. Such encoded patriarchal ideologies reinforce ideas that women are easily influenced sexually without the need for affectionate intimacy. And female fans learn "that their bodies are what men desire, not their minds or ideas" (Andsager and Roe 2003: 94). Many female artists in the industry have thus used their sexuality as a marketing tool, while their music readily embodies the gendered stereotypes that are openly reinforced within popular music at the time. Music videos have therefore been readily criticized for the reinforcement of outdated, harmful sexual stereotypes.

In recent years, female musicians have spoken out about the persistent sexism in the pop music industry and the continued sexualization of women in media representations. Björk, for instance, has denounced the prescribed gender roles, with females being allowed to be singer-songwriters but only as long as they sing about their boyfriends. She critiqued that female artists are frequently critiqued if they sing about "anything other than love, relationship and motherhood" and that "sexism had also affected her career as a DJ" (BBC 2016; Guardian 2016). Along similar lines, Scottish singer Lulu states that sexism is now far worse than in the 1960s, with record label executives forcing young female singers like Disney's Hannah Montana star Miley Cyrus to "strip off" (Turner 2015). Indeed, Miley Cyrus' controversial performance alongside Robin Thicke at the MTV Video Music Awards 2013, and their respective videos for 'Wrecking Ball' and 'Blurred Lines', are recent examples of rampant sexism and implied misogyny in mainstream popular culture. Due to her hyper-sexualized displays, with her profanity-laden interviews, near-naked stage performances, photo shoots, and music videos, Miley Cyrus has become the object of public disdain and described as "the naked twerking whore", whom mothers would not want their daughters emulating (O'Donnell 2017: 112). Similarly, Nina Minaj's 'Anaconda' (2014) is explicitly about sexism, and particularly about black female sexuality in the context of the male-driven hip hop world. Even so, many critics have hailed 'Anaconda' as a feminist anthem pushing boundaries of black female sexual expression, arguing that Minaj subverts women's objectifying role for the male gaze of a patriarchal society. The lyrics of the main, rapped verses tell of relationships with two different men, while boasting about the phallic sexuality of her ex-boyfriends, as well as sex, money, and excitement (guns and drugs). In the coda, Minaj famously does a lap-dance on/for Drake, and when he lifts a hand as if to touch her body from behind, she slaps it and strides away off stage. The video deploys different color demarcations to highlight different sexual persona, and in terms of overall audience address, the video falls within the scope of the "female gaze" (Bradby 2016).

Meanwhile, Lily Allen's video for 'Hard Out There' has been heavily criticized as an example of anti-black feminism and racism, as she pathologizes and fetishizes women's bodies by positioning herself above the women of color, while reducing them to hyper-sexualized mute bodies—dehumanized proxies of patriarchy, assumed to have neither brains nor agency (Sidiqqi n.d.). Instead of using them as props, she blames them with contempt for women's self-inflicted struggles in the music industry. While naked bodies make money, they are continuously used to sell products. Moreover, women of color are continuously marginalized from both the music industry and mainstream cultural critique. Scottish singer Lulu also raised the critical issue of ageism in the entertainment industry, which is evident in widespread prejudice against older artists in television and the belief that "it's all about young people" (Turner 2015). Numerous inciting incidents that depict and construct women and men into roles similar to those once portrayed by MTV thirty-five years ago show the continuing cycle of sexism in the music industry:

> Anyone who aspires to be a "woman in rock" (or pop) is only able to inhabit that scene as an 'other'. They exist in a place where they're only seen as women, as being to be looked at first, and as such can be relegated to subordinate status as any moment … It also goes without saying that, for the most part, these ideals are being played out in a decidedly heteronormative and cis-centric sphere, and also largely among white principals; the othering that goes on with sexual orientation, race, and able-bodiedness also screws in societal perceptions of who the "default" might be (Johnston 2016).

Arabpop. The sexualization of the female body through mediated representations is also present in popular music from other parts of the world. In recent years, Arabpop, in particular, has become increasingly westernized (Usher 2007) and constitutes quite a different musical aesthetic than Arabic popular traditions:

> The Arab music world is sharply divided between music of the "golden age" (1930s–70s) and the Arabpop phenomenon that has emerged since the 1980s. Although originally incorporating influences from European music, the music recorded by the likes of Umm Kulthum, Mohammed Abd-Wahab … [etc.] came to signify high art and Arab uniqueness. When, in the 1990s, Arabpop singers started to record songs by these canonic artists in electronic, danceable arrangements, it evoked some enraged responses (Regev 2013: 53).

Two female artists, Haifa Wehbe and Ruby, and their pop music performances help to illustrate this. Both artists have on numerous occasions come under fire for exploiting their bodies in a sexualized manner. The sexualized nature of both artists is in some part likely to be influenced by western culture, as the birth of music telelvision and the more recent event of the internet have enabled youths around the world to experience western popular music. Perhaps, then, artists like Haifa Wehbe and Ruby represent "tamer" versions of what the West has made popular. Indeed, young musicians in the Arab world see the attraction of western popular music and therefore attempt to create their own music "by combining old and new, Arabic and Western" (Mahdi 2003: 141). Contemporary popular music proves all the more attractive "when it is offered along with seductive female dancing [which] angers the conservative Muslims and older parents" (ibid.). However, it is still questionable whether the sexualized nature of their music is wholly influenced by western pop music, or whether their play with an "exotic" sexuality resonates with "the insistent claim that the East was a place of lascivious sensuality" (Kabbini 1986: 6). Here, one must consider the European concept of exoticism or orientalism, which is in fact "a discourse framed by the responses, adaptations and contestations of those whom it constructed as objects" (Lewis 2004: 2). In other words, exoticicism was reinforced by the acceptance of European stereotyped views about Middle Eastern people by Arabs themselves, and in particular notions surrounding the sensual oriental woman for the pleasures of the male gaze. Edward Said similarly observes that "the Arabs have participated and continue to allow themselves to be represented as Orientals in this Orientalist way ... I think the Arabs keep themselves collectively in a way that is subordinate to and inferior to the West, and in fact fulfills the kinds of representations that most Westerners have in their minds about the Arabs" (Edward Said, in Jhally *et al.* 2005a: 10).

An examination of the comments left by the viewers of these videos on YouTube shows that many are actually not from the Middle East, and seem attracted by the aesthetic nature of the videos, and the image and look of the artists themselves. In the video for 'Ragab' (2005), Lebanese singer Haifa Wehbe plays on her own sensuality and mysteriousness. As she arrives during the song's opening, the view changes to that of two men who are so struck by her presence that their mouths open in amazement, as though they have never seen a woman like her before. The viewer's view of Wehbe is restricted up to this point, as the camera focuses either on one part of her body (and never the face), or the view comes from behind the reeds in the river on which she is travelling, which suggests a voyeuristic, secretive gazing at her body. Although at first it would appear that Wehbe has some sort of power due to her attractiveness, she is in fact ignored by the two men, whose attention she requires, which is suggestive of an ongoing gender divide. The video for Ruby's 'Enta Aref Leih' suggests less voyeurism, but is still highly sexually suggestive, as in some scenes the camera is positioned above her, depicting her as a submissive and subordinate female. The fact that Ruby is known only by her first name is further suggestion of the mysterious. Her namelessness reflects the earlier mentioned representations of the exotic, in which "the subjects are not named as individuals" (Sturken and Cartwright 2001: 103), and resonates with male Victorian travelers' views of oriental women as a "sub-group", "doubly demeaned (as woman, and as 'Orientals')" (Kabbini 1986: 7).

The location of both videos is interesting, but for different reasons. The setting in Haifa Wehbe's video is, from a stereotyped western viewpoint, a traditional Arabic village. Ruby, by contrast, is performing in what seems to be a European city, even though most of the time she is dancing in "exotic" clothing, thereby creating a deliberate sense of otherness. This is most obvious when she is seen walking down a crowded street amidst western passers-by both at the beginning and end of the video, with Ruby wearing clothing that resembles a belly-dancing costume, which she then proceeds to dance in. A few seconds into the video, a man is seen staring at Ruby as she walks down the street, either because of the revealing nature of her clothing, or the fact that she looks out of place, and signifies the exotic other. While the music and image of artists like Haifa Wehbe and Ruby would be regarded as increasingly westernized, it is clear that both artists play with stereotyped notions that place oriental women as mysterious, alluring, and sensual. There are, of course, plenty of artists adhering to more traditional modes of musical expression, yet this is increasingly seen as unattractive by youths in favor of artists like Haifa Wehbe and Ruby, whose work clearly resembles western practices surrounding the sexualization of the female body for the pleasures of the male gaze.

Racism(s) in Popular Music in Neoliberalism
In neoliberal culture, racialized narratives continue to be expressed through and experienced in popular music, and the remnants of racist identity constructions still reverberate today with persisting racism and economic disadvantage in the UK, US, and elsewhere. Much contemporary popular culture continues to be shaped by a pervasive race consciousness, hegemonic ideals of white supremacy, and racism. Race is still an important means for certain social groups to classify their own and other people's identity. Central here is the idea that whites and non-whites have fundamentally opposed

natures, which is captured in various ways: white versus black, white versus non-white, European descent versus non-European descent, West versus East, self versus other. These dichotomies characterize everything that is not western and thus "foreign", and are established, maintained, and negotiated exactly in order to evoke notions of inequality, of subordinate and dominant groups, of groups who are different and opposed to each other. They serve the politics of othering on the basis of race, which is highly political as it serves to define the deviant, unnatural, and strange based on it being deemed "outside" of the normal and part of the self. Binary oppositions help to construct and maintain the idea that westerners are superior to their others. Accepting western values, judgments, beliefs, and cultures as normal, natural, and ideal means to assume eurocentrism, rendering western values central, while relegating others to the periphery. It also means that non-whites adopt the values and beliefs of the dominant culture, perhaps even losing much of their own cultural identities. Racist and populist music reveals some of the most stereotyped conventions of racism. Critical conceptualizations of racialization thereby allow us to problematize the power produced by racialization.

Obvious racist stereotypes in mediated representations are rare today, but there still exists a kind of racism that is more subtle and hidden. Some contemporary representations of race continue to associate "black" people, specifically young men, with crime, violence, drugs, gangs, and teenage pregnancy, which is most evident in hip hop and rap. Hip hop, like other forms of African American culture, emerged in the "ghettos" of the USA, and is historically rooted in the enforced removal of native Africans from their homelands during European colonialism, which was a major period in recent history from which "black music" has assumed a sense of "blackness" as an important marker of shared racialized identity. It is the reason why bold generalizations about blacks pertain, and why black people are rendered as opposite to the white, Euro-American status quo, and defined by otherness and difference. Yet stereotypes in hip hop have served dominant groups in their maintenance of power over subordinate groups, while this power over mediated representations—the right, ability, and access to the media to make representations—has historically been upheld by white people (CEOs, executive directors of powerful media conglomerates). Mediated representations in much commercialized hip hop continues to epitomize a "white" view of the world (Jhally et al. 1999, 2007). While the western world has seemingly eradicated much of the obvious racial dubiety in policy and law,[5] race is still widely accepted and used within popular discourses and everyday imaginations of the world. As a source for human identification and division within the contemporary world, race in neoliberal culture still generates inequalities and reinforces hegemonic—albeit subtler—ideals of white supremacy.

Subtler forms of racism lingering in much contemporary popular culture became a focus of attention at the 2017 Grammy Awards in Los Angeles, which caused furore surrounding Adele's victory over Beyoncé for the album of the year award, the top prize at the Grammy Awards. Adele herself appeared unconvinced during her acceptance speech, saying "I can't possibly accept this award" and addressing Beyoncé directly: "You are our light. And the way that you make me and my friends feel, the way you make my black friends feel, is empowering!" She then snapped her Grammy in two to share it with Beyoncé. The issue is around the huge commercial success and creativity of R&B and hip hop, yet the album of the year prize at the Grammys has usually been awarded to white artists, with only a few exceptions. Black artists like Beyoncé, Kendrick Lamar, Frank Ocean, the Weeknd, Pharrell Williams, Kanye West, and Drake have been shortlisted in the past few years, but have lost out. Many of these artists are not marginal who have been overtaken by more mainstream artists, but are the main drivers of contemporary popular culture: "They are hit artists, the most-talked about artists of the moment" (Hann 2017: 2). Artists themselves have spoken out about the pervasive racism in the music industry. In 2015, Rihanna revealed that despite her huge success her "race" frequently plays a role in her business dealings, and she criticized the ongoing racial profiling and racist assumptions people make based on her skin colour (NME News Desk 2015). In the *NME* interview, she said:

> I have to bear in mind that people are judging you because you're packaged a certain way—they've been programmed to think a black man in a hoodie means grab your purse a little tighter. For me, it comes down to smaller issues, scenarios in which people can assume something of me without knowing me, just by my packaging.

Consequently, many contemporary (predominantly female) artists actively and purposefully engage in a body politics of skin bleaching/lightening/toning, which has become part of their "celebrity persona" construction and production of the self. Skin color is the most visible signifier of racial difference, and it continues to be a global issue as a marker of otherness/sameness in societies structured by racial dominance (Tate 2016: 2). The issue is colorism, prejudice based on actual skin tone, which continues to be a persistent, discriminatory problem for people of color (Hunter 2007: 237). The color complex that it produces has spread around the globe, in part through media images, and helps to sustain the multibillion-dollar skin bleaching and cosmetic surgery industries. The practice of skin transformation and shade shifting through bleaching/lightening/toning is widespread and well-established among women globally due to a global cultural preference for white/light skin and its link to white supremacy (Nakano Glenn 2008: 282), which is amplified, particularly for black women, through the prevalent discourse of a desire for whiteness/lightness because of the impact of global white supremacy. Skin bleaching/lightening/toning is thus a transracial global phenomenon, and is complexly interwoven within global capital and the profits of multinational corporations and small entrepreneurs. It is enabled by a multimillion-dollar global pharmaceutical and cosmetics industry, which is predominantly based in Europe and the US. Three of the largest corporations involved in developing the skin-lightening market are L'Oreal, Shiseido, and Unilever (Nakano Glenn 2008: 296). By 2018, sales of skin lighteners—pills, potions, creams, soaps, lotions, suppositories, laser treatments, intravenous drips, injections—are projected to reach US$19.8 billion, with Japan (especially older women) being the largest market, but they are also commonly used in some African and Asian nations (Li *et al.* 2008), and among dark-skinned people in Europe and North America, the Caribbean and Latin America (Nakano Glenn 2008). Mercury is a common ingredient in skin-lightening products, and is used for the face, body, vagina, and anus (Tate 2016: 9).

In popular music, Michael Jackson's alteration of his racially marked features has received by far the most attention in public and scholarly discourse as an artist who "has made ample use of skin bleaching agents and heavy white pancake make-up" (Davis 2003: 82). Media critics have increasingly turned a critical eye on celebrity appearances, stating about Beyoncé, "with her tumbling blonde hair, the world's highest-paid black music star of all time looked more Caucasian when she appeared this week" (Paris 2015: n.d.). A Google search on "celebrities skin bleaching" quickly brings up a string of websites claiming celebrities like Rihanna, Beyoncé, Janet Jackson, Nicki Minaj, Eva Longoria, Jennifer Lopez, Lil' Kim, and Sammy Sosa, while advertising the "best skin lightening products" to their readers.[6] Indeed, celebrity endorsement of skin-whitening products is a key marketing strategy for the global beauty and cosmetics industry:

> One of the most controversial celebrity endorsements came in 2007 when mega-successful Bollywood actor, Shah Rukh Khan endorsed the skin-lightening product, "Fair and Handsome". Created by the British company, Unilever, and marketed as the masculine companion product to best-selling Fair and Lovely, Fair and Handsome became the first major skin-lightening product mass-marketed exclusively to men. Khan's endorsement was read by the Indian public as an endorsement of skin-bleaching itself and as an

endorsement of a strongly colorbased system of privilege in India ... Similarly, U.S. baseball star Sammy Sosa, originally of the Dominican Republic, recently attracted international media attention when he appeared at the Latin Grammy Awards with notably lighter skin than he had during his career in Major League Baseball ... Sosa has suggested that he is negotiating an endorsement deal with the cosmetic company that manufactured his skinlightening cream (which he has refused to name in public) ... His de facto celebrity endorsement of skin-bleaching elicited significant feedback including a televised ridiculing from former NBA basketball star, Charles Barkley. Despite the media furore, Sosa's actions reinforce the idea that skinbleaching is a mainstream route to building racial capital (Hunter 2011: 147).

Cultural Appropriation in World Popular Music. Some contemporary artists like Gwen Stefani, Katy Perry, and Avril Lavigne have been heavily scorned for cultural appropriations in their music videos and appearances, with some critics going as far as saying that "Katy Perry is pop culture's most prominent purveyor of racist cultural appropriation ... Cultural appropriation is not flattery or appreciation. It's offensive and disrespectful to your fans, many of whom are having a hard time still liking you, since they're disappointed by a string of racist stereotypes" (Clifton 2014: 2). This criticism is a response to Perry's music videos and live appearances, such as 'This Is How We Do It', a 1995 R&B hit song, in which Perry appropriates African American and other racial stereotypes; or 'Dark Horse' where Perry plays around with stereotypes of Ancient Egypt, including the mysterious magic of the Arab world and racial divisions between white-skinned pharaoh and dark-skinned servants, and showing a man wearing a pendant with the Arabic word for "God" being burned down by a lightning strike (which caused a storm when 50,000 Muslims petitioned the video to be taken down for its blasphemous content); and 'Birthday' with Perry representing a "yarmulke-wearing, afro-sporting Jewish comic [Yosef Shulem] who 'for a price' will 'do a funeral'" (Elan 2014b). During the 2010 Coachella Music Festival, Perry wore her interpretation of Native American female attire, while in 2013 Perry opened the show at the American Music Awards with a performance of 'Unconditionally' in Japanese geisha dress style, while the spectacle included a cherry blossom rain shower, *taiko* drummers, and a shrine for the Japanese religion of Shinto. In the 2014 performance of 'I Kissed a Girl' during her Prismatic tour, Perry surrounded herself with "very curvy black women dressed as mummies ... These back-up dancers were all outfitted with exaggerated red lip paint, likely done for artistic purposes, but also bringing to mind perceptions of black people as having relatively bigger, fuller lips than Caucasians and other ethnic groups" (Clifton 2014: 9). Attracting similar accusations of cultural insensitivity and racism,

Avril Lavigne's 'Hello Kitty' video depicts the singer as a forty-something, "surrounded by four identikit, glassy-eyed Japanese dancers as she enjoys sushi, sake, and shouts random Japanese phrases ('KAWAII!', 'ARIGATO') in an exaggerated child's voice" (Elan 2014b: 2). Lavigne was criticized for using Japanese women as "props" and imitating the "cute" Kawaii subculture. While artists have defended their appreciation and celebration of the different cultures they imitate, they have been scorned by critics and the public alike for their distasteful and ignorant ethnic stereotyping.

The reductive treatment of non-western cultures by artists like Perry and Lavigne are subtle forms of racism, based on cultural stereotypes and ideas of the other. For instance, the appropriation of the *bindi*, an ancient religious adornment, as a quirky sign of otherness by famous celebrities like Björk, Siouxsie and the Banshees, Vanessa Hudgens, Sarah Hyland, Selena Gomez, Gwen Stefani, Iggy Azalea, Katy Perry, and Azealia Banks (Elan 2014a) has come under sharp attack by critics for being insidious forms of racist cultural theft. Critics of such cultural appropriations argue that "capitalism makes it easy to take something that is spiritually and culturally significant to a group of people and make it available for widespread production because 'it's pretty' and it will 'sell well' ... So many pop stars are accessorizing themselves with ... our own culture ... For them, it's cool" (Berumen n.d.). Meanwhile, music festivals have started to address the issue of cultural appropriation by banning headdresses simulating the sacred creations of Native American spiritual leaders and tribespeople. For instance, the 2014 Bass Coast electronic music festival in British Columbia (Canada) and the 2015 Montreal Osheaga Music and Arts Festival did not permit festival-goers to wear the Native American feathered headdresses in a public effort to respect the dignity of the aboriginal people (Lynskey 2014; Marsh 2015).

Cultural appropriations in contemporary popular music are not new at all, and much popular music has been similarly littered with exoticized symbolisms that evoke the "faraway" since the beginnings of the music industry. Many 1960s rock groups, including the Butterfield Blues Band and The Beatles, were inspired by Indian music and musicians like Ravi Shankar. In 1961, John Coltrane recorded a song called 'India', while on the Butterfield Blues Band's album *East/West* (1964), guitarists Mike Bloomfield and Elvin Bishop sought to recreate the atmosphere of Indian music. The Beatles' song 'Norwegian Wood' (1965) is the first popular song that features the actual *sitar*, which was, following the tritest orientalist principles, played in a western fashion, with a total absence of the drones that typically stem from *raga*, the modal system of Indian classical music. The song started a trend that has continued within pop and rock, thereby linking the sitar with the exotic. For instance, so-called raga rock (rock music based on a few raga ingredients, such as the lowered seventh degree of the major scale) became prominent among groups such as The Rolling Stones, The Yardbirds, The Kinks, and The Who, and many US psychedelic bands during the 1960s. They developed a strong infatuation with Indian meditation and yogis, delving deeply into the exotic East, often for drug-related reasons. Indian art music has played an interesting role in feeding exoticist imaginations in the West, further exemplified in the collaborations between sitar virtuoso Ravi Shankar and violin virtuoso Yehudi Menuhin, flute virtuoso Pierre Rampal, jazz musician Paul Horn, minimalist composer Philip Glass, and several others, including George Harrison. And women, too, have constructed orientalist ideologies in their music, whether musically or visually. The singer and composer Sheila Chandra has treated diverse musical influences from "East" and "West" with wit, intelligence, and sensitivity.

Orientalist Pop. Western musical appropriations of the "East" can be conceptualized through Edward Said's "Orientalism" (1978), which examines the ways in which Europe during the period of the late nineteenth/early twentieth century has understood cultures beyond the "oriental line". Orientalism is a European method for understanding unfamiliar "Eastern" cultures (Jhally *et al.* 2005a; Said 1978: 3). The character of Orientalism coincides with colonialist acquisition and conquest of the Middle East, both ideologically and militarily, by the British and French, which was marked by a "scientific movement" (MacKenzie 1995: 9; Jhally *et al.* 2005a) that led to a discourse central to establishing difference, superiority and inferiority, power and worth—othering. The politics of othering is reflected in orientalist artwork, literature, and music during the nineteenth and twentieth centuries. Music, photography, and other forms of representation were central to the production of Orientalism, through which western culture has attributed qualities of exoticism and barbarism to cultures in the Middle East, and thereby establishes those cultures as other. The concept of the Orient also defined Europe, and yet Orientalism served to set up binary oppositions between the Occident and Orient, through which negative qualities were attributed to the latter. European paintings often cherished a mysterious and exotic idea of the imagined Orient,[7] including artwork by Delacroix, Ang, and Gerome, while literary works, such as those by Disraeli and Flaubert, reflected odalisques, Arabic hostesses, exotic heroines (the Queen of Sheba, Cleopatra, Salome, Salammbô), and many other female characters. Photography similarly reflected this trend of the gaze at the other, specifically in colonialist visual anthropology, which extended also to poetry, notably the depictions by French poet Gerard de Nerval based on his "voyage to the Orient" (Jhally *et al.* 2005a).

The depiction of female sexuality is noteworthy in Orientalism, which reflects a certain tradition of white men travelling to "faraway" places for personal encounters with native women. Representations of women were created and perpetuated by men (Lewis 2004), and these operated within the binary imagination of civilization vs. nature, white vs. other, and male vs. female, while establishing the oriental (harem) woman as exotic, different, and other. Similarly, Hollywood films on the Arabian nights conveyed an "exotic, magical quality [and] the sheiks in the desert ... galloping around and the scimitars and the dancing girls" (Edward Said, in Jhally et al. 2005a). The 1934 film *Cleopatra* similarly constructs the ideology of oriental women as the "sexually manipulative" (Shohat 1997: 23) exotic other, and depicts "Babylon as sexual excess ... the orient as the scene of carnal delights" (ibid.). Extending this argument to women in East Asia, visual representations of the Orient show the "western construction of the 'orient' as a sexualised, and sexually compliant, space that is ripe for conquest and rule. The Asian woman's perpetual sexual availability for the Western male" (Heung 1997: 160). Consequently, the Orient becomes an imagined place of pleasure, travel, and escapism for European males, "a kind of mysterious place full of secrets and monsters ... 'the marvels of the East'" (Edward Said, in Jhally et al. 2005a). Yet, while oriental women were stereotyped in this way, European women too became subjected to a form of othering on the basis that if the male European traveler seeks pleasure and romance in the Orient, it must be assumed that he cannot be satisfied by European women, notably Anglo-European women, which rendered them reserved and dispassionate. Indeed, Anglo-European women were "placed as other and inferior in the gendered divides of European art and society" (Lewis 1996: 5), even though they were simultaneously placed as superior in the West/East divide of colonialism.

In opera, classical composers of the nineteenth century similarly tried to evoke, romanticize, exorcise, assimilate, and suggest the other and "faraway" by using unusual instruments and employing various musical styles and unusual sounds. Mahler, for example, "turned the supposedly eastern pentatonic scale into one of his own trademarks and underpinned it by an exotic-sounding orchestration" (MacKenzie 1995: 159). Meanwhile, Saint-Saen's opera *Samson et Delilah* (1877) signals otherness through musical materials that depart from western stylistic norms and evoke "underlying binary oppositions between a morally superior 'us' and a dangerous 'them' (collective 'other')" (Locke 2000: 104). The use of the *femme fatale* in the opera plot signifies women in the Orient as exotic and seductive, and it was not unusual at the time to represent the oriental woman as a seductress, who would lure away the European male. Europeans adopted eastern iconography into their art forms, thereby discursively constructing particular ideologies about the Orient that could later also be marketed for western consumption.

Popular music expressions during the twentieth century similarly absorbed exotic symbolisms and sought to evoke the faraway, while becoming thoroughly objectified and commodified for western consumption. For example, the album cover of Israeli pop icon Ofra Haza's *Shaday* (1988) evokes orientalist notions. It depicts the singer wearing jewellery and eye-shadow typically evoking the Middle East, seemingly reaffirming prejudiced views of gender roles: Haza's downward look with a certain expression of angst in her face evokes notions of sensitivity and vulnerability. Folding her hands as if symbolically to cover her face, similar to a veil's function, further supports the idea of the "oppressed woman" in the Middle East. At the same time, the image contains sexual promise and eroticism by depicting her as an "alluring woman", an exotic treasure made mysterious through her sparkling costume and the symbolism of the veil that hides her from the viewer and evokes connotations of the harem. The choice of representation suggests tradition and an idealized past, an escape from the modern world. It reflects the ways in which Orientalism is used to assign certain, highly sexualized, yet at the same time innocent attributes to women in the Middle East. East Asian popular musicians often similarly evoke stereotypical orientalist representations. For instance, Thai artist Tata Young and Japanese artist Utoda Hikara both sing in English, but "their music videos projected more sexually assertive identities than those found in their earlier Thai and Japanese work" (Benson 2013: 28), thereby utilizing orientalist ideologies of the sexualized sensual woman in order to market their music for western consumption.

Besides imagery, orientalist ideology is also evoked in popular music through moving images, combined with verbal and non-verbal clues and settings, a powerful example of which is presented in Sting's 'Desert Rose' (1999). The video to the song depicts Sting as a lone traveler in the desert, equipped with a handheld camcorder and chauffeured in a black luxurious Jaguar by a female driver. The song works at numerous levels of denotation and connotation, while combining visual, linguistic, and musical codes to construct an orientalist discourse (see also Bloechl 2005). Textually and visually, this song evokes a world of fairy tales, the world of 1001 nights, evoking fictional, historically past worlds. Sting sings of dreaming of an oasis and love. It contains sexual promise through the signifier of an imaginary, mysterious woman from the desert (desert rose). The landscape places the woman outside time in a natural environment (desert), and outside or beyond the modern, civilized world, stretching back timelessly. It offers escape from the modern world, while positioning the imaginary woman as an exotic treasure (as a desert flower, and sweet desert rose), an object that can be possessed by the white man (Sting). It also stereotypes Middle Eastern women as sexy and different. The quality of exoticism is attached to a place, connoting a nostalgic sense of an earlier era, conjuring the male traveler as a person who moves through distant, exotic terrains. For instance, a quick search for the song lyrics online quickly reveals two versions, one version referring to her veils, while another version instead referring to her shadows (in refrain 2, line 6). The song is selling difference by promising the (white, male) viewer a particular kind of authentic, exotic experience. By encoding the song with the aura of the exotic, the listener is promised a virtually authentic experience as musical tourist. Such visual images "invite the viewer/consumer to desire the role of the liberated traveler through an exotic locale. They do encode products and saleable experiences with the aura of the exotic. The consumer is promised a virtually exotic experience" (Sturken and Cartwright 2001: 105–106). Musically, the song is based on the usual pop aesthetic, which, upon Sting arriving in a modern, civilized part of the world depicted via a nightclub setting, concludes with a live duet performance with Algerian raï singer Cheb Mami and *darabukka* players, thereby constructing a distinct Arabic music feel that serves to re-emphasize the intended meaning of the song.

Another example of orientalist representation is Sarah Brightman's *Harem, A Desert Fantasy* (2003 [DVD]). The DVD is a mixture of performance footage and other recordings, notably pop-like songs with a strong underlying dance beat, and has been described as "a one-hour soundscape that brings to life all the magic and mystery of the East through hypnotic rhythms and gorgeous epic settings. Filmed at ancient sites in places such as Morocco and Egypt, this desert fantasy takes the viewer on a dazzling musical journey of cinematic proportions" (liner notes of the DVD). The DVD cover and text are selling to the audience a heightened sense of exoticism through stereotypical clichés that reconstruct the difference of the Middle East, using terms like magic and mystery, hypnotic rhythms, epic, ancient, desert, dazzling, and cinematic, which stand in stark contrast to western values and beliefs in rationalism and reason, rhythmic structure, objective and scientific, modern, and developed (emphasizing the western gaze at the other). The website similarly constructs orientalist representations of the Middle East:

> A musical fantasy becomes a visual feast—teeming with epic and timeless settings, shimmering colors, and sensuous images—in the new TV special inspired by Sarah Brightman's new worldwide hit recording Harem on Angel/EMI Records. Filmed on location throughout ancient Morocco, *HAREM: THE SARAH BRIGHTMAN SPE-*

> CIAL – A DESERT FANTASY lends a new dimension to the experience of the recording, on which Brightman's soaring soprano reaches into a new creative dimension, inspired by the sounds and images of the Middle East of legend (www.wliw.org/productions/harem. html, accessed 1 October 2010).

Sarah Brightman herself explained that "I wanted to record an album with a Middle Eastern feel ... Harem means 'forbidden place' in Arabic ... I have always loved that whole Arabian Nights feeling. Much of what we have created derives from my childhood reading. I was a C.S. Lewis fan. I like the idea of parallel worlds, faraway lands, mystery" (EMI Canada 2003), which is equally reflected in the music and video. Together with producer Peterson, Brightman sought to write a new repertoire of syncretic music that combines the "new and old" and bears an instrumental sound that is both western and eastern. The artifical, deliberate construction of otherness is immediately evident when considering the title track, which is actually an adaptation of 'Canção do Mar', a classic Portuguese *fado* song, and thus clearly far removed from Middle Eastern culture. Yet to Brightman, the melody of the song and ancient inspirations of fado apparently have a connection to Middle Eastern sounds, for which Brightman and producer Frank Peterson wrote new lyrics. Brightman said that, "I've loved this song for ages. In our version, I wanted it to have a contemporary, Arabian Nights feel – love, the desert, passion and fire but also with a dance feeling" (EMI Canada 2003). Other songs on the album feature guest appearances by orchestral musicians and virtuoso instrumentalists, notably classical violin superstar Nigel Kennedy and singer Kadim Al Sahir, as well as Natacha Atlas, Ofra Haza, and Shweta Shetty. While these collaborations may enhance the "Arabic" appeal of the album, visually the video is far from a realistic representation of men and women in the Middle East. The setting is often overdone, playing on stereotyped ideas about oriental women and men set in assumedly Arabic deserts and harems, amidst which Brightman is suggestively gyrating in glittery outfits over a heavily synthesized dance beat, rendering the entire setting utterly unrealistic. Throughout, the singer is depicted in an exaggerated orientalist fashion through her clothing and behavior, enhanced by the set, props, and actors used in the music video.

Orientalism continues to play a significant role in commercialized popular culture. Myths surrounding orientalist representations in popular culture that result from capitalist intentions in order to create a panoptic view of exoticness and otherness are easily spread in today's culture and accepted as "true" reality, in turn becoming constructed hyperreality in the form of distorted knowledge and its consumption. This process provides the conduit for the permeation of western knowledge and eurocentric perceptions of the norms, values, and beliefs of non-western, non-European cultures, which does not lead to a cosmopolitan utopia, but has, to many critics, achieved the antithesis of it.

Musical Transnationalism

Since the late 1980s/early 1990s, academic thinking has moved away from the theory of cultural imperialism and toward explanations of globalizing trends through the lenses of musical transnationalism and hybridization in order "to refer to the creative practices employed by pop-rock musicians in many countries when they merge and fuse elements of traditional music with pop-rock" (Regev 2013: 101). Musical transnationalism and hybridization are the result of the major changes brought on by global media and technologies, increasing (human) migration, modernization and Westernization, and musical commodification throughout the previous century (Titon *et al.* 2018: xvi). Rather than the result of imperial imposition, imported cultural goods have been a vehicle for the modernization of national culture. Cultures have always been in flux and hybridized, and globalization is in fact uneven in its impact across the world. New popular music is constantly produced by altering styles, maintaining old values or new ones, and adapting new music according to local circumstances. Cultural materials that originate in the West flow into non-western countries where people perceive them as models of modernity, and selectively adopt elements and components and merge them with indigenous or traditional materials. Western modes of being and behaving have been successful as many non-westerners were eager to learn the ways of the West in order to succeed. Indeed, people always tend to copy those people who have succeeded. Thus, if some musical traditions have been eroded, it is because of the rise of a mass public, empowered by US-invented mass capitalism, consumerism, and (apparent) democracy. The impact of the West, including pop-rock music, is now universal (Zakaria 2008: 78). Modernization or westernization is part of a historical development with a certain degree of inevitability.

Some of this "new" hybrid material flows back to metropolitan countries to be hailed as genuine, albeit exotic, expressions of contemporary culture, where it often exerts influence on western artists. Localized forms of culture continue to create hybridity and heterogeneity. Local discourses and practices help to resist and shape people's perceptions of dominant western culture, often indigenizing music to serve their own cultural interests. In this process, dominant western culture has been deconstructed, altered, and reassembled in such a way that the resulting new forms resonate with and respond to local everyday life. The newly emerging musical forms, both in western markets and elsewhere, are marked by hybridization and syncretism, in which the global and the local exist in a more complex interrelationship (Stokes 2007: 5–6). Cultural globalization has thereby led to a growing connectivity, proximity, and overlap between popular music cultures around the world.

The concept of a totalizing US-dominated cultural imperialism is thus a somewhat contentious issue. The working of the music recording industry itself promotes cultural hybridization. The major labels own growing portfolios of record labels, including well-known smaller labels, in different territories globally, specifically when the signed artists promise high degrees of corporate success. In doing so, the majors are able to monitor independent labels who engage in innovative practices, while avoiding the risks involved in signing artists before they have reached some popularity. Smaller companies are thereby in an interdependent relationship with the dominant corporations, a relation through which the major labels can also manipulate new market cycles and niche markets. With the imprints, the major labels can indulge in innovative practices while spreading the element of (financial) risk involved. Thus, the organization of the music business (involving niche markets alongside big hits and blockbusters) seeks to ensure that neoliberal capitalist strategies and economies of scale manifest themselves in the ongoing integration and concentration of the Big Three. The absorption of small labels by the major corporations means the distribution of increasingly wide-ranging repertoires in different geographical markets and musical genres, marked by increasing musical hybridization and diversification. At the same time, it is important to acknowledge that local alternatives in popular culture, both in the West and beyond, are constantly revived and revitalized. Theodor Adorno's critique of the complete commodification and standardization of culture in capitalist societies has thus proven to be outdated for contemporary theories of musical globalization in neoliberal capitalism (see also Manuel 1988: 7–15). While Adorno may have been right to argue that economic globalization is replacing Europe's "high" culture with a new aesthetic based on the image industry in fashion, lifestyle, and popular music, his critique is informed by earlier forms of capitalism, characterized by large-scale production of standardized goods for mass consumption. His thesis regarding the standardizing impact of the "culture industry" thus relates to the Zeitgeist of his contemporary age. Furthermore, Adorno's particular brand of aesthetic philosophy concerning popular culture, including music, was based on a schism between the classical arts (so-called high-brow) and popular culture. It is not unreasonable to argue in a more positive light that contemporary postmodern culture is, in fact, a liberating response to modernism and the valorization of the old elitism of "high" culture. This response is liberating as it is marked by democracy, freedom, eclecticism, irony, and innovation.

Aesthetic Cosmopolitanism
The resultant "singular world culture" (Regev 2013: 3) is characterized by an increased availability of types of music to many people and an emergent network of musical interrelationships transculturally. Andrew Killick (2014) proposed a tree metaphor in order to illustrate the global interrelatedness of world popular music today, while Motti Regev used the term "aesthetic cosmopolitanism" to describe the global cultural condition of neoliberalism, by which he means

> the ongoing formation ... of world culture as one complexly interconnected entity, in which social groupings of all types around the globe growingly share wide common grounds in their aesthetic perceptions, expressive forms, and cultural practices (Regev 2013: 3).

Accordingly, globalization is marked by transnational, multi-directional flows, including counter-hegemonic ones, and its impact has been such that emergent global communities and global cultural networks constantly continue to evolve. Key concepts in the approaches that stress these flows and networks are hybridity, creolization, complexity, mixture, fusion, and deterritorialization. This conception of globalization is based on the understanding that late modern culture is one cultural space—"a single world cultural web" (Regev 2013: 7).

With the arrival of modernity, global innovations such as travel, radio, and television have allowed music distribution to transcend national and international borders with the primary purpose of reaching global consumers. Resulting from these technological innovations, music could become a commodity for media and music TNCs to manipulate and sell back to consumers through standardized means. Intercultural global exchanges, combined with economic pressures, have promoted stylistic borrowings and cross-fertilizations between different cultures, leading to the existence of hybrid popular music, alongside a desire to celebrate, resist, and oppose negative aspects of globalization and convey a more democratic sense in and through popular music. Moreover, music production and consumption by the new "prosumers"—the digital music consumers in the new global age—is celebrated as a positive consequence of globalization, which has surpassed previous methods of music production and consumption. The new prosumers of music, the "digital natives", are much more effective at consuming and distributing music than their predecessors (Mundy 2001: 10). Due to the global popularity of digital communication and the advantages that this service has provided, major record labels and TNCs are no longer able to acquire full control of the production, consumption, and distribution of music. The technological consequences of globalization therefore propose that music production and consumption have reached a certain level of musical autonomy and democratization.

Popular music thereby has, through its seemingly endless re-contextualizations and meaning re-attributions, contributed to a world marked by increasingly global cultural diversity, hybridization, digitization, and musical participation, which have become considerable factors within the current global age—the new globality. Their existence means that contemporary culture has become increasingly cosmopolitan in nature, marked by "cosmopolitan borderlessless" (Urry 2003: 6). Cosmopolitanism is a particularly relevant and useful term, since it helps us move away from grasping globalization as a single system, and toward more "scalar" thinking about the multiplicity of global social and cultural processes as these are marked by cultural and institutional specificity (Delanty 2006: 27; Stokes 2007: 5–6). The academic literatures usefully differentiate between different types of cosmopolitanism to denote the various ways in which difference and otherness are regarded and understood. Sociologist Gerard Delanty, for instance, argues that "the very notion of cosmopolitanism compels the recognition of multiple kinds of cosmopolitanism, including earlier kinds of cosmopolitanism, and which cannot be explained in terms of a single, western notion of modernity or in terms of globalization" (2006: 27). An "early" type of cosmopolitanism involves the philosophical cosmopolitanism referred to by Immanuel Kant, who stressed the need for a world community and world governance based on the notion of human interdependency and shared morality, purporting a particular stance toward difference characterized by openness to and tolerance of diversity and otherness. More recently, relevant discourse on cosmopolitanism comes from sociology with a frequent differentiation made between "true/real" cosmopolitanism and "banal/trivial" cosmopolitanism, the latter to include consumption-based cosmopolitanism (Scheibel 2012: 5–8) which is marked by "acquisitive consumption, and the control of others" (Stokes 2007: 10).[8] These types of cosmopolitanism have little to do with Immanuel Kant's liberal-enlightenment discourse,[9] and yet they are particularly pertinent for the discussions on globalization, capitalism, and identity. So, while on the one hand, globalization has been scorned as nothing more than banal cosmopolitanism in the context of neoliberal and entrepreneurial urbanisms which territorializes difference and normalizes acceptable and unacceptable others, and thereby reinforces the binary opposition between self and other informed by the contested politics of race, gender, class, and so forth, it is also seen by many musicians, critics, and academics alike as a form of cosmopolitanism that resonates more closely with Enlightenment's philosophical cosmopolitanism, an ideal form of diasporic cosmopolitanism underpinned by neo-Kantian cosmopolitan values, in which "there is genuine acceptance of, connection with, and respect and space for the cultural other, and ... the possibility of a togetherness in difference" (Sandercock 2003: 2). The work of popular musicians around the world who have sought to relate their practice to the values of democracy, justifying innovative approaches to musical material and performance practice in terms of democracy, must clearly be placed in this context. Globalization, then, has also effected positive consequences for individuals, societies, and cultures across the globe.

An example of aesthetic cosmopolitanism is the internationally successful song 'Treaty' by the Australian Aboriginal band Yothu Yindi, fronted by singer Mandawuy Yunupingu. The song combines "traditional" Aboriginal (Yolŋu) with western musical features, and reflects the ways in which musicians take a part of their culture and repackage it for a western, mainstream audience. The song has reached the status of national anthem in Australia, and has gained recognition and acclaim well beyond national borders. It became a number-one hit, the first ever to be sung in a Yolŋu language:

> We were forming the Yothu Yindi band at that time, never coming up with a hit song. We were looking for that one song to break it for us. So we just combined *djatpangarri* with the modern beat, and that was the breakthrough ... We blend two cultural aspects, which is important to have because we live in [two cultures] ... in a contemporary modern Australian thinking and life, but we also want to sustain and maintain our own traditional ... knowledge production ... It's just our way of making sure that we don't lose aspects of one [culture] because you need one to inform the other (Mandawuy Yonupingu (1956–2013), former front singer of Australian Aboriginal band Yothu Yindi, interview footage, previously available at http://thepuredrop.com.au/ep_mainstream/ accessed 1 November 2010).

Yet, even though the song is based on an international pop style format, it was not written entirely with western concepts and ideas in mind. Yunupingu instead sought to address the absence of a Treaty or reconciliation for the Aboriginal people. The song's verses are interspersed with passages in the Yolŋu language, accompanied by the sounds of traditional Yolŋu instruments such as the *yidaki* (didgeridoo) and clapsticks, which act as pivotal markers of local identity. The verses and rhymes, which are all sung in English, speak up about pivotal issues concerning Aboriginal rights and agendas in Australian society today. This blending of traditional with western pop-rock aesthetic is not seen as a threat to the integrity of the music, but instead creates the advantage of reaching younger people as long as the important elements of tradition are maintained:

> There are layers of knowledge [in the song] that is still in its original form ... If you draw that conclusion in mind, and if you are ... a good artist, then you would avoid the destruction [of music] by making sure that the elements that you've been trying to bring about and keep the other intact, can be arranged, then you are a great artist for keeping that for the next generation (ibid.).

The hybridization of some aspects of culture is a powerful method in engaging different cultures globally. Hybridity is indeed "a strategy of the dispossessed as they struggle to resist or reshape the flow of Western media into their culture" (Suárez-Orozco and Qin-Hilliard 2004: 130). 'Treaty' is an example of reshaping Aboriginal music and blending it with western pop-rock musical aesthetics as a means of raising political awareness and preserving Aboriginal culture (Corn 2009: 30).

Expressive Isomorphism

To talk about aesthetic cosmopolitanism in world popular music is not to reject the general idea of the global dominance of western musical styles and aesthetics. On the contrary, Regev acknowledges "the pervasiveness of pop-rock styles and genres ... across the world" (2013: 32), which has resulted from the fact that "local popular music has been gradually taken over by the [mainstream] pop-rock aesthetic" (ibid.: 54) and "national fields of pop-rock became isomorphically similar" (ibid.: 90). This in turn led to the ubiquity and omnipresence of pop-rock styles and genres in late/neoliberal modernity, "especially in urban settings, all over the world. They are crucial elements in the cultural design of urban environments and audio-visual products like film, television series, and advertisements" (ibid.: 157). The global popular music field is thereby dominated by western pop-rock mainstream and supplementary sub-fields of local, ethnically-flavoured indigenous genres. Regev adopts the term "expressive isomorphism" to describe "the process through which national uniqueness is standardized", thus world popular music is being dominated by the pop-rock aesthetic, both quantitatively and qualitatively.

The worldwide influence of western musical ideas and aesthetics is evident, particularly, in the omnipresence of musical styles like progressive rock, punk, metal, electronic dance, hip hop, and ethnic rock, as well as the phenomena of the female superstar or diva (e.g. Madonna, Umm Kultum) and the rock auteur (e.g. Bob Dylan, Thomas Mapfumo), as well as the typical electric, electronic, and amplified sonorities, including the electric guitar and sounds generated by synthesizers, samplers, and other electronic sound generators that characterize the pop-rock mainstream. These musical styles, ideas, and aesthetics have expanded globally to create similar soundscapes and aesthetic environments around the world, particularly in urban environments. Motti Regev adopts the term "expressive isomorphism" to describe the process of musical interaction and absorption "through which national uniqueness is standardized so that expressive culture of various different nations, or of prominent social sectors within them, comes to consist of similar—although not identical—expressive forms, stylistic elements, and aesthetic idioms" (2013: 11). This standardization occurs "in modes ranging from sheer duplication to local adjustment and modification ... of the pop-rock mainstream" (ibid.: 32). The global field of world popular music—or "pop-rock music"—is dominated by Anglo-American music production, meaning mechanisms, and evaluative criteria, and this dominance is indeed substantiated through charts of best-selling and most-played music.

The key to understanding the global omnipresence of the western pop-rock mainstream, then, is *not to regard it as imperial imposition*, but as the result of cosmopolitan omnivorousness—that is, "enlightened eclecticism" or "humanist openness" to cultural diversity (Regev 2013: 15)—and as a symbol of status and distinction among the new upper-middle classes. Since the 1980s, "the cultural tastes of elite groups have become less connected to the fine arts and increasingly eclectic ... posit[ing] a change from 'univore' tastes for high culture to more 'omnivore' tastes in the last few decades" (Taylor 2016: 39). There are several assumptions that account for the emergence of omnivorousness, which include the growing sophistication of the mass media, the rise in education levels and white-collar occupations, the baby boomer generation's continued interest in their own youth culture, and the emergence of "cool capitalism" (McGuigan 2009). Omnivorous, undiscriminating consumption and taste cultures including popular culture have in turn shaped the emergence of new musical practices by artists and producers, which merge and blend exogenous and indigenous cultural elements so as to modernize local and national cultures. Accordingly, "cultural imperialism" no longer sufficiently explains both the imposition and subsequent acceptance of pop-rock music due to people's genuine belief in its cultural significance and artistic value. Musicians have been self-mobilized into adopting pop-rock music, which was not a move forced upon them by the industry, but rather a move of "willful embracement" (Regev 2013: 97). In doing so, fans, musicians, critics and media professionals, and music industry personnel have all played a role in the absorption and valorization of the pop-rock mainstream in local or national contexts. Music cultures around the world today consist of Anglo-American mainstream pop-rock music and local-language, indigenous popular music (e.g. "popular traditions"), composed primarily of electric and electronic sonorities.

The emergent musical practices are marked by hybridity and self-selected musical adaptations. Regev describes these "new" global electro soundscapes as "aesthetic cosmopolitan landscapes", "places where one feels local and global at the same time" (2013: 171). Regev's "aesthetic cosmopolitanism" marks the global cultural condition in neoliberalism, which has at its core "the shriveling and withering of cultural otherness" (ibid.: 179).[10] National uniqueness becomes transformed in this process to emphasize pluralism, fluidity, relativity, and openness to otherness. Since the 1990s, and with the emergence of digital technologies and the internet, world popular music is marked by increased stylistic diversification in accordance with trends globally and locally. Along global trends, for instance, diversification is manifested by global electronic music, global hip hop, and global Bollywood. Local stylistic trends, meanwhile, rendered the Anglo-American mainstream less relevant to "world popular music" cultures. In some instances, artists have occasionally produced their own variants of global stylistic patterns and successfully forayed into the global field, such as the teen pop idols of K-Pop and J-Pop in the 1990s and 2000s. International world pop stars, who also became part of the World Music craze in the West, are further examples of local musicians who have entered the international field of popular music with occasional success.

Global Hip Hop. Along global trends, diversification in neoliberalism is most clearly manifested by global hip hop, which has seen a rise in popularity from the late 1980s onwards and gradually established itself as a global music genre. Initially seen as "black" music, rap music emerged in the late 1970s as part of a wider hip hop culture in the South Bronx in New York—primarily among migrant African Americans and Puerto Ricans—that included musical and extra-musical signifiers, such as modes of dress, language, and so on. It was quickly taken up by residents in other American urban neighborhoods, notably in south-central LA, Houston's fifth ward, Miami's Overtown, and Boston's Roxbury. Hip hop has increasingly been adopted by a much wider ethnic audience inside and outside of the US, and was diffused across the world and appropriated by artists in all sorts of countries, especially those associated with more recent international migration, such as Sweden, France, and Germany. It is largely a product in cities of the diaspora, particularly among the more depressed urban groups with imagined links to distant "sources" and roots in Africa. Thus, rather than being the exclusive domain of black Americans used for promoting a kind of black separatism, rap has been appropriated by Europeans, Americans, Latinos, Turks, Africans, French Arabs, Iraqis, Aborigines, and others, giving it new languages and supporting the fact that "music cannot be seen as racially 'owned'" (Longhurst 2007: 146). For instance:

> In France, hip hop developed in the outer suburbs of Paris and ... Marseilles ... of West Indian, African or Maghrebi descent; the leading performer, MC Solaar, was born in Senegal ... Marseilles group IAM [has] members from Senegal, Madagascar, Algeria, Spain and Italy ... Similarly in Germany, rappers were often young people in migrant guestworker [*Gastarbeiter*] families from Turkey and Morocco (Connell and Gibson 2003: 184).

Hip hop was also appropriated in places without a history of international migration, but where there were significant ethnic minorities, for example among young Maoris in Auckland or young Aboriginal Australians, and predominantly in urban settings. Aboriginal hip hop groups emerged during the 1990s, linking rapping with black nationalist politics, which resonated with New Zealand's hip hop scene that

> commonly mobilized the rhetoric of black pride and unity apparent in Afro-American rap, translating earlier Aboriginal political movements centred on land rights and cultural survial for younger generations [and] transformed [black politics] into indigenous Australian circumstances—particularly their political focus and use of visual symbols to affirm local cultures and attachment to land (Connell and Gibson 2003: 189).

Meanwhile, in Brazil the meanings, stylistic features, and essence of hip hop are expressed differently in São Paulo, Rio de Janeiro, and in commercialized samba-hip hop fusion, reflecting the music's "political importance in highlighting the gulf between rich and poor, black and white" (Denselow 2007b). In São Paulo, for instance, Brazil's most militant hip hop band Racionais MCs, known since the early 1990s as "the boys of the poor São Paolo suburbs", delivers a politically charged rap in Portuguese to the youths of the predominantly black shanty towns to the south of the city that reflects the split in Brazil surrounding issues of wealth and race (Denselow 2007b). Meanwhile, in Rio de Janeiro hip hop has become the second most popular style after funk in the favelas, with artists like MV Bill known for his controversial songs that depict gang culture, police violence, and gangster lifestyle, which to him reflect the "hidden reality in our daily life". Despite the controversial nature of his songs, MV Bill, who still lives in the notorious favela of Rio, "City of God", has won awards from the United Nations for giving hope to disenfranchised youths in a place of sadness, violence, prejudice, and lack of opportunities

(Denselow 2007b). In contrast, Marcello D2 is a Brazilian hip hop artist who started writing songs about police violence, then changed direction in 2003 with a syncretic musical style that merged rap and samba in order to reach a more mainstream audience. His songs and videos make use of "classic" samba artists, and reflect the way in which samba became fashionable with a new generation of predominantly white youths as it is performed in Rio's more affluent, bohemian quarter (Denselow 2007b). Generally, Brazilian hip hop in its evolved forms continued to serve a social function, rather than being hijacked by commercial interests, tackling issues that are rarely addressed in other Brazilian music, while criticizing the massive gap between rich and poor, and giving a voice to youths who have no voice and opportunities.

Existing in various locations around the world today, hip hop is a transnational musical form that uses black music and liberation theory as a base, and through which artists can resist the trappings of their respective cultures. It reflects that music in both the homeland and diaspora is never static, but a living product of synthesis and hybridity. In the US alone, examples of hip hop artists include white rappers like Third Base, Tony D, Vanilla Ice, and Eminem; ethnically-mixed rappers like Rebel MC and Neneh Cherry; Latino rappers like Kid Frost; and black rappers like KRS-One. Lines of division between ethnicities and music are thus blurred, which renders language at the core of transnational hip hop expression, as "music and language remain potent and ubiquitous markers of ethnic identity" (Connell and Gibson 2003: 134). Language is an important cultural and political signifier of national difference, especially since English dominates world popular music. To this end, language can be an important means and tool for artists and audiences to engage in nationalism in various ways:

> For some years, Aboriginal rap music in Alice Springs, central Australia, simply copied African American music; efforts to encourage the use of local referents (let alone language) initially foundered on the delight that dispossessed Aboriginal youth had in using such words as "motherfuckers". Similarly, in Tanzania, rap groups initially took wholly derivative American names, such as Niggers with Power and Rough Niggaz, and wholly American dress, hairstyles and language use, before subsequently rapping in Swahili, and covering local themes, such as the rise of AIDS and promiscuity (Connell and Gibson 2003: 131).

> In Auckland, young Maoris valued American rap music above all ... Maori rap groups performed lyrics in opposition to racism and police harassment ... and in post-apartheid South Africa hip hoppers used ethnicity as a symbol of strength and resistance. Hip hop

> emerged in southern Italy, in Ireland, where lyrics focused on issues of high unemployment and the cost of living, and in Japan, where rap performers used their musical style to differentiate themselves from the "mainstream" youth of Japan ... In Micronesia there was even Yap rap ... In Mexico, the group Control Manchete ... were using local words ... In southern France, the Fabulous Trobadors rapped their nostalgia for a medieval, less centralised world ... but in support of the anti-racism and Afrocentrism of hip hop ... In many of these places rap existed where there was virtually no established black population; in Newcastle, England, a hardcore of hip hop enthusiasts believed [in hip hop's] relevance for their own marginalised, white working-class experience ... In the Netherlands, white Dutch preferred "Nederhop"—the rap produced by white performers... (Connell and Gibson 2003: 186).

The reasons for using local language are varied: they may be cultural, economic, and/or political. In using their own language, including local forms of slang, rap artists emphasize local experience and localized sub-cultures, stressing difference and often marginality. Thus, over time, lyrics, styles, and delivery become adapted to particular migrant circumstances, a process also often termed glocalization. At the same time, hip hop connected people across most of the African diaspora through a pan-African consciousness. Here, blackness is theorized through notions of contemporary migration and diaspora and the complex, multi-sited, fluid identities that these produce. In hip hop culture, diasporic, transnational peoples are engaged in a dialectic of opposition and resistance to the hegemonic logic of multinational capital (Bhabha 1990), reflexive of a certain liberatory character of global, diasporic practices. An example of this use of transnationalism as a counter-hegemonic political space is found in the musical practices of non-white and white hip hop artists across the globe. Transnational practices surrounding hip hop culture are potentially counter-hegemonic, but they are by no means always resistant. The examples here illustrate this by showing the way that the black diaspora has been imagined, represented, and challenged. In doing so, blackness is regarded as a political signifier; it is, like race and racism, a social construct that is discursively created.

Hip Hop in Germany. Hip hop culture has also become popular in Germany, which has become an ethnic melting pot, in which Turkish, Tunisian, Ghanaian, Kurdish, white German, and other youths have found their own, personal connection to the genre. Here rap is not limited to migrants from Africa alone, but is adapted by people from different ethnicities and classes. Thus while youths of different ethnicity are involved in rap, how do white Germans or rappers of Turkish or Arab descent relate to the notion of blackness? If blackness is so important in African American rap (Baker 1993; Cross 1993; Rose 1994), how do youths of other ethnicities relate to the music? Hip hop culture became a part of German youth culture during the 1980s when youth from migration backgrounds came into contact with American youth culture that existed on American army bases in Cold War Germany (Verlan and Loh 2006), specifically in Berlin, which served as an "ideal" breeding ground for German hip hop. Isolated from the rest of the country at the time, young Turks and Arabs living at the border to the east of Berlin drew upon similarities to the living conditions of black youth in the US. Being of different ethnicity meant being different to the rest of the German youth, and hip hop reflected this sentiment. Coincidentally, Berlin had always been an important site in rock mythology (Connell and Gibson 2003: 104–105), and music infrastructure was already in place before rap swamped the city; this preexisting music scene helped to fuel the imagination and determination of young kids to "make it" through music.

Resonating with the development of rap elsewhere, early German rap was performed almost entirely in English to express feelings of isolation and draw attention to the living circumstances of youths. Yet the use of their local language, combined with a growing confidence, maturity, and innovation, became gradually more prominent, well after gang culture, a certain style of clothing, break-dancing, and graffiti were adopted in German hip hop culture. Indeed, "language is of obvious cultural significance, especially as English dominates popular culture and popular music" (Connell and Gibson 2003: 131). The deliberate change toward rapping in German can be seen as an act of rebellion against Anglo-American corporate hegemony, the driving force behind the global music industry. In turn, it broadened the local, German-speaking audience as it allowed youths who do not speak English to comprehend the lyrics, which is vital to the very essence of rapping. Yet, while on the one hand, the use of local, comprehensible vernacular broadens the German audience, on a more global level it also limits the economic possibilities for the artists. As German is a minor language in the context of the global music market, which is characterized by its widespread aversion to foreign-language music, thus making it very difficult for non-English singing artists to break into, rapping in German obviously means to limit the potential audience. These struggles are not unique to German rappers, but are similarly faced in rap scenes around the world.

Besides language, and somewhat reflexive of the feuds in American rap between West-coast and East-coast rappers, some German rap also places a strong emphasis on locality, which reflects the concerns in more recent academic discourse that focuses on notions surrounding identity, place, and space (Stokes 1994, 2004; Forman 2002; Krims 2003; George 2007). Thus place is an important factor for the lyrical content of much German rap, and songs reflect the context and proximity of specific places and localities, which shall be explored here by looking at four different rappers from different German cities, while illustrating their differences in lyrics and style. German rap, then, reflects an identity that is both global and local, on the one hand belonging to the subculture of hip hop, a global culture with a collective frame of mind, and on the other hand belonging to a specific local scene, which can differ significantly from one another. Local surroundings and social backgrounds thereby heavily shape the parameters in which hip hop is constructed. Thus, despite being a worldwide subculture, "the glocalization of rap [is] still very much concerned with roots, family, locality and neighborhood" (Mitchell 2005: 111). In German rap, in particular, local references can be found in the majority of the lyrics, further distinguished by the different accents of rappers. It would indeed make little sense for a German rapper to rap about life in Compton or New York.

"Black rap", place, and ethnicity. AZAD (from Frankfurt) and Sido (from West Berlin) both hail from cities with a high percentage of immigation, which has shaped their style of rap as being heavily linked to gang culture and gangster lifestyle, similar to American "gangsta rap" that emerged in the early 1990s. Born in Iran, AZAD is of Kurdish origin and grew up as an immigrant in the German financial capital of Frankfurt where rap groups first formed in the 1980s, and which were initially influenced by their American counterparts that featured on local and national radio and MTV Europe. The first prominent Frankfurt-based rap group was White Nigger Posse, but groups quickly moved away from their American heritage and sought to inflict their own particular form of "lived" ethnicity, which required its own local and particular way of expression (Connell and Gibson 2003: 185). Initially, rap groups used German lyrics, but this shifted later toward more particular forms of lived ethnicities of second- and third-generation migrants, notably Turkish rap. In Germany, "the process of localisation of hip hop thus went from slavish imitation of an overseas genre, to the development of a national form and finally its localisation in terms of the concerns and aspirations of particular ethnic groups" (Connell and Gibson 2003: 185). In AZAD's rap, certain similarities to Afro-Amercian rappers can be drawn on the basis of his relatively poor upbringing and migrant background, and yet his lyrics are not directly concerned with blackness. Nonetheless, AZAD adopts certain canonic topics like isolation, otherness, and difference. Frankfurt is the financial capital of Germany, with a high percentage of millionaires living close to the city, yet

it is also known as the city of differences due to its large population of immigrants and low earners. This shared feeling of otherness is shaped by ethnicity, gender, and class, and serves as the impetus for AZAD to separate himself from the cultural norm and construct his own "authentic" identity among his peers that he expresses through music.

The authenticity debate is poignant in this context, with hip hop fans often expressing a strong desire for "their" rap stars to be "real" in terms of living the life they rap about. These demands for authenticity come primarily from white listeners, whose knowledge of "authentic" black life usually comes from an essentialized notion of race and blackness (Werner 1999: 317). The image of the "authentic" rapper is thereby a stereotype, one that white rappers like AZAD readily tap into. AZAD's lyrics are sprinkled with his own Kurdish language and local Frankfurt dialect, and marked by his frequent use of swear words. His rap also reflects the circumstances of the community of poor, different, and marginalized immigrants in Frankfurt, which is not bemoaned, but celebrated as "real" and as a better alternative to the social norm he does not feel he belongs to. The lyrics to his song 'Napalm' (2005) show just this by targeting "fakes": "inauthentic" rappers that are not "real", who are imitating gangster lifestyle in order to sell records, similar to the dominant gangsta rappers in the US. Frankfurt serves as the blueprint for his local identity, and he aspires to be part of the rich and wealthy world he is surrounded by, yet his social upbringing, class, and ethnicity pose obstacles to him. While AZAD seeks to liberate himself through the avenue of ethnicity, he can only achieve this within the boundaries of local acceptance so not to lose his authenticity in the eyes of his peers.

Another rapper from the gangsta rap genre is Sido from Berlin, who, far more than AZAD, adopts the conventions of US gangsta rap surrounding gang culture and the criminal underworld. His posse is from the Märkische Viertel in Berlin, a so-called Großwohnsiedlung (large living estate) with a dense, relatively homogenous architecture marked by high-rise blocks of flats, and a social hotspot in the German capital. In his song 'Mein Block' (2004), Sido raps about his world being just this one tower block where he has everything he needs, namely "drugs, friends, and sex". Similar to AZAD, his use of language is littered with "lower" class expressions, including extensive use of swear words. By making direct reference to his local posse in his music, Sido constructs a strong connection to a shared sense of locality and localized identity that is not marked by ethnicity, even though some members of his posse have migrant backgrounds. Indeed, "the posse [is] the fundamental social unit binding a rap act and its production crew together. It creates a relatively coherent or unified group identity that is rooted in place and within which the creative process is supported" (Forman 2002: 176). In hip hop, the posse is based on solidarity between the group members and plays an important part in supporting a fellow artist's career, which is evident in the creation of the label Aggro Berlin that has enabled other members of Sido's posse, such as Fler and B-Tight, to gain popularity and credibility following Sido's commercial success. The posse has thereby helped in the "rise of artist-owned labels [which] brought an increased emphasis on regional and local affiliations and an articulation of pride and loyalty in each label, artist roster, and the central locale of its operation" (ibid.: 174). Sido and the Aggro Berlin label are prime examples of this in the German context, as the artists represent the label on a nationwide scale and promote each other, while continuing to emphasize their local identity and locality in their music. The posse and an artist's connection to "place" are thereby incredibly important to remain an aura of authenticity and "keeping it real" in the eyes of their local fans by "authentically rapping about situations, scenes, and sites that comprise the lived experience of the 'hood'" (ibid.: 180). Interesting here to note is Sido's exaggerated gangsta image, which may be understood as an attempt to stress his street credibility and seek heightened acceptance from peers within the context of his white ethnicity.

Both AZAD and Sido are rooted in their local posses and thereby reinforce notions of place and locality in their music, which they maintain through their lyrics and support network of local friends. Both artists rap about place and trying to "big it up". Their style of gangsta rap with its strong affiliation to place and the criminal underworld is in part shaped by their social upbringing. While AZAD comes from a migrant background, Sido grew up in a lower-class area of Berlin, and both have arguably not received the best of education, all of which is mirrored in their language use, which is marked by rude, colloquial, even simplistic forms of speech. Both artists create a parallel utopian world for themselves within the hard reality of violence, drugs, and sex, coupled with aspirations for financial success, flash cars, jewellery, and sexualized women, in which the posse serves as a substitution for the real family. While hip hop has grown out of the experiences of black youths, both AZAD and Sido do not share the same ethnicity, and yet absorb the culture and lifestyle of black rap artists in their music; this may be due to the fact that their working-class and, as in AZAD's case, migrant backgrounds resonate to a certain extent with the experiences of black artists, to whom music has played an important role in "the project of emancipation" (Gilroy 1993: 74). Their ethnic, socioeconomic, and gendered roots thus play a significant role in efforts of self-identification within the context of a white, Christian, middle-class dominated society. While the black community in the US has sought to compensate, oppose, and fight the feeling of being peripheral to the white racist, imperialist mainstream culture, so too do both German rappers highlight their feelings of marginalization and helplessness within their own social circumstances marked by drugs, gang culture, violence, and poverty within a white, Christian, affluent society.

"White" message rap. While gangsta rap as a subgenre of hip hop is generally seen at the opposite spectrum of "message rap" (Forman 2002), the latter has also been adopted in the German rap scene. Message rap in the US was used to establish connections between the black communities and raise awareness about their struggles within a white-dominated, racist culture: "Message rap, especially from 1987 to 1994, arose as part of a deliberate effort to forge links across the diverse social settings and urban landscapes that divide and separate black youth throughout the country" (Forman 2002: 185). In German message rap, by contrast, local identities were formed differently due to class differences, whereby rappers from middle-class backgrounds have adapted notions surrounding black nationalism and identity in their own, very unique ways. German message rap similarly seeks to establish connections between certain communities and raise awareness of their struggles, yet the focus is not on black youth but more generally on the socially underprivileged. This broadens the appeal of the music on the one hand, and at the same time emphasizes the makeup of German society as a multiethnic/multicultural melting pot in the heart of Europe.

An example of message rap is presented by the rap group K.I.Z. (pronounced "kids" in German) from Berlin, which consists of three rappers and a DJ, who come from various parts of Europe (Tarek was born in Freiburg, Bavaria and lived in Spain for most of his youth; Maxim is of French origin; Nico is a Berlin-native; DJ Sil Yan Bori is of a migrant background). This patchwork of nationalities and different cultural backgrounds is reflexive of Berlin's melting-pot identity, and is significant to the ideology and cultural identity of the group. All members of K.I.Z. enjoyed higher education, which is evident in the music and lyrics.[11] In their song 'Selbstjustiz' (2009) (Vigilante Justice) from their album *Sexismus gegen Rassismus* (Sexism against Racism), the group raps about social problems in Berlin and in Germany more generally. Domestic violence, corruption, xenophobia, criticism of capitalism, avarice, and anti-Muslim politics are all topics covered in the song. The song is sung collectively by all three rappers, who take one verse respectively, each taking different perspectives to social problems. The song reflects the group's adoption of message rap within the context of German society, and therefore constructs, resonates with, and reflects the lived experience of particular local identities. With references to places like "Cotti" (Cottbusser Tor, a square in Kreuzberg, an area dominated by Turkish immigrants and renowned for drug dealing) and the "Kiez" (a city district where illegal activities are common, including drug use and distribution, prostitution, and black market dealings), and public figures like "Kaiser Wilhelm" (German Emperor during the early twentieth century, founder of German imperialism, and Prussian ruler until the end of WWI) and "Ackermann" (Josef Ackermann, chairman who turned the Deutsche Bank into a global operating institution, while releasing 18 percent of the workforce to cut costs), the song is highly critical of German society. Rapping about these historically, economically, and culturally grounded topics is unusual, and may thus be of specific concern to more educated people who are able to relate to the issues at stake. K.I.Z.'s message rap is thereby heavily influenced by their middle-class upbringing, education, and collective identity as "mainstream" German citizens. Another contributing factor is the group's connection to the local Berlin punk rock and left-wing scene. For example, the group is managed by Berlin-local "Archie Motherfucker", former lead singer of Berlin punk band Terrorgruppe. In an online interview that focused on education, Maxim talks about the importance of reading and acquiring knowledge, and specifically mentions Marxism as an important source of reading (iChance 2009). The group's cultural identity is thereby shaped by a somewhat philosophical stance, even though they work within the boundaries of rap, while producing a musical alternative that moves away from the gang ethos and highlights the centrality of the message. In this context, it is therefore more meaningful to talk of a collective, rather than a posse, in which K.I.Z. share a common identity through their musical involvement, while at the same time also expressing their own personal identity.

An example of white, middle-class message rap is presented by Curse, who does not come from a large city community, but from the small town of Minden. To Curse, it would make little sense to rap about inner-city life, gang culture and its troubles, or about blackness and black identity, as he has a different set of experiences that have been adapted in his rap music. His song 'Freiheit' (2009) from the album *Freiheit* provides an interesting, if contrasting, example of German message rap. The main hook is a sample of German singer Marius Müller-Westernhagen's song 'Freiheit' from the late 1980s, which reflects the common practice of sampling in rap, and yet the choice on which the sample is based emphasizes a particular period in German cultural history, namely the reunification of Germany in November 1989. The first verse of the song talks about what freedom means to Curse himself before discussing the importance of freedom for underprivileged people. Curse's song is not about actual places, events, or people, but is more concerned with his personal interpretation of an abstract idea. Curse adopts a far more philosophical approach to rap than the previously discussed rap artists, and takes a more culturally sophisticated approach to rap more generally. Reflecting on his own experiences, Curse raps, without any noticeable accent, about the inequalities in the world and that "not everyone should take their freedom for granted". The absence of accent is important here, as it reflects the locality where "high German" is spoken. In direct contrast to gangsta rappers' ego-centric and inward-looking concerns, Curse's message rap sets its focus on others. More generally, German rap is marked by notions of race, class, and place, while absorbing a range of substyles, such as gangsta rap and message rap, which play important roles for rappers in positioning themselves and justifying their existence within the global world of hip hop. German rappers resist, challenge, adapt, and transform themes of blackness and black identity in their music, thereby creating a pan-national, global form of hip hop that resonates with and reflects their own, often unique, circumstances and experiences. In doing so, German rappers have established their very own brand of rap music, in which national identity plays a lesser role in favor of locality and localized experience.

Hip hop is an interesting music genre that is historically rooted in the enforced removal of native Africans from their homelands during European colonialism, a major period in recent history from which hip hop has assimilated a sense of "blackness" as an important marker of shared racialized identity. As a highly politicized expression by Black Nationalists, hip hop has given a voice to a black community otherwise underrepresented and remains directly connected with the urban street culture from which it emerged. Having grown out of the experiences of black communities in the US, it became adopted by youth across the globe who often feel a certain connection to the experiences of impoverished, disenfranchised, and marginalized black youth cultures from which hip hop first began. Yet the term must of course be regarded as arbitrary on the basis that the cultural significance of the label "black" is socially constructed, forged by common political, economic, and geographic conditions. The label "black" has grown out of the essentialist views of the modern era with its search for objective and universal truth. There is thus an inherent danger of essentializing hip hop as a black cultural form that fails to acknowledge the fact that hip hop also attracts youths from diverse sociocultural, geographical, and other backgrounds. Hip hop has developed into a simultaneous global and local music genre that is a dynamic cultural force with rootedness in the development of western capitalism, and in this process has been transformed into a primary expression of global popular culture, thereby enabling global representations of historically underrepresented communities within a system of global communications constituted by flows. "Black culture" has thereby become global culture, its styles, musics, and images "crossing with a range of different national and regional sensibilities throughout the world and initiating a plurality of responses" (Bennett 2000: 137). Thus "black music", although crudely adopted by the music industry as a means of genre categorization, reflects and resonates with the formations of identities on a global and local scale. Hip hop has thereby also become the voice of peripheral, marginalized youths, and plays a central role in the expression and experience of whiteness. The essentialized whiteness of cities like Berlin and Frankfurt facilitates highly particularized responses to the "black" notions of the hip hop style that specifically play on notions of class, ethnicity, and place, which "amounts to a celebration of blackness in the absence of blackness" (Bennett 2000: 152). And yet again, it is important to acknowledge that such cultural associations are socially constructed through discursive practices. Blackness or whiteness, through the lenses of national and transnational hip hop and rap, then apply to continually re-made and new hybrid identities.

Global Bollywood
Global Bollywood is another example that exemplifies aesthetic cosmopolitanism in neoliberal culture. Indian film music (Indipop) is part of popular culture in which heterogeneous class and regional forces are blended. It is a result of the increasing deregulation of domestic industries, the participation in global capitalist economy, and the subsequent "economic liberation" policies that emerged in the early 1990s, characterized by a shift toward market-driven policies. As "India is undergoing a new stage of integration into the global economy that cannot simply be accounted for ... by 'cultural imperialism'" (Zuberi 2002: 239–40), changes in the Indian media industries toward the neoliberal model contribute to India's development into a global consumer society. The developments in India reflect the latest stage in the evolution of globalization, and the Indian film industry plays an active part in the global, transnational economy, facilitated by the global media, and particularly the new information and communication technologies. The Indian film industry serves as a powerful example of the ways in which globalization is transforming indigenous and national cultural formations.

A brief historical overview shall illustrate the syncretic evolution of Indian film (after Manuel 1988: 176–86). Early Indian films borrowed extensively from Hollywood and Europe, yet after 1912 became more and more a homegrown domestic entertainment form guided by indigenous aesthetics and conditions. Before the 1940s, the film industry was more decentralized, using diverse languages and often regional music, as films were produced in several urban centers in the country. The 1940s–1970s saw a dramatic reorganization of the Indian film industry, which evolved from a handful of family-run businesses to a vast corporate industry. Moreover, while in early films actors were themselves vocalists (e.g. K. L. Saigal), since the 1940s songs have been recorded by "playback" singers and actors mime. Films of the 1940s and 50s reflected sentimentality and concern about the fate of the family in a rapidly westernizing and modernizing urban milieu, with a trend toward melodramatic escapism. From the 1950s onwards, Indian films increasingly absorbed western musical elements, including instruments like the violin, clarinet, and saxophone, rhythms like the foxtrot and polka, and chordal harmony. Since the 1970s, Indian cinema has continued to evolve into a more complex and varied business, with an increasing overlap between commercial exploitation films and art films. Filmmakers increasingly stressed more "masala" (spice) and violence and eroticism, the new heroes being "angry young men" whose peripheral or antagonistic relationship to society seems to reflect an increasing social disillusionment and alienation. They incorporated elements from contemporary western pop, including disco, synthesizer, traps, bass, and electric guitar, while cabaret scenes often portrayed rock bands. Film songs were lengthened to an average of five minutes to fit with the standards for western LP and cassette recordings. The only Indian element to remain was the characteristically ornamented vocal style. The films seldom portray actual poverty, but take place in mansions, palaces, chic cabarets, and immaculate gardens. The heroes and heroines are themselves rich, celebrating synthetic, urban, westernized luxury. Films can be seen as responses to a mass desire for escapism, and as reflections of the rampant consumerism of the Indian bourgeoisie and the ideology of the affluent corporate producers. Indeed, Indian film music is marked by a homogenous vocal style, lush orchestration, corporate origin, and the glittery world of unreal cinema. Via the evolving media and digital technologies, including internet, satellite TV, video compact discs, or DVDs, films and their songs today reach ever larger Indian and non-Indian audiences worldwide. It has literally become the "people's" music and is consumed by an immensely broad and diverse portion of the populace in India and the diaspora.

Film producers and their companies dominate the music industry, yet transnationals are keen to step into this market. In their quest for expanding markets and profitability, the global media organizations have adapted their outputs to cater for local tastes. MTV, for example, has adapted to local audiences by being renamed MTV India and cutting down on its American content, mixing it with local news in India. The strategy of MTV India lies in the recognition that "in the Asian market, success lies in localisation ... [so] we reflect audience tastes with Hindi film music" (Zuberi 2002: 241). Interestingly, there is an increasing use of English words and phrases in song lyrics, which reflects MTV's encouragement of a hybrid urban language—Hinglish

(Hindi and English). As a result, local broadcasting is a mélange of locally produced and imported items. MTV, and music television as technology and cultural form more generally, has become a key institution in defining the direction of India's media culture. Meanwhile, deregulation and privatization of the national media have had a massive impact on a global and local level. The Indian media industries look outwards, seeking to maintain dominance in the South Asian region, and use the diaspora market to expand their influence. De-territorialization (the movement of people, goods, businesses and services) is another pivotal factor in the success of the Indian film industry. The emergent transnational diasporas produce the conditions for new hybridized cultures and identities. As a result, media organizations can expand their economic and cultural power beyond national and regional markets to include South Asia, Southeast Asia, Africa, and the Middle East, and market their products among diasporic populations in Europe, North America, and Australasia.

Film music is itself an essential component of this mass culture. It is the largest category of popular music in South Asia and provides the model for much of the popular music outside the cinematic world (Manuel 1988: 172). Virtually all film music is vocal in style with distinct ornamentation and melodic nuances. Songs (filmi music) are central, if not essential, in Indian movies, and music directors and composers are often better paid than actors or film directors. The music serves to broaden a film's audience beyond language barriers and to express otherwise unarticulated sentiments, such as falling in love. A typical song scene may take place in a garden, mansion, or cabaret, where the hero and heroine dance as they mouth the lyrics in a dance style that is a hybrid of Indian classical folk and western elements. The often overt eroticism of film dance also compensates for the strict censorship restricting sex and kissing on screen. Film singers are as famous as the actors themselves, who usually sing the songs in Hindi or Urdu. There are typically eight to ten songs per film, which have become the pop music of the day. The syncretic nature of Indian cine music has contributed to a culture in which western musical elements, including instrumentation, have been blended together with Indian classical and folk elements. Filmi music is typically commercialized syncretic music, absorbing elements from Indian art music, western art and popular music, and other features, including folk elements, *ghazal*, *qawwali*, and traditional styles. Melodies tend to be based on diatonic scales, to which western harmonies are added as background. Indian instruments, especially the *tabla* and *dholak* drum, are often combined with western instruments, including congas and orchestrated violins. The folk-derived *kaherva* and *dadra tals* (in eight and six beats) are the predominant meters, while the vocal timbre, particularly among female singers, is remarkably stereotyped. A large percentage of North Indian film songs of the past decades have been sung not only in the same vocal style, but by the same woman, Lata Mangeshkar, who has recorded songs for over a thousand Hindi films since the 1940s. Film music is pre-composed and recorded, while being restricted to CD-tracks' four-to six-minute length. Filmi music is produced for secular mass entertainment that creates escapism and fantasy. It involves a star system consisting of playback singers, composers, and actors, combined with speech, dance, and drama. For most Indian spectators, the effect is not unnatural, but rather a continuation of the traditions of the folk theater forms, where speech, song, and dance are tightly integrated into a unified dramatic style. These mass-produced catchy tunes are commodities with a certain mass market in mind, conditioned by globalization, mass culture, and a centralized music industry. Consequently, it reflects the new sociocultural identities in urban centers, which are regarded as being hybrid and syncretic (see also Marre and Charlton 1985e).

An interesting example of Indian cinema is the film *Devdas* (2002), described as the most lavish, expensive Bollywood production to date that continues to be distributed worldwide to international (and not only Indian) audiences. In its plotline, musical choices, and distribution, *Devdas* builds on multilayered diasporas and evokes notions of globalization. The film is about Devdas who shared his childhood with Paro; their love intensified when they reached adolescence, but Paro was to marry another man, which completely shattered Devdas who turned to alcohol. Even the devotion of a beautiful courtesan Chandramukhi did not ease his pain, and only death would provide a solution. The film's opening is framed by a scene in Devdas' family home, a western mansion (icons are both Indian and western and point toward upper class or caste), with family members (and Paro, the heroine) depicted in "traditional" clothes, attitudes, and mannerisms: for instance, Paro is overtly feminine and humble in contrast to the free-spirited, open-ended fun staged by the dancers. Devdas (the hero) returns as a westernized "man of world" from his studies in England, marked, for instance, by his class-distinctive clothes and heteronormative masculinity combined with coolness (e.g. when catching a fly), which positions him as a modernized, diasporic business man in his own country. Later on, when the parents announce the arranged marriage between Devdas and another woman, the music shifts decisively to Indian instruments. The main tune riffs on American stylings of western pop with an Indianized vocal sound, which is at times perhaps more Indian in character owing to the use of Indian traditional instruments. Visually, the film blends traditional Indian elements (e.g. interior, clothing, behavior, class, plot, texts, music, etc.), which literally underscore "the local" as the unchangeable foundation of life with western elements (e.g. the setting, interior, Devdas' clothing, values, music, etc.) to weave a web of global cultural strands. Musically, the film combines local vernacular roots with western sources, including classical music. *Devdas* presents an array of diasporic and global sensibilities by sketching out a society that is both segmented (traditional versus modern; western versus Indian, etc.) and integrated (merging the various). The overlay of western sounds adds layers of meanings that move the discourse toward the global, though from a local perspective, marked by class orientation, sentimentality, the westernized business man image, and a burning light (a western symbol for "burning love"). All of these features show worldwide style sources, while staying within a familiar genre model, and so represent an efficient eclecticism. The film clearly targets a global audience that might be Indian or non-Indian, and reflects the fact that the commercial entertainment industry seems to create a diaspora of taste as well as population, evident in the fact that Indian film has become as powerful as western musicals. Huge posters in bright colors advertise the movies, with gigantic pictures of the stars who have the status of superstars and are immensely powerful figures in Indian society and the diaspora.

The Indian film industry Bollywood is a major competitor to the long-term dominance of America's Hollywood. It is an emerging cultural force that explicitly challenges American themes and assumptions about the filmgoing public. Indian films have thus become symbols of successful resistance to western cultural imperialism, even while incorporating elements of Hollywood commercialism, thus illustrating the culture clash and paradoxes of globalization. Bollywood provides an important example of syncretic popular culture that involves a globally powerful film industry and its aligned music recording industry. Aesthetic cosmopolitanism, fusion, and crossover in world popular music is the epitome for globalization, and a "western" musical genre to emerge in the 1980s exemplifies this most directly—World Music. As a kind of pseudo-genre, World Music is characteristic of both hybridity and authenticity, which resembles a kind of paradox between the mixing of musical styles, on the one hand, and a desire to leave a musical "tradition" intact, on the other. Artists who "make it" as World Music stars must therefore tread a fine line between hybridity and authenticity and navigate carefully around western ideas of "authentic hybridity".

Notes

1. An example of the manifestations of neoliberalism in China, for example, is provided by P. David Marshall's account of the peculiar T-shirt phenomenon among Chinese university students, which he reads as a presentation of the branding of the self (2016: 28–35). This expression of individuality is a celebration of entrepreneurialism and a reflection of the freedom of the individual, and thus an extension of neoliberalism and neolib-

eral subjectivity. Marshall thereby concludes that while this individuality is not quite the same in the Chinese context, it is influenced by neoliberalism, but within the context of internal Chinese politics and identity tensions (33). Another useful contribution is made by Park, Hill, and Saito (2012) on the manifestations of neoliberalism across a number of East Asian states, including Japan, South Korea, Taiwan, Hong Kong, Singapore, Malaysia, and Thailand. Manifestations of neoliberalism in music-specific contexts are explored in a special issue, "Music, Music Making and Neoliberalism" (León 2014), with articles exploring the impact of structural changes on musical activities in South India, post-socialist Albania, Peru, South Africa, and Thailand.

2. This is particularly evident in the "creative industries" program of the so-called "knowledge economy" promoted by New Labour during the late 1990s and through to 2010 that sought to combat the decline in manufacturing industries.

3. This trend is also visible in the growing personalization of electoral politics, notably in the "totally personality-based election campaigning" (Crouch 2004: 26, 102–103) of recent years, which used to be characteristic of dictatorships and authoritarian regimes. This personality phenomenon is a consequence of some of the problems of postdemocracy (Crouch 2004: 28). P. David Marshall (2017) speaks of the way that brand culture has shaped political discourse in that nowadays we think of politicians and parties as political brands. In the attention economy, the political brands have to work in a manner similar to the commercial economy (2017: 2). See also Olczyk and Wasilewski (2017) for an example of political branding in Poland.

4. See also http://www.islandrecords.co.uk/island-life/ (accessed 28 November 2017).

5. Until recently in the United States, blackness was integral to the legal systems of different states to legitimize slavery and racial subordination. Under the Jim Crows law, what constituted a "black" person varied between different states: "In Alabama, Arkansas and Mississippi, anyone with a 'visible' and/or 'appreciable' degree of 'Negro blood' was … a black person whereas in Indiana and Louisiana the colour line was drawn at one-eighth and one-sixteenth negro blood respectively" (Longhurst 2007: 119).

6. E.g. http://beautifulwhiteskin.com/skin-lightening/celebrities-rihanna-beyonce/ (accessed 12 May 2017).

7. For examples of orientalist artwork, see http://www.orientalist-art.org.uk/ (accessed 12 December 2015).

8. For useful overviews on cosmopolitanism from sociology, see also Beck and Grande (2010: 417–19); Calcutt, Woodward, and Skrbis (2009: 170–72); Delanty (2006: 28–36).

9. Within the context of European cosmopolitanism, there exists a paradox between the persistence of Enlightenment culturalism and ethical universalism that leads to the rejection of those who are inadequately cosmopolitan (Calhoun 2009: 649). Enlightenment cosmopolitanism is therefore also flawed and used here as an "ideal type" (after Max Weber).

10. Aesthetic cosmopolitanism is the outcome of musical developments since the 1950s, beginning with imitations of Anglo-American rock in many countries and a gradual move, during the 1970s, toward localized pop-rock versions, including "national rock" styles that rose to national dominance in many countries; and followed (during the 1980s) by domesticated or locally-produced forms of pop-rock music becoming fully legitimized and consolidated in many parts of the world.

11. Indeed, K.I.Z. are known for their wit, irony, and provocative tactic of challenging and subverting established norms and behaviors in German society, culture, and music, including gangsta rap. See, for instance, http://www.gea.de/nachrichten/kultur/k+i+z+pubertierende+klassenclowns.640731.htm (accessed 24 January 2016).

3 Globalization and World Music

During the 1980s, transnational entertainment corporations successfully marketed predominantly Anglo-American pop-rock music around the globe. Meanwhile, major cities around the world witnessed the emergence of local centers of musical production and distribution, recording and disseminating globalized music styles, allowing local music and stars to acquire a new legitimacy via new standards of professionalism. While much of this repertoire was produced locally, most of this music had little or no direct influence on the western marketplace. Yet this began to change, marked by a trend of wholesale migration of music recording industries to Europe, notably to Britain and France, where recordings of non-western musicians were made and marketed to western enthusiasts and diasporic migrants. For instance, both the former Ghanaian record industry and Kenyan center for the East African music industry, including multinationals like HMV and Decca, abandoned the region due to piracy, which meant that much of the legitimate West and East African music industry moved to European cities. These fed back into the global music business, as local music producers provided marginal markets and "raw" musical material for international music consumption, made possible through new recording technologies and the internet. The boundaries between mainstream and marginal music became fuzzy. The twin pressures to expand the global market for Anglo-American pop-rock and create new alternative genres and audiences within the western market grew ever stronger. An important milestone in this international influence and musical interchange commercially was the Beatles' promotional relationship with Indian *sitar* player Ravi Shankar in the 1960s, as well as The Token's hit 'The Lion Sleeps Tonight' (number one in 1961), which sparked a growing interest among western musicians and audiences in "unusual" musical sounds from other parts of the world.

The growing interest in foreign music cultures by western artists and audiences eventually gave way to the emergence of a new commercial pseudo-genre of World Music, "the soundtrack to the most recent regime of globalization" (Taylor 2014: 194). World Music manifests the processes and dynamics of globalization, as it has grown out of waves of cultural exchange, movement, and appropriation. Globalization is a vehicle through which cultural forms and practices spread globally and new hybrid forms of cultural expression emerge, and originated out of the mixing and matching of pre-existing local, usually national, forms. It means that cultural forms, practices, and expressions come into contact with one another and in this process are reshaped. Under the impact of globalization, it makes no sense to imagine anything like cultural purity as a result. World Music is the very embodiment of the globalization of culture.

The Birth of World Music in Britain

In 1980s Britain, popular music was dominated by glitzy, artificial, chart-friendly pop that reflected (rather than challenged) the excesses and glamour of life. Audiences and musicians looked for fresh and new music that was not mainstream or overtly commercial. They longed for more authentic and meaningful, virtuosic, and culturally-connected music that they could get from roots music and jazz in the 1960s and from punk music in the 1970s:

> At the dawn of the 80s, in an age of spandex and synthesizers, many music fans were becoming bored with the pop charts and hungered for a new music that could excite them once again. Where music from the rest of the world had once been regarded as mere exotica, there was increasingly a sense that World Music could be the future of pop music (Cooper *et al.* 2013).

A spark of interest and new curiosity about the world's cultures was ignited, as more distinct and specialized music emerged alongside rapid growth in product range and promotional support by both the recording and aligned entertainment industries, as well as Labour government support. The post-punk scene of the early 1980s saw the first WOMAD festival in July 1982 where British indie bands like Echo and the Bunnymen performed alongside musicians from around the world, such as the Drummers of Burundi (see Chalcraft *et al.* 2011: 31–34, and Magaudda *et al.* 2011: 64–65, for useful discussions on WOMAD). The careers of many World Music artists began in the punk movement, notably with musicians such as Joe Strummer (The Clash), Jah Wobble (Public Image), Charlie Gillett, and Billy Bragg who dabbled in world sounds (Arts Council England 2005: 5). At the same time, some radio broadcasters, notably Alexis Korner, Charlie Gillett, John Peel, and Andy Kershaw, began to venture into new musical territory, with "eclectic playlists including a diverse range of African, Latin, and Caribbean music" (ibid.).

This growing interest in new sounds coincided with a celebration of multiculturalism, promoted at government level under Labour, who, in response to the increase in racism in the 1960s and 70s, passed the Race Relations Act

(1976) and created the Commission for Racial Equality. UK cultural policy began to actively promote multicultural arts and music. For instance, in 1985 the Music Advisory Panel of the Arts Council England promoted the creation of two multicultural touring circuits, the AMC (Asian Music Circuit) and ACMC (African and Caribbean Music Circuit) to assist a small, but growing network of music promoters. The funding organization Visiting Arts was set up and funded its first African band as early as 1979, followed in 1981 by funding the first World Music event at the Commonwealth Institute, and in 1982 by funding the first WOMAD festival. In 1986, the Arts Council England committed 4 percent of its expenditure to the promotion of African, Caribbean, and Asian arts and music, continuing to provide funding to a number of pioneering organizations, tours, and festivals throughout the 1980s (Arts Council England 2005: 6). For instance, the promotional organization Arts Worldwide brought non-mainstream international artists, mostly from Africa, to tour in the UK. Arts Worldwide founders, Anne Hunt and Mary Farquharson, also decided to release records by the non-Western artists they had brought over due to the growing demand for recordings from the concert-going public. The label World Circuit Limited was born, and Nick Gold, who at the time volunteered on a work placement for Arts Worldwide, got the job of overseeing the recording projects. A few years later, in the early 1990s, Nick assumed sole ownership of World Circuit, and was instrumental in discovering and developing some of the finest and most successful World Music projects of the last two decades (Krüger 2015: 187).

Small, independent record labels emerged, including Stern, Globestyle, Earthworks, Cooking Vinyl, and World Circuit, and a few records broke through to the mainstream, notably *Le Mystere des Voix Bulgares* (1986) and Paul Simon's *Graceland* (1986). By the mid-1980s, there existed a small, but vibrant, scene of enthusiasts and organizations who

> had adopted a range of terms to describe the music they recorded and promoted: worldbeat, ethnobeat, ethnic, international pop, international folk, roots, tropical, and of course, World Music, to name but a few. Confusion in the sector led to confusion in the record stores. Haphazard cataloguing made it difficult for the increasing number of record buyers to find or browse CDs of international music. Some kind of standardization was needed (Arts Council England 2005: 7).

This development ultimately led to the birth of World Music as a commercial genre, which is tied closely to the economic, social, cultural, and technological manifestations of globalization (White 2012: 1). The term "world music" first appeared in the 1960s, notably in American academic circles where it was introduced as a populist alternative to the discipline of ethnomusicology, as well as in American commercial music circles where "world music" was "sold as primitive, exotic, tribal, ethnic, folk, traditional, international, and nostalgic music" (Feld 2000: 10). The mid-1950s onwards witnessed a considerable rise in the popularity of Indian classical music, sparked by the championing of the music of Ali Akbar Khan and Ravi Shankar by concert violinist Yehudi Menuhin, both in America and the UK. Ravi Shankar, specifically, influenced a number of 1960s musicians, notably George Harrison, who played the sitar on The Beatles' song 'Norwegian Wood' in 1965. During the 1960s and 1970s, many mainstream artists adopted non-western music in their own music, "albeit sometimes as an exotic novelty on cheesy flower-power anthems" (Arts Council England 2005: 4). Some underground outlets for "world music" included the 1970s American magazine *Sing Out!* with their flexi-disc releases, followed in the 1970s by the (short-lived) publication, *Collusion*, edited by David Toop, Sue Steward, and Steve Beresford (Anderson 2000).

Yet it was during the 1980s, with the rise of British popular music studies, that non-western music became more thoroughly approached from the global music industry perspective, with the emergence of the new commercial genre of World Music in Britain driven primarily by marketing concerns:

> In the 1980s, some British music fans were searching for something new. The answer lay somewhere out there, but how to find it over here? Where do you put a Bulgarian factory workers' choir and some guitar-slinging hot shot from Guinea Bisseau, how do you put them in a record shop? ... What could we have? Ok. Tropical? Well, that leaves the Bulgarians out ... World Beat ... Maybe someone said ethnic ... World Music, and everybody went "Yeah, that works!" (Andy Kershaw, in Cooper *et al.* 2013).

This brief excerpt above refers to the three meetings between various World Music record companies and interested parties in June and July 1987, which included representatives from GlobeStyle/Ace Records, Crammed US/freelance, WOMAD, Oval, Channel 4, Folk Roots/Rogue Records, AWW/World Circuit, Sterns/Triple Earth, Triple Earth/Sterns—Triple Earth, Blues & Soul, and Hannibal (fRoots 2000). Held at the Empress of Russia in St John Street, Islington, on 29 June 1987, the main aim and purpose of the first meeting was to discuss how to broaden the appeal of this new musical material, and how to sell, promote, and market non-western musics:

> Roger [Armstrong; GlobeStyle] felt that the main problem in selling our kind of material lay with the U.K. retail outlets and specifically the fact that they did not know how to rack it coherently. This dis-

couraged them from stocking the material in any depth and made it more difficult for the record buyers to become acquainted with our catalogues. The initial purpose of the meeting was to encourage the retail trade via various concerted efforts as follows. 1. It was agreed that we should create a generic name under which our type of catalogue could be labelled in order to focus attention on what we do. We discussed various names for our type of music(s) and on a show of hands "World Music" was agreed as the "banner" under which we would work. Other suggestions were "World Beat", "Hot...", "Tropical..." and various others. It was suggested that all of the labels present would use "World Music" on their record sleeves (to give a clear indication of the "File Under..." destination) and also on all publicity material etc. [...] 2. A representative of each record company present spoke about their various methods and problems with distribution. [...] 3. Five possible sales devices were discussed. They are as follows: a. Browser card containing "World Music" heading and individual logos of companies involved; b. NME "World Music" cassettes to which each company would contribute material; c. *Music Week* advertorial; d. Counter leaflets/joint Catalogue/Poster; e. Hiring a joint PR; f. World Music chart. [...] It was also suggested that Andy Kershaw might be persuaded to do a run down of this chart on his show regularly. This whole campaign would start mid-September and run through October, which would be designated World Music month (fRoots 2000).

Besides deciding on how the CDs should be racked, the meeting's participants also agreed to share the fees for a marketing consultant and costs for creating CD dividers labelled "World Music", which proved to be hugely successful, as record shops now had a convenient category to rack the most diverse "exotic" recordings. The accompanying press release summarized the meeting as follows:

> At a meeting on the 29th June '87, representatives from most of the main independent record labels dealing with international/ roots music discussed ways of achieving a greater awareness of their music in the retail trade, in the press, and among the public. One of the problems perceived as hindering the development of this music is the haphazard racking of the records in the shops. As the labels concerned have a very wide spread of music in their catalogues, many shops willing to stock this material could benefit from expert advice about this specialised (but not specialist) music. It was agreed that the term WORLD MUSIC would be used by all labels present to offer a new and unifying category for shop racking, press releases, publicity handouts and "file under..." suggestions. This means that you no longer have to worry about where to put those new Yemen-

ite pop, Bulgarian choir, Zairean soukous or Gambian kora records. We shall be making October "WORLD MUSIC" month, heralded by an NME cassette, a dealer campaign and extensive promotion and advertising in the popular press (Press Release 01 – World Music 2000).

During the 1980s, World Music was still largely signified by, what Steven Feld called, "pop star collaboration and curation" (2001), most notably between Paul Simon and Ladysmith Black Mambazo for his album *Graceland* (1986); Peter Gabriel and Nusrath Fateh Ali Khan and Youssou N'Dour; David Byrne and Latin musicians for his album *Rei Momo* (1989) as well as with musicians from Papua New Guinea; and Kate Bush and The Mysterious Bulgarian Voices; to name but a few. Toward the end of the 1980s/early 1990s, pop star curation continued to dominate much World Music repertoire; however more distinct models of musical collaboration were emerging, for example Peter Gabriel's Real World label and co-founding of the WOMAD festivals, as well as his collaborations with numerous musicians, notably during the so-called Real World recording weeks. Other examples included Mickey Hart's collaborations with Tibetan monks, and African and Indian percussionists on his *World Series* (Rykodisc) and *Endangered Musics Project*; Henry Kaiser and David Lindley's collaborations in Madagascar; David Bridie's collaborations with Papua New Guinean musicians (*Not Drowning, Waving*) and Aboriginal, Islander, and Melanesian musicians; and Ry Cooder's collaborations with Hawaiian, Mexican-American, African, and Indian guitarists, and Cuban musicians (Feld 2001, 2000). For instance, the Grammy-winning album *Talking Timbuktu* (1994), a collaboration between Ali Farka Touré and Ry Cooder, sold over half a million records, an incredible figure for an album of its kind, and brought the World Circuit label international acclaim (Krüger 2015).

The 1990s saw increasing marketplace success of World Music, as the genre no longer relied on pop star collaborations for sales and witnessed significant growth in product range and promotional support of the recording and aligned entertainment industries. This time saw the proliferation of record labels devoted to World Music. Musical highlights at the time included Salif Keita, Nusrath Fateh Ali Khan, Fela Kuti, Ali Farka Touré, Youssou N'Dour, and World Circuit's *Buena Vista Social Club* (1997), the biggest-selling World Music album of all time, which elevated the Cuban artists to superstar status (with their own solo records released through World Circuit) and led to the phenomenal rise in popularity of Cuba's rich musical heritage, all of which has contributed to a massive boom in Cuba's tourist and recording industries (Krüger 2015: 187). The 1990s saw the rise of "global dance", a thriving sector that included Massive Attack's hugely successful remix of *qawwali* music by

Nusrath Fateh Ali Khan. In terms of print media, the magazine *Rhythm Music: Global Sounds and Ideas* was launched in 1991, followed by *RootsWorld* in 1993, *World Music* in the mid-1990s, and *Songlines* in 1999; the listener guides *The Virgin Directory of World Music* (Sweeney 1992) and *World Beat* (Spencer 1992) appeared; the first *Rough Guide to World Music* (Broughton et al. 1994) and the subsequent two-volume reference books *World Music: The Rough Guide* (Broughton et al. 1999; Broughton and Ellingham 2000) were published. Meanwhile, in 1990 the American music magazine *Billboard* reinstated World Music as a sales tracking category and began charting its commercial impact (Feld 2000). Moreover, radio, television, and the internet increasingly featured World Music with tremendous record industry and fan support, reflected by the rapid expansion of new airline World Music channels, video and television series, and thousands of internet websites devoted to the promotion and merchandising of World Music. Sales were supported through the development of stores and mail-order catalogs, alongside email "info-tisements". Some corporations even developed tailored marketing plans to align their products with World Music, for example the Putamayo compilations that are omnipresent in Starbucks and other chains (Feld 2001; see also Kassabian 2004).

The noughties gave rise to an even wider range of venues, festivals, and events, including World Music *melas* and carnivals designated to world, traditional, folk, and culturally diverse musics in the UK. Asian dance music continued to grow with "stars like Apache Indian, State of Bengal, and Asian Dub Foundation, who made their first appearance in the UK Pop Charts" (Arts Council England 2005: 10). The growing British Asian underground scene has rivalled Ibiza's dance club scene with ease. World Music continued to be promoted via the media, notably by BBC Radio 3 presenters Andy Kershaw, Lucy Durán, Verity Sharp, and Fiona Talkington, as well as through the creation in 2002 of the Award for World Music. Many mainstream artists continue to take inspiration from World Music, notably Damien Albarn (Blur, Gorillaz) and Robert Plant (Led Zeppelin), "being the most high-profile new converts" (ibid.: 13).

The Brand Warehouse of World Music

World Music, or certain kinds of music within World Music, provide an interesting example of branding, even though musicians in the World Music category are less often discussed as brands, as they tend to be too marginal to be swallowed up by the mainstream music industry. Tim Taylor describes World Music as a "brand warehouse" (2016: 93), with its own record labels, sections in record stores, radio and television programs, magazines, internet sites, book publications, festivals, music tourism (e.g. Songlines Music Travel), and more. An interesting example is World Circuit's "Buena Vista Social Club" brand, which signifies an unmistakably Cuban music subgenre within World Music by distinguishing its individual artists' releases with a recognizable brand name such as "Buena Vista Social Club Presents Ibrahim Ferrer", or "Buena Vista Social Club Presents Omara Portuondo", conjuring up a romantic exoticism and emphasizing a back story that is not easily forgettable (Sisario 2006). "Buena Vista Social Club" plays on the fraternity of nostalgia in "a lost musical paradise", while the film behind the music centers around remembrance and rediscovery, which made the music even more appealing (Sisario 2006). In other words,

> through repackaging Cuba's abandoned musical past, it presented a very different country ... In an age of increasing globalisation, the feeling of stepping into a world on the verge of disappearance seemed irresistible. The worldwide success of Buena Vista Social Club showed how music from other cultures could be presented to a global audience. It was no longer enough to have the right sound (Cooper *et al.* 2013).

Music brands play important roles for marketing and commercialism, which are often manipulated in such a way as to tap into the beliefs and pleasures of consumers so as to resonate with their identity (Burton 2005: 71). To its audiences, World Music is a source of private interests, emotional pleasure, and personal identification: "Branding is another way of putting something in its place, making it knowable and accessible to potential consumers and creating an emotional connection to it" (Taylor 2016: 93). Branding thereby reflects the growing conceptions of identity as a "personal" conception of selfhood in neoliberal consumer culture:

> The ideology of identity has become a potent way for many to attempt to ground themselves and to differentiate themselves from others [which] is accomplished through the consumption of certain means of communication and not others, ensembles of commodities and not others, as in that brand of shoes, that brand of shirt, that style of haircut, that brand of cellular phone—that is the primary means of fashioning identities today. The consumption of music is part of this project of identity construction, and for some social groups, particularly youth, a potent part ... One consumes goods to make oneself; one even consumes other modes of selfhood to make oneself as a way of demonstrating one's agential selfhood to oneself and others (Taylor 2016: 66–67, 69).

World Music functions as a constructed concept that results from the exchange between the music industry and the audiences of World Music. The construction of a genre brand thereby serves the market interests of the music industry to streamline musical production, and it becomes a source of private interests, emotional pleasure, and personal identification for consumers. The new style of World Music can be understood "in terms of supply for a social market, in which existing and new social groupings are constantly in demand for cultural products in order to maintain and construct their sense of difference and distinction" (Regev 2013: 82). Genres start by establishing stylistic conventions or formula of some kind (Burton 2005: 68), which help the audience to relate to and identify with World Music, and gives the producer a clear foundation on which to create World Music. The semiotic dimension is crucial for genre construction, which concerns the "whole" musical experience, including sound, visuals, lyrics/language, performance style, and behavioral norms. The conventions constituted by the genre of World Music are determined partially in terms of its subject matter. World Music usually encompasses traditional, popular, and hybrid musics from outside the "normal" Anglo-American popular and classical music canon, as well as some "minority" musics from Europe and America, such as Bulgarian choirs, Spanish *flamenco*, Portuguese *fado*, or Louisianan *cajun* music. On the one hand, World Music has thus become defined as "fusion music" that results from the blending of musics from around the world, absorbing so-called (non-western) traditional and (western) popular musics. On the other hand, World Music also includes some American and European "minority" musics, so the subject matters for inclusion in the genre are not exclusively determined by their geographical origin. Moreover, since its conception in the 1980s, the scope of what constitutes World Music has increased immensely. A good example of a newer style called World Music 2.0 is Schlachthofbronx, two Bavarians who have become increasingly crucial figures on the global bass scene blending together dancehall, rave, dub, dubstep, Brazilian *baile* funk, New Orleans bounce, Trinidadian *soca*, and other styles to create a new blend of world dance music (see also Schlachthofbronx GbR 2018).

Authentic Hybridity

The genre conventions for World Music are not prescribed to subject matter alone (even though it does play a large part), but an important role is also played by ideas surrounding authenticity. To put it simply, a World Music artist is accepted by critics and audiences if they perceive the musician and her or his music to be an authentic representation of the culture from which she or he hails. Yet World Music artists often disagree. Angelique Kidjo, for instance, complains in her introduction to the recent *Music Hound World* book that

> critics generally want a musician from a foreign country to stick to a pure tradition; he has to be "authentic". Well, there are "purists" and "traditionalists" in just about every form of music. But it was never part of the original World Music concept to tell artists what to do, just to help them sell records ... I don't detect that being on the agenda of any of the original World Music plotters. Yes ... it did later pick up a small selection of shysters, control freaks, newage knob-twiddlers [sic], self-glorifiers and sick California crazies with a weird and varied selection of personal agendas (Anderson 2000).

Among musicians, audiences, and critics, there clearly exist disagreements as to whether musicians should "keep it real" (Murphy 2007: 48–52). Talking of authenticity in this context, some understand "real" music as an authentic expression of cultural identity. The term authenticity is thus often used to refer to traditional music that is embedded within the context and lived experience of "the people" (the folk; the rural). The western perception of authenticity has its roots in the European romantic celebration of the "native" as being more real, and therefore authentic, than the civilized westerner (Frith 2000: 308). More specifically,

> the search for authenticity in the social and material world, as well as concerning the person (in psychoanalysis) began at the end of the last century, at a time when citizens in the newly industrialized countries had an unprecedented variety of goods, lifestyles and artistic expressions at their disposal. This new range of choice in combination with a disrupted social order, demanded an active positioning of the self. Authenticity became to be an orientation device and a mark of distinction (Gebesmair and Smudits 2001: 112).

According to this Romantic idea, cultural purity, rather than hybridity, became the measuring device for authenticity. In today's world, however, the concept of authenticity is in fact incompatible with the reality of globalization. Some scholars, notably from popular music studies, have thus questioned the concept of authenticity altogether (Leonard and Strachan 2003: 164), arguing that music is only inauthentic in the framework of an essentialist and dichotomous understanding of authenticity (e.g. rural versus urban; traditional versus modern; and so on). Authenticity should instead be understood as a socially and culturally constructed concept, informed by ethnocentrism in people's search for the other.

Tim Taylor differentiates between different kinds of authenticity. He suggests that World Music of the 1980s and early 1990s was marked by "authenticities of positionality,[1] emotionality, and primality[2]" (2016: 90), while more current World Music often draws on authenticity of emotionality, which refers to "the kind of raw emotions that people ... are thought to possess and express in their music" (2016: 91). Branding World Music, or some kinds of music within the genre, for instance, plays on authentic means for artists "to appear in native garb, whether or not they actually wear those clothes outside the concert hall" (Taylor 2014: 197). Authenticity is thereby constructed and maintained through musical and extramusical activity that includes image and visual style, rules of behavior and etiquette, language, proxemics, and kinesic codes, and so forth. Such musical and extramusical practices resonate with the musical tastes and preferences of the audiences of World Music, who in turn ascribe certain meaning and value to the musics they listen to and consume. Musical audiences therefore determine and model the musical and extramusical conventions specific to musical genres. A musician's image, clothing, and performance style, as well as the discourses around him or her, determine the construction of a distinctive "music personae" or "music brand" (Lieb 2013; Taylor 2016: 54–62, 80–117), which is in turn used by consumers in their own processes of identity formation and maintenance. Yet musicians and/or their producers may apply genre conventions too loosely in terms of the characteristics that are accepted by audiences as constituting the genre, which may lead to considerable disagreement and rejection. Thus genre conventions do not exist in some vacuum independent from audiences. World Music artists and/or producers must be careful about the ways in which World Music is marketed—presented, positioned, packaged, and so forth—within the "expected" conventions of the genre.

World Music encompasses a huge variety of musical styles and so is not determined by one homogenized musical taste. To many consumers, World Music products mark a democratic desire and expression of solidarity with peoples from other cultures. (There may, of course, also be consumers who simply have an escapist desire for "aural tourism" [Howard 2009].) Since its conception, World Music is thus often packaged and presented to its western consumers as an educational cultural experience. World Music is usually promoted via displays of expertise, evident in lengthy explanations and descriptions of the music and cultural context inside sleeve notes, and thereby marketed for "proper" appreciation that assumes some kind of academicism from the consumer. Similarly, Morley describes World Music as "something that was packaged and presented as educational, as something you visited, if at all, out of a sense of duty" (2010). World Music has thus connotations with educational music. In turn, the "serious" World Music consumer seeks an "authentic" musical experience, whereby the music must be "true" to its own origins and not be hampered by western commercial interests. It may be argued that such a view of the authentic in World Music ("authentic and true" versus "commercial and banal") has grown out of the "long European Romantic celebration of the native (the peasant and the African) as more real (because more natural) than the civilized Westerner" (Frith 2000: 308). In academic circles, World Music is thereby often scorned for banalizing difference (Guilbault 1997) or for constituting neo-orientalist musical appropriations (Stokes 2007: 5), a view that suggests that the dominant (western) culture "is reinforced by matching the familiar to the exotic Other" (Howard 2009: 5). In other words, while in the commercial sphere World Music is often celebrated as an authentic genre by establishing and maintaining carefully selected genre conventions in order to please audiences, in the academic sphere World Music is often seen as nothing more than "commodified forms of hybrid collaborations ... [that are] greying cultural distinctions" (Howard 2009: 5).

Commodified Authenticity
A good example to exemplify the commodification of authenticity in World Music is the Bhundu Boys, who are perhaps one of the earliest non-western artists to achieve commercial success in Europe. After achieving a relative level of success in their home country Zimbabwe, the Bhundu Boys were "brought over" to the UK by two independent Scottish entrepreneurs, Doug Veitch and Owen Elias, who had found their recordings on cassettes in Zimbabwe. The band's first two albums, *Shabini* (1986) and *Tsvimbodzemoto* (1987), both sung in their native Shona language, were released on the small independent label Discafrique and, with the championing of John Peel and Andy Kershaw, gained positive critical attention and publicity in the music press and reached the British independent charts (Denselow 2007a). Their sound was signified by a cross-fertilization of traditional African rhythms and western guitar pop before being introduced to the British music market, but it was still considered to be "based on tradition, although the music would have been 'modernized' to some degree as a result of structural and contextual changes" (Brusila 2001: 40). This certain familiarity with western pop resonated with the taste of western audiences, while the fact that they also maintained African traditions meant that the Bhundu Boys were "both accessible and authentic at the same time" (ibid.: 55). This authenticity was understood within the context of the rock discourse of the 1980s: "A combination of simple raw talent and hard work [combined with] the general approach to music-making ... congruent with the guitar band aesthetics common among indie and roots enthusiasts" (ibid.: 40–41). Upon pressures from the media to name their musical style, the Bhundu Boys called it *jit*, and so they became known as a *jit band* or *jit jive band* in Britain.

After their early success, the Bhundu Boys signed a lucrative deal in 1987 with one of the major transnational companies, WEA (Warner). Being inspired by British pop of the 1980s, the band wanted to make a record that was closer to British pop than their earlier Zimbabwean recordings. Their sound became heavily commercialized for a mainstream taste, with the resulting album *True Jit* (1987) featuring a pop song format with more polished westernized sound, English lyrics, brass sections, and pastiches of the band's glossy visual image that conformed to, what may be described as, a colonialist and orientalist perspective of what Zimbabweans should look like (Thomson 2006). Jo Haynes describes the process as follows: "Although it [World Music] may have derived its 'authenticity' from the significations of racial difference manufactured in modernism, it has been 'constructed and commodified through the effect of transnational capitalism'" (2013: 65). Musical westernization driven by the logic of neoliberal capitalism reflects the often-criticized workings of some music industry companies with their sole ambition to produce and sell World Music for profit to their target audiences, whereby local music from elsewhere is processed in such a way that it is readily marketable to certain western (mainstream) audiences. It could be argued that this practice is a deliberate attempt to maintain the notion that Anglo-American, hegemonic culture and music are of a higher calibre than foreign music culture, and that in order for the latter to be successful globally, it must meet particular (western) musical standards, as economic success in the western world is the "ultimate" form of success. In doing so, the original style, meaning, and sound of the musics are altered, resulting in a "falsified" and "inauthentic" representation of World Music cultures.

Despite WEA's attempt to market the Bhundu Boys for western tastes, the album *True Jit* (1987) did not resonate with the expectations of the audience, and was poorly received by British critics and the public alike. The band was neither acceptable for a mainstream pop music audience, nor authentic enough for the World Music fans. For instance, "the media's response was either confused or outright negative. Some writers did accept the record as the product that the band wanted to make ... However, particularly the British 'roots' media wanted to distance itself totally from the band's new style" (Brusila 2001: 46). This shows that the (perhaps) abrasive tendencies by some dominant music corporations, as well as the musicians themselves in their attempt to move from peripheral niche markets to the mainstream international pop market, to westernize World Music provides opportunities for audiences and critics to resist the standardized and "inauthentic" feel of the music and culture. In many instances, audiences, consumers, and critics activate their own perceptions and understanding of World Music by deliberately opposing the "falsified" version presented to them, and thus "in opposition to a process of capitalist globalization commanded by the large multinational corporations" (Lechner and Boli 2005: 154). The Bhundu Boys recorded a second album with WEA, *Pamberi* (1989), which was a deliberate attempt to return to the "roots" music style of their earlier recordings combined with features of progressive pop, and which received more favourable responses in the World Music media. Yet after the failure of *True Jit*, WEA's interest in the band had waned, and so their contract with WEA ended in January 1990 after only two and a half years. Interestingly, the British press and media often brushed aside the interests and motives of the musicians, and instead blamed the record company and producer for the changes in the band's musical style and sound. For instance, BBC's World Music DJ Andy Kershaw criticized that "The dick-head who sat down at WEA Records and said, 'Hey, I've got an ideaaaa! It's going to be Robin Millar!' should be taken out and publicly put to death" (Brusila 2001: 46–47). In the World Music media, the Bhundu Boys thus became a symbol of the banalizing influences of modern pop, technology, and westernization (ibid.: 48). Clearly, the Bhundu Boys achieved success in the British independent music market early on when they were representative of their country by adhering to their "original" sound (even if somewhat westernized), and by doing so maintained their national identity and, with it, authenticity. This example shows that

> the discourse of World Music, anchored in the self-definition of the "West", tends to portray the musicians as "Others", that is, as representing the "Rest". Thus, the musicians and their music come to signify something that has been lost in the more "modern" West. The key to an artist's success in the World Music market seems to be a successful negotiation of the tensions that these expectations create. In order to please the Western audience, the artist must be *both accessible and "authentic"* at the same time ... What is most important is not how truthfully the musical structure follows some "traditional" style, which would be explained to be "pure". Instead, the crucial issue is to what extent the music fits the Western listeners' ideas of what makes the music genuine instead of corrupt and this validation depends largely on the listeners' own cultural background (Brusila 2001: 52, original emphasis).

Very often, we understand the music through a fundamentally western perspective that leads to some of the music's meaning becoming "lost in translation". Bohlman discusses the ontologies of World Music and how our preoccupation with treating music as "a 'thing' that possesses meaning" prevents us from understanding the music from a global viewpoint; we largely "impose a western ontology where it does not belong" (Bohlman 2002: 6), and so World Music is often enjoyed and understood on a relatively vicarious level.

Diasporic World Music
Besides questions surrounding, what Taylor termed, "authenticities of positionality, emotionality, and primality" in World Music of the 1980s and early 1990s (Taylor 2016: 90), more current World Music often draws on authenticity of emotionality, and thus World Music artists' raw emotions that they express through their music, alongside other strategies for its success. A good example is Nitin Sawhney, a diasporic Indian-British producer and composer who incorporates musical styles from around the world in his music. Despite Sawhney's dislike for the term World Music ("World Music is a crazy term; it's another way to marginalise and generalise music from other cultures that people don't want to give an equal platform to—an excuse for apartheid in record shops" [Sawhney 2006]), he won the BBC World Music Award in 2003. Nitin Sawhney incorporates a vast repertoire of styles into his compositions, including Asian influences, jazz, and dance music. His "work has combined Bach and Bollywood, electronica and sitar, with voices ranging from Enoch Powell to Nelson Mandela" (Sawhney 2006). His song 'Nadia' (1999), for example, features a drum and bass rhythm complemented by a female vocalist singing Indian *raga*. By fusing influences from Asia and Europe, the music is made far more accessible to western (often diasporic, cosmopolitan) consumers, and thus tends to do well in the World Music market: "Just as there are 'new diasporas' in the 'New Europe', for example, the musics of those diasporas are most audible and effective as world music" (Bohlman 2002: 118). Musical expressions of diasporic experiences often exert certain themes that relate to the social situation of migrant people. Multiculturalism, spirituality, and politics are all prominent narratives in diasporic World Music. Addressing emotional themes of belonging becomes a vehicle for imagining a sense of place to supplant the condition of placelessness. This can be seen in Sawhney's song 'Immigrant' (1999): "*Will you take me there, to a distant place I've never been before, I could leave this world, I could follow you like oceans to the shore.*" Meanwhile, collaborations with Paul McCartney, Norah Jones, and Nusrat Fateh Ali Khan helped Nitin Sawhney to build bridges to the western mainstream.

Besides musical characteristics that evoke and resonate with the personal (real and/or imagined) experiences of World Music consumers, it is also important to consider the ways in which World Music artists might actively promote themselves in the twenty-first century. In previous decades, it was a common premise that a World Music artist would need to rely solely on a record label for promotion and marketing. However this is no longer the case:

> The major recording corporations no longer are considered the only site of agency in the global circulation of musical style. A number of analyses stress the importance of state, civic, and other institutional sponsors of World Music scenes, radio and television broadcasting, small independent record labels, academic ethnomusicology programs, civic arts exchanges, and concert-promoting organizations (Stokes 2004: 50).

Nowadays World Music artists have the freedom and ability to control how their music is promoted and circulated, often under the management of independent record labels. Nitin Sawhney has released material under the independent Pinnacle Records, and he manages to promote his music via a wide range of platforms, from advertisement, film, television, theater, and even public lectures for Ted Talks, thereby utilizing the promotional possibilities of cross-media marketing. World Music artists also have opportunities to utilize creative and modern promotional platforms to expose themselves to the global audience. Indeed, due to globalization and the development of streaming services, such as YouTube and SoundCloud, people are now listening to more music than ever before. While there is a whole new population of artists gaining exposure through the internet, it is also proving far easier for World Music artists to push their careers online. An online profile to promote a World Music artist is of huge importance, given that streaming services are able to share music and information around the world at the click of a button, making for an easily reachable audience.

The Virtuosic World Music Genius
The above examples illustrate the role played by the constructed concept of authenticity in World Music, which often determines whether a musician or group achieves success and becomes a "star" in the western World Music or (even) mainstream pop music industry. The western star system is clearly rooted economically and based on the current oligopolization of the music industry, in which a selected number of artists generate the majority of revenue. In this system, "stars" are often musicians, whose past sales are taken into account to guarantee the success of future deals (Frith *et al.* 2001: 35). They are products of the market, yet at the same time also possess unique, distinctive talents, personalities, or musical characteristics. The musical career of Nusrath Fateh Ali Khan serves as another example of the formation of a World Music star and his introduction in western culture. Nusrath Fateh Ali Khan was a famous Pakistani singer known for his aptitudes in traditional *qawwali* music, a devotional, religious musical genre from the Indian subcontinent that shares characteristics with classical music of Pakistan. The term itself applies to both the genre and experience of its performance, to which Qureshi (1986)

refers as "the devotional assembly of Islamic mysticism, or sufism" (xiii). Musically, *qawwali* acts as mystical poetry, punctuated by a powerful, ceaseless rhythm. Spiritual experiences rely on the Islamic practice of *sama*, which means "listening", especially to words considered sacred or inspired (Newell 2007: xvii). The function of the performance is ultimately to arouse euphoric, divine states of ecstasy in participants and to focus attention toward the spiritual master (God).

Despite its religious functions, Khan successfully established *qawwali* in secular, western markets, and aided in its "transformation from an 'exclusive' art form into a 'popular' form of entertainment" (Mirza 1986: 189). In the 1970s, Khan's *qawwali* music was distributed through a small record label located in Birmingham. To British Asian audiences, Khan was already an established icon and regarded as "transcend[ing] the boundaries of faith" through his performances (Cooper *et al.* 2013). His significance remained within Asian cultures until his appearance at the World of Music, Art and Dance (WOMAD) festival in 1985. Khan performed alongside the British post-punk band The Fall and the rock band New Order. This ground-breaking performance lasted for four hours, over five times the scheduled time-slot. The mass of spectators who came and remained throughout the performance inspired a revelation in Khan: western audiences were not only interested, but supportive of his music and vocal talent. Khan's success as a *qawwali* singer in both western and non-western circles is revealed in the "ritual of solo performance", which Edward Said describes as the exaggerated, extreme nature of performance (1991: 3–4). The spectacle of Khan as the solo *qawwali* vocalist (although accompanied by a group of *qawwali* singers) is coupled with his demonstration of virtuosity, which has the effect of an onslaught on the audience's senses, leaving it speechless (ibid.). Khan's performances have often been described as transcendental, by which he communicated directly with the "soul" of his listeners via their senses. Relevant here is the concept of "heroic individualism", historically realized through the emergent concept of selfhood and the idea of "genius" that emerged in the late eighteenth century with Beethoven (DeNora 1997; see also McGuigan 2016: 156), and continued with the concept of the "performing virtuoso" in the early nineteenth century with Paganini and Liszt (Samson 2003). Khan similarly epitomizes the notion of the "virtuosic genius" by the way in which he wowed his audiences via sheer vocal mastery, executive ability, superhuman technique, and endless improvisation, even though Khan's virtuosity posits a qualitatively different mode of rarified performance than was common among the extrovert virtuosi of the Romantic era, and through which Khan acquired the persona of the divine messenger of *qawwali* music.

Meanwhile, collaboration with recognized performers, such as Peter Gabriel, was key to the establishment of Khan as an authentic World Music artist, as people who appreciate and support Gabriel's musical career trust his judgments regarding new artists and genres. Gabriel has been responsible for a number of successful World Music artists, arguably due to the weight his name carries. Understandably, it can be argued that World Music artists collaborating with established western artists hold an advantage over those seeking to independently break into western markets. However such cynicism colors the integral concepts of collaborative artefacts, implying they are merely the works of marketing strategies. Yet collaboration also serves to create something richer and deeper. It allows for creative discussion and contribution, as people of varying dispositions and disciplines are brought together with a common aim. Collaboration, therefore, is no longer a strategy of the oligopoly. Rather, World Music artists also benefit from both the creative input of those they collaborate with, and the subsequent partnerships they form. Either way, collaboration remained an integral constituent to Khan's success. In 1990, Khan was approached by the Real World label's producer, Michael Brook, to work on his first collaboration album. Khan's arrangements drifted away from the traditional, incorporating westernized instrumentation such as mandolin and guitar, in order to aid in the introduction and appeal of Khan's *qawwali* music to western ears. However, the authenticity of such works can also be questioned. By altering traditional, sacred arrangements, Khan risked misinterpretation of his art as disrespectful, which is exemplified in Khan's album *Musst Musst* (1990). Khan's extensive improvisation during recording sessions, which lasted as long as half an hour, problematized the editing process. Since Brook did not fully understand the sanctity of Khan's lyrics, the tracks were amended, modified, and shortened in order to aurally please westerners. The result, however, was an album consisting of lyrically incoherent songs. The fundamental, religious connotations of *qawwali* were ultimately lost. Here it can be argued that World Music is merely a celebration of multicultural art within westernized constraints, as his experimentations were seen by his Asian followers as a defilation of the sacred form of *qawwali*. Despite this, the album *Musst Musst* peaked at number fourteen on the Billboard Top Music Album charts in 1991.

Khan's success may be explained less so in terms of authenticity, given his frequent departures from the traditional aspects and characteristics of *qawwali*. While Khan sang in his native language, he seemed to possess the ability to transport (western) listeners in ways that were "liberating and glorious" through his talent alone (Hilburn 1996). At the same time, Khan's western arrangements appealed to westerners as he was still preserving a traditional or "ethnic" quality. As Khan received more attention, his popularity grew. By 1991, he was an established World Music star, collaborating and performing with artists across the globe. The repetitive, engulfing nature of Khan's *qawwali* captured the interest of the emerging UK dance scene, as the culture called for new, distinctive sounds. It reflected a trend during the 1990s in the "rise of club and dance music [which] sucked in and sometimes spat out various world musicians whose works were sampled and remixed to the thump of drum machines" (Arts Council England 2005: 10). Global dance music became a thriving sector. For instance, British trip-hop group Massive Attack, one of the most influential British groups of the 1990s, was inspired by Khan's *Musst Musst* and subsequently released a hugely successful remix of the track. The commercial success of both the remixed track and the original album inspired British Asian dance producers, such as Talvin Singh, to discover a new musical identity by implementing samples of audio taken from music of their own tradition. As a result,

> World Music (in a modified form) was now being brought to an even wider, even younger audience. And although many "traditionalists" regarded it as the worst kind of commercial "contamination" of traditional music (especially since the music was not live) the World Music touring circuit easily expanded to take in clubs and venues, such as The Shrine … created in the image of Fela Kuti's Lagos venue (Arts Council England 2005: 10).

Before his sudden death in 1997, Nusrath Fateh Ali Khan had developed from WOMAD spectacle to World Music stardom. He provides an interesting example of how experimentation and "incorporation" (Kheshti 2015) of traditional music for western tastes have a significant impact on listeners' positive reception of "difficult" music such as *qawwali*. World Music artists like Khan challenge notions of tradition, with the resultant hybridization problematizing the idea of "authentic" World Music. The World Music that western consumers are exposed to, therefore, often does not faithfully represent authentic tradition. This shows that authenticity is socioculturally constructed by musicians, producers, and audiences in unique and often highly subjective ways.

Moving between Cultures
Youssou N'Dour is a World Music star whose musical career and creative output has been subject to the authenticity debate surrounding World Music. Born on 1 October 1959 in Dakar, Senegal into a family of *griots* (his mother, Ndèye Sokhna Mboup, was a griotte).[3] N'Dour had his first success at the age of thirteen performing a song with the Dakar Star Band, the biggest Senegalese band of all, which he joined properly at the age of sixteen in 1974. Ini-

tially imitating and performing Cuban-style music, which, like other forms of copyrighted music imitated across Africa, became scorned as "foreign" (Murphy 2007: 46), the Star Band increasingly Africanized their music during the 1970s by introducing more percussion instruments, specifically the local *tama* talking drum, among other types of drums. Renamed Super Etoile de Dakar and subsequently Super Etoile, the band coined the musical term *mbalax* to describe their new blend of Afro-Caribbean music, western pop, and Wolof folk music. This music became popularized among local Africans as dance music, while the traditional, and thus authentic, stylistic and musical elements of *mbalax* are mostly reflected in the complex polyrhythms (performed by the drums) and abrupt tempo changes. This is audible in the continuous, varied repetitions and variations of basic musical units, and successive entries of new instruments or voices. These complex rhythms are marked by shifts of emphasis in bringing out new rhythmic parts and patterns.

Visually, too, we can note the "Africanized" image of Youssou N'Dour. Both the original (1988) and re-released (2006) album covers of *Immigrés* depict the singer behind an earthy background with somewhat rural connotations, wearing a traditional Islamic garment and cap, reflexive of his actual image of a "good non-smoking, non-drinking Muslim [who used to live] with his parents in the Medina quarter in Dakar" where he grew up (RFI Musique 2014). The drum is noteworthy too, instantly signaling the local African rhythms that mark the music of the album. The lyrics are pivotal too, playing into strong ideas of local identity. Singing in his local Wolof language, N'Dour's lyrics often invoke Senegalese history and culture, particularly that of his own ethnic group, the Wolof, which has been accredited to his lineage to a long line of griots. Reading the lyrics, we get a sense that N'Dour clearly views himself as a griot, as he engages in story-telling, disseminates news, helps people to understand their world, giving admonitions, and keeping watch (Taylor 1997: 130).

While N'Dour's earlier music is clearly a reflection of place and locality, and thus authenticity, N'Dour turned toward and adapted his music for an international western market in his later career, during which his music became increasingly marked by westernization to varying levels (Murphy 2007). Although marketed as World Music, his later music reflected N'Dour's desire to break into the lucrative western music mainstream of international pop in a drive for commercial success. While he was already an established popular music star in Senegal, N'Dour only became known to the West during the World Music boom in the 1980s. He secured a record deal with Virgin Records, with whom he released albums such as *The Lion* (1989) and *Set* (1990). N'Dour gained massive media exposure through his performances with stars like Sting,

Tracy Chapman, and Peter Gabriel during the Amnesty International World Tour in 1988; he had already supported Gabriel's Secret World Live Tour in the US in 1986. Their collaboration continued when Gabriel joined N'Dour on his single 'Shaking the Tree' (1990), a track from N'Dour's album *The Lion* (1989), which reflects the ways in which he westernized his music to break through to the western market, and for which Peter Gabriel acted as production adviser. This album was a hugely expensive undertaking: while *mbalax*, the Africanized musical style pioneered by N'Dour, was the main driving force, the music was combined with synthesizers and sophisticated arrangements requiring the highest tech studios. Critics saw in this album the deformation of his music, as it no longer sounded like an authentic, local expression of cultural identity. Yet even though N'Dour was highly popular in the World Music community in the West, his record sales remained modest, and Virgin ended the contract in April 1991.

N'Dour was subsequently offered a record deal by Sony, who released the single 'Seven Seconds', a duet with Neneh Cherry. The song is an atmospheric and international pop tune. It features no particularly African sound in that it is devoid of the musical trademarks of Senegalese *mbalax*, even though N'Dour sings parts of the lyrics in the Wolof language. The song was a commercial hit worldwide (with 1.5 million copies sold), through which N'Dour became known to the western general public and those who would usually be more attracted to British and American music. The song reflects how music becomes altered in style beyond recognition and devoid of any local and national distinctiveness. It enabled N'Dour to break through on the international scene, which benefited his subsequent album *The Guide [Wommat]* (1994), as it quickly entered the European charts and markets outside of Africa. Besides a cover song of Bob Dylan songs 'Chimes of Freedom', and 'Undecided', a single that was remixed by the French duo Deep Forest, the music generally adopts the conventions of international rock. Meanwhile, his 2000 album entitled *Joko: From Village to Town* similarly aimed at the international market, featuring contributions from guest stars including Peter Gabriel and Sting. In this album, N'Dour makes the most significant alterations to his music in a continued attempt to break into the western mainstream music market. The album moves away from pure African sounds to experiment with international pop, so that instead of abrupt tempo changes, polyrhythms, and N'Dour's unusually piercing vocals, the music is heavily produced and based on steady, regular rhythms, synthesizers, and toned-down vocals. For instance, in 'New Africa', the final track of the album, the sound is heavily produced, maintains a slow tempo throughout, and utilizes synthesizers to accompany the vocals. The album cover art for *Joko: From Village to*

Town (2000) is noteworthy too: Behind a grey background, which is set off by modern graphic effects in red tones, the cover depicts a close-up, frontal shot of the musician's face that stares directly at us, giving a feeling of confrontation and assertiveness. N'Dour's face is somewhat whitened, playing down his "blackness" and reflecting a more artificial (instead of natural) light. The musician's assertive facial expression, together with the use of colors and lighting, evoke a sense that N'Dour is a "modern" musician. Visually, it reflects the influences of urbanism and modernity that characterize the music on this album. Youssou N'Dour provides a fascinating example of the ways in which musicians often willingly alter their style, even beyond recognition, so that it bears little resemblance to the music available in their own cultural contexts. Indeed, N'Dour sought to translate his music for the West so as to break into the lucrative music mainstream of international pop, leading him to produce a completely different style of music that is genuinely not the same as the music listened to in his African home country (Murphy 2007: 55). It is the expression of a modern, commercial sensibility that incorporates western musical elements to form something new. In other words, commercialized popular music that is produced as a result of desire for commercial success is not necessarily the popular music heard in the country in which it originated. Here, we tend to find a different popular music, as traditional culture, religion, and lifestyle continue to play an important part in people's lives.

Even so, however, N'Dour's westernized music has been regarded as reflecting a kind of resistance to the homogenizing forces of globalization by addressing more local concerns. For instance, the song 'Leaving [Dem]' on the album *The Guide [Wommat]* (1994), while reflecting a contemporary western rock aesthetic, addresses issues surrounding the dichotomy between modernity and tradition:

> Rather than becoming modern and moving ... from the country to the city, N'Dour instead tells us of wanting to move the other direction: he has had enough of modernity, thank you very much. He is interested in cultivating older ways of interaction, through one's friends and family, rather than the faceless, impersonal postcolonial city (Taylor 1997: 128–29).

Themes of modernization and colonialism/post-colonialism characterize much of N'Dour's later music. Meanwhile, David Murphy (2007) shows that alongside the music marketed to consumers and audiences in the West, N'Dour also maintained different repertoires aimed at Africans in local markets. For instance, the track 'New Africa' on the album *Joko: From Village to Town* (2000) also appeared on a cassette titled *Diapason Plus [Extra Groove]*, a live album released for the African markets, yet here the track is rendered as a different version, and

> at the point where the Western version ends, the Senegalese version bursts into an explosion of polyrhythms as N'Dour continues to invoke the names of great African figures but in a joyous and exuberant celebration of Senegalese dance music... [Thus,] the Afropop we hear in the West is not necessarily the popular music of Africa. In Senegal, 'New Africa' is a very popular dance track that conveys a sense of exuberance, of Senegalese, and more generally African, self-confidence, while in the West it is transformed into a middle of the road, new age evocation of Africa, in which cultural difference is safely packaged for Western consumption (Murphy 2007: 55).

While N'Dour was keen to achieve a global, increasingly homogenized, soft rock style aimed at western audiences, he was also prone to maintaining a local Afropop music that resonated with the experiences, beliefs, and concepts of the Senegalese people. Murphy stresses the problematic nature of thinking along binary oppositions that divide between modernity and tradition, assuming that "modern" western music is commercial, homogenized music, while "traditional" African music is "authentic", local music. Instead, he reminds us that the different kinds of repertoires, the local music aimed at Senegalese audiences and the global music aimed at the international western market, are *both* reflexive of a dynamic, hybrid, urban Senegalese culture:

> I wouldn't want to define myself. But there are two ways I see myself. One is to appeal to my African audience and the second is to leave myself open to other influences and other cultures (Youssou N'Dour, quoted in Taylor 1997: 136).

The rise of the commercial category of World Music in the West epitomizes the development of globalization and, with it, debates on commodification, power, and identity. Situated in multiple cultural and economic networks, some World Music artists reinvent and revive traditions; others stir national political consciousness or contribute to political movements, while many seek to achieve commercial success. As a product of globalization, World Music is a contemporary cultural expression entangled in both hybridity and authenticity. As a commercial product, World Music is a powerful illustration of the complex ways that the global and the local are articulated, manipulated, contested, and constructed. Meanwhile, some World Music has acquired a sense of "coolness" in neoliberal culture, a word that is ubiquitously used presently around the world. Coolness is a sensibility now widely embedded and at the very heart of mainstream (world) popular culture under neoliberal capitalism.

Notes

1. Authenticity of positionality "refers to expectations that musicians be downtrodden or from a poor or dangerous part of the world" (Taylor 2016: 90).
2. Authenticity of primality refers to "Western expectations that non-Western musicians were closer to nature, to the earth, than modern Western musicians" (Taylor 2016: 91).
3. For detailed discussions on the activities of Wolof griots in Senegal, see Panzacchi (1994).

4 The Cool Culture of Neoliberal Capitalism

In the age of neoliberal capitalism, the ideology of cool determines cultural production and consumption. The concept of cool has become a focal point of world popular culture, and is widely acknowledged as a global phenomenon, influencing a diverse range of contemporary trends and fields from food, music, and fashion to technology and cinema (Belk *et al.* 2010: 186; McGuigan 2012). The ideology of cool marks the logic of neoliberal capitalism. Tim Taylor asserts:

> I would now go so far as to put it this way: What is the cultural logic of neoliberal capitalism? It is the hip and the cool. That is, knowledge of the hip and the cool is the source of cultural capital today; and what drives the cultural industries is the production of the hip and the cool. In terms of cultural production, workers frequently use the term "edgy" to describe the sort of work that they want to produce, which, it is hoped, will be thought of as hip or cool by consumers ... To repeat ...: I regard the hip/cool/edgy as the cultural logic of neoliberal capitalism (or one cultural logic of neoliberal capitalism, certainly the hegemonic one) (Taylor 2014: 195, 197).

Coolness today is pursued through consumption, and it is a key motivator for teens, youth, and young urban professionals, the "culturati taste leaders" (McGuigan 2016: 37), who represent the largest consumer group of popular culture. Coolness is hugely important and influential for marketers, who engage in the relentless market research practice of coolhunting (Goodman 2001; McGuigan 2009: 110). The driver of producerly consumption is the ideology of the hip and the cool. This marks a historical shift in the control of cultural capital away from social elites and toward the workers in the cultural industries and, more generally, creative industries, members of a new class, the so-called "new petite bourgeoisie" (Bourdieu 1984) or "new (technocratic) bourgeoisie" (Taylor 2016: 64). This new class includes the cultural intermediaries of advertising, journalism, marketing, public relations, and media and culture generally, whose numbers have significantly increased since the 1940s. Its members are engaged in a struggle for distinction (in the Bourdieuan sense), yet they do so by blurring the boundaries and discarding the "old" hierarchies between high art and culture and commerce and mass popular culture. They "find what is hip, cool, and edgy and ... both promulgate this ideology and employ it to sell anything" (Taylor 2016: 63). Cultural producers thereby cultivate the tastes and habits of consumers in order to dictate supply. McGuigan speaks of "cool seduction" in consumer culture to describe the cool rhetoric of advertising today, not dissimilar to Marxian commodity fetishism. Coolness is thus applicable to the sphere of cultural production and communication of meaning in cultural artefacts, and is often articulated in the language of creativity and artistry to the point that "human creativity is squeezed by economic considerations" (McGuigan 2016: 40). As a way to enhance coolness, the advertising industry has cultivated the idea of agency in the consumption of lifestyle and fashion, evident in the appropriation and revitalization of various consumer materials by members of subcultures "for their own negotiated, very public presentations of meaning [and] the very public display of the self" (Marshall 2016: 82). And it is not only cultural commodities produced by the cultural and creative industries (advertising, fashion, film, television, and so on), but the commodities of other industries too that are increasingly culturalized, whereby all sorts of goods become desirable and consumed for their perceived coolness.

The Origins of Cool

The word "cool" comes from the West African *itutu* ("mystic coolness") to describe composure in battle and emotional control in public community rituals of music and dance. In dynamic expressive performances, cool is a kind of spiritual calm and force of community, enacted, for example, by the master drummer (Dinerstein 2017: 53–55). While the continuity of West African retentions in the musical cultures of the Mississippi Delta and New Orleans is untraceable, literatures nonetheless suggest that West African cool spread with slavery to the US, where its quality persists until today within the jazz tradition (Dinerstein 2017: 57) and shaped a culture of disaffection in response to discrimination that emerged at the margins of US culture. Coolness was characterized by rebellion through "sullen detachment from and contempt for the conformist mainstream" (McGuigan 2016: 76). The cool person, although perpetually alienated, adopts a balancing strategy of submission combined with subversion. Coolness is a social term directly related to youth and the now that refers to an ironic stance, aloofness, insider knowledge. Coolness also points toward a certain generational tension as a distinct feature of the neoliberal imaginary in a manner that makes sense to peculiarly individualized young people, including the rejection of "dinosaur attitudes" apparently held by older generations. Cool is "good", but uncool is not. Coolness is a set of shared meanings, including self-presentation, language, values, and artistic expressions, all of which represent group membership (O'Donnell and Wardlow 2000: 13). Coolness derives from imitation of other cool people, and from conforming to behaviours within a particular subculture (Warren and Campbell 2014: 543). Coolness is a combination of three character traits: narcissism, ironic detachment, and hedonism (Pountain and Robins 2000: 5). Yet, given the concept is inherently fluid across time, places, and cultures, and therefore culturally defined and continually changing, coolness is problematic to define as a coherent concept (Ferguson 2011: 267).

In its evolved form, coolness is intrinsically American. Its evolution as a cultural phenomenon was shaped in the first decades of the twentieth century, which were marked by profound changes in the social contours of American life, notably by young people, African Americans and women, and visible in the emergence of Hollywood, modernist literature and art, youth entertainments, jazz, new technologies (radio, film, and the automobile), and the increasing diversity in America's booming cities. The concept of cool converged African-American (the American working-class male) and Anglo-American (the Victorian gentleman) archetypal modes of masculine behavior, but increasingly shifted to the heroic ideal of the slightly aloof rogue figure of the untameable, self-sufficient male "tough loner" (Dinerstein 2017: 8–9, 53). Coolness became a personal stance associated with dignity in oppressive circumstances, which can be located in popular music and literature in the 1920s, particularly black American jazz culture and later, especially during the mid-twentieth century, also in white jazz circles:

> As Ted Giola has noted, the trumpeter Miles Davis, nicknamed "the Prince of Darkness", epitomised cool with his abrasive attitude towards the audience, particularly the white audience, and his generally detached and even foreboding presence on stage. The 1954 release of the long-playing record *Birth of the Cool* was pivotal to the spread of studied disaffection amongst hipsters, both black and white (McGuigan 2016: 36).

Through music, style, slang, humor, and physical gesture, the jazz musician, "global culture's first non-white rebel", was the emblematic cool existential figure in post-war US cities, practicing cool for survival "through rituals of self-affirmation" and "public assertion of the self-in-resistance" (Dinerstein 2017: 12). Cool jazz was a black response to the need for black entertainers to mask their feelings and smile in front of whites ("the grinning black mask" [ibid.: 42] or "Tomming" [ibid.: 44]), for example in blackface minstrelsy in the 1870s. Jazz saxophonist Lester "Pres" Young disseminated the word and concept of cool into jazz culture in the early 1940s. He was the first to use the saying "I'm cool" as an expression of "being relaxed and under control, and in his own style" (Dinerstein 2017: 19), while rejecting "Tomming" as a means of accommodation to a white social order and as a symbol of black male limitation. Young's cool self-expression extended to the strategic use of sunglasses (he was the first jazz musician to wear shades on stage), recognizing "the use of shades as a mask to deflect the gaze of others without causing conflict and to create an air of mystery" (Dinerstein 2017: 50). Indeed, wearing sunglasses turns a person into a "cool medium", creating a sense of visual mystery in the observer (McLuhan 1964: 53). Sunglasses convey transformative iconic power, when considering "Schwarzenegger donning shades as the Terminator, Clint Eastwood's Dirty Harry specs, Corey Hart's ode to wearing 'Sunglasses At Night' or Bob Dylan's ever-present Wayfarers" (Jackson et al. 2013: 111). In jazz, specifically,

> sunglasses became a key element of the stylistic rebellion of black jazz musicians in the postwar era; in effect, wearing sunglasses at night was the primary symbol of the cool mask (Dinerstein 2017: 50).

Coolness as black self-expression and self-presentation in response to the white gaze of superiority quickly spread to other cultural expressions like film noir, Beat literature, and abstract expressionism as a "rebel masculine sensibility", and by the 1950s, cool came to represent cultural resistance to all authority. During the 1960s and 70s, cool became the key ingredient to a surging underground, counterculture aesthetic in rock 'n' roll, journalism, film, and African American culture, marked by antiauthoritarianism and openness to new ideas (Smithsonian 2014a). While youth culture increasingly embraced the pursuit of wealth, coolness has since the 1980s entered the mainstream and is no longer associated exclusively with black culture, disaffection, and resistance, although African American culture remained central to its growth. Rebellion became co-opted and sold as an integral aspect of the cool aesthetic, from highbrow fashion to mass-culture video games, from hip hop to grunge, from skateboarding to the internet, from street graffiti to MTV. Young black men responded to the appropriation of cool by the dominant white society by recasting it as "chill" and "chillin'" in the early 1980s. Many cool figures from the past ("Astaire and Rogers in the '30s, Brando and Elvis in the '50s, Dylan and Hendrix in the '60s, Madonna and Prince in the '80s" [Dinerstein 2017: 15]) shaped the new music icons of cool around the world, enabled by global communication and markets. Cool spread worldwide through the global impact of musical practices and tastes in jazz, blues, gospel, swing, soul, R&B, and rock 'n' roll, along with the style and slang, and the physical gestures and kinesthetics that informed each genre. Representatives of the legacies of cool include Bessie Smith, Miles Davis, Billie Holiday, Frank Sinatra, Muddy Waters, Elvis Presley, James Brown, Bob Dylan, Jimi Hendrix, Deborah Harry, Marvin Gaye, Chrissie Hynde, David Byrne, Madonna, Prince, Afrika Bambaataa, Kurt Cobain, Selena, Shawn Carter (Jay-Z), Johnny Cash, and others (Dinerstein 2017: 15; Smithsonian 2014b). Coolness became America's chief cultural export. In the new capitalist context, coolness is often scorned for its pretentious style, superficial rebellion, and faddish consumerism (Dinerstein 2017: 21). Even so, contemporary usage has been shaped by four core African-American cool concepts from the postwar era:

> Cool the first: to control your emotions and wear a mask of cool in the face of hostile, provocative outside forces. Cool the second: to maintain a relaxed attitude in performance of any kind. Cool the third: to develop a unique, individual style (and sound) that communicates your personality or inner spirit. Cool the fourth: to be emotionally expressive within an artistic frame of restraint, as in jazz, acting, or basketball. *Cool* is also the term used to express aesthetic approval of such performance ("Cool!") (Dinerstein 2017: 39).

Neoliberal Capitalism as Cool Capitalism

In his *cool capitalism* thesis, Jim McGuigan (2012, 2016) asserts that coolness is more than a mere discursive practice and affective code. It is also a social practice and connected to working life under neoliberal conditions. Cool capitalism means neoliberal capitalism across the globe. Neoliberal capitalism is cool capitalism, while its legitimacy reaches into people's everyday life. The most tangible manifestation of cool capitalism to most people is in consumer culture and representations of cool commodities. Promotional culture is thereby marked by cool seduction and acutely brand-aware commodity fetishism. As a global phenomenon and feature of Americanization, cool capitalism incorporates the signs and symbols of disaffection into capitalism itself. In the neoliberalized art world, for instance, artists like Damien Hirst are celebrated by art critics for his apparent subversive and controversial aesthetic. Mass popular culture similarly incorporates signs and dispositions of disaffection and dissent, yet in doing so renders them somewhat neutral in their subversive intent. Fashion companies like Nike and Gap, as well as Steve Jobs' Apple, for instance, have drawn on counter-cultural themes and symbols to sell their rebel products. These corporations are prime examples of postmodern consumer capitalism:

> Nike in casual wear and Apple in communication technology ... are especially pertinent examples of the culture and political economy of transnational capitalism today, since both have cultivated counter-cultural and rebel brand identities. Such "cool" identities might at one time have been connected to anti-capitalism, but that is no longer so. These rich and powerful corporations are the epitome of cool capitalism (McGuigan 2016: 58–59).

More recently, Nike has branched into a new market by developing a performance *hijab* aimed at Muslim women athletes (Kleinschmidt 2017), a move that is regarded by many Muslim women as the co-option or selling out of this Muslim feminist symbol.[1] Disaffection, such as left-wing radicalism or Muslim feminism, becomes fused with commercial culture, fashion, and celebrity obsession, which effectively contributes to the neutralization of critical opposition to neoliberal political economy. Consequently, coolness is projected as a "façade" to contemporary neoliberal culture that incorporates dissent and distracts actual attention away from "dirty secrets" (like garment manufacture by children for very little pay and under dreadful conditions) (McGuigan 2016: 4). The cool façade is made up of seductive symbols and experiences of everyday life and absorbs ostensibly rebellious or non-conformist sentiments. It masks and cools anger and disaffection at the deeply exploitative capitalist system. Yet in doing so, dissent or disaffection are, in effect, neutralized.

In much popular culture, coolness has been indirectly or directly related to black culture and historically been associated with masculinity, yet it is not exclusively so today. In the global music business, coolness is often ascribed to masculinity and postfeminism. Popular music styles like hip hop, rock, heavy metal, and glam rock exemplify rebellious coolness, as these play on notions of cool hyper-masculinity and queering, thereby incorporating dissent and disaffection toward cultural hegemony. Postfeminist artists like Britney Spears, Beyoncé, and Lady Gaga have acquired the status of cool through the absorption of feminist ideals into mainstream popular culture. Yet for females, coolness is usually based around their visual appearance. For males, what they do and say conveys coolness. Meanwhile, World Music, the soundtrack to neoliberal capitalism, can sometimes signify the hip and the cool, specifically through branding processes that conjure imaginations surrounding authenticity and identity in the consumers of World Music. In short,

> [E]ven now, with the idea of cool long since commodified and diffused into the vernacular, so to say "he's cool" or "she's cool" still carries a social charge of charisma, style, and integrity, of having developed an edge to walk that is all one's own. It remains an honorific redolent with populist admiration (Dinerstein 2017: 25).

Branding the Cool Celebrity Persona

Cool emerged as a distinct form of American musical expression. Cool spread globally with evolving technologies and markets, and the word "cool" has been introduced into many languages across the world. Today, its aesthetic is most often used in advertising cool, trendy commodities, and promoting urban lifestyles and contemporary self-fashioning. Central to the ideology of cool is branding, which today determines and confers value. Branding plays a critical, if not central, role for all commodities today in a globalized, highly mediated, and neoliberal capitalist economy (Klein 2010). The successful global firm "concentrates on the sole task of developing brand images ... just to associate brand names with attractive images, concepts, celebrity figures" (Crouch 2004: 37). This is made possible by the globalized structure of the global firm that out-sources and sub-contracts more or less every ancillary activity, except the capacity of a strategic headquarters to make financial decisions, and which "manages the brand, but has very little to do with actual production" (ibid.). In doing so, branding has become a central concept in neoliberalism. A brand seeks to create "an emotional connection to a product, giving it a real personality, almost so that it becomes a valued and trusted friend ['brand personality'], something known and understood" (Taylor 2014: 196) and is "another way of putting something in its place, making it knowable and accessible to potential consumers and creating an emotional connection to it" (Taylor 2016: 93).

Information technology is of great assistance to the global firm in running its complex organization and managing the brand. Although the branding of products (physical brand) has always been present (branding originated in the late nineteenth century with the packaging of products), in neoliberal capitalism branding has become "a more intense, frequent, and dominant strategy" where every commodity is treated as a brand (Taylor 2016: 54). Today vast advertising and marketing industries revolve around what makes a brand attractive and the revenue produced by that brand. They strive to add value to products by establishing brand names and associating them with distinctive characteristics (Achacoso 2014: 9; Montoya and Vandehey 2002: 10). This evolved from simple logo designs to creating entire visual identities for companies or products that portray their style and brand personality to the public. Branding is a way to create value in non-economic terms, while also having significant economic implications so that a brand competes better in a crowded marketplace. The goal is to create a "brand personality" and infuse a product with human characteristics, so that consumers connect emotionally and create lifelong relationships based on love, trust, and belief. It is believed to help consumers to navigate the crowded marketplace, and to identify with the brand by appealing to the senses of touch, taste, hearing, smell, and seeing through its distinct imagery, language, and associations.

Branding around personalities has become increasingly popular over the past twenty years and has developed into a dominant concept within marketing. Creating brands around personalities, that is, human brands or "productized celebrity person-brands", specifically, is highly lucrative in today's media-saturated society (Fournier 2010: 38). Personal brands instantly communicate simple and clear feelings about a product, and underpin important concepts like market positioning, consumer experience, and management of performance. Personal branding is intrinsically linked to our fascination with people, since consumers are most likely to relate to human brands. Personal brands have the effect that consumers seemingly build relationships with celebrities and therefore feel they are not purchasing from a complete stranger, but rather a familiar face (Vesey 2015: 1002). Brand persona familiarity is thus important: for consumers to connect with an artist is key in creating "familiarity in an unfamiliar world" (Montoya and Vandehey 2002: 4), an essential factor of branding and the reason why it is so powerful.

Music Branding
In their marketing book, *Hit Brands*, Daniel Jackson, Richard Jankovich, and Eric Sheinkop (2013) show how to establish music as part of a brand's marketing and communication. The argument is based on the idea that there exists a direct link between music and a brand's income. Music is a social currency today: in 2012, the top most followed and watched people on Twitter, YouTube, or Facebook were music artists. Music creates positive emotional states in humans, providing both cognitive and social benefits, and this seems to be the case globally. Music also fulfill's a fan's desire to be seen as cool (Jackson et al. 2013: 146). The economic value of creating an association/connection between a brand and a hit song has been well-known to marketers and advertising agencies since the dawn of recorded music. The earliest use of music to sell products was in the early twentieth century through jingles, which became an effective marketing tool and started a lasting trend in advertising. The most impactful jingle hit was Coca Cola's 'I Want to Buy the World a Coke' in 1971, which was personally meaningful to customers and became a worldwide phenomenon. Music has also been used in retail and corporate environments, which have been literally "filled" with music and sounds to soothe consumers (muzak elevator music), to motivate consumers (McDonalds), or to engage consumers (T in the Park music festival), and every major retail or hospitality brand uses music today as a central component of the consumer experience. From the 1960s until 1980s, music also became increasingly appropriated in

advertising, first using popular hits and gradually licensing less well-known music. A dramatic milestone in this regard was Moby's *Play* (1999), with all eighteen songs being licensed for use in commercials, television shows, films, or video games, many prior to the album release (Jackson *et al.* 2013: 27). The album became the top-selling electronica album of all time, which shows the way that commercials have become the new promotional channel for artists and their music. A brand, through its indirect role as a distributor of music, is thereby a serious force for breaking new music. The 1980s also saw the rise of the tour sponsorship industry, with the Rolling Stones' tour sponsorship agreement with Jovan Musk in 1981 being one of the first prominent examples. By the mid-1980s, marketing and music tie-ins had become the norm.

Brands are aware that music is a powerful way to engage their audience. Known as music branding, brands use music and sound as a tool in their marketing and communications to make emotional connections with an audience and help them develop an affinity to the brand. Disney developed one of the most successful unifying music strategies to use music as part of its corporate identity, ranging from physical spaces to social and emotional connections to the brand. One strategy of music branding is to create a unique sonic logo like "La Figura NESCAFÉ" to ensure the consistency in a brand's sonic heritage (Jackson *et al.* 2013: 48–52). Brands also need music, particularly "hits", in order to create "value" between brand, customers, musicians, and agencies. Brands invest millions of dollars in sound and music across their entire marketing and communication platforms in order to associate themselves with music and stars. In order to harness the power of music for their brands, big brand businesses like Diagaeo or P&G have begun to employ heads of music, or, like Converse, have launched their own recording studio, Converse Rubber Track (Jackson *et al.* 2013: 165–75). Meanwhile, advertising agency networks (like the Big Five Omnicom, WPP, Publicis, IPG, and Havas) have developed network music offerings. The aim is to embed their sonic brand logo into a pop song, as in the case of Coca Cola and K'naan's 'Wavin' Flag'. Today, music branding includes online website soundtracks, brand-promoted live events, artist partnership/sponsorship relations, content offerings (compilation CDs, free downloads, free streaming), chyrons on ads, and more.

With the demise of physical sales of recorded music due to digital downloads, the music industry has slowly shifted its focus (besides live concert and radio plugging strategies) toward building capability to advise brands, and to license their music and artists so as to bring value to brands. Indeed, the evolution of new technologies, companies, and business models, notably Napster, since the start of the twenty-first century, has resulted in a significant disruption in the music industry, which in its Golden Age enjoyed decades of supremacy and controlled the music market in its entirety to the point that it was near-impossible for new artists to have their music heard without being signed and owned by a label: "record labels offered artists a road to stardom paved with gold ... and groupies" (Jackson *et al.* 2013: 123). The arrival of the internet brought an end to the physical music product, and record labels lost their control over music creation, marketing and promotion, and distribution. The music industry was slow to adapt, first attempting to fight the disruption via legal attacks against the new technology companies and their digital consumers, and gradually developing means to reconfigure their product in the new online business model, with iTunes being the solution, a trend also mirrored in the advertising industry with its move toward digital platforms for promotion and marketing.

Today the global music industry, in its traditional role as record label, has lost a significant degree of relevance in the music landscape. This has triggered a critical paradigm shift in the working relationship between brands, music, and advertising. Licensing music to brands has become a steady and important line of income for the music industry, which explains the huge interest today in how big music labels can get involved with brands. Similarly, the advertising industry has in turn looked toward music to beat back the detrimental effect of new technologies and to harness the emotion-evoking power of music to create distinctive and real connections between brands and their consumers (Jackson *et al.* 2013: 139). Since the early 1990s, the music and advertising industries have begun to work together and have partnered their roster of hit artists with big brands. The economic benefit is three-directional—brand, music company, advertising agency—while music offers brands and advertisers a way to stay relevant and fresh with their target audience: "With that, music and brands went from casually dating to married with three kids—and we see the offspring of this marriage every day" (ibid.: 140). Consequently, the music industry has evolved into the B2B2C (Business to Business to Consumers) music industry (ibid.: 12). Apple, a technology hardware manufacturer, is often regarded as the ultimate example of how a brand harnessed music's potential through its iTunes music download service and iPhone to create value for its brand via emotional connections between its products and consumers. Consequently, brands have become the curators, developers, and providers of new music to the point that "consumers now consistently ... look to them [brands] for what's hot [and] to achieve the level of cool and social inclusion they aspire to, and include them in the brand's new, hip music community" (ibid.: 148–49).

Brands are the curators of cool today, which they aspire to fulfil by looking to the global music industry. This paradigm shift is the reason why musicians and artists today are affected by branding processes and brand management, and are frequently discussed as brands. Consequently, "the ideology, discourse, and language of branding now powerfully shape considerations of musicians' sound and image" (Taylor 2016: 55). Since the introduction of promotional videos in the 1970s and the emergence of MTV in the 1980s, there have been huge changes in the way popular music is experienced and sold (Goodwin 1992: 195; Railton and Watson 2005: 52), which has opened the opportunity for cross-capitalization through various media avenues (Fournier 2010: 39; Lieb 2013: 107). In short, music marketing combines the marketing of goods with brand personality concepts: a music brand is a construct of human agency or brand performance delivered by the artist, conscious brand building efforts, such as advertising, and prior product experience, including the artist's reputation and past service delivery (Dann and Jensen 2014: 1639). Popular music is considered as one of the most portable and affect-laden cultural products, therefore corporate interest in the role of brand building is generally based around enhancing emotion-based qualities to convert them into surplus value. The branding potential for artists ties in with celebrity culture and celebrity as "consumer role model", which first emerged in the US during the 1920s and 1930s (Meier 2011: 399). The image associated with a celebrity is transferred onto the brands he or she endorses, which is then interpreted by consumers through consumption (Borucka 2013: 196). The "celebrity persona" conjures up several qualities from the fictional world to the everyday, a seriality that is very much connected to neoliberal patterns of entertainment (Marshall 2016: 48). This seriality produces a structure of familiarity for the audience (a kind of typecasting) and a structure of performance for the artist, of which Eminem is a good example:

> Eminem is a stage name for a person sometimes called Marshall Mathers; but Eminem takes this a step further and produces beyond a character in its integration of the personal—a real *personage*, Slim Shady, to inhabit his music and its stories. To further complexify this construction, Eminem relies on the production of his stories with elements that appear to be from his everyday life ... His characterizations, because of the emotional depth he inhabits through his rapped stories, betray a connection to his own psychological state. Following in the history of popular music performance where the singer-songwriter's work is seen by all to present a version of the public self that is closer emotionally to the private self, we once again see how the seriality of performance begins to produce a blended public persona. Rap music has inherited this seriality of produced identity from twentieth-century icons of the singer-songwriter and its display of the public-private-self—in reverse order, from grunge to punk, from folk to blues (Marshall 2016: 62).

Considering this alongside brand extension, artist brand endorsement is an important way of enhancing an artist's narrative and image, with notable examples including Madonna and Louis Vuitton and Dolce & Gabbana, Jay-Z and Duracell, Nicki Minaj and Pepsi, Jennifer Lopez and L'Oreal, Justin Timberlake and Givenchy, and more. Brand endorsement has grown out of the Hollywood star system since the twentieth century, which models the ways that movie actors, singers, musicians, and sports people are recruited today on the basis of their celebrity status for the endorsement of consumer products (McGuigan 2009: 92). "Posh" Spice, for example, has featured regularly as a fashion icon in various celebrity magazines like *Heat*, *Hello* and *OK!* Artists' behaviours, image, and presentation in- and outside the musical sphere are therefore carefully managed in order to "protect" their overall image. Branding power therefore works for or against artists. An example is the steep decline in sales for Justin Bieber's fragrance when his "poor behavior" was reported in the media, which weakened his fans' emotional attachment. Celebrity brand ambassadors are an integral part of the brand itself.

The combination of "successful pop record" and "media image" has had the effect that some top-selling artists have established a strong sense of persona—a brand for marketing and promotion, for which lifestyle and fashion are the underlying principles. Many musicians today are co-branded by partnering their brand persona with another brand to achieve reach. Thus, besides press attention, artists actively seek out new distribution channels for both their music and brand persona, adopting almost the stance of "mini-conglomerate" in themselves marked by synergy and cross-media marketing. Hip hop rapper Jay-Z provides an example of a successful cross-media brand. Having set up his own sub-business Roc-Nation (part-funded and owned by Live-Nation), which creates revenues from music sales, artist management, and touring, Jay-Z also branched into the service industry by co-founding a chain of sports bars and night clubs called the 40/40 Club, while Roca-wear clothing lines, coupled with his own line of footwear for Reebok and transnational advertising campaigns, such as his deal with Coca Cola, further strengthen his worldwide fan base. In 2013, Jay-Z partnered with Samsung for the release of his album *Magna Carta Holy Grail*, who bought one million albums to entice Samsung users to download an app in return for a free copy of the album.

Another successful example of a branded artist is boy band One Direction whose extensive use of social media is unprecedented. Indeed, "social media has become the new radio; it's never broken an act globally like this before" (Needham 2012). Facebook, Twitter, and other social networking sites give fans direct access to the musicians, their day-to-day thoughts, personalities, and images. This connectivity has brought fandom to new extremes, evident in the Channel Four documentary *Crazy About One Direction* (2013) which showed how fans, so-called "Directioners", usually girls aged between ten and twenty-two, use Twitter to feed their drug-addiction-like obsession with the band by sending death threats to the band's girlfriends, or by using information on Twitter to follow the band around the country. Parallels can be seen here with Beatlemania, but social networking has enabled a kind of obsessive super-fandom. Following their appearance on the 2010 series of the *X Factor* (note that they did not win the competition, indicating the insignificance of the public vote regarding who is chosen to be branded as a "global star"), One Direction were signed to SYCO, a global production joint venture between Simon Cowell and Sony Music Entertainment combining music, television, film, and digital content, and subsequently marketed for consumption. They are told what to wear and what to say on social media, and are a product of meticulous branding, as former SYCO Marketing Director Mark Hardy explains:

> The essence of the strategy was not to position One Direction as demi-Gods but as "my mate" all girls could have access to 24/7. Behind the scenes we did extensive social media training with the boys so they understood how to respond to a tweet (Ibrahim 2013).

In recent years, there has thus been a shift away from demographic-based marketing and toward a psychographic-based approach, which entails a focus on thought and vision of the audience, rather than their age and ethnicity, so that if an eighteen-year-old and thirty-year-old both like Britney Spears, it is because of the qualities she expresses, not because of the age of her fans (Lieb 2007: 10). Developing brands around musicians has allowed the music industry to recoup losses encountered due to music piracy that resulted from digitization, evident in the recent emergence of 360 ("multiple rights") deals, which grant the record companies a percentage of profits for all revenue generated by the artist, including record sales, touring, merchandising, licensing, endorsements, book publishing, and acting. This has led to even heavier branding as the focus shifts away from music and toward the artist's image. For female artists this meant that marketability is shaped by youth and beauty, which has become as important as musical ability and skill. Relevant here is the concept of "the enterprising self"—an entrepreneur of itself—that reflects a new body politics associated with healthiness and fitness, self-improvement, autonomy, and enterprise training, and which is one of the reasons why popular culture has adopted language like "beyond the sell-by date" (McGuigan 2009: 144). The primary concern is how to sell music rather than make it, whereby the customer experience is key (Gervais *et al.* 2011: 40). Signing with a music label automatically puts an artist in competition for marketing funding against other artists in the label, and this puts pressure on the artist to adhere to the label's instructions or to "play the game" in order not to be dropped (Lieb 2007: 21). Personal branding also provides the opportunity for marketers to adjust flexibly to circumstances, allowing the brand identity to be strategically changed and updated over time, although it is recognized that personal brands also have a significantly shorter life span than physical brands. So in order to stay in the spotlight, artists must evolve as the world does, and the fact that they have the ability to do so heightens branding power, as they are able to adjust styles and reflect the audience's needs. This shows that while branding is an aesthetically and visually driven concept, it is indeed dependent on cultural and contextual factors.

Through personal branding, revenue is thereby inevitably tied up in the artist's brand; this, it is argued, destroys artistic purity and authenticity. Indeed, artists who have lent their image to sell product have in the past been said to "sell out". However, the connection between music and branding has become increasingly customary due to technological, economic, and cultural changes, and it is now often seen as good business sense (Hesmondhalgh and Meier 2015: 107; Klein et al. 2016: 1). Entrepreneurship is "hip" in the contemporary music industry and enhances an artist's overall image. Jay-Z is a clear example of this. The release of celebrity-branded products often coincides with record releases, which creates additional publicity. For instance, Justin Timberlake's signing as creative director for Bud Light Premium corresponded with the release of his single 'Suit and Tie', which was included in the advert along with Timberlake himself (Kim 2013). The imagery and branding surrounding Timberlake's album emphasized luxury. By endorsing a "premium" product and sharing co-ambassadorship with Jay-Z, he was positioned as an upscale pop artist. Meanwhile, Beyoncé is another artist who has achieved enormous impact beyond the realm of pop music and entertainment. Regarded as a highly successful entrepreneur, one of Beyoncé's latest products was a sports fashion line introduced in 2016 to enhance the ultimate Beyoncé brand (Muchitsch 2016: 1). Such strategic positioning is employed by the music marketers and brand authors to leverage a specific aspect of an artist's persona. The branding of aesthetically pleasing artists through cross-media marketing exemplifies Baudrillard's theory of "simulacrum—an endless cycle of repetition and stagnation" (1994: 1), as media appearances, social or otherwise, are vital to the success of a branded artist, hence the vast amount of money spent on producing cross-media promotional packages. The pantheon of the branded artist is therefore representative of the elevation of the visual in the West.

Branding has become indispensable in today's neoliberal culture, and in the over-crowded music market branding is not only beneficial, but necessary in order to stay relevant and profitable. Music branding, in particular, illustrates the increasing blurring of the distinction between branding and entertainment, in which "hit brands" are the ultimate goal (Jackson *et al.* 2013). Yet the highly commercialized nature of branding and capitalizing on artists and their music produces "processed" music, which diminishes artistic autonomy, ownership, and involvement, and instead determines and reinforces an artist's identity. Artists rarely express themselves in a natural, organic way when artistic contents are connected to brands, since their image and identity are carefully and self-consciously calculated in order to appeal to different taste groupings identified by the music label and advertising agency (Negus 1992: 62). Being a successful artist has little to do with quality records, but rather with media manipulation and image creation with the aim to achieve audience identification. Music branding is therefore about leveraging and emphasizing different aspects of an artist's appeal, which is most often defined by gender. Visual appeal is critical, allowing an artist to remain recognizable even when the music is turned off. Particularly for female artists, marketing efforts have become more extreme in order to achieve recognition, since brands built around female artists have shorter lifespans. Consequently, the gender roles represented in the music industry have become increasingly narrow. Constructs of masculinity and femininity are based around what is deemed to be cool in order to appeal to the consumers of neoliberal cool culture.

Patriarchy and Resilience in Neoliberalism

Relevant here is the Robin James' concept of "multi-racial white supremacist patriarchy" in neoliberal culture (2015: 11), which has replaced bell hooks' white supremacist capitalist patriarchy. Given that neoliberal ideology conceives of everything in economic terms, this has changed how gender and race work. In neoliberalism, the old binary divisions that were used to regulate, objectify, and exclude have gradually been replaced by the "acceptance" of all sorts of differences, at least on the surface, in "the new, supposedly more diverse, tolerant, and progressive post-racial, post-feminist mainstream" (ibid.: 168). Femininity, blackness, queerness, disability, class, and so on, have been updated in neoliberalism's preferred mode of deregulation. Sexism and racism, at least in visible form, are inconsistent with the "neoliberal myth of postracialism and postfeminism" (ibid.: 113). Yet, in those instances where sexism and racism are visible, multi-racial white supremacist patriarchy makes this sexism and racism *look black*, which is clearly evident in much contemporary commercialized hip hop, in which specific people and populations are rendered responsible for the "backwards" and inefficient or unhealthy phenomena of sexism and racism. Early twenty-first-century globalized western race/gender/sexuality/capitalist hegemony is thereby marked by the techniques of resilience and (black) exclusion, which works as follows:

> Resilient populations who can overcome their race/class/gender/sexual/immigrant/religious/damage *in socially profitable ways* move closer to the center of white supremacist privilege, whereas less resilient, precarious populations move further and further from this center. Resilience *deregulates* the work of racialization, gendering, sexualisation, bodily normalization, and so on; it treats racialization/gendering/sexualisation/etc. like a deregulated marketplace... [Multi-racial white supremacist patriarchy] *is absolutely anti-black, anti-queer, ableist, and misogynist.* It is a strategy for producing blackness, queerness, disability, and femininity as mutually-intensifying feedback loops for precariousness (James 2015: 15, 17, original emphasis).

Neoliberal upgrades to capitalism and to ideology have impacted on contemporary world popular music, and coolness provides a useful lens through which to understand the way that contemporary pop-rock styles have been "upgraded" to integrate them more fully into contemporary neoliberalism. Cool neoliberal pop-rock music is resiliently noisy, which contemporary western pop audiences hear as music (James 2015: 43). Hip hop illustrates just one way that modernist pop music has been upgraded so that its logic and aesthetics are compatible with neoliberal norms and ideals. From the perspective of late twentieth-century mainstream American pop music aesthetics, early hip hop was literally noisy, and its disruptive noisiness resembled a powerful critique to the established WASP (white-supremacist-capitalist-patriarchy) hegemony (see the discussions about Public Enemy in Chapter 5, who framed their political critique as an attempt to "Bring the Noise"). In the twenty-first century, hip hop's sonic and racial noise is no longer a disruptive force, but a profitable feature, even though it continues to be associated with racial blackness. Yet its noisiness is no longer perceived as a disruption of mainstream tastes or hegemony, and is often directly appropriated by big business, for example in advertisements for all sorts of products. Neoliberalism thereby co-opts negation and opposition (e.g. queer negation, critical black aesthetics) and redistributes "their negative, critical force [while] putting it in the service of privileged groups" (ibid.: 56). The conquest of cool in contemporary pop-rock music represents the mainstream co-optation or gentrification of racial, gendered, etc. negativity.

Neoliberal culture also upgrades the male gaze: instead of objectifying women (being looked at), it subjectifies women (overcoming),[2] and makes looking ever more efficient and profitable (James 2015: 89). This is particularly evident in postfeminist thinking. It places agency upon women through deregulation and resilience, as women are "free" to overcome the male gaze. Women are assumed to be already damaged by patriarchy in neoliberal thinking and thus engage in performances of resilience, prepared to meet any and all challenges, including emotional and affective labor on oneself and one's corporeal schema: "Women must, for example, display their bodies as objects of *self-love* and admiration: flawed bodies and damaged psyches must be explicitly transformed into normal bodies and healthy psyches" (ibid.: 168). Traditional forms of misogyny are not resolved or fixed, but instead solicited and incited for different, non-traditional uses, which in turn reinforces and strengthens white patriarchy. Resilience is profitable for neoliberal capitalism: it "makes women marketable sexually (as femme), ethically (as 'good'), and commercially (as productive laborers)" (ibid.: 86).

Resilience is found all over contemporary pop-rock music, and white pop divas like Avril Lavigne, Kelly Clarkson, and Taylor Swift express their own brands of good-girl resilience: Lavigne's 'Girlfriend', Clarkson's 'Since U Been Gone', and Swift's 'We Are Never Ever Getting Back Together' are all about post-breakup resilience, giving a sarcastic middle-finger to the undeserving ex. Their brands of femininity are constructed around the neoliberal overcoming of pain caused by failed romantic relationships and ex-lovers (James 2015: 152). Resilience is expressed through the focus on the individual self. Taylor Swift's resilience is clearly displayed in her responses to media scrutiny and criticism, through which she manages the self. For instance, Swift's 'Shake it Off' ([1989] 2004) is a resilient way to deal with the dissection and scrutiny of her life under the media gaze (Finlay and St Guillaume 2017: 39). Resilience is thus a political, ethical, and aesthetic ideal to be achieved *individually*—through the neoliberal postfeminist self. Looking at resilient overcoming in neoliberal culture is thereby a deregulated visualization that upgrades the older "male gaze" or "controlling images" theories. Visualization is typically built on sensory overload, the aesthetic equivalent to the "shock" in Naomi Klein's "shock capitalism" (2007). The pleasure in resilient looking derives from "resiliently overcoming damage—that is, from making oneself into ... the ideal form of neoliberal human capital" (James 2015: 97–98). While artists use "shock" to different extents, shock-doctrine methods generate a surplus of aesthetic pleasure in being overwhelmed by dissonance. In neoliberal culture, dissonance and transgression then become normalized and recycled into raw materials for the neoliberal culture industries.

Resilience discourse is vividly present in contemporary world popular music, which is "performed as a spectacle for others [to] be seen and heard" (James 2015: 88), while shock-doctrine methods frequently serve artists to "turn damage (incoherence, accidents, chance occurrences) into a performative resource" (ibid.: 101). Resilience means to recycle suffering and pain inflicted by damage into learning, and visualize struggle and/or triumphant overcoming of this damage. The examples that follow reveal the racialized and gendered economy of neoliberal capitalism and its resilience narratives, which are grouped thematically under the umbrellas of cool masculinities and cool postfeminism.

Cool Masculinities

Coolness is gendered, since it is historically ascribed to masculinity rather than femininity. It is determined by "male" individualism that requires distance from the feminine and particularly from maternal notions (Fraiman 2003: 11). The concept of cool is thereby often regarded as a male phenomenon, and today it is often intrinsically linked to black popular culture (Holmes and Negra 2011: 191; Nancarrow *et al.* 2001: 313). Coolness provides a powerful explanation for the current popularity of hip hop and its huge branding potential.

Contextualizing Hip Hop Coolness
Hip hop is arguably the epitome of cool in 2016. Regarded by some as the new rock 'n' roll, rappers continue to establish themselves as cultural icons and powerful brands (Balaji 2012: 314). Hip hop's success has grown out of a combination of cool capitalism and a rebellious attitude, perhaps most directly exemplified by the phenomenon of "bling" (McGuigan 2009: 95–96). Hip hop is a prime example of "black cool" in its embrace of capitalism and, with it, the neutralization of rebellion and disaffection in black culture:

> The spectacular incorporation of rap represents the astonishing capacity of cool capitalism to repackage virtually anything for mass distribution. So even the most brutal, misogynistic and homophobic features of some strands of rap and hip-hop culture became another consumer item, to be tasted and discarded at will (McGuigan 2009: 98).

Hip hop is historically a male-dominated genre, fraught with notions of hardness and hyper-masculinity, and criticized for perpetuating negative stereotypes of young African American men who glorify violence and objectify women (Steinberg *et al.* 2010: 264). The genre's transition from a subculture to mainstream popular culture over the last thirty years has meant a constant strive to sustain a "pure" identity based on authenticity and (street) credibility, or "keeping it real". Being authentic and credible are essential to being considered cool and ultimately determine an artist's success. Authenticity and street credibility in hip hop are achieved by using "bottom-up" branding processes and establishing layers of creative intermediaries between the artist and corporate decision makers. Intermediaries, such as the record label Cash Money, founded by Birdman, an established rapper and producer, guide the creative process to ensure it meets the corporation's requirements, while recognizing regional trends, legitimizing the artist's street credibility, and ensuring authenticity. Intermediate hip hop labels themselves must therefore be deemed street credible and authentic in order for the rapper to be considered cool (Borucka 2013: 206). Cash Money represents such "big" names as Drake and Lil Wayne, who often reference the label in their songs, and yet they are usually owned by one of the Big Three who construct powerful brand extensions around a rapper's image. Brand extension into different products and services beyond hip hop is crucial to the economic success and longevity of an artist (Lieb 2007: 202). Brand extension is defined as the use of an established brand name in order to enter new product classes or categories, and the hip hop genre has the largest breeding ground for such endeavors (Borucka 2013). The emergence of 360 deals reflects this trend (Bouton 2010). For example, Lil Wayne, in collaboration with his imprint company Young Money Entertainment, which is owned by Universal, created a successful line of what many youths regard to be cool merchandise. Other successful brands in hip hop include Sean Combs (Diddy), Dana Owens (Queen Latifah), 50 Cent, and Beyoncé with her House of Deréon fashion line.

It is commonplace for rappers to mention their own brands in a song: for example, Beyoncé's husband, Jay-Z, mentioned his clothing line Rocawear extensively in the song 'All I Need', which supports brand recognition and conveys the notion that the brand is cool (Oliver and Leffel 2016: 44). In their embrace of entrepreneurship as both a practice and a masculine ideal in the first decades of the twenty-first century, "Hip Hop artists not only brag about their entrepreneurial skills in their songs, they are CEOs of multiplatform brand enterprises" (James 2015: 116), and Jay-Z often raps about his boardroom strategy. Jay-Z is now regarded as a successful businessman through the careful marketing strategies spun around his brand, but he still needs to retain his authenticity and street credibility which are integral to hip hop culture (Balaji 2012: 311). Another brand building technique is to feature artists in a range of publications, an example of which is Kendrick Lamar, whose interviews were published in various non-mainstream music blogs, as well as in large high-brow publications such as *The Guardian* (Fields 2014: 31). Large corporations thereby build a rapper's brand and gain access to wider consumption markets, while still ensuring that the rapper's authentic and, importantly, cool image is retained (Negus 1999: 490). Hip hop entrepreneurship has become a means for black masculine resilience, that is, a way for black men to overcome stereotypically black masculine pathology and to move closer/into the respectable "multi-racial white supremacist patriarchy" society (James 2015: 116).

Hip hop entrepreneurship is often framed in terms of a gendered resilience narrative, exemplified in the "war-on-drugs racialized, gendered, and class-inflected damage [as] the very basis of entrepreneurial rap success game" (James 2015: 116). Coolness is thus evoked in the language used by rappers, and music corporations encourage artists to rap what is deemed cool in wider hip hop culture—drugs, crime, sex, and violence—to enhance a rapper's black masculine brand persona, which stands in stark contrast to political or underground hip hop with its focus on inequality, racism, and urban storytelling. For instance, the term "dope" is used by hip hop artists to mean "cool", which relates to the slang for street drugs and evolved as good, cool quality hip hop practice that gets artists "high". Ice-T explicitly described this metaphor and its usage in hip hop in his song 'I'm Your Pusher' (1988). Rappers who veer from this stereotype in mainstream hip hop are a rarity, which of course contributes to the performance of a specific black masculinity. Authenticity and street credibility are often constructed by rapping about where artists are from—their locales. By referencing specific places, rappers often associate their identity with the ghetto, despite the fact that the vast majority of their audience is not from or accustomed to such communities. For example, Drake often raps about his humble beginnings, but has been heavily criticized when it emerged that he was brought up in a fairly upper-class suburb in Toronto (Roberts 2013). Being perceived as non-mainstream and untainted by commercialism are key to a rapper's perceived status, particularly within the early stages of his career and when the brand is being established. Because of this strong link between cool, hip hop, and locale, record labels make efforts for rappers to gain approval, acceptance, and street credibility within the local area prior to rolling out distribution on a global scale. They use street teams and guerrilla marketing strategies in order to create a grassroots following and keep brands on trend, which contributes to an overall edgy and cool image (Balaji 2012: 315). Members of street teams are usually teenagers or young adults, who are part of the local hip hop scene and are seeking a way into the music industry. They work in areas and underground venues that are deemed to require the most street credibility from rappers.

Another key to hip hop's success is the use of stereotypes of specific black masculinity (Bradley 2012: 57). In other words, black males are often expected to produce a particular brand of black masculinity (Belle 2014), which in turn contributes to the narrowing of masculinity. In order to be deemed cool and credible, men within hip hop must perform black hyper-masculinity, internalize exploitative representations of women, and promote patriarchy and sexism. Consequently, gender has become a particularly pivotal theme since the 1990s when hip hop from Los Angeles became more prominent, with rap lyrics seemingly promoting more violent solutions to black problems, while disseminating a gang worldview and denigrating women. Hip hop has since become more insular, sexist, misogynistic, and violent. Black men in hip hop need to be perceived as "untamed, uncivilised and unfeeling" (hooks 2004: 171). They need to express hardness through references to violence, drugs, and sex. Sex plays a frequent role in enhancing black men's coolness and appeal to audiences (Belle 2014), whereas depictions of women in hip hop are limited to being accessories and sexual servants in positions of objectification (Aubrey and Frisby 2011: 478; Ralph 2006: 71). Women's provocative clothing and submissive dance styles serve to enhance the coolness of the male rapper. This racialized hyper-masculinity is not only enacted through the subordination of women (sexism), heterosexual performance (heteronormativity), and ideals surrounding toughness, hardness, and competitiveness, but also through the marginalization of gay men (homophobia) (Renold 1997). Commercialized hip hop exploits specifically black women's bodies as objects of male sexual pleasure (voyeurism), and revives forms of misogyny, where black women are treated with disrespect, hatred, and disdain, and at times subjected to violence. Women are typically defined by their relationship to cool black men, which evokes a space for male exclusivity. In using sexist and misogynistic terminology, young male fans can identify with a particular black male position. Such valuations of "black" power are problematic for women of all ethnic backgrounds. It shows how race and gender are often interwoven in complex and multifaceted ways in contemporary cultural politics.

Misogynistic aspects are particularly evident in gangsta rap, where black women's bodies "have been reduced to isolated body parts and defined solely by their sexuality" (Jhally et al. 2007). For instance, in the video for 'Tip Drill' by Nelly (tip drill referring to "runnin a train on a girl", e.g. several men lining up to have sex with a woman), Nelly is seen swiping a credit card on a woman's bottom. Other hip hop videos depict black women being "showered" with bank notes by disdainful men, treating them like strippers or prostitutes. Through misogynistic displays of black women, male black rappers are represented as seeking to empower and assert themselves, and to gain social and cool status through clothing, jewellery, money, cars, drugs, and weapons. By subjugating black women in particular, male rappers are depicted as creating a sense of superiority in a "me-against-the-world" mentality. Indeed, in gangsta rap there is a connection between gangster lifestyle, gun violence and crime, drug use, misogyny, and powerlessness (economic, political, and so forth) in a white-dominated capitalist society. Implicated in these social commentaries is thus the notion that gangsta rap simply popularizes criminal lifestyles, which is often simply "dismissed by many as vulgar, profane, misogynist, racist, anti-semitic and juvenile" (Forman and Neal 2004: 357). There is a clear need for a fuller understanding of why such lifestyles are constructed and popularized by the media corporations, including the appeal of status afforded to gangster lifestyle (e.g. the God Father figure) or the commercial promise associated with exaggerated representations of urban icons such as drug dealers and pimps. Consequently, gangsta rap forms of hip hop have become the "typical soundtrack" of a racially and male-defined urban landscape, which is shared but rarely shaped by young black women, who are instead defined by an imagery of "ho's and gold-diggers, backstabbers and ballbreakers" (Reynolds and Press 1995: 298).

N.W.A.'s (Niggers with Attitude) 'Straight Outta Compton' provides a powerful example of gangsta rap's gender politics, whose lyrics portray hate, sexism, and misogyny. For instance, the title track's lyrics reflect a street mentality of individualism, as they portray no sympathy for a woman who is the victim of a shooting. As a further example, Broadus (Snoop Dog) frequently utilizes words like bitch, ho', hustler, player, and Mack-daddies. The song 'Aint No Fun (If the Homies Can't Have None)' on his debut album *Doggystyle* (1993) depicts blatant disrespect, even hatred, for women. Typical of gangsta rap videos is the depiction of women as only interested in a man to exploit him financially while she degrades and humiliates him, within a male-female relationship often devoid of any sense of romantic love. Rappers' sexist outlooks are often represented through the "bitch" character, a (black) woman who is money-hungry and shallow. The distinction between women and bitches is significant, as rappers maintain power over the definition of "woman" and the criteria to place women in either category. Women's rights, concerns, and desires are poorly, rarely, or never represented in these musical constructions. Instead, women of color are blatantly mistreated as objects and props that are barely clothed, continually gyrating, and readily available for the sexual pleasure of cool black men.

Cool masculinity in gangsta rap has certain resonances with the jazz slang "playing it cool", which was used by jazz musicians to describe an emotional mode and style of aesthetic detachment evident in cool jazz of the 1920s. Playing it cool was the direct opposite to "being a fool", which meant "to be vulnerable and open to love and warmth [and] sincere and emotionally open, wearing your heart on your sleeve, being an eager beaver" (Dinerstein 2017: 24). The cool man resembled a new style of American manhood through the coarse and vulgar working-class and gangster figure, which emerged in Hollywood film during the studio era with its depictions of violent and misogynistic masculinity. Glamorizing increasingly regressive and violent masculine ideals, American popular entertainment thereby shaped ideas surrounding American manhood as an expression of male violence, misogyny, and homophobia (Jhally *et al.* 1999). In constructing the cool masculine façade, hip hop represents the continuation of a stereotyped fantasy that has its roots and causes in "imperialist white supremacist capitalist patriarchy" (hooks 2004: 17) and continues in neoliberal "multi-racial white supremacist patriarchy" (James 2015). As bell hooks has argued, the excessive misogyny in hip hop results from executives' "racist ploys to scapegoat black men, making them seem responsible for the misogyny that is actually a central feature of white supremacy, too" (James 2015: 114). And yet neoliberal popular culture makes visible sexism and racism *look black* (i.e. white supremacy is multi-racial, including everyone except blacks) (ibid.: 113). Consequently, black rappers have been the scapegoats of white supremacist patriarchy, who are constructed and represented in hip hop as non-resilient, working-class, non-bourgeois, urban-black individuals who are usually embodied in thug stereotypes. Feminized, racialized, and socio-economically-inflected "damage" is profitable to hegemonic institutions *as damage*, which resembles an exception to the neoliberal myth of post-identity inclusion. This type of masculinity remains toxic for society, and is thus excluded:

> Whereas Modernist and Postmodern white supremacist aesthetics treat blackness ... [as] an "otherness machine", in MRWaSP [multi-racial white supremacist patriarchy], non-exceptional blackness works instead as an *affective amplifier*. Because some styles of blackness [middle-class, cisgendered, normatively hetero- or homosexual] are conditionally incorporated within MRWaSP's privileged mainstream, they don't generate "otherness" as efficiently as do newer, more exotic and unruly racial identities do [*sic*] (James 2015: 154).

Moreover, visualization in neoliberal culture racializes particularly "non-resilient" women as black, which separates out "toxic" black women from everyone else (James 2015: 103). This portrayal of hyper-masculine identities of black men and misogynistic images of black non-resilient women at the expense of perpetuating stereotypical representations of black masculinity is used by record company executives purely for financial gain. And the continued oppression/exploitation of non-bourgeois black men and non-resilient black women evidences that multi-racial white supremacy is not really post-identity (e.g. multi-racial, multi-gender, etc.) after all. Although hip hop strives for perceived authenticity and credibility, demonstrated in its bottom-up branding approach, it is ultimately controlled by record company executives who dictate the limited narratives it supports. Across hip hop, black men are thus "repeatedly portrayed as violent, drunken, misogynistic savages [which represents] some of the most racist images in media history, harkening back to D.W. Griffith's controversial 1915 film *Birth of a Nation*, which justified white supremacy by representing black men as animalistic, boorish abusers of white women" (Jhally *et al.* 2007). Consequently, coolness as a survival strategy in imperialist white supremacist capitalist patriarchy has cost the black male an enormous price:

> While it represents black identity and pride in the ghetto, such "compulsive masculinity" in that context is also seriously damaging to both women and men, not to mention the druggy lifestyle, disorganized sociality and violent criminality associated with it—which is by no means confined to working-class black males in the USA (McGuigan 2016: 36).

Other Masculinities and Cool Queering
Coolness today is not only about black American culture and is not unique to hip hop alone. It is global and colorless today. Coolness has also been hugely relevant in the success of earlier musical styles, as noted earlier, including rock and heavy metal. Indeed, there exist many similarities in the performance of a specific hyper-masculinity across these music genres, and hip hop is often regarded as the new rock 'n' roll (Balaji 2012: 314). The "conquest of cool" in rock music coincides with the cool sensibility of 1950s American mainstream, marked by "the rise of rebels without a cause", who objected to middle-class life and business (McGuigan 2016: 26). The countercultural movement of the 1960s, one of the most powerful social movements in American history, was less a push for civil rights and rather "anti-consumption in orientation, hoping to chart a path toward greater social freedoms and equality. And it was accompanied by a soundtrack ... rock and roll [that] produced bountiful profits for the record industry" (Taylor 2016: 41). Thus the counterculture and, with it, the cool pose and "creativity" caught on quickly in corporate America and elsewhere.

In the music industry, male bodies have also become objectified and eroticized, particularly male rock stars, who have been turned into cool objects of voyeurism and desire. Rock musicians often embody a rebellious, anti-establishment, even left-liberal or radical political ideology (Walser 1993: 109), alongside a carefully constructed sex symbol image, with obvious examples being Elvis Presley, Robert Plant, Jon Bon Jovi, and Michael Hutchence. A November 1967 article in *Vogue* magazine, "Love, Mysticism, and The Hippies", for instance, included a photograph of Jim Morrison, which firmly established Morrison as a cool sex symbol to women.[3] The photograph, which was shot by Alexis Waldeck in 1967, shows Morrison in an open leather jacket exposing his chest and wearing a woman's belt as a necklace. Model Donna Mitchell is to his right, her hand on his chest and leaning in to Morrison. The reaction to the photograph almost instantly transformed Morrison into a cool sex symbol. The *Village Voice*'s Howard Smith (who would interview Morrison in 1969) said, "If my antenna are right he could be the biggest thing to grab the mass libido in a very long time, I have never seen such an animalistic response from so many different kinds of women" (Cherry 2015).

Coolness in rock and heavy metal is achieved through the staging of fantasies of hyper-masculine virtuosity and control through their vocal extremes, guitar power chords, distortion, and loud bass and drums. Visually, heavy metal musicians express a kind of hyper-masculinity, as they appear as "swaggering males, leaping and strutting about the stage, clad in spandex, scarves, leather, and other visually noisy clothing, punctuating their performances with phallic thrusts of guitars and microphone stands" (Walser 1993: 109). When combined to produce intricate virtuosic performances, the myths of the genius and suffering artist are actively constructed and revalidated, which can be hugely supportive in enhancing an artist's cool image.

The 1980s marked a shift in representations of masculinity in British mainstream pop toward "a more sensitive, less macho type" (Hawkins 2006: 280). This was a period marked by the "new" male in British society, during which mainstream fashion became more popularized. This period saw the "eroticisation of the male image within popular culture [which] moved gay erotica and the fetishism of maleness into the mainstream marketplace" (Hawkins 1997: 120–21). This new camp sensibility was particularly expressed through narcissism. Continuing this trend well into the 1990s, representations of masculinity often blended "the soft and hard: a chiseled masculinity framed by beautiful clothes, makeup, and flawless complexion" (ibid.). Thus, besides more traditional modes of hyper-masculinity, this period also saw men who liked shopping and paid attention to their own appearance, accompanied by the emergence of the homosocial gaze. The resultant mix of representations, the "new bricolage of masculinity" (ibid.: 120), marked a new kind of masculinity, which "challenged traditional norms of virility and toughness [and] reject[ed] conventional masculinity by distancing itself from heteronormativity" (Hawkins 2006: 281). This was evident in the emergence of "queer" personalities, including Marc Almond, David Bowie, Boy George, Jarvis Cocker,

Elton John, George Michael, Morrissey, and Jimmy Summerville, and "queer" bands, including Bronski Beat, the Communards, Culture Club, Depeche Mode, Frankie Goes to Hollywood, the Pet Shop Boys, and Soft Cell, entering the British pop music scene. The musicians and groups played on their queerness through camp mannerisms so as to represent a more ambiguous masculinity and challenge gendered stereotypes. As pop artists, they symbolized the disruption of gender and sex norms, and, through gender-bending spectacles, played out an emphasis on being "different" and, ultimately, cool.

Androgynous spectacle was one means to express the new sentiments surrounding masculinity during this time. For example, androgynous metal, also known as "glam metal", included less emphasis on musical complexity, originality, and virtuosity in order to emphasize visual displays of androgyny (Walser 1993: 128), for example in the loud fashion statements of musicians like David Bowie, Jeffree Star, Boy George, Marilyn Manson and others, which challenged and transformed hegemonic masculine ideology. In heavy metal, specifically, androgyny

> is the adoption by male performers of the elements of appearance that have been associated with women's function as objects of the male gaze—the visual styles that connote ... "to-be-looked-at-ness". The members of bands like Poison or Mötley Crüe wear garish makeup, jewellery, and stereotypically sexy clothes, including fishnet stockings and scarves, and sport long, elaborate "feminine" hairstyles (Walser 1993: 124).

The musicians also often use "colorful makeup; elaborate, ostentatious clothes; hair that is unhandily long and laboriously styled" (Walser 1993: 131). Presenting masculinity as an androgynous spectacle is a fairly recent phenomenon, which results in a kind of glamour being attached to cool male objects of desire. Bands like Poison and Judas Priest have succeeded in a genre normally dominated by virtuosity, since their musical simplicity complemented their androgynous visual style and helped them forge a constituency. Bands like Poison have claimed the powers of spectacularity for themselves.

The use of androgyny in heavy metal challenged masculine "harder" styles of rock and heavy metal by blurring hegemonic gender boundaries and questioning the "natural" exclusiveness of heterosexual male power. It is often seen to subvert male heterosexual privilege; indeed, with an implicit alignment to homosexuality and crossing of gender boundaries, androgynous displays threaten patriarchal control and power, and this resistance came to be regarded as cool. Even the use of "non-masculine" instruments in heavy metal (e.g. keyboard) evokes homosexual conventions, which "continues to resonate with camp, with being different, with being 'other' or, at worst, with being threatening and deviant" (Whiteley 2005: 133). Heavy metal musicians have indeed recognized the ambiguities of androgyny and its association with the homosexual gaze, and developed compensatory strategies. Aerosmith's 'Dude Looks like a Lady' (1987), for instance, confronts gender stereotypes and anxieties evoked by androgyny, confronting the "problem" of gender bending with the tone of mock hysteria: the singer Steven Tylor represents a feminized image on stage through his facial expressions, dance moves, and dress style, counterbalanced by his actual involvement in bodybuilding and martial arts, which reaffirm conventional patriarchy.

Thus, by incorporating gender-ambivalent and queer representations, artists have succeeded in constructing coolness around themselves. Signifying an artist as queer (rather than being queer) in mainstream pop has been shown to achieve high record sales, popularity, and control. Appearance (rather than self-representation) is the determinant factor in their cool appeal through the spectacularization of gender play that mocks masculine conventions. Queering—the disavowal of the explicit homoerotic—parodies male domination and is essentially threatening and provocative, key ingredients of cool. In the music industry, therefore, queering is only acceptable as long as it is maintained and dependent on patriarchal control. Queerness thereby becomes naturalized and rationalized in heterosexual terms, and so reinforces conventional masculinity, even while queerness undoubtedly challenges traditional behavior associated with conventional masculinity. As a result, mainstream pop stars must negotiate a sensitive relationship between queerness and masculinity, which may be interpreted as nothing more than "gender tourism" (Hawkins 2006: 289), a criticism held against pop stars like Prince, Madonna, U2, and others (e.g. U2's members dressed up as queers on the cover for *Achtung Baby*) for using queerness as a strategy in their music. For instance, Madonna's explicit usage of queerness has been criticized as being nothing more than reinforcing "the very dead ends (objectification, control, violence) from which feminism has fought to free women" (Gill 1995: 175). The intentions of these artists are seen in this context as purely theatrical. In doing so, queerness becomes a commodified signifier of the hip and the cool, and appeals to an audience that likes to think of themselves as edgy and different. Even so, Madonna has entered the status of a "cool legacy", who has transformed the postfeminist landscape of American culture by combining dance-driven spectacle, erotic exhibitionism, and artistic omnivorousness. She is undoubtedly the most important female musical artist in recording history, with an immeasurable influence on such cool postfeminist music divas as Lady Gaga and Pink (Smithsonian 2014a).

It is precisely for this reason that Madonna's 1983 photograph was included in the "American Cool" exhibition at the Smithsonian National Portrait Gallery in 2014 (see http://npg.si.edu/exhibit/Cool/images/madonna_full.jpg, accessed 4 September 2017).

Prince. It was during the late 1980s that one of popular music's biggest stars was catapulted into superstardom while reflecting the changing attitudes in society toward sexuality, identity, and patriarchy. No other artist captured more clearly the idealism of cool than Prince. Born in Minneapolis in 1958 and signing with Warner at the age of nineteen, Prince represented a huge change of attitude toward ethnicity and sexuality in popular music. Prince is widely recognized as taking ideas surrounding gender and sexuality into previously unexplored arenas: a concert in 1980 would feature the young musician dancing in bikini briefs, high heels, and a trench coat. Indeed, "he became the pimp and the whore in the same body" (Jones 1998: 62). Prince was also the first African American musician to deal with sadomasochism. In his early career, Prince was often described by critics as having two interests, music and women, and the fact that he wore plentiful makeup and high heels seemed to make him a threat to men, rather than to women. The writer for *Vogue* fashion magazine, for instance, wrote that "one minute he is drooling, hip pumping, sex-crazed deviant, the next he's ethereal ... His gender bending has never called into question his heterosexual orientation ... acting female is merely a way of playing out his own sexual desire ... the dandy whose bare, hirsute chest suggests an animal lurking" (ibid.: 118). His masculine persona, however, stands in stark contrast to his more feminized demeanor and singing style. Although Prince's performances have often seen him paired with incredibly gorgeous (and semi-nude) women, he often appeared wearing just as much makeup and played the onstage role of the dominated, rather than the dominator. In the video for his song 'Kiss', the female guitarist Wendy sits on a stool playing the guitar, while Prince dances around her "as the half-naked sex object" against a backdrop of vaginal imagery where the "only deep male sound (to contrast Prince's falsetto) comes out of ... the female dancer" (ibid.: 109). Prince often sang in falsetto voice, which lends his persona a gentler, romantic, feminine side, even when singing the "dirtiest" lyrics and holding his guitar as a phallic symbol. Even when rapping, Prince was often known to present a feminist message. The song 'P. Control' ('P' standing for pussy) sees Prince explaining how "women should never be slaves to men, and they always hold the power" (ibid.: 246). Indeed, Prince has often included lines denouncing violence to women, though he has received criticism for songs like 'Lady Cab Driver' and 'Gett Off'—a song detailing twenty-six positions in a sexual encounter, while scorning his love interest for her desire to eat ribs since "them hips is gone"—for promoting misogynistic messages. Nonetheless, Prince has always given great respect to women (O'Brien 2002). Said to be his "waking fantasy", Prince has generally preferred working with women, who have been empowered as a result. Perhaps Prince's most explicit postfeminist moment was in the classic 'If I Was Ur Girlfriend' (1987), a song that sees Prince—or Camille, his alter ego, his feminine side with a voice that has a heightened pitch—acting to be as close to his partner as she is with her girlfriends, representing "his desperate plea to girlfriend Susannah that he would … stop seeing other women, he'd like to be a sister to her" (Jones 1998: 128). He begs, cries, and pleads with his partner; he offers to wash her hair, dress her, and in the final act of the song offers to "dance a ballet … will that get you off?" The desperation in this song is not just sexual, but a desperation to connect spiritually, mentally, and emotionally. Prince—his image, music, and relationship with women—is clearly a representation of cool queering, while highlighting the fact that patriarchy is as much a struggle and pain to men as it is to women.

Cool World Music
World Music similarly signifies coolness. It can provide a certain edginess or coolness that results from unfamiliarity with new sounds, the anxiety of the other, or simply from exoticism. A current example of World Music that evokes the ideology of the cool is the Malian Tuareg musicians known as Tinariwen, who have managed to gain popularity and success in the international mainstream pop music market. This is significant, as foreign acts rarely get the opportunity to break through to the mainstream market. Historically, most of the greatest commercial successes have been enjoyed by western musicians, largely due to the oligopoly that the western economy holds over record companies and the music business more generally. Despite this, some World Music acts have moved beyond their own cultural and geographical borders, and have gained recognition and success in the western mainstream market, yet this is still rare, as non-western artists are often marginalized in the World Music category, which in itself is not considered profitable enough for "big" record companies to exploit commercially. Most of the time, non-western musicians enter the World Music niche market, with its cultural, rather than commercial, demand for World Music. Urry attributes this to a more cosmopolitan, postmodern perspective that has come to permeate western society, saying that "such a cosmopolitanism presupposes extensive patterns of mobility, a stance of openness to others, a willingness to take risks and an ability to reflect upon and judge aesthetically between different natures, places and societies" (Urry 1995: 145). Such a cosmopolitan perspective of the world and

the cultures within it has been made possible by immigration, greater social equality, and tolerance, and by the massive role that the media now plays in our society. Media have the power to raise awareness of foreign cultures, and this results in a curiosity for the music and forms of artistic expression that different cultures practise. Often people in the West are drawn to these cultures as an other, a "mysterious" culture unlike our own, and that is both alien and relatable to us.

Figure 4.1: Screenshot depicting members of the band Tinariwen in traditional costume in desert-like surroundings to evoke images of the Saharan desert. Source: Cooper *et al.* 2013. Reproduced with permission by BBC WORLDWIDE LEARNING.

Tinariwen sing in their native Tamasheq dialect (with occasional sections in English), and the message of Tuareg liberation has always been at the very core of Tinariwen's mantra. For instance, their 2014 album *Emmaar* "is dominated by angry political comment and world-weary laments that are aimed at a Malian, not western, audience" (Denselow 2014). Yet without translation, a western audience cannot understand the meaning behind their politically motivated lyrics. It is then interesting to determine whether Tinariwen's appeal rests in their lyrical message, or in the musical signifiers they communicate, or in the images and stories they spin around themselves:

It was no longer enough to have the right sound. Music would also need to be accompanied by a strong story and some photogenic characters. And like a mirage, one band emerged from the sands of the Sahara with the perfect backstory. "The legend has it that they went into battle with AK47s and electric guitars strapped to their backs" (Andy Kershaw). Tinariwen were the Touareg nomadic warriors that rose from the desert wars of Mali, bringing with them a slow African blues groove. "Lots of bands know how to rock, very few know how to roll. And Tinariwen, by God, they know how to roll. There's a slightly menacing quality to them. A kind of gang quality that I have not really seen since the heyday of the Clash" (Andy Kershaw) (Cooper *et al.* 2013).

Tinariwen is largely a guitar-based group, and the music reflects a western blues and rock influence, which the group absorbed into its music and spread via home-made cassettes throughout the Sahara. The musical similarities to western music makes Tinariwen more accessible and may explain the group's ever-growing popularity as a World Music act. Indeed, instrumentation is an important signifier within music, and Tinariwen's identity as a guitar-based band places it in a global guitar culture that perhaps gives the group an advantage over world acts that use unusual instrumentation. The guitar is "a globally mobile instrument whose form, tonal textures and associated playing techniques are the product of its appropriation and use in a variety of locally specific musical contexts" (Bennett and Dawe 2001: 1). Moreover, "the electric guitar is probably the most iconic instrument of pop-rock ... [and so] adoptions of electric guitars by musicians in different parts of the world gained the symbolic meaning of joining the ranks of the pop-rock aesthetic" (Regev 2013: 49), thereby joining the ranks of a line of guitarists like Jimi Hendrix, Jimmy Page, and Eric Clapton. In terms of sound, Tinariwen has appropriated the electric guitar to encompass a range of musical influences from Africa, the Middle East, and America. The African influence is perhaps the most obvious, as they employ a range of characteristic techniques, including call and response, repetitive rhythmic cycles, and a "buzzy" timbre. Turino explains how in African music "the multiple layering of different rhythmic patterns creates a tension and, at times, an ambiguity such that a listener can hear and feel the same music in a variety of ways depending on which rhythmic part or pattern he or she is focusing on" (Turino 2001: 171). This is demonstrated well in 'Iswegh Attay' (2011), a song from Tinariwen's fifth album *Tassili*, which begins deceptively simple with a soft melody line, but then integrates an unpredictable, rather complex percussion track that makes listeners pay more attention to the individual instruments and rhythms. There are also notable Arabic inflections in the vocal part and a blues influence in the guitar track, a combination of musical features that make Tinariwen's musical style unique indeed.

The music is more specifically known as Tichumaren, which is synonymous with the Tuareg rebel movement between the Malian government and Tuareg rebel forces during the 1990s, which Tinariwen have always closely identified with. Some of its members have historically been involved in military activity with the Tuareg rebel movement, and their exile from Mali led to them becoming known as true representatives of the Tuareg's "nomadic" lifestyle:

> When Lybian ruler Gaddafi was gathering young Tuareg men to fight in his territorial wars, the founding members of Tinariwen who were exiled by the Malian government answered the call. "In the earliest days of the Liberation Front, we decided to make some cassettes to get out to our people. We had no radio stations, nor any other way of getting news out to our people, the Tuareg, to encourage them to express their grievances. The only way of doing that was to get them to listen to our songs. That's how the group was created. (Hassan Ag Touhami). "The truth is when you talk to a lot of Tuareg ... [and] say how did you first become aware of the Tuareg cause, it would be because we listened to a cassette of a song by Tinariwen" (Andy Morgan) (Cooper *et al.* 2013).

This historical/emotional context imbibed the group with an element of authenticity, a quality that is actively sought out in the World Music industry where cultural issues and politics are often at the forefront of media attention. For example, *Songlines*, a London-based, English-language magazine dedicated primarily to popular musics from around the world, "is a window into the politics and modes of political engagement of the many actors—including musicians, journalists, consumers, record labels and academics—who constitute the World Music scene" (Wagner 2014: 201). In World Music, this authenticity often manifests itself "in the form of a particular affect—rage. Does the musician display anger about her racialized/ethnicized subject position and what is thought to have happened to her people?" (Taylor 2004: 86). In the case of Tinariwen, there is certainly an element of "rage". For example, their 2011 song 'Tenere Taqqam Tossim' from their aforementioned album *Tassili*, a hypnotic, guitar-driven piece that ends with the lyric (translated) "*I cry out to God on high/To bring my people together/In unity*", makes clear that Tinariwen's message has remained relatively fixed since their inception in the late 1970s, which can largely be attributed to the fact that the Tuareg people still have no autonomy and that the problem remains largely unresolved (Amico 2014).

Another trait of authenticity is the band's priority of message over profit. For instance, in their early career Tinariwen would provide free recordings to those who gave them blank cassettes, and it is important to understand that this ethos was not just exclusive to Tinariwen, but to all Tuareg people who considered themselves Ishumar. After the droughts in the Sahara desert in the 1970s that left the population with only 20 percent of their livestock, the Tuareg people realized that they could no longer survive via outdated means of pastoral living. They subsequently spread across the African continent and became employed in various sectors, educating themselves, and spreading their message of Tuareg unity, and those who actively supported this forward-thinking mentality were known as Ishumar/Ashamor (Lecocq 2005: 94). It could be argued that Tinariwen's use of electric instruments, and their later involvement with music videos and other forms of modern media, placed them within this spectrum. "Musicians would perform at ishumar parties where those who had cassette recorders recorded the sessions, which were then copied by new listeners" (ibid.: 97). This ethos has a startling similarity to that of punk rock in the western world, and it is easy to see how this genuine expression of anger, rebellion, and independence might chime with a punk rock-inspired western audience.

Even so, it took around twenty years for Tinariwen to achieve success outside of their Tuareg society, made possible through recognition by a French group known as Lo-Jo who supported the Malian Festival au Désert (Amico 2014). Producer Justin Adams describes his first encounter of Tinariwen in the Saharan desert as follows:

> It was really like a Western movie ... you know ... the Seventh Samurai. It was like that because one by one the dudes turned up, you know. Then there was the day when this thin guy with sort of tangled hair turned up where we were staying, and he just came, you know, quiet to the point to be this completely introverted-looking guy [sic], and he sat down in the tent where we were having tea and he got his guitar out. And it was, you know, a moment that still sort of sends shivers down my spine thinking of, because he started to play the guitar so gently, you know, touching the strings, and this absolutely mesmerizingly beautiful scales [sic] and then hit a gentle rhythm and then started to sing. And there must have been 10 or 15 Tuareg men and women sitting round in the tent and when he hit the chorus, everybody started singing. You know, everybody knew the song. It was clearly a kind of anthem written by this guy, and I could tell that we were sitting with an absolute master (Justin Adams) (Cooper *et al.* 2013).

To western music producers, Tinariwen's lead singer looked like Jimi Hendrix, which further authenticated the group's rock image. Tinariwen were subsequently promoted at the Malian Festival au Désert, and it was at this annual gathering of Tuareg people, which only turned into a festival in the late 1990s (Amico 2014: 87) that Tinariwen became subjected to the western conquest of cool:

> They do this fantastic thing where the women sit in circles and are playing the tindé drum, and suddenly on the horizon you see camels coming at top speed toward you. These guys with all the veils and in amazing costumes, *looking cool as hell*. And they come as close as they can to the circles of women, like young guys on motorbikes [rrrrrhhh], showing off basically. Then they start to control the camel and they circle the group, and this is where they do this kind of thing where they control the camel, and the camel ... dances to the music (Justin Adams) (Cooper et al. 2013).

Tinariwen's appeal of cool in the eyes of western music industry professionals who attended the Malian festival led to slots at British World Music festivals like WOMAD, the most prominent multicultural festival devoted to the celebration of new, alternative forms of music (Hutnyk 1998: 402), and subsequently more mainstream pop festivals, such as Glastonbury and Coachella, as well as appearances in the US. Indeed, festival appearances are hugely effective for promoting their music, given that "the contemporary proliferation of music festivals is remarkable—big, small, conservative, radical, alternative; every demographic and niche audience is catered for" (Connell and Gibson 2014: 117). Tinariwen's appearance at Glastonbury is significant, as they represent one of the main World Music acts who have crossed the line between independent and mainstream. This cross-over is further evident in their rise in popularity among indie rock fans, which came from their participation in the Arts Council-funded Africa Soul Rebels UK tour in February 2005 (alongside Daara J and Rachid Taha), which was promoted, marketed, and packaged in a deliberately "rock 'n' roll way":

> By not marketing it as World Music [they] attracted a different kind of crowd and a different kind of coverage. The age range was lower. By not having a "niche mentality" [they] were not in a niche ... This wasn't just the usual World Music crowd ... Many people in the crowd would normally consider themselves indie/rock fans looking for something a bit different but with attitude (Arts Council England 2005: 15).

As Tuareg rebel music started to reach new audiences in Europe and the US, it became known as desert blues, resonating closely with the Tuareg's word *asuf*, meaning non-physical pain used to describe their music. Explaining their success in the mainstream pop music industry, the musicians themselves said that, "we realized there was a nostalgia in our music that could reach out to everyone" (Cooper et al. 2013). Tinariwen's rise then, like their rise in Tuareg society, could be said to have been achieved through their carefully constructed indie rock promotion during the band's live performances at western mainstream festivals and events, while spreading the political message of the plight of the Tuareg people. Indeed, indie rock has become a firm part of the neoliberal ideology of cool: "Indie-inflected music serves as a kind of Trojan horse. Consumers feel they are discovering something that they believe to be cool and gaining admittance to a more refined social clique" (Sisario 2010: 10). Tinariwen have successfully tapped into the appeal of cool through their ability to present an authentic past to a modern audience. Tinariwen demonstrate powerfully that musicians who have the "right" sound, who are accompanied by a strong story, and who come with some photogenic characters can become successful by tapping into the appeal of the cool. It is then easy to understand the attraction that Tinariwen would hold for western pop music fans.

Postfeminism as an Ideology of Cool

In popular music, coolness is also linked to postfeminism (Bartlett 2002; Holmes and Negra 2011: 176), which emerged in the late 1980s/early 1990s. Postfeminism can literally be seen as an "after"-feminism in response to the apparently perceived failures of second-wave feminism. Postfeminism is a "softer", even neoliberal, women's movement that has existed alongside third-wave feminism (1999–), which is traced to the emergence of the Riot grrrl feminist punk subculture, and fourth-wave feminism (2012–), which is associated with the use of social media to protest against harassment, sexual assault, rape, and other forms of female oppression. Postfeminists embraced new forms of non-feminist femininity, while not conforming to traditional forms of subjectivity, leading women to accentuate feminine characteristics while at the same time claiming male privilege and attitudes (Gamble 2001a, 2001b; Hollows 2000). Postfeminism thus seemed to evolve from the many frustrations felt regarding feminism, while developing from a fragmentation within second-wave feminism as it intersected with other disciplines, such as psychoanalysis, cultural studies, and black feminism. So while feminism strengthened the position of women in spite of men, postfeminism began to work alongside men. Postfeminism rejects metanarratives and positivisms in search of absolute or universal truths, and instead focuses on the differences and multifaceted experiences of women. Postfeminists acknowledge the many different female cultural expressions, and reject the idea that for a woman to be a feminist role model she would have to adopt masculine traits (Whiteley 2000: 3). The theories surrounding postfeminism thus rework original feminist writings and argue that there is nothing "wrong" with women or men, and women should not have to adopt masculine traits to succeed in their fight for women's rights. Both men as well as women should simply be regarded as human beings, and thus equal (Nicholson 1997).

The emergence of postfeminism must be contextualized within the "individualization thesis" in neoliberal culture, which is of broad significance to the quality of life for younger people. Contrary to Romantic individualism, which "is a little-realized value of bourgeois society" (McGuigan 2016: 156), individualization is a compulsory necessity, an obligatory, institutionalized, and collectively shared condition under neoliberal capitalism. It does feel like freedom, which, combined with lonely responsibility, can be both exhilarating and terrifying. It is about cultivating self-discipline under surveillance in highly precarious, insecure, and stressful working conditions within the creative industries of neoliberal capitalism. "And individualized life, cool and apparently 'free', on the one hand, is an uncertain and precarious life to lead, on the other hand" (ibid.: 43). While this can be quite possibly terrifying for the newly emerging creative class, "the precariat", it has also been a liberating change in life situations. Young professional people, including women, who previously had been denied choice, have much greater agency since the 1990s, liberated from patriarchal control and with improved opportunities for employment and self-realization: "They are much freer than their mothers were. Assumptions about women's prescribed social role have been called definitely into question, and there is much greater formal equality between the sexes, particularly in affluent segments of the world's population" (ibid.: 42). Under neoliberal conditions, there has been a progressive loosening of gender constraints, which also means that production and consumption are no longer simply equated with masculine and feminine according to older binary oppositions. Indeed, masculine consumption has been cultivated just as women have also progressed upwards, albeit still disproportionately, in labor hierarchies.

Postfeminism is often criticized as "anti-feminist" in that its theories and practices naturalize and commodify feminism for use in popular culture (McRobbie 2009). Indeed, the 1990s was an era when the popular music business presented many female artists who seemingly waved the flag of feminism (e.g. Jewel, Alanis Morissette). Riot Grrrl's mottos and catchphrases, such as "girl power", were assumed by the capitalist music corporations and mass media. "Girl power" as a phrase emerged in 1987 by a London-based acapella all-girl group called Mint Juleps in a song entitled 'Girl to the Power of 6', and subsequently used in a fanzine by punk band Bikini Kill, after which it also became spelled as "grrrl power" due to its association with Riot Grrrl. In 1996, the slogan "girl power" became synonymous with the Spice Girls, which in turn subverted the meaning of girl power and consequently became inconsistent with the empowerment that it was originally intended to evoke (Hopkins 2002). While the Spice Girls did to some extent promote female power in their own, unique ways and within the context of a highly commercialized music culture, the group had in fact paid no attention to the manner in which they intended to empower young females, and thus "diluted [girl power's] radicalism" (Leonard 2007: 159). Consequently, the legitimacy of the feminist movement in popular music has been questioned, specifically in regards to the punk genre that characterizes much of the Riot Grrrl movement. As both punk and feminism have historically been grassroots movements, their emergence as "popular" rendered them apolitical or as co-opted (Tasker and Negra 2007). For feminism (or punk) to become co-opted for mass-produced, globally distributed products aimed at girls and women puts into question its perceived authenticity. These growing concerns resonate in the criticisms of more recent artists such as Pink, Avril Lavigne, and the Donnas who are commonly referred to as "punk", "punky", and "pop punkettes".

Postfeminist popular music thereby reflects the way that "'cool' has traversed the political landscape from the "left" to the "right", thereby reversing its meaning. It is now more a sign of compliance than of resistance" (McGuigan 2016: 36). While feminist musicians have attempted to radically challenge women's place in music, and have helped to introduce issues related to gender inequality and difference, these representations are still often disseminated by patriarchal and male-dominated music corporations. Feminism has not impacted upon popular music to the point where it universally changed the marginalized, exploitative, and suppressed positions of women in neoliberal popular culture. Much current popular music still remains dominated by men, and reiterates and reinscribes the fact that certain genres are still a man's world. Managing a short-term female brand often focuses on aesthetic appeal, rather than content, in order to be profitable (Lieb 2007: 194). Female artists are usually expected to be both beautiful and sexy, regardless of their musical capabilities. To do so, neoliberal bodies require constant processes of self-discipline and self-surveillance (Gill 2007: 155). This is a feature of cool postfeminism in neoliberal culture, in which white femininity ideals have become iconic and marketable as cool, as have notions of hyper-sexuality (Holmes and Negra

2011: 195). Cool postfeminism is structured by a "current of individualism", which introduces a certain kind of self-regulating and self-reinventing subject explicitly directed at women: "To a much greater extent than men, women are required to work on and transform the self, regulate every aspect of their conduct, and present their actions as freely chosen" (Gill 2007: 164).

Gendered sexual attractiveness is not a new phenomenon, and most representations of female sexuality throughout the twentieth century prescribed value to white middle-class bodies and heteronormative codes of behavior (Deliovsky 2008: 51). Beauty, entertainment, and fashion industries have since become intertwined to commodify female attractiveness, which is typically linked with feminine sexuality and beauty. Females encompass a better niche market than males, since they relate to easily marketable products and goods, such as accessories, clothes, make-up, and perfume. Emergent market categories such as tweens and teens are considered key to profit margins (Lamb *et al.* 2013: 168). Using attractive girls and young women in magazines, television, music videos, movies, and social media helps companies to sell their products, since attractiveness in females is significantly linked to being deemed cool by teens and young people (Ivaldi and O'Neill 2008: 402).

Many current female artists in mainstream popular music are marketed by their female attractiveness and sexuality, and their music co-opts musical styles that once signified resistance, such as punk, indie, hippy, grunge, and avant-garde, to denote coolness, which when combined contribute to the branding of a cool postfeminist image. Feminist resistance strategies have been co-opted and domesticated by multi-racial white supremacist patriarchy and turned into resilience discourse, just like the musics of oppressed groups have been co-opted and domesticated, while turning "these noisy monstrosities into gaga-style pop aesthetics" (James 2015: 165). The musical styles that were once associated with feminism, resistance, and girl power have become highly commercialized, yet they may still carry, if somewhat diluted, a certain feminist cultural connotation that is appealing to young consumers. This has the consequence that this co-opted resilience is a normalizing, rather than a critical counter-hegemonic practice. Musical style thereby helps to accentuate the brand, particularly in the early stages of an artist's career, and can help an artist become unique and more identifiable.

Clearly, then, there exists a close link between attractiveness, feminine sexuality, and coolness in neoliberal culture, whereby gendered stereotypes are commonplace. Managing a short-term female brand means utilizing stereotypes and ideals deemed attractive, feminine, sexual, and cool among fans and audiences. An artist's hair, make-up, and clothes all contribute to feminine attractiveness (Milner 2004: 5), as does sexualized behavior, as well as their ability to sexualize aspects of themselves that are not inherently sexual (e.g. Lamb *et al.* 2013). The converging industries commodify female sexuality across the entire media landscape, positing sex and sexuality as the key components for consumption to ensure that their cross-capitalization efforts are successful. Female artists are branded as cool postfeminist women, as young people are unlikely to purchase products from artists deemed uncool. This is a key feature of cool postfeminism, in which ideals of white femininity, including hyper-sexuality, have become iconic and marketable as cool (Holmes and Negra 2011: 195). Female artists are styled in such a way to denote coolness, drawing on fashion influences from punk, indie, hippy, grunge, and avant-garde. Artists like Britney Spears, Jennifer Lopez, Katy Perry, Nicki Minaj, Lady Gaga, and others all encapsulate this western beauty ideal and feminine hyper-sexuality.

An interesting example is Lady Gaga, who achieves coolness through her shock tactics and hyper-sexualization (like, for instance, her music video for 'Telephone' (2009), or her appearance at the 2010 MTV Video Music Awards wearing a dress made of raw beef, or her appearance wrapped up in a hooded floral top as if being wrapped up in gift paper to celebrate the release of her debut fragrance, Fame, in 2012), which in turn enables her to distinguish herself as a non-conforming individualist. Her coolness resonates with a certain ideal type, namely "a rebellious attitude, an expression of the belief that the mainstream morals of society do not apply to you" (Pountain and Robins 2010: 188). This has been a successful technique for Gaga to create publicity and gain notoriety, while fitting into her constructed and well-established brand image. Miley Cyrus adopts similar shock tactics through her nakedness, twerking, and provocative comments while seeking to establish herself as an adult through her videos. The brand of sex-positive feminism self-identified by Miley Cyrus is marked by an *individual* empowerment strategy—individualism—and freedom of choice, by women embracing sexual desires and playing with sexuality, which are promoted by third- and fourth-wave feminism (O'Donnell 2017: 114). Yet Cyrus' cool postfeminism does threaten feminism itself, given the issues surrounding her self-constructed hyper-sexualized persona and self-identified brand of feminism. Lily Allen similarly conforms to popular music culture's demands for provocative images, for instance in her salacious and (for some) racist lyrics and video for the 2009 song 'Hard Out Here?', which is read by some critics as anti-black feminism (Siddiqi n.d.). Lady Gaga, Miley Cyrus, and Lily Allen are thus "at least part of the same construction of scandal and attention seeking that is ever present in contemporary entertainment culture" (Marshall 2016: 26). Due to brand consistency, however, shock tactics are not always effective for female artists, given that the scrutiny of both their private and professional lives leaves little scope for forms of rebellion within the pop genre (Vesey 2015: 998). To counteract this limitation, female artists are therefore still branded via their attractiveness, feminine sexuality, and non-feminist coolness. So while sex and sexuality are harnessed as a marketing tool to convey a sense of rebellion and rejection of societal order, this is done in such a way, usually by emphasizing ideals of beauty, that still renders the female artist "safe" for her young audiences, and thus consumable.

The commodification of feminism—by disregarding it and playing on feminine and hyper-sexualized qualities for financial gain—has also been termed as "postfeminist entrepreneurialism" (Vesey 2015: 999) and "neoliberalization of feminism" (Prügl 2015). It is limited by gender conventions and capitalist reliance, and thus does nothing more than fetishize female power. This culture reinforces neo-traditional aspects of femininity by emphasizing feminine glamour (McRobbie 2004: 260). Glamour is a slippery concept, yet still often today

> relies on its strong connection to the star of classic Hollywood, where the notion of glamour and its associated fur, slinky dresses, and attitude were an expression of the modern woman negotiating her public place in the contemporary world. But it is a soiled concept ... [since] as the twentieth century progressed ... even the idea of glamour became associated with tackiness (Marshall 2016: 20).

Glamour and all its accoutrements of seductive and sexualized image allow female artists to temporarily inhabit that celebrated identity space. The commodification of female empowerment—the struggle and ambiguity surrounding women's roles and feminism—through beauty ideals like feminine glamour and female sexuality thereby devalues feminism. Postfeminism provides opportunities for constructing feminine coolness, which, while broadening concepts of femininity in some way, is "ultimately absorbed by the status quo, serving rather than resisting the needs of a capitalist value system" (Holmes and Negra 2011: 193).

Female Cool Celebrities
Postfeminism, then, enabled a new mode of femininity that entailed narratives of emancipation and hyper-femininity, individuality and makeover, irony, and consumerism. Combined, these narratives—feminist, anti-feminist, capitalist—are the gendered manifestation of neoliberal governmentality (in the Foucauldian sense) (Muchitsch 2016: 5).[4] These narratives have been vividly evident in pop music since the 1990s and are markers of cool postfeminism in contemporary popular culture.

Britney Spears' 'Toxic' (2003). Britney Spears is an artist who has paved the way for the branding of cool postfeminism. Spears emerged in the early 2000s, which marked a turning point for female musicians in the context of brand extension. Through their strategic marketing of branded products, namely fragrances, artists like Spears paved new avenues for future generations of females within the music industry by capitalizing on hugely successful perfumes aimed at their tween/teen audiences. The emergence of brand extension in music also provided scope for further profitability through body lotions, special edition fragrances, and gift sets. These entrepreneurial efforts allowed Spears to evade her approaching "shelf life" and image discrepancies, for instance her volatile marriage to Kevin Federline and changing appearance and behavior (Vesey 2015: 999). In so doing, Spears and others were pioneers for the embodiment and effective "intimacy" that makes consumers feel closer to their idols (Keel and Nataraajan 2012: 692). Even so, brand extensions surrounding female artists are usually limited to the beauty and fashion industries.

Britney Spears is an artist firmly situated within cool postfeminism, whose music, lyrics, and videos illustrate the intersection between female attractiveness, feminine sexuality, and coolness. While albums like *In the Zone* (released in 2003) hit #1 in the Billboard 200, and songs like 'Toxic' received awards, including a Grammy for Best Dance Recording and was one of many of her records to top the charts, Spears' highly publicized life has led many parental groups to express concern about the "mixed signals" that her music and public persona send out to their adolescent children (Hawkins and Richardson 2007: 607). The video of her first single 'Baby One More Time' saw Spears as a pretty seventeen-year-old "strawberry blonde" adolescent dressed in school uniform. This video stood in stark contrast to the highly sexualized Spears shot shortly after for the *Rolling Stones* cover, pictured sprawled out on a bed in only her underwear. It was widely perceived that Spears conducted herself in a way that simultaneously signified immaturity and eroticism. 'Toxic' was a single released from her fourth album and was surrounded with as much controversy as the rest of her subsequent career. The music video employs the technique of "temporal disjunction" found in neo-noir films, which employs the strategy of flashbacks to gradually reveal a significant past event in the plot:

> Thus when Spears' character chances upon her lover in the shower with another woman in a rapid-fire montage of three musically accented shots, located almost subliminally toward the end of the video (each lasting less than a second), it is this composite event that motivates the storyboard of events and character changes that precede and follow it in the chronology of the video (Hawkins and Richardson 2007: 608).

The use of *film noir* is noteworthy here, which in itself is deemed cool, since it represented a rebellious artistic response to Hollywood (Dinerstein 2017: 73–120). The neo-noir motif continues throughout the imagery within the video through the use of its lighting conventions (much of it is backlit by sunlight), which establishes and reinforces the portrayal of the female protagonist as a *femme fatale*. Spears morphs into three characters that seem to pander to masculine fantasies and desires. The first character is an air stewardess, who wears heavy make-up and provocative clothing, drawing on gendered stereotypes surrounding the "trolley dolly" associations with the profession, where the main requirements are to be attractive and "bend over backwards" to serve and please all "who fly with you". Throughout the video, Spears plays the part of the sexual aggressor, and in the first sequence she pounces on a male passenger and kisses and gropes him in the aircraft lavatory, which actively simulates the revered "mile high" fantasy. The man is in disguise and holds a key to a secret research facility, and once she has had her way with the passenger she emerges with the key. Spears' aggressive kissing and sexual grinding seem to position her as the aggressor and as using her sexuality to get what she wants as a strong female. However, with the man emerging from the lavatory with a smile, it seems he got what he wanted out of the exchange too. Close-ups are focused on Spears' body throughout the exchange: her lips and bottom are made the prime focus of the scene, which places her under the male gaze. The specific focus on parts of the body emphasizes the fetishistic, eroticized clothing and returned gaze, as Spears looks directly into the camera in the knowledge that she is being looked at, which in turn signifies Spears' acceptance of and submission to the male gaze. With the audience placed in the position of identifying with the sexualization of Spears' body parts, Spears' aggressive assertiveness is transcended into the act of performance, with Spears performing in a manner that satisfies male sexual desires.

The second character Spears morphs into is a tight leather-clad redhead who straddles a motorcycle with muscular actor Tyson Beckford. Again she is deemed as the strong independent female, as she karate-kicks her way into a high-tech research lab where she obtains the poison needed to extract her revenge. However, the fetishized male gaze is ever present as the camera focuses on her tight leather outfit and stiletto S/M inspired leather boots. The motorbike serves as a prop for eroticized display. Beckford is in the driving seat with control over the vehicle, which signifies that the male viewer is in control of Spears. Vocoded (digitally manipulated) vocals and shattered glass provide the build up to the final camera transition, which coincides with the reprise of the song's chorus. This time, a dark-haired "futuristic female warrior, cartoon-like neo-noir Spears scales the wall of a building with sci-fi suction pads in order to secure the man from the shower before administering the poison he evidently deserves" (Hawkins and Richardson 2007: 609). This final character uses her sexuality once again to get the male character to succumb in order to achieve her goal. There is also a fourth character that is interpolated with each of the other sections, with Spears wearing glued-on jewels and little else, adopting poses resembling those of a lap dancer. Her nakedness apart from the jewels seems to elevate her into a position that commands admiration and signifies her as precious, much like the diamonds the jewels seem to emulate. However, as she writhes around on the floor, gyrating seductively and looking straight into the camera knowingly, it signifies again that she is adorned for the pleasure of the male viewer. Spears knowingly encourages the admiration that a half-naked woman, sexually gyrating, would demand from a heterosexual male viewer.

The narrative of 'Toxic' is strongly musically-driven. Throughout the song, the lyrics imply a specific relationship in the heavy reliance on I/you. Spears sings about the addictive love/lust that she is feeling for an assumed heterosexual male, which is further enforced through the narrative of the video. Her voice has a breathy delivery, connoting a sense of intimacy. While Spears' vocal timbre emphasizes sexual connotations, it also engages extra-textually, "not least with her own previous recordings, but also in the media reports and myths about her" (Whiteley 1997: 265). The criticisms within the media surrounding Spears' inappropriate integration of the binary oppositions of immaturity and eroticism can also be indicated by her vocal deliverance. In 'Toxic' and other early songs, Spears' "whiny vowel sounds, guttural groans, and lingering liquid phonemes signify both immaturity and eroticism, as do the accompanying visual representations" (Hawkins and Richardson 2007: 615). The close-up on Spears' lips as she sings "*The taste of your lips*" from the chorus emphasizes the sensual act of kissing that she is singing about. The repetition of "*I'm addicted to you*" signifies the loss of control and powerlessness felt by Spears, who is under the spell of her lover. Spears also draws on the contrasting notions of poison and paradise in her lyrics. In the chorus, "*The taste of your lips*" is later referred to as the "*Taste of the poison paradise*", which seems to imply that although the love of which she sings is venomous (poison), it is also pleasurable (paradise). This could be seen as supporting notions that allow for bad behavior within a heterosexual relationship. The exceptional degree of technological manipulation of Spears' voice is somewhat similar to other pop artists' use of vocoding, notably in Madonna's 'Music' and Cher's 'Believe', and Spears' vocals are similarly digitalized "to invoke a multiplicity of the self through the body [which] is teamed with the digitalized animated woman that panders to the desires of the mainstream gaze" (Hawkins and Richardson 2007: 616).

Meanwhile, a violin motif is heard throughout the song, but in narrative terms is most prominent at about the center-point (01:49) and at the end, as neo-noir Spears finally morphs back into her role as stewardess (03:16) (ibid.: 610). The violin motif has a distinct Arabic character that connotes notions of exoticism (ibid.). The fast tempo and exotic strings combine to create a sensory overload and work to place Spears in a position of the exotic mystique.

It could of course be argued that Spears' aggressive sexual assertiveness can be read as a celebration of female power and sexual freedom. Throughout the video of 'Toxic', she is the sexual aggressor and uses her feminine mystic style to lure the men under her power before achieving her ultimate goal. However, 'Toxic' may also be read as yet another example of the sexualized nature to which the female form is subjugated within the mainstream music industry. But it is really more complex, since 'Toxic' uses the typical methods and aesthetics of post-cinematic media to adopt a style of visualization that is distinctively postfeminist. The video contains all the main elements of Robin James' "resilient looking" in neoliberal culture (2015): first, by affirming the damage (e.g. her lover in the shower with another woman); second, by recycling this damage into feminine subjectivity and human capital (e.g. Spears as three in-control characters who eventually executes her lover through poisoning him); and third, by establishing men as the source of ongoing patriarchal damage. While Spears may objectify herself in front of the camera, she is also fully aware of the male gaze and its feminizing damage, thereby transforming this performance from a damaging to an empowering experience, and thus demonstrating her resilient subjectivity. 'Toxic' thereby forms part of a set of subsequent music videos, in which resilient women spectacularly execute supposedly misogynistic, undeserving men.

Beyoncé's 'Video Phone' (2008). Beyoncé, or "Queen Bey", arguably the most globally successful female pop star of the contemporary era, is another cool postfeminist artist, whose image is strongly informed by neoliberal governmentality, individualization and a multi-faceted self, and larger-than-life stardom, all of which exemplify successful neoliberal entrepreneurship (James 2015: 44–45; Muchitsch 2016: 1). Many of her songs, such as 'Run the World (Girls)', depict messages of multi-faceted postfeminist femininity and female empowerment, often through the body "as women's source of power" (Gill 2007: 164) alongside notions of traditional femininity and sexuality, motherhood, entrepreneurship, capitalism, and power, which together represent a key element of neoliberal postfeminism (Muchitsch 2016: 4). Beyoncé's 'Video Phone' uses methods and aesthetics to adopt a distinctively postfeminist and post-racial style of visualization (James 2015: 107). Like Spears' 'Toxic', 'Video

Phone' contains the key elements of resilient looking in neoliberal culture. First, 'Video Phone' critiques the male gaze as damaging to women by recognizing the artifice of the camera and its associated sexism and racism, both in its title ('Video Phone') and visuals, which substitute the cameras with men's heads, and thus establish the camera's gaze as male. The male gaze subjects Beyoncé to feminizing damage, namely by chopping and fragmenting her image (techniques of classic cinematic feminization), and objectifying her while she performs sexualized dance moves in revealing clothing for the male gaze.

'Video Phone' then transforms this damage into feminine subjectivity and human capital: Beyoncé is fully aware and in command of the feminizing damage; the male gaze may damage her, but she can handle and control it, a clear marker of feminine resilience. Beyoncé's character affirms that damage as empowering. She overcomes the damage of the male gaze by capturing, torturing, and eventually executing the camera-headed male dancers and male gazer, a stereotypically misogynist black man, and by positioning herself as a presuming entrepreneur via the video phone (you can't *really* look at me), instead performing for the video phone and for (viewers') computers, smartphones, and tablets. Beyoncé's character is not subjected to the traditional male gaze with its clear subject/object dichotomy, as she positions herself as "a distinctly *feminine* 'data self'" (James 2015: 110), turning herself into "content" to be uploaded, shared, and circulated virtually across social media platforms.

However, her performance doesn't liberate Beyoncé from patriarchy, but it incorporates her more fully into multi-racial white supremacist patriarchy: 'Video Phone' connects non-bourgeois black men (and women) to the ongoing patriarchal damage of the male gaze. It is non-white men who represent the male gaze in 'Video Phone'. The male gazer is a man of color, while Beyoncé's lyrics signify him as a member of working-class, non-bourgeois urban black culture, a representative who typically remains at the margins of middle-class, multi-racial respectability. Through their excessive misogyny in genres like hip hop, black rappers have long been scapegoats to white supremacist patriarchy, and videos like 'Video Phone'

> update this trope to function in a MRWaSP (multi-racial white supremacist patriarchy) context. Non-bourgeois black men must be eliminated by female characters so that dominant society can prove it is *both* post-racial (they're bad because they are misogynist, not because they are black) and post-feminist (misogyny is limited only to this "primitive", backwards subgroup from which women can defend themselves) (James 2015: 114).

Beyoncé's character's resilience is thus both gendered and racializing.

Lady Gaga's 'Bad Romance' (2009) and 'Telephone' (2010). 'Telephone' shares with 'Video Phone' the collective overcoming of stereotypically misogynist black men and presents heteromasculine sexuality as predatory. It fully reflects the neoliberal "resilient looking" narrative of feminine resilience and anti-blackness, "as though black men were singularly responsible for patriarchy's monstrous excesses, and overcoming patriarchy was simply a matter of punishing or eliminating black men" (James 2015: 133). In other words, 'Telephone' frames black men for the damage caused by the male gaze. The opening depicts Gaga being taken to her cell in an all-female prison and later being bailed out by Beyoncé, teaming up to poison Beyoncé's ex (and patrons) in an American diner. The "ex", a black male, is repeatedly constructed as stereotypically misogynistic and brutish: He calls her a bitch, gazes upon her breast before acknowledging her face, confronts a customer, and gropes another woman. Beyoncé and Gaga overcome this misogynist damage spectacularly—they kill him. Moreover, they also kill the other seemingly *non-bourgeois* patrons, and thereby extend their own personal patriarchal damage (e.g. the male gaze, anti-blackness) to the American nation's history of misogyny and racism. Their "post-execution dance party" dressed in American flag costumes and matching nail art thus looks like an Independence Day celebration.

A central feature of Gaga's creative output is the musical sartorial and visual appropriation of the traditionally oppositional subculture of goth, which ranges from industrial and electronic body music (EBM) to the more straightforward goth-pop of Siouxie and the Banshees, Depeche Mode, and Bauhaus, and through which she proudly demonstrates her resilient looking. Gaga's visual style is heavily influenced by goth fashion and aesthetics, which is vividly absorbed into 'Bad Romance', one of her most popular and highly regarded songs where she uses "goth monstrosity to demonstrate the grotesqueness of traditional gender and sexual norms/identities" (James 2015: 130), including the male gaze, the trafficking of women, and rape culture, which are evoked and amplified by the disgusting, monstrous, distorted bodies and movements. In other words, 'Bad Romance' highlights the grotesqueness of heteropatriarchy's desire (e.g. romance), and presents "normal" heterosexuality (e.g. the male gaze, sex trafficking, rape) as monstrous and horrific. The opening features bodies in bondage wear, high-heeled platform combat boots, and furniture in Victorian style, with Gaga wearing razor-bladed eyeglasses and barbed-wire manicure. White caskets labelled "monster" and adorned with a red Christian cross are seen in the "Bath House of Gaga" (in reference to Bauhaus), out of which emerge Gaga and six dancers dressed in skin-tight latex bodysuits like an eyeless tree monster. The dancing is anything but sexual, while a nude Gaga later emphasizes (through reptile-like features on her back, while wearing the mummified body of a long-fanged bat on her head) her grotesqueness rather than sexual desirability. The video depicts her being commanded by men to dance for them while offering bids, with one man, the video implies, nearly raping her at a point when Gaga morphs into an insect suit with lobster-claw heels—a praying mantas who eats her mates after copulation. 'Bad Romance' then depicts Gaga in a flame-throwing bra to immolate both the (presumed) rapist and bed upon which the violent act was presumed to happen. 'Bad Romance' is a clear example of neoliberal "resilient looking", in which the female character acknowledges and spectacularly overcomes her patriarchal damage, whereby "damage" (e.g. the male gaze, sex trafficking, rape) is made vividly visible in the video.

Lady Gaga's unique style has become known as "Gaga feminism", "a highly aestheticized, gothy variation on resilience discourse [and] the neoliberal co-optation of queer riot sound and queer monstrosity" (James 2015: 136). Gaga feminism uses patriarchal damage (e.g. the male gaze, human trafficking, sexual assault, domestic abuse, rape) and transgressions, and reframes them as pleasurable experiences and normalizes gender trouble. Her "spectacularly monstrous, disgusting, macabre performances" (ibid.: 135) thereby help Lady Gaga to construct a unique, cool postfeminist Gaga brand and to achieve mainstream success in the neoliberal music industry. Yet, like Beyoncé's postfeminism, Gaga feminism is also a culturally racist feminism that provides only a narrow path for female agency and empowerment, producing (non-bourgeois) blackness as exception to the patriarchal status quo. Gaga feminism fuels multi-racial white supremacist patriarchal strategy used by neoliberalism to elevate its imperatives like development, capitalization, flexibility, globalization, and so forth. As James (2015: 138) puts it, "neoliberalism needs privileged folk to individually 'go gaga' so that society (relations of privilege and oppression) can stay the same".

Coolness is an arbitrary and intangible concept that has shifted over time in popular culture. At one time, the Beatles would be the coolest thing; in another one Lady Gaga, Beyoncé, or Britney Spears. For instance, when Last.fm published a list of "the most unwanted scrobbles" in 2009, which contained tracks that were most frequently deleted by the Last.fm community from their scrobbles in the preceding month, artists with the most deleted scrobbles included Lady Gaga, Britney Spears, Katy Perry, Rihanna, Beyoncé, Miley Cyrus, and many more mainstream artists, many of whom also had the "guilty pleasure" tag attached to them (Lamere 2009). Interesting questions can be asked about how many female acts were included on the list. Is it not cool to listen to female artists? And can female artists be cool? It is hard to be female and cool. And yet many postfeminist female artists are branded as cool. As an ideal type, coolness is often described as "resistance to authority through creation and innovation" (Botz-Bornstein 2010), but creativity and innovation have historically been associated with male and masculinity. For female artists to be cool, they have to revert back to well-established gendered conventions that have shaped the global music industry throughout its history. Coolness is thereby inherently gendered. Coolness for females is based around their visual appearances, while for males what they do and say conveys coolness. And how this is perceived by consumers is dependent on cultural and contextual factors, one of the key reasons why any questions about deleted scrobbles on Last.fm are critically inconclusive.

Nonetheless, coolness is a defining feature of contemporary commodification practices in popular culture, including music. It is the logic of neoliberal, open-market capitalism, the most recent regime of globalization. Coolness has led to the redefinition of cultural capital in society, in which the cheapest commodities are seen as cool. It confers status through knowledge of the cool, which marks a historical shift in the control of cultural capital away from social elites and toward the new technocratic bourgeoisie. To them, all sorts of goods become desirable and consumed for their perceived coolness, which is enhanced through branding. In popular music, this is achieved through person branding and establishing a brand persona around particular artists, a shift away from music and toward an artist's image. Indeed, "the pop star is the ideal neoliberal subject—the corporate person, entrepreneur of herself, pure spectacle constituted by media feedback" (James 2015: 145). The neoliberal brand persona must express/visualize the resilience narrative that fans and critics expect: she must evoke and locate damage, and spectacularly overcome it. In an overcrowded music market, branding is necessary to stay relevant and profitable. Artists' images, identity and visualization techniques are therefore carefully and self-consciously calculated, constructed, maintained, and, if necessary, adapted. Consequently, the gender roles represented in the global music industry have become narrower than ever, constructed around what is deemed to be cool in order to appeal to the consumers of today's cool popular culture.

Technologies of Cool

While it may be true that technology is fundamentally changing who we are and what we do, debates and ideas surrounding the impact of technology have been on a spectrum from utopian to dystopian (Marshall 2016: 64). Utopian discourses around technology point to elements of exhilarating empowerment, while dystopian views center on the sense of powerlessness and manipulation. For more than thirty years, internet culture has led to a new cultural condition around the world. The utopian view regards technological consequences of globalization as positive and proposes that music production and consumption have reached a certain level of autonomy, which suggests that a true democratization of music has occurred. Revolutionary technological advances, it was believed, would liberate people from banal cultural commodities and enable greater participation in cultural activity, genuinely empowering the customer in many ways. Indeed, computer audio-file players, combined with the platforms made available by the internet, established full-fledged participation in aesthetic cultures of pop-rock in countries for which western music was initially an import (Regev 2013: 133). Internet platforms include platforms of streaming, including internet radio stations, Napster, YouTube, and mp3 blogs, and platforms for downloading music, including internet music stores and file-sharing (P2P downloading). While these internet platforms meant that corporate record sales were declining in the 2000s, people gained unprecedented access to a seemingly unlimited scope and amount of information, including experiential musical knowledge through the possibility of immediate engagement with recordings, live concerts, and documentaries. The socio-cultural structures of connectivity and integration are global in scope, facilitating organization of geographically dispersed fans in the forms of scenes and subcultures. Internet culture thereby "afford[s] fans unhindered intensive engagement with almost endless amounts of local and global music" (ibid.: 137). Moreover, digital and mobile technologies of communication have facilitated the movement of people and the flow of information in recent protest movements. The new global age of digital music consumers has thereby surpassed previous methods of music production and consumption. This new participation has been labeled "*produsage* to describe online experience, where the individual is no longer an audience member but a hybrid of producer and user that is engaged in her media consumption/production" (Marshall 2016: 65). The powers and communities produced through this networked individualism are seen as something to be celebrated.

The development of both the worldwide web and browser software made the internet accessible to the mainstream population, and has since been offering seemingly limitless information and data, and unprecedented possibilities for interactivity. In its rapid rise in popularity, the internet has changed the ways in which people interact with information, consumption, and other people through the emergence of WebTV, internet telephony, online publications of news, online advertising, fashion and lifestyle, value-added content, and online music. Online music has proven to be extremely popular, as listening to music using an electronic medium is experienced as a less drastic change for music consumers than, for instance, the reading of a print newspaper on a screen (OECD 2005: 13). Digital content and digital delivery of music have become increasingly ubiquitous. The growth of broadband and further technological innovations have triggered the growth of new online music services, which have changed the ways in which music is accessed, listened to, and consumed, and has had a positive impact on the time people spend listening to music. In other words, the digitization of music is believed to have increased the total hours of listening to music, which overall may be regarded as a positive consequence of globalization.

Yet at the same time, the unauthorized downloading of copyrighted content over the internet has raised considerable concerns for the global music corporations, posing a serious threat to the music, and film and TV industries (McGuigan 2009: 84). Specifically, the music industry, which held around 94 percent of its global record sales in OECD countries in the early noughties, with the US, Japan, and the UK being the largest markets (OECD 2005: 20), experienced a pronounced drop in overall revenue from 1999 to 2003 and, with it, concerns about the enforcement of intellectual property rights, caused by unauthorized sharing of copyrighted music, as digital recording now enabled master-quality copying in large quantities. The year 2004 marked a turning point when a range of legitimate, licensed online music services, such as Apple iTunes, became available as a result of legal actions and anti-piracy measures by the music industry. This was accompanied by significant public information campaigns about the illegality of file-swapping. The outlook for the music corporations since 2005 has been more positive due to the rapidly increasing sales of digital music services, the rise of the mobile phone, and the popularity of other formats like DVD, Blu-ray, and others. The number of legal music downloading sites has since grown, and record companies have since made large parts of their repertoires available online, which includes pay-per-track and subscription services. Instrumental to the changes in the online music landscape have been Apple's pay-per-download iTunes and the streaming subscription service Napster.

In the new digital music model, artists, majors, and publishers have so far retained their creative roles, while new players are involved in digital music stores, with essential functions that include digital content creation (e.g. content creation, production, sales and marketing), digital asset management (e.g. rights clearance, hosting, encoding, billing software), and digital networks and devices (e.g. delivery over networks, devices to listen to music). The impact is thereby twofold: Music can be consumed more rapidly and directly, and a new set of players have become essential to the online distribution of music. It has proven that A&R is increasingly done over the internet, that physical retailers are no longer the last link to consumers, and that distribution is directly possible from artist to consumer. The internet accommodates cheap promotion and lower entry barriers for newer artists, which means that online music sales can result in a broader audience taste and less concentration of music sales by individual artists. Consequently, diversity in music genres and styles has been increasingly promoted, which clearly marks a positive consequence of globalization. Meanwhile, peer-to-peer file-sharing networks are an innovative communication technology allowing individuals to "interact directly, without necessarily going through a centralized system or hierarchy. Users can share information, make files available, contribute to shared projects, or transfer files" (OECD 2005: 73), which has numerous advantages for education in the form of e-learning and communication. Many musicians have "embraced the internet as creative and inspiration-enhanced workspace where they can communicate, collaborate, and promote their work" (ibid.: 80). The internet has thereby enabled a much more direct relationship with their fans. The internet has also meant lower barriers to entry for artistic creation, as there are reduced/no costs for physical pressing and distribution, combined with fewer costs for finding new talent who can now be "discovered" through music promotion sites like MySpace and SoundCloud. The internet has thus positively altered the market conditions of artistic start-up, which goes further into opportunities for participation in digital music practices, whereby network users—prosumers—have become important participants in the whole chain of content creation, production, marketing, promotion, distribution, and consumption.

With the emergence of the internet, the music recording industry has faced serious challenges in competing with "free" digital music, accompanied by the current moral panic surrounding the illegal file-sharing debacle. To critics of globalization, then, the age of digital music provides *the* conditions for achieving artistic autonomy and independence, and emancipation from the exploitative and alienating forces of global capitalism, and for circumventing the practices of the major labels, triggered by unauthorized file-sharing and downloading, which has impacted on the music recording industry's control over the commodification, standardization, and homogenization of popular music. Thus, while western cultural domination coexists with localized forms of popular culture and the western conglomerates still dominate the popular music market, this phenomenon has been significantly undermined by the internet and musical digitization, as it means free, ubiquitous music for consumers and the democratization of musical participation, whether during listening and socializing to, performing, or making music. Technological advancements and the interconnectedness via the internet have meant that ripping and burning on home PCs is a form of resistance to the transnational corporations' control over musical manufacturing, distribution, marketing, and promotion. Resistance, in simple terms, means autonomy, that is, complete independence for artists and audiences. To (leftist) critics, then, this stage of globalization has ultimately meant the antithesis of commodity fetishism and musical standardization.

Communications "from below" undoubtedly evoke optimism to fulfil some kind of cultural radicalism. However, the media corporations reacted quickly to this cyber anarchy by bringing the virtual spaces into the commodity market system and subjecting them to advertising, exemplified, for example, by the buy-out of MySpace by Rupert Murdoch in 2006 (McGuigan 2009: 84). Such ideals as expressive communicative freedoms brought about by the world-wide web are therefore not facilitated under neoliberal arrangements, which cleverly combine corporate manipulation and citizen empowerment. While some cultural commodities, such as music, could be considered to convey or evoke deeper or more profound meanings, and could thus be considered to be special or more compelling than other commodities, they are still commodities. With the advent of interactive, social-networking media, the hyperactive cyber producer-consumer has become "the lynchpin conceptual source of neoliberal, free-market capitalism" (McGuigan 2016: 52). Technological innovation supports automation, which evidently aims to reduce labor power, costs, and boost profitability, and "not some public-spirited policy of freeing people for comfortably-off leisure activity" (ibid.: 183). Technological innovations have also tended to destroy traditional crafts and de-skill traditional artisans.

Moreover, technological innovation in communications since the time of mass migration and urban industrialism meant mobile privatization. In the music recording industry, mobile privatization began with the invention of the Sony Walkman in 1979, which led to a new kind of revolution in people's relationship to recorded music, namely by creating a private audio space within public physical space. The widespread social and cultural acceptance of listening to music "privately" in public marked a shift in the decline of the public as a direct effect of neoliberalism. This type of technology was followed by the 2G mobile phone in the 1990s and the online iPhone and smartphones soon thereafter. Cellular phones are ubiquitous around the world today. Their emergence meant a hyper-individualization in neoliberal culture. With the advent of the iPhone, telephony was combined with digital music consumption. These "all-purpose mobile communication devices" are the coolest commodities today (McGuigan 2016: 55) and have acquired the status of "Apparatgeist" (McGuigan 2009: 125). Online mobile phones, tablets, and laptops mean an ever more mobile and privatized way of life, and are deeply entrenched in young people's patterns of daily use. Mobile privatization is thus a characteristic feature of modern life, which effectively combines "much greater actual and virtual mobility, on the one hand, with an increasingly cocooned, individualized and perhaps isolated social existence, on the other hand" (McGuigan 2016: 127).

Digital and gadget technologies, or so-called all-purpose mobile communication devices, including smartphones and Apple products (iPod, iPhone, iPad), are surrounded by a veritable explosion of commodity fetishism and cool seduction, and are believed to be essential to modern urban life under cool capitalism.

> [T]he industry behind online culture cajoles, seduces, and invites the user to move into becoming part of a different public sphere ... defined not by citizenship but rather by participation and, maybe even more significantly, revelation ... We are encouraged to participate in order to reveal elements of ourselves [which] has an economic motivation (Marshall 2016: 76).

Communication gadgets are also tokens of global exploitation of cheap labor elsewhere in the world. Everyday life under neoliberal capitalism is thereby marked by a proliferation of heavily fetishistic, although useful, communication gadgetry, which are designed in such a way to be extremely seductive, and at the center of both meaning construction and circulation and capital accumulation. Online platforms such as MySpace, Facebook, Instagram, Google+, LinkedIn, Pinterest, Tumblr, and so forth serve their users in the construction and production of a public self:

> We are constantly laboring on the presentation of ourselves for public consumption. Visibility, reputation, impression management, and impact are at play as we work and labor on the production of our online and public personas ... The sad truth of this persona production is that our labor is a massive information source that feeds the new structure of consumer culture, the new formation of advertising, and the new focused efforts to connect industries to help us construct smart public visions of ourselves (Marshall 2016: 6).

Social media are market research and advertising tools "to the cool machineries of capital" (McGuigan 2016: 38), designed for subtle manipulation and surveillance by consumers. The mobile private person, accompanied by a personal soundtrack, online and in constant touch, "is the ideal figure of cool-capitalist culture in the sphere of consumption and, to an extent, production as well" (ibid.: 39). Under neoliberal capitalism, the ideal today is the free movement of networked individuals. Mobile privatization is the epitome of sociocultural experience, through which the individual is naturalized into commodity fetishism and cool seduction. Thus dystopian critiques of the internet imply that technologies have facilitated the expansion of a culture of surveillance for the purpose of marketing and advertising, and governmental surveillance to combat illegality and potential terrorism, as well as the threats to privacy, including identity theft.

Cool capitalism illustrates "our" cultural complicities with white supremacist patriarchy and the persistence of racism and sexism in cool popular culture globally, while cool technologies have contributed to the veritable explosion of commodity fetishism and cool seduction under cool capitalism. Cool (neoliberal) popular culture extols celebrity and success, and promotes and celebrates values of the public self and possessive individualism. This development has thoroughly undermined egalitarianism, which calls into question the legitimacy of globalization and global hegemonic capitalism. We are in an age of interregnum, the historical point of postdemocracy, and this raises questions about the idea of active democratic citizenship, and how this activism is mobilized through and manifested in world popular music practices.

Notes

1. I am grateful to my colleague, Dr Fatima Khan, for informing me about this example during an informal conversation at work whilst she was finalizing an article about this same issue.
2. Robin James (2015) suggests that neoliberalism has led to the subjectification of women, meaning they must first recognize/acknowledge and then "overcome" the damage caused by contemporary hegemony, namely multi-racial white supremacist patriarchy (MRWaSP), and also show/display their overcoming of this damage—their "resilience"—for others to see ("looking").
3. For the actual photograph of Jim Morrison and Donna Mitchell, follow this link: http://doorsexaminer.com/doors-history-november-15-1967-jim-morrison-appears-in-vogue-magazine/ (accessed 29 November 2017).
4. Foucault's neoliberal governmentality represents both an extension and intensification of modern disciplinary regimes, which describes the shift toward individual self-disciplining, by firstly invoking individuals as entrepreneurs of their own existence, and secondly revaluing and regarding the body as a window to "successful" identity.

5 Popular Music in Postdemocracy

> Democratic politics ... needs a vigorous, chaotic, noisy context of movements and groups. They are the seedbeds of future democratic vitality (Crouch 2004: 120).

Globalization has shaped a popular culture that extols celebrity and success, and that promotes and celebrates values of the public self and possessive individualism. It has thoroughly undermined the egalitarianism that underpinned the welfare state, with painful consequences for socially vulnerable groups, including women, ethnic minorities, the young and old, the disabled, and so forth. Neoliberal culture has meant that since the 1990s, state policies have favored the interests of the wealthy and socially advantaged, who have benefited most from the unrestricted operation of the capitalist economy (Crouch 2004: vii).[1] The globalization of business interests and fragmentation of the population have meant that political advantage has shifted away from desires to reduce inequalities of wealth and power. The legitimacy of globalization and global hegemonic capitalism has thus been called into question routinely, given that the neoliberal project is truly hegemonic on a global scale. There have been innumerable sites of political contestation to globalization, including feminist, gay, and anti-racist campaigns. As neoliberalism became established, though, radical political culture changed to move away from the earlier "social critique" of capitalism that called into question the poverty, inequality, opportunism, and egoism associated with capitalism. From the 1970s to the 2010s, criticisms of capitalist civilization were predominantly marked by "the artistic critique" that voiced anger at "disenchanting and inauthentic features of capitalism, often combined with a general sense of oppression [with] demands for autonomy, liberation, authenticity and singularity" (McGuigan 2016: 54). Critical opposition to capitalism has thereby been somewhat marginalized in neoliberal times, rendering campaigning social movements of peace, equality, feminism, ecology, and so forth as sources of resistance to neoliberalism crucial for a twenty-first-century democracy. Capitalism, instead of suffering retreat, is strong and global, and despite interesting movements and forces, nothing is cohered to challenge and counteract global capitalism (Marshall 2016: 37).

Sociologist Colin Crouch (2004) describes the current period as "postdemocracy", a new historical point in the parabola of globalization, marked by the strengthening of the global firm—large corporations that have outgrown the governance capacity of individual nation states—with its political importance, and the decline of the working class, both numerically and increasingly disorganized and marginalized within that life, and the growth of a powerful political class of political advisers and business lobbyists. State provisions for ordinary people's lives have become increasingly insignificant. Consequently, ordinary people are apathetic about politics, being "reduced to the role of manipulated, passive, rare participants" (Crouch 2004: 21) with no or little interest in citizen involvement. Many countries have undergone complete commercialization of public services, including education, health, and other parts of the welfare state. Satisfaction with the conditions of liberal democracy has produced complacency with the rise of post-democracy, in which "there is little hope for an agenda of strong egalitarian policies for the redistribution of power and wealth, or for the restraint of powerful interests" (ibid.: 4). Global capitalism thereby leads to apathy, lack of affect, and depoliticized attitudes among young people around the world, who are "quite simply, 'cool' about the state of the world and how broken it seem[s]" (Cazdyn and Szeman 2011: 162).

The postdemocratic age means the trivialization of democracy due to the political and governmental control of privileged elites characteristic of pre-democratic times, signaling a crisis of egalitarian causes and politics that has rendered them increasingly impotent. Governments have meanwhile become fundamental for anti-egalitarian tendencies in postdemocracy, and so egalitarians "must learn to cope with it—softening, amending, sometimes challenging it—rather than simply accepting it" (Crouch 2004: 5). The shift toward postdemocracy raises questions about the idea of citizenship and signals a paradox in western democracies, in which "democracy has moved into a parabola" (ibid.: 5). This is the concern of the final chapter with its focus on the active democratic citizen, illustrating how this activism is mobilized through and manifested in world popular music practices.

Citizenship

The quality and character of social, democratic citizenship were historically linked to the welfare state during the mid-twentieth century, the heyday of "unrestrained capitalism" (Crouch 2004: 97). Social citizenship stood at the opposite end of market competition and profit, and the inequalities of the capitalist component of society. Today, in postdemocracy, these assumptions are seriously challenged as the maximization of markets, private ownership, and big business' ability to interfere with government stand in stark conflict with other (social) human goals. Since the arrival of neoliberal hegemony, the democratic rights of citizenship have been lost. Yet a more optimistic stance is possible, which recognizes two concepts of the active democratic citizen today: positive citizenship, marked by collective identities and their expression of shared interests; and negative citizenship, marked by protectionist activism against others, especially the state. Causes and pressure groups, organizations, self-help groups and communitarian networks, charities, and individual activists provide some of the answers for the present predicament, driven by both left-wing and right-wing rejection of big business interests, the monopolization of politics, and the retreating welfare state. While it is impossible to see any major reversal of capitalist practices in the music industry and, with it, the growing (political) power of the global firm, actions to try to shift away from the inexorable drift toward postdemocracy in all spheres of life are possible, including policies and actions available to concerned citizens themselves. Indeed,

> the search must therefore be for ways of retaining the dynamism and enterprise of capitalism while preventing firms and their executives from exercising power to a degree incompatible with democracy (Crouch 2004: 105).

Critical disquisition to postdemocracy centers around the counterproject to the hierarchical world of cultural domination, also recognizing that people are not a passive echo of dominant culture and stirring optimism concerning the influence of campaigning social movements on mainstream political agendas. What can the active, positive citizen do to bring to terms global financial capitalism and its product of postdemocracy? Active democratic citizenship seeks to address the "big issues" of politics and allows more optimistic views in favor of what a globalized world can potentially offer. Active citizenship and, with it, alternative and oppositional thinking, seek to overcome the impasse of neoliberal culture and policy. Active citizens critical of cool-capitalist culture engage with lifeworld issues often aesthetically and emotionally; this engagement or activism, in the realm of culture, is felt and expressed passionately and experienced as especially meaningful. Robin James talks about "a social justice strategy" (2015: 172) that, most and foremost, requires consciousness-raising and the recognition that the background conditions for multi-racial white supremacist patriarchy continue to support the vitality of only certain kinds of life.

Popular musicians and artists have long recognized that music can function as a catalyst for social change, a means for political communication, and an expression of democratic citizenship. Many popular musicians around the world have sought to relate their practice to the values of morality, humanitarianism, and democracy, justifying innovative approaches to musical material and performance practice in terms of democracy. Many musicians and musical activists seek to address the major imbalance between the role of corporate interests and those of other groups. Sonically noisy, some pop-rock music bears the aesthetics of "riot sounds" as anti-racist, anti-queer, etc. political responses to neoliberalism (James 2015: 69). Meanwhile, social inclusion projects have been championed globally as models of democratic process, while experiments in group improvisation, audience participation, and online networked performance seek new kinds of emancipation and egalitarianism in the name of musical democratization. Individual celebrities, too, become actors and agents to effect change in this highly privatized and individualized world, becoming involved in activism, charities, and philanthropy for altruistic purposes. For instance, rock artists like Paul McCartney and Brian May have fought animal rights by condemning proposals to bring back fox hunting in the UK (Lester 2015), while Bono with his (American Express) consumer/corporate-invested RED Campaign has provided funds to combat AIDS in Africa (Marshall 2016: 81). The charity single 'Do They Know It's Christmas' (1984) and the subsequent Live Aid Concert at Wembley Stadium in 1985, organized by Bob Geldof and Midge Ure, raised awareness about and funds for the famine in Ethiopia. Posthumous celebrity activism in tribute of Freddie Mercury by fellow band members, including the Freddie Mercury Tribute Concert for AIDS Awareness in 1992 with support from the likes of David Bowie, Liza Minnelli, Annie Lennox, George Michael, Elton John and others, the resultant EP 'Five Live' (1993) and DVD of the Tribute Concert (2002), and the 1996 exhibition of photographs of Mercury in the Royal Albert Hall in London, Japan, and other European cities, all in support of the charitable work of the Mercury Phoenix Trust, have provided significant funds to NGOs worldwide to help try to eradicate HIV/AIDS (Bennett 2017). Meanwhile, Taylor Swift has been actively engaged in extensive philanthropy, charity, and "meet-and-greets" with fans with disability. Yet, while most music celebrities no doubt believe in their causes and their advocacy provides much-needed exposure, celebrity morality and humanitarianism have become central in celebrity brand management in the twenty-first century, raising, in some instances, questions about the hypocrisy of "selling via activism" (Rocavert 2017: 14). Taylor Swift's pop activism with fans with disability, for instance, raises questions about the perpetuation of problematic representations of disability (Finlay and St Guillaume 2017: 36).

Some music celebrities have aligned themselves directly with politics and politicians, such as Katy Perry's support of Democratic presidential candidate

Hillary Clinton ('Roar and Stronger'), Fleetwood Mac's backing of Bill Clinton ('Don't Stop'), or will.i.am's support of Barack Obama ('Yes We Can') (Jamieson 2016). Kid Rock is notoriously known for his support of Republican candidates, including Mitt Romney (in 2012) and Donald Trump (in 2016), and he sells Trump merchandise on his website. Kid Rock's political views tend toward the libertarian and are strongly anti-left, and in a 2015 interview with *Rolling Stone* he referred to Obama as "Obummer" (Guardian Music 2017). Meanwhile, in June 2017 grime MCs championed Labour leader Jeremy Corbyn in the lead-up to the general (snap) election in Britain through a live music event in north London that was organized by Grime4Corbyn, a grassroots campaign group to encourage electoral registration among Black and Minority Ethnic (BME) youth (Duggins 2017a). The campaign group created a pro-voting registration website, featuring the track 'Corbyn Riddim', which sets a Corbyn speech to a bombastic instrumental (Duggins 2017b).

While democracy is a highly contested category, one that has been imagined in many different ways, many popular musicians believe in the "democratic" nature of music and their musical and extra-musical practices in their fight for particular kinds of freedom and equality. Their musical practices embody democratic processes. Music can be a metaphor and model for democracy in the work of activist musicians (Love 2006). Activist musicians often address fundamental problems of social justice and difference in neoliberal democracies, which have historically assimilated difference. Democratic practices do not change power relations in society, which are deeply embedded in the dualistic thinking in western culture through which the other is colonized by a variety of processes that assimilate difference. The music of activists from the feminist and civil rights and anti-racism movements, specifically, engages deep, fluid energies of civil society by modeling a concrete democratic conversation that embraces humanity, justice, and equality. Active citizenship means to mobilize new social identities by recognizing

> their outsider status in the political system, and to make both noisy and articulate demands for admission ... We have already seen how feminist movements have provided very recent, very major instances of this. Ecological movements provide others. This constant scope for new disruptive creativity within the *demos* gives egalitarian democrats their main hope for the future (Crouch 2004: 116).

Clearly, then, many popular musicians around the world believe in the democratic nature of music and their musical practices in their fight for particular kinds of freedom and equality, evident in the work of activist musicians involved in the multiculturalism, anti-racism, feminist, and other, even far right, movements. They address fundamental problems of social justice and difference in neoliberal democracies, which have historically assimilated difference and are deeply embedded in the dualistic thinking in western culture through which the other is colonized by a variety of processes. Popular music thereby engages deep, fluid energies of civil society by modeling a concrete democratic conversation that embraces humanity, justice, and equality.

World Music and Democracy

Democratic concerns, coupled with resistance to globalization, can be seen in the workings of the independent music record labels, which are less tied to the corporate structures, and so also release music records from more varied musical styles and/or grassroots music. The independents are also more willing to take risks, musically, politically, and financially, that the major labels are not willing to take. As a product of globalization, World Music is inextricably tied up within these debates. Yet World Music has, at times, ignited pessimism about the historical, political, and economic subjugation and exploitation of the third world by powerful capitalist corporations. For instance, the resilient echoes of postcolonialist discourse have criticized forms of musical collaboration, particularly in the context of World Music, with dreary accusations of "appropriation" and as benefiting from western positionality. World Music became frequently scorned as "'colonial', the music of 'conversion' or 'tourist' music" (Day 2008: 92), and "thwarted in the literatures as 'exotic', with a tendency to exoticize and overemphasize those styles and genres of indigenous pop-rock that appeal to western ears as authentic in an essentialist way" (Regev 2013: 27).

The Bhundu Boys serve as a powerful example of the criticisms surrounding musical commercialization that show how World Music is used in profit-driven ways. Along similar lines, Youssou N'Dour has been heavily criticized by critics, scholars, and fans for compromising his music for economic reasons: "As his fame and popularity have grown, N'Dour has had to face criticisms that his music, which was, early on, a conscious attempt to re-Africanize Senegalese music, has become too slick, too commercial, too western" (Taylor 1997: 134). Musical collaborations have been scorned by some as being "neo-colonial" or "tourist music" (Day 2008: 92; Howard 2009), while some western artists and their corporations have been criticized for being "cavalier and negligent, if not outright exploitative" of world sounds (White 2012: 198). Scorned as musical appropriations, the apparent "neo-colonial othering" in commercialized popular culture has transformed history "into an exotic cultural spectacle [and] becomes a marketable commodity for metropolitan consumption" (Huggan 2001: 115). Such criticisms resonate with pessimistic views that "neoliberal globalization is America's attempt to remake the world in its own image, a form of neo-Darwinist colonisation" (Lechner and Boli 2004: 160), and thus conceiving myths through misrepresentation and simulation in popular music practices. To ethnomusicologist Martin Stokes, pop star collaborations constitute nothing more than neo-orientalist forms of musical appropriation:

> [M]ore recent, mass-mediated kinds of cosmopolitanism ... involved musical encounters orchestrated by prominent rock and pop stars in the west: Peter Gabriel, Brian Eno, Robert Fripp, Transglobal Underground, Sting, Natacha Atlas and others ... Though billed as exchanges and fusions, they graft exotic sounds onto a western rock and pop musical infrastructure and as such constitute—in my mind—a musical prolongation of nineteenth century orientalism ... [T]he cultural politics of these musical "exchanges" rarely attract comment, let alone criticism. And Gabriel, Eno, Fripp *et al.* are serious musicians, after all. Most of us are inclined to give them the benefit of the doubt, I guess. We might consider this particular kind of cosmopolitanism, then, as appropriation by musical neo-orientalists for a western market in exotica (Stokes 2007: 8).

The validity of the binary opposition between authenticity and commercialization is difficult to sustain, and debates surrounding authentic and true versus commercial and banal music must be approached more carefully, as it would be misleading to view some music as a raw material that is simply mined by corporate interests. Indeed, ownership of musical styles is difficult to apportion. Much popular music around the globe is the result of the musical creativity of the musicians, so "any ideas that these are innocent noble savages who are gonna be corrupted by Western influences is rubbish!" (Andy Kershaw, in Cooper *et al.* 2013). Ian Anderson put it as follows:

> Nowhere in any of this was there the faintest whiff of exploitation, exclusivity, cliques, ghettoization, conspiracies, cultural imperialism, racism or any of the other nonsensical-isms that have been chucked at the notion since, often by people who ought to know better and in the end do little more than expose their own foibles. It was simply a great idea, followed up by a lot of unprecedented co-operation between enthusiasts (very few thought of each other as business rivals) who wanted others to have more opportunity to share their enthusiasms. Yes, it was good for business, but by being so it was automatically good for the incomes of the artists too. Of course ... one can see that having such a simple concept without any baggage was still likely to bring problems. Even if the original idea was virus-free, it was bound to get thoroughly bugged as others logged on (Anderson 2000).

Indeed, it begs the question whether critics of World Music (notably ethnomusicologists) have actually spoken with and listened to the voices of Peter Gabriel, Ry Cooder, Sting, or other World Music artists and producers to gain a fuller understanding of their perceptions and intentions? How and why do such criticisms proffer that "for Gabriel, Africa is an antidote to the modern West, with its categorical and rigid distinctions between spirituality and sensuality, the body and technology, nature and culture" (Stokes 2012: 113)? Is that *really* how Peter Gabriel regards Africa? Lucy Durán, in her recent article titled "Our Stories, From Us, The 'They'" (2014), critiqued this trend in the academic literatures of making sweeping assumptions about the thought processes, strategies, and motives of World Music artists and producers, "question[ing] the methodology of writers who feel they can speak for the views and attitudes of record producers without consulting or interviewing them directly" (133). Durán specifically refers to a chapter, "World Music Producers and the Cuban Frontier" from the book *Music and Globalization: Critical Encounters* (White 2012), in which she found "a marked tendency to attribute 'these foreign producers of Cuban music' [Durán is included here] with identical characteristics, thoughts and motives, almost like a kind of oldschool anthropological view of the 'tribe'" (2014: 134). She goes on to ask:

> The World Music industry has had its fair share of criticism from academics. But I baulked at the idea that "all these producers" (though unnamed) behaved and thought uniformly. I felt uncomfortable about the underlying pejorative tone of these assumptions. Did they all act like "old colonial traders"? Did they feign a "vague sympathy for the Cuban regime" in order to do business on the island? Did they really all cultivate an "image of cosmopolitanism"? Who is actually being described here? As someone who was involved in the presentation of Cuban music in the UK during the 1980s, following closely the developments of *Buena Vista Social Club* and other albums produced by Nick Gold, and also as someone who wears three hats—that of academic, journalist and music producer—I do not recognize either myself or my colleague Nick Gold in these descriptions ... Why were our views not elicited? I am reminded of a Malian proverb, often quoted by Mali's iconic desert musician, Ali Farka Touré: "If you shave the head of a man, he must be present" (Durán 2014: 134–35).

If ethnomusicology is the study of humans making music, then surely such a top-down approach toward academic writing about World Music raises ethical concerns and serious questions around power and representation. Aren't western record producers humans too? And if only "other" people's voices are valid in ethnomusicological research and writing, doesn't that too resemble some form of exoticist academicism? Indeed, listening to their voices reveals a desire toward active democratic citizenship through the producing, recording, promoting, and so forth of World Music. Disregarding artists' and producers' desires and motives for musical modernization and/or collaboration as mere "appropriations" should thus be viewed with extreme caution. Consequently, "one conclusion, in the context of such academic analysis, is that we need more critical encounters between the creative industries and academics. Both voices need to be heard, in conversation, discussing processes of production" (Durán 2014: 137). Addressing the disparity between the deleterious worldviews presented by hegemonic western institutions and actual reality, it could be argued that those very critiques have gone too far. Western conceptions of the "non-West" (Said 1978, 2003) have stretched too far in the opposite direction, forbidding all cross-cultural interaction whatsoever. Immersed in the discourse of "neo-post-colonialism", such thinking thwarts any attempt to bridge the gap between cultures constructed by overzealous cultural relativism and post-colonialist liberalism. Musical hybridity and democracy are thereby regarded as opportunities and positive consequences of globalization.

Musical Incorporation
A more fruitful way of looking at the phenomenon of musical collaboration and mixing is, what Roshanak Kheshti termed, "musical incorporation" (2015) in the context of a transformed, contemporary World Music industry. Incorporation refers to the ways in which people absorb that which they want to make their own. It conveys that the hybrid musical forms come to the listeners through noble and respectable methods, as opposed to through theft, which is typically the way that appropriation is thought of. By incorporating different sounds, musicians incorporate the cultural, historical, racial make-up of these sounds into themselves. The musical endeavors of Peter Gabriel, Youssou N'Dour, and others may therefore be understood within this transformed sense of appropriation in World Music. Indeed, many of the attendees of the infamous 1987 meeting are "far from being hard-bitten music execs, they still get emotional when they encounter something new and ring all their friends" (Arts Council England 2005: 8). World Music thus also ignites optimistic views about the exuberance of new world popular musics created and owned by musicians themselves, and about World Music consumption as a gesture of solidarity against the conglomerates. Indeed, independents such as Peter Gabriel's Real World offer a positive balance by promoting World Music artists to the western-buying populace in highly ethical ways with an emphasis on human rights, fair pay, and cross-pollination between different musical cultures (White 2012: 200). Real World's aim is to provide talented musi-

cians from around the world the opportunity to gain reach beyond their own geographical boundaries, and thus makes an important contribution toward cultural exchange, knowledge, and appreciation of other cultures and their musics:

> Before Real World, only with great determination, or a lot of travelling, was it possible to access music by artists working outside western Europe and North America. Now, you can stroll into high street stores and find CDs of music from every continent, many of them bearing the Real World colour bar logo. There is an enormous variety of styles, moods and genres on CDs that bear this logo (Real World Records 2017a).

Ian Anderson further argues:

> It's not all positive, but World Music (or Musique du Monde in neighbourly Paris) is way ahead on points. It sells large quantities of records that you couldn't find for love or money two decades ago. It has let many musicians in quite poor countries get new respect (and houses, cars and food for their families), and it turns out massive audiences for festivals and concerts. It has greatly helped international understanding and provoked cultural exchanges—people who've found themselves neighbours in the same box have listened to each other and ended up making amazing music together. Oh, and it has allowed a motley bunch of enthusiasts to not yet need to get proper jobs. I call it a Good Thing, and just feel a bit sorry for people with the thinking time on their hands to decide they hate World Music ... Lighten up, guys, it's only a box in a record shop (Anderson 2000).

Due to globalization, World Music has gained many followers in the western world over the last three to four decades, seeing the rising popularity of World Music stars such as Buena Vista Social Club, Youssou N'Dour, and Mariza. Globalization has fueled the education of consumers about different cultures, traditions, histories, and creativities around the world. It has created access to the rest of the world through travel, migration, and tourism. In terms of music, globalization has brought not only musics from other cultures to the western sphere, but it has also initiated a desire in many artists to work collaboratively with foreign musicians, wherever "foreign" may be for them. Thus, even if the World Music industry may be regarded as a "cottage industry" within the music business with generally low record sales, World Music continues to contribute to the diversity of live and recorded music by new, non-mainstream artists.

Peter Gabriel's Real World. World Music celebrates "what is arguably our greatest achievement—multiculturalism" (Patience 1998: 6), and perhaps one of the greatest proponents of this idea is Peter Gabriel. Throughout a long career of writing, performing, and producing, collaboration and musical heterogeneity were some of his most enduring themes. Gabriel was one of the principal organizers of the WOMAD foundation (World of Music, Art and Dance) and associated festival events (the first festival was held in 1982), the goal of which was the bringing together of musicians from all over the globe. Yet in the early 1980s, artists who performed at the WOMAD festival could not get a record deal in the UK, so Amanda Jones who ran a small label called WOMAD Records approached Peter Gabriel regarding the recording of world artists. Gabriel felt persuaded and created Real World Records; one of the first records released on this label was with the great qawwali singer Nusrath Fateh Ali Khan. In its thirty-something years' existence, the label has produced around 160 titles, many of which are the result of collaborations or fusions between musicians from different parts of the world or producers and artists from different backgrounds (Amanda Jones, interviewed in Maas and Zeppenfeld 2009). The idea behind Real World Records is *collaboration* on the basis that "when people are concerned with purism, they are denying the ability of a traditional artist to grow as an artist" (Michael Brook, interviewed in Maas and Zeppenfeld 2009).

In 2008, the *Big Blue Ball* album was released, which is the product of many years of collaboration between artists and producers from different parts of the world. The album grew out of so-called recording weeks in 1991, 1992, and 1995 when Gabriel invited musicians playing at the WOMAD festival to meet, jam, swap musical ideas, play, and consolidate musical material. The recorded material generated was immense until Stephen Hague began sorting through it. After fifteen years, the resultant *Big Blue Ball* album represents one of the greatest examples of musical hybridization and cultural cross-fertilization to date. Its release was accompanied by a visual art exhibition around its theme, at the center of which was a three-dimensional ball mapped out by whiteboards featuring video messages from places around the world, which sought to transform the large flatscreens into futuristic paintings. To Peter Gabriel,

> *Big Blue Ball* is I think an act of globalization. It's an act of trying to bring the world together and to explore it. Globalization I think has had a bad publicity. As I think of myself as a global citizen, you know, I still have attachments to my country but I live and work with people from all around the world, and my life is so much richer. I've learnt so much more from having done that (Peter Gabriel, interviewed in Maas and Zeppenfeld 2009).

5 Popular Music in Postdemocracy 239

Figure 5.1: Album cover of *Big Blue Ball* (2008). This album was the product of several years of collaboration between artists and producers from around the world. The album represents one of the greatest examples of musical hybridization and musical cross-fertilization to date. @ *Big Blue Ball*. A Real World design, by Marc Bessant. Courtesy of Real World Records Ltd. Reproduced with permission (licence reference 201611-06).

Gabriel's recording approach is shared across many of his albums, for instance the exact same "status" is afforded to Gabriel's session guitarist, the English-born David Rhodes in terms of the recording mix. His Real World recording studio in Bath, which he founded around 1986, also evokes democracy. The studio was built around performance to make people feel comfortable, so there is no artificial separation between recording space and control room to break down the division between them and us. Gabriel continues to explain that

> you can tell how civilized a person is by where they put the boundary between them and us and, the idea being, the more people you could include in the us-bracket, the better things will likely to be... It's very easy for us to think of others as them, and as soon as you start that division you have enshrined a problem (Peter Gabriel, interviewed in Maas and Zeppenfeld 2009).

Moreover, globalization in fact supports Peter Gabriel's, and many of the musicians he has collaborated with, human rights activism by embracing globalizing technologies (see Witness Org 2014), which in turn resembles a means of resistance to the negative globalizing tendencies. Notable here is his work with Youssou N'Dour in raising awareness of AIDS in Africa, or his efforts to preserve music and arts in Cambodia:

> I think we are at a unique point in our evolution because for the very first time, anyone on the planet can communicate with anyone else on the planet in the same way I can go into Google Earth and actually go down to the tree in my garden. I should be able to ... drill down and zoom in to the person who has lost their house in the cyclon, who has got HIV, who is in a warzone and hear their experience, their story, not in the words of the news channel, but in their words, so they can speak for themselves and be seen and heard. So I would call that a fundamental human right. And something we can now do with this technology, layer one, we have thought of Witness.org. Witness.org is a human rights organization we started about 16 years ago to try and encourage the use of technology in human rights campaigning. And the dream is that anyone that has bad stuff happening to them might be able to upload video images or photos or text of what's going on, of their story and their experience. The power of observation, which was used to control people in old-world speak ... is now being reversed on its head and is allowing ordinary people to control those in power. Layer two is connectivity and campaigning. Having told these stories, you know the people who care about them or might care about them and the people who are campaigning about them, how do you connect them around the world in such a way to make a difference (Peter Gabriel, interviewed in Maas and Zeppenfeld 2009).

In embracing globalization, Peter Gabriel is also critically aware of the absence of global governance for a global civil society and thus conceived (together with Richard Branson) the idea of The Elders. They proposed their idea to Nelson Mandela, who brought together The Elders in 2007 to form "an independent group of global leaders who work together for peace and human rights" (Elders 2014). The potential of globalization, offered to us by the benefits of mass communication and technologies, cultural cross-fertilization, and multiculturalism, is very high and one of great humanitarian value. It indeed provides opportunities for greater cross-cultural understanding and appreciation. Many similar contemporary musical practices may be understood within the context of a diasporic cosmopolitanism underpinned by neo-Kantian cosmopolitan values, in which there is a genuine acceptance of the cultural other and the possibility of a togetherness in difference.

Feminism, Resistance, and Popular Music

One major form of resistance and disruption to neoliberalism and postdemocracy has been the political mobilization of women. Historically, women gave little autonomous expression of their demand, given their roles as guardians of the family and lack of organization, so not to upset the (gendered) status quo. Indeed, "to articulate a feminine vision is to criticize a masculine one" (Crouch 2004: 61). Since the 1970s, there has been a mobilization of female identities and their political expression, which began with a small group of intellectuals and extremists and grew into a major social movement beyond official feminist movements, even though "feminist pioneers might not have had phenomena like Girl Power in mind when they sought to mobilize their sisters" (ibid.: 62). Nonetheless, the movement for political autonomy for women "has constituted a democratic moment within the overall framework of the onward march of post-democracy, reminding us that major historical tendencies can be contradicted" (ibid.: 63).

The singer and musician Ani DiFranco once suggested:

> All decent people, male and female, are feminists. The only people who are not feminists are those who believe that women are inherently inferior or undeserving of the respect and opportunity afforded men. Either you are a feminist or you are a sexist/misogynist. There is no box marked "other" (1998).

DiFranco's words have high relevance in today's media landscape in which music carries a powerful message and a moral responsibility. The feminist movement has played a significant role in challenging the hegemonic order of the global music business and wider society, as these were shaped by, what bell hooks calls, "imperialist white supremacist capitalist patriarchy" (hooks 2004: 17). Feminist popular music has thereby functioned in opposition to the cultural hegemonic norm, and in doing so, revealed, challenged, and resisted stereotypical and oppressive role models, and hence unequal power structures. Feminism has attempted to radically challenge women's place in the global music industry. This section includes a historical development of feminism, starting with the development of second-wave feminism in the late 1960s and early 1970s, and how this movement has been challenged by several other feminisms, including psychoanalysis, which became hugely influential in the latter part of the 1970s and led to postfeminism. Feminism, as it is known today, is a multifaceted and contested term based on the collective belief that "women, purely and simply because they are women, are treated inequitably within a society which is organized to prioritize male viewpoints and concerns" (Gamble 2001b: vii).

Feminism grew out of the activism that addressed the suffragette movements of the late nineteenth century, opposed women's oppressions in equality, and aimed at changes within society. Subsequently, steps toward the "women's liberation" movement were taken by members of left-wing university/college campus organizations in the mid- to late 1960s, which grew out of the fact that women, while taking the same risks as their male counterparts (like getting arrested or expelled from college) never held lead roles within their campus protest organizations, and proposals to include gender discrimination in the meeting agendas were rejected by their male peers. Women thus started their own activist groups, a historic split in the counterculture, reinterpreting Marxist approaches toward institutionalized power relations (e.g. in education, law, and marriage) in private life, such as domestic work and sexual relationships. Such early forms of feminism were limited to a small group of intellectuals and radicals, and thus often ridiculed by the popular media. The feminist movement became later (from the 1960s until 1980s) known as second-wave feminism, which was created by largely middle-class women concerned with counterculture in the US and addressed the inequalities of the legal system. Feminism became increasingly a movement against sexual oppression, a desire for equal rights for women, and generally a protest against the hegemonic order and, with it, "racism, capitalism, hetero-normativity, classism, and cultural and political imperialism" (Garrison 2004: 185). Pragmatic second-wave feminist thought focused on equality and saw political areas, such as equal pay and career opportunities, as essential. Feminist theories and practices thus have become hugely diverse, but to simplify the matter feminism is often regarded simply as a movement seeking to change and improve the social, cultural, and political position of women, tainted by feminism's often misinterpreted reaction to men. Indeed, feminism seemed to give women permission to unleash their rage and hatred at men, but it did not allow men to think about the art of loving men (hooks 2004: xii). Second-wave feminism has often been criticized for falling into the trap of agreeing with patriarchal ideology, that is, a general assumption that the areas in which men dominate are of most value. Consequently, second-wave feminism "encouraged women to *become* like men" (Whiteley 2000: 76), a view challenged later by postfeminism.

During the 1960s, the impact of feminism on popular music was certainly limited. While prior to rock 'n' roll, music performed by women made up one third of all singles sales, with the arrival of rock music (and after the British rock invasion into the US), female artists' sales decreased to 6 percent of the top 50 singles in 1969 (Chapple and Garofalo 1977: 277). Similarly, the number of pop songs that implied sex, and the number of females as initiators, significantly increased between the 1960s and 70s. In much pop music, women were portrayed as sex objects to be directed at the male gaze. Thus, male dominance in the rock music business continued in both the representations and musical careers of female rock stars, and female music artists of the counterculture era suffered due to the dissemination of their public image remaining in the hands of male gatekeepers of popular culture. The late Sheila Whiteley explained that "both the lifestyle and the musical ethos of the period undermined the role of women, positioning them as either romanticized fantasy figures, subservient earth mothers or easy lays" (2000: 23), and during the mid- to late 1970s, despite feminist advancements, music journalism continued to represent female musicians in this way.

Thus, within the dominating hegemonic practices in the music industry, women who embodied feminist ideologies, whether consciously or subconsciously, found it hard to be taken seriously in a music business dominated by men. They tackled this problem in various ways. Early blues singers of the 1920s such as Bessie Smith Janis challenged lingering nineteenth-century beliefs that women were naturally passive, pure, and passionless (Sheehan 2017). They also refused to be defined by negative white/black stereotypes that equated black women as hypersexual. The subject of Smith's blues included queer desire, infidelity, and intimate partner violence. Blues women also paved the way for gender bending, playing with bisexuality and queer desire long before Little Richard, David Bowie, Grace Jones, Annie Lennox, and others. Joplin, for example, adopted masculine traits at the expense of her feminine qualities in order to be accepted within the rock music genre at the time, regardless of her singing talent and strong personality. For women to represent hard, aggressive performers, it was thus necessary for artists like Janis Joplin to be branded as "one of the boys" (Leonard 2007: 37), with descriptions of her physical appearance often demoting her looks to the realms of strange, unattractive or even abnormal in an attempt to limit the disruptive potential of her self-assured sexuality and confidence. The struggle for women can be located within the dichotomous binary between "masculine authenticity" versus "female artificiality", and the construction of women as "fragile pop singers" that limited and marginalized them to the status of backing singers in the world of rock (Coates 1997: 53). Women were thereby constructed as the other in society (Cook and Tsou 1994). In neoliberalism, women also continue to be disadvantaged in employment in the cultural sector, and have typically remained near the bottom of corporate hierarchies, with comparatively few women in a position of power and control (McGuigan 2009: 184; McRobbie 2016).

Feminist Movements and Musicians
Feminism encouraged female artists to participate in popular music. Feminist support networks emerged to support female participation in popular music by providing material resources such as musical instruments and technology, training, as well as confidence. During the late 1960s/early 1970s in both the US and Great Britain, women-targeted music with feminist and lesbian lyrics

emerged from numerous bands and solo artists. There was also a growing trend toward establishing women-only groups, workshops, rehearsals, and dance and performance spaces, all of which reflected a sense of feminist collectivism and community among female musicians (Cohen and Leonard 2003: 75). During the 1970s, new women-run music businesses were established, such as Olivia Records (1973) in the US. Various other feminist initiatives to emerge in recent decades included music festivals that showcased the work of female musicians, including the annual Chard Festival of Women in Music in England, promoting folk, classical, jazz, and contemporary music; the New Zealand Composing Women's Festival with concerts showcasing a vast array of styles from jazz to opera to hip hop; or Michigan Womyn's Music Festival, an event completely built, staffed, and run by women. Motivated by the desire to challenge male dominance within mainstream rock music and increase the prominence of females in music-making, these festivals helped to challenge the inequalities prevalent in the production of cultural artefacts, while raising the profiles of female artists and offering a platform for creative expression. A very current example of female empowerment is the Australian *Women in Pop Magazine*, whose first issue was published in 2017, which is dedicated to giving female pop artists from around the globe "the attention they deserve" (Women in Pop 2017) with the aim of reversing the "injustice towards female musicians" (Dawson 2017).

Riot Grrrl. During the early part of the 1990s, a feminist networking group labelled "Riot Grrrl" was promoted by musicians and performers within the underground rock music communities of Olympia, Washington, and Washington DC in the US, which aimed to empower girls and women, enlighten them to the prospect of becoming involved in the production of music, and to challenge restrictive gender roles that had previously deterred the participation of women in the rock music scene (Leonard 1997). Often associated with third-wave feminism, Riot Grrrl is an underground feminist hardcore punk movement that "foregrounded women's involvement in the music making process ... transforming the male-dominated song tradition into an expression of femininity" (Bock 2008: 6). The Riot Grrrl movement was fundamentally opposed to the overtly masculine customs of the music industry and actively sought to challenge the dominant roles of males. It was created by women for women. Indeed, "Riot Grrrls' explorations of assertiveness, confidence, and agency traits rarely afforded to female youth in the public sphere, are evident in much of the writing and imagery associated with this community" (Kearney 2006: 69). Riot Grrrl soon expanded its network to the UK, Canada, and other regions within the US, which resulted in the establishment of extensive (print and electronic) "zine" networks and an abundance of dedicated Riot Grrrl websites, and the creation of numerous female-centered punk rock bands. The production of Riot Grrrl zine articles and their differing distribution networks were particularly prominent during Riot Grrrl's existence and had a fundamental cultural impact throughout its movement. Besides female empowerment, Riot Grrrl bands often addressed issues such as rape, domestic abuse, sexuality, racism, and patriarchy. For example, a group of young females affiliated with Riot Grrrl organized a one-off event in 1995 called Free to Fight! with the objective of providing empowerment and addressing violence and ill-treatment, which was followed by an album compilation and zine comprising women's recollections of mistreatment and male harassment, both of which were distributed through private record shops and helped to finance complementary self-preservation classes for women.

Connections to punk music underpinned the DIY culture and "amateurist ethos" inherent in punk as a catalyst for the Riot Grrrl movement in the US, where punk represented a move away from the mainstream hippie music dominating the 1960s and offered an alternative, more aggressive and assertive approach to music-making. Punk was identified with notions of resistance not only musically, but also in terms of its distinct fashion and lifestyle, while challenging—visually—the mainstream culture by standing out from the crowd and being noticed. Through mode of dress, which typically consisted of school uniforms combined with bunched hair and ribbons representative of childhood, riot grrrls sought to challenge traditional conventions of beauty and femininity. "Hello Kitty" accessories were particularly popular due to the cat motif's association with childhood, even though the brand was thoroughly entwined in western capitalism. Many Riot Grrrls bands labelled their bodies with words like "slut" and "whore" as both a protective and assertive means of communication, and thereby "to shock and confront gender conformity" (Leonard 2007: 121). Interestingly, why the Riot Grrrl movement was centered on the punk scene, at least to a large extent, is somewhat unclear, since 1970s punk in Britain was not at all female friendly. While there was an increase in female performers toward the end of the 1970s, punk was particularly restrictive toward women in that it did not afford female musicians the opportunity to explore the limits and confines of their gender. Riot Grrrl is thus often regarded as a musical genre that grew out of indie rock and was inspired by the punk scene, which subsequently grew into a musical movement, in which women could express themselves equally to men. In doing so, the Riot Grrrl movement helped females to make their own mark in a male-dominated punk scene:

> Riot Grrrl made punk once again accessible to females and a place for the enactment of femininity. In a playful—but always confrontational—manner, riot grrrls reclaimed the punk stage, which they were forced to leave during the hardcore era (Bock 2008: 53).

One of the most prevalent impacts of the Riot Grrrl movement occurred within the musical sphere. During the peak of the Riot Grrrl movement, some of the pioneering Riot Grrrls bands (e.g. Bratmobile, Bikini Kill) worked with large record labels like K Records, thereby gaining a higher level of exposure in both the independent and commercial press. Yet, in order to challenge and undermine the capitalistic working practices of major record labels and their corporations, many Riot Grrrl bands started their own indie labels, most notably Mr Lady (formed by Kaia Wilson and Tammy Rae Carland) selling female-produced media, including music and film, with "bigger" bands like Bratmobile and Bikini Kills later also forming collaborations with independent record labels and subsequently forming their own indie labels (Kearney 2006). Lyrically, Riot Grrrl bands were confrontational, coupling "obscene lyrics [with] frilly frock" (O'Brien 2002: 166), while challenging male dominance combined with confrontation and dismissal: "Babes in Toyland's Kat Bjelland ... looking like a five-foot-something porcelain blonde, spat out songs about 'dirty motherfuckers' and potential rapists" (ibid.). For instance, many of Bikini Kill's songs are concerned with "sexual and physical abuse of women", while also tackling "girls' concerns about being unable to meet society's beauty standards and ideas of femininity" (Bock 2008: 91). The lyrics of 'Don't Need You' (1994) by Bikini Kill provide an interesting example in this context, while also reworking crude words like "whore" that many Riot Grrrls displayed on their bodies as a protective strategy: *Us punk rock whores don't need you.*

Meanwhile, early festivals operated as a catalyst for inspired action between females, while encouraging females to actively involve themselves in music and form their own bands. The last "official" Riot Grrrl conventions on record were held in 1995 in Los Angeles and Chicago (e.g. Midwest Girlfest), followed by gatherings in 1996 in Santa Barbara, Seattle, Portland, Philadelphia, and New York, which included political workshops and discussions of race and class privilege (Marcus 2010: 326). Subsequently, the Riot Grrrl movement splintered due to the mediated misrepresentations of its core message. Many followers felt that the feminist movement had been co-opted by the music business and that its politically radical aspects had been subverted by the Spice Girls' adoption of the "girl power" message. Nonetheless, similar gatherings inspired by the Riot Grrrl movement have been held since, notably the Ladyfest Art Festivals in cities worldwide; the queer-art Homo A Gogo festivals on the West Coast; and the annual Southern Girls Conventions (from 1999 until 2008). More specifically, Ladyfest first emerged in 2000 "in commemoration of riot grrrl" (Leonard 2007: 163) as a week-long event comprising art, performance, and musical activities, and aimed to drive forward the impetus that Rior Grrrl previously created, notably by offering a friendly and welcoming environment to female-centered musicians, groups, and performances. Its primary objective was to increase the presence of female musicians within indie and punk music scenes where females were/are often marginalized, and in doing so to continue the objectives of the Riot Grrrl movement to empower and promote female musicians. In 2001, Ladyfest was held three times in the US, followed in 2002 by nine events in the US, which triggered a rise in awareness and geographical spread as far as Indonesia and South Africa. The festival organizers developed a website to promote the Ladyfest brand to potential festival coordinators, which since led to more than 100 Ladyfest events being held globally. Ladyfest is often referred to as a DIY festival as it draws upon "aesthetics circulating within the punk and post-punk music scenes" (Leonard 2007: 164). A spin-off is the all-female rock music camp, which originated in Portland, Oregon, in 2001 and is now a global phenomenon, offering music lessons, workshops, instrument maintenance, silk screening band T-shirts, magazine making, and the like. The Girls Rock Alliance is the global umbrella organization that unites the camp leaders across the world, while Girls Rock Foundation, headed by artists such as Tegan and Sara, Kathleen Hanna, and Beth Ditto raises funds for the camps. London hosted its first camp in 2016, described by London branch leader Geraldine Smith as a "very positive and creative response to sexism in the music industry" (Singh 2017).

The Riot Grrrl movement also gained momentum and popularity through a variety of media, most notably a network of zines, which provided a communication platform for music-related matters and issues surrounding gender and sexuality. Zine articles also confronted taboo issues and sensitive matters, such as "date rape [and] abortion rights" (Whiteley 1997: 238). Zines were often handwritten by individuals, including hand-drawn sketches and embellishments, incurred inexpensive production through photocopying, and were circulated during Riot Grrrl performances, by post, and later electronically. Some zines adopted names like "bitch", "angst girl", and "odd girl out", thereby posing an aggressive challenge toward traditional notions of femininity, and often used alternative (incorrect) spellings like "luv" and "womyn" to challenge notions of conformity to middle-class expectations (Kearney 2006: 160–63). Importantly, zines have resisted corporate co-option by being self-produced in small quantities and distributed within the alternative feminist community for no/minimal profit. The Riot Grrrl zine network thus provides a striking example of resistance to capitalist ideologies through its conscious attempt to "exist outside the institutions that support commercial youth culture" (Kearney 2006: 68).

The Riot Grrrl movement opened the punk scene to females and helped reclaim its performance space for female musicians and audiences alike, notably also by participating in slam dancing in the mosh pit, the area directly in front of the stage, thereby challenging their supposed prohibition toward male counterparts. Riot Grrrl also provided a safe space to hear the voices of victims of crime and actively contributed to safeguarding, protecting, and supporting females. Riot Grrrl provided many females with the impetus to form bands, collaborations, and networks with similarly-minded females. In doing, so, Riot Grrrl imparted significant empowerment to females.

Ani DiFranco's Righteous Babe. Ani DiFranco is a champion of feminism in popular music and the concepts that surround it, while also facing criticism for her role in the feminist movement. Starting her own music label, Righteous Babe Records, at the age of nineteen, DiFranco has long been hailed as a pioneer of the DIY method of creating and releasing her own music. Her independent label Righteous Babe is based on an alternative economic model. Through musical and other forms of activism, independents seek to oppose the exploitative, capitalist structures of the major labels and support artists whose music would otherwise not be heard, while treating them fairly:

> The whole idea I had about not signing with a record company was about not participating in a corporate system, which I think homogenizes music, commercializes it, co-opts it, and you know, basically takes culture from people and sells it back to them—sucks the life out of it (Ani DiFranco, in Jhally *et al.* 2005b).

DiFranco first gained popularity in the early 1990s and saw her popularity rise among the major labels' feminist-constructed artists, including Alanis Morissette, Jewel, and PJ Harvey. Their rise triggered DiFranco to ask important questions about the role of women within the music business. Her popularity, reputation as an independent woman artist, and lyrical content have led her to become associated with feminism. In her song 'Not So Soft' (1994), DiFranco sings, "*I always wanted to be commander-in-chief of my own one-woman-army*", while telling the story of being in a boardroom with male chief executives at a record company and experiencing her period, which stains the white chair she sits on, clearly a statement against the much-hated corporate music industry and the men who run it whom she has rallied against. Meanwhile, in 'Face Up and Sing' (1994), she sings "*some guy tried to rub up against me on a crowded subway car*".

DiFranco clearly conveys her frustration with having to deal with sexism and misogyny in the everyday life of the global music industry. Her idea of feminism, while cautious about its use, may be described as "self-determination", whereby "every woman has the right to do whatever she needs to do" (1998). Even while she is recognized as a feminist figure, some critics regard her, and with it her beliefs and lyrical contents, more as a postfeminist. DiFranco has indeed explained that her sexuality is beyond categorization as she has had relationships with both men and women. In numerous interviews, she has expressed frustration at being labelled a "man hater" (when singing about women) and traitor (when singing about men) by some lesbian fans. While her gay female fans are her strongest supporters, they are also her biggest detractors, particularly when DiFranco married a man, which made her position as a feminist icon a controversial one. Even so, DiFranco once said that she regards herself as a "vehicle through which women could project their own goals of self-empowerment". If feminism is, as noted earlier, a movement toward positive change in the context of resistance and democratic citizenship, DiFranco is clearly a crucial figure.

Feminist Arabpop. Arab women have often been stereotyped as passive, voiceless, politically apathetic, and religiously repressed. But Arab women have long been committed to fighting for a more equitable society as active political players in trade unions, grassroots activism, and other political organizations. Social movements around the Middle East have thereby challenged preconceptions of the traditional role of women (Khan 2011). Arab pop, too, serves as a powerful avenue for Arab feminist expression. A recent example has been the music video for 'Hwages' (2017), translated as "Concerns" and interpreted by some media outlets as "God, Rid Us of Men!" (Desk 2017). The song was directed by singer Majed al-Esa who works for the Saudi production company, 8ies Studios. Known for his ability to take classic music and poetry, and transform them to cater for contemporary music tastes, Majed al-Esa also created the hugely successful 'Barbs Dance' (2015), a highly "addictive" dance tune across Saudi Arabia, which was similarly seen as provocative and immoral by conservative Saudi leaders (Observers 2016). His latest song 'Hwages', with its critical lyrics and symbolic visuals that mock patriarchy and misogyny, has been hailed as a feminist anthem from Saudi Arabia across the region.

The video's opening depicts three women dressed in *naqab* (a veil that covers the face with only the eyes uncovered) and colourful shoes and printed dresses, getting into a car that is driven by a young boy. The feminist critique is instantly obvious, as women are not allowed to legally drive in Saudi Arabia and obtain a driving license, or go out in public without their (male) guardians. They decide to swap the car for rollerblades and scooters, scootering and blading down the street amid an upbeat and energetic soundtrack, "hitting up" a basketball court, shooting hoops, even performing "cool" tricks with the basketball, riding a carousel, and dancing unabashedly, much to the dismay of the men around them who are seen shaking their heads at the expressive dance moves. The video moves on to the White House press room which is signed "House of Men", and overseen by a cardboard cut-out of president-elect Donald Trump, while listeners hold up deliberately misogynist signs and placards of women's faces crossed out. They then go bowling with pins incorporating men's faces. Lyrically, the song is highly critical of patriarchy, singing in Arabic "If only God would rid us of men!", an obsolete phrase used in the conservative region of Al-Qassim. In the second half, the song's rhythm changes and the dialect changes from the Al-Qassim region to a Saudi Bedouin dialect when they sing several phrases from an old Bedouin song.[2] Other lyrics include "*May men go extinct, they cause us to have mental illnesses*", referencing the lyrics of a 2014 protest song in Saudi Arabia (Hughes 2017), and "*They are making us go crazy*" (Desk 2017).

The song has taken the internet by storm, with some viewers branding it disgusting, offensive, and extremely inappropriate (Godden 2017; Hughes 2017), as well as receiving critical acclaim from parts of the Saudi community: "The new generation of women [that] is different from the past", according to one of the oldest newspapers in Saudi Arabia, *Al-Bilad* (Elizabeth 2017; O'Malley 2017). To many feminist thinkers, the song and video celebrate female empowerment and rights, and deliver

> a stark political and cultural message about the perception and freedom of women, most notably in a country that asks them to wear "modest" clothes, limit their interaction with men, forbids them from opening a bank account without a male guardian or driving their own cars and often shames them for competing in sports (O'Malley 2017).

Feminist Afropop. Gender inequality is similarly an issue across the African continent, that is being addressed by supergroup Les Amazones d'Afrique in their album *République Amazone* (2017). Les Amazones d'Afrique is a collective of twelve female west African musicians, comprising Grammy-winning Angélique Kidjo, Mariam Doumbia of the legendary duo Amadou and Mariam, international popstar and Nigerian singer-songwriter Nneka, Kandia Kouyaté, Mamani Keita, Mariam Koné, Massan Coulibaly, Mouneissa Tandina, Pamela

Badjogo, Rokia Koné, Madina N'Diaye, and Madiaré Dramé. Collectively, they are campaigning for gender equality and voicing their discontent against gender inequality and patriarchy in West Africa, including polygamy, forced marriage, sexual violence, abuse, and domestic violence. Sung in English, French, Bambara, and Fon, the songs tackle love, oppression, and female empowerment of women across Africa. The project has grown out of the realization that "What we found out was that female repression in the continent and in the world, is something that touches every woman. It's not a question of colour, or culture. It's something generic. All women can relate to it" (Brinkhurst-Cuff 2017). In doing so, Les Amazones d'Afrique continue a long tradition of west African female empowerment such as Adelaide Smith Casely Hayford, known as the "African Victorian feminist", who set up a girls' school in Freetown, Sierra Leone; and Margaret Ekpo, Funmilayo Ransome-Kuti and Gambo Sawaba, who fought in Nigeria's twentieth-century independence and emancipation movement. Moreover, their crowdfunding campaign helps finance the work of the Panzi Foundation, led by Doctor Mukwege in Bukavu (DRC), which has provided healing support to more than 80,000 women, nearly 50,000 of whom are survivors of sexualized violence (Real World Records 2017b).

Black Nationalism and Resistance in Political Hip Hop

Besides resistance to gender inequality and masculine hegemony, race is often used in various contexts to fabricate "authentic" notions of blackness and, in some cases, black nationalism as a response to white power and resistance to white hegemony. While some commercialized hip hop serves the powerful white male-dominated corporations to construct negative stereotyped representations of black youth, much rap music in fact also depicts the cultural "reality" of black men's experience in relation to the police and unjust authoritarian practices. Regarded as the critical voice of the "underclass black youth" (hooks 2015 [1990]: 27), some rappers deliberately create hip hop as a counter-hegemonic response to white power. Hip hop's rap carries a "'message of disaffection and rage' associated with alienated youth in the inner cities of the United States" (Connell and Gibson 2003: 132). The lyrics are crucial in evoking "the anger and violence of inner-city life" (ibid.: 133). Technology was paramount too, as DJs began to experiment with different records, voices, and sounds (e.g. sampling), which was in part influenced by Jamaican DJ music cultures. One of the pioneers of developing this eclectic mix of musical elements included Afrika Bambaataa, and the first commercial records started to be released in 1979, key singles being 'Rapper's Delight' by The Sugarhill Gang (1979) and 'The Adventures of Grandmaster Flash on the Wheels of Steel' by Grandmaster Flash (1981).

In its development, early hip hop can be seen as a challenge to the authority and legitimacy of specific state systems, including repressive, post/colonial, nationalist, and capitalist structures. Much rap music has since been a means for liberatory expressions and other nationalisms. Black nationalism, for instance, acknowledges and celebrates a pan-African identity across different cultural forms, including music. In doing so, music provides "a potent post-colonial demand for radical emancipation from oppressive social circumstances, in contrast to more repressive images and concepts of the 'exotic', where ethnicity was simplified and vulgarised for popular or commercial effect" (Connell and Gibson 2003: 129). Considerations of black nationalism are therefore crucial in considerations of popular music, which has often constituted a primary means through which people seek to mark out their cultural territory. Black nationalism could be said to embrace ideologies that emphasize an intense identification with an imagined ideal nation. Nationalism is thereby an ideological response to a perceived mismatch between reality and an imagined ideal nation. The conception of a nation, which is the primary determinant of nationalist ideology, constitutes a kind of imagined community that is tied together through imagined allegiances, commonality between its members, and faith.

While nationalism as a political ideology first emerged in the nineteenth century in Europe, localized musical traditions and popular music practices have played a key role in nation-state building projects through their nationalist appropriations. In recent decades, shaped by globalization and global movement, traditional regional styles have been increasingly hybridized with other musics to produce a rich and fluid national musical style that is preferred by the liberal "global" youths. Thereby national identities have been both embraced and contested in the transnational practices of much popular music. The new popular music is marked by a proactive stylistic hybridity to reflect the new critical identities in opposition to older, more "conservative" identities. Various forms of rap music exemplify this shift in nationalist musical practice, which is reflexive of the "new" musical nationalisms that have emerged in recent decades. These "new" nationalisms are often articulations of a post-colonial predicament, in which the West constructed an image of the former colonies as "subaltern", that is, the consumable, available, conquerable Other, but also constructed an image of forcibly moved, dispossessed, and dislocated black people, who, in the aftermath of the abolition of officially sanctioned racism, had to negotiate an identity for themselves that both rejects this history and simultaneously embraces the trauma of that history.

Black nationalism is therefore a response to white extrinsic racism that meant the systematic oppression and economic exploitation of people who are not classified as white, and the infliction of suffering on people of all racialized classifications. Black nationalists of the 1960s advocated "racial solidarity", which carries the language of intrinsic racism, while using race as the basis for moral solidarity, which is most commonly expressed in varieties of Pan-Africanism. Pan-Africanism presupposes black people as being of "the same race", and thereby "responded to their experience of racial discrimination by accepting the racialism it presupposed" (Appiah 2012: 391), even though race is obviously not a biological or natural category. Black nationalism is thereby based on a shared race that provides the basis for solidarity, and where racism is implicated, it is intrinsically applied in its nationalist discourse. One of the founding members of black nationalism, Alexander Crummell, utilized the metaphor of the family and family feeling to exemplify the meanings of a shared race and race feeling, similar to feelings of community.

Public Enemy
Chuck D, frontman of Public Enemy, delivers a highly charged black nationalist rap. Also known as a "lyrical terrorist", Chuck D has been acknowledged as the inventor of political hip hop, holding the conviction that music has the power to remove presidents, and whose ultimate aim on Air America was to attach George W. Bush and the conservative right in the US (Morley and Evans 2004).[3] Chuck D is often regarded as "rap's sharpest, deepest thinker", who in the late 1980s started off with his rap group Public Enemy, while stirring up hope (or fears) that "hip hop could affect a revolution in American culture, arousing the anger of dispossessd black people by talking politics over unsettling grooves" (ibid.). Chuck D is driven by an idealistic vision of a black community informed by the belief in the trancendence of race. Growing up in a decade of radical political change, following the civil rights protests that finally effected equal rights for black people after 150 years of slavery and discrimination, Chuck D idealized Mohammad Ali, the born-again Muslim radical who transformed resentment and resistance into a kind of street poetry, the beginnings of rap. Yet the 1960s until the 1980s were marked by Republican right-wing politics that were detrimental to the black communities, described by Chuck D as "R&B, Reagan and Bush", and hip hop soon became recognized for its potential and power. In 1986, Public Enemy were signed by Def Jam, which marked the beginnings of radically blistering rap against the "powers that be", most evident in their song 'Fight the Power' (1989), recorded for the Spike Lee movie *Do the Right Thing* (1989). Overnight Chuck D became the spokesperson for a whole generation of profoundly alienated young black people, who no longer identified with the old songs of the civil rights movement, which did not allow them to express their anger. Thereby hip hop

became a form of political activism that addressed issues of police brutality, education, and other issues in black culture. Until hip hop became hijacked by the corporate machinery of the global music industry "as a billboard for hyper-capitalist excess and the shiny MTV world" (ibid.), and thereby packaged and marketed by the promotional agencies and largest record producers in the world, Chuck D viewed hip hop as black people's CNN, a genuine political threat to the "powers that be", which they represented musically, visually, lyrically, and personally. For instance, Chuck D's affiliation with the nation of Islam and Black separatism, which sanctioned Islamic fundamentalism, represented a serious threat to the hegemonic political and economic order in the US.

As hip hop became hyper-commercialized in the early 1990s, Chuck D continued to be the "militant mouthpiece for an abstractly violent form of black nationalism that owes its uncompromising stance to the Black Panthers" (Morley and Evans 2004). Moreover, when the "illegal" downloading of music first became an issue, Chuck D challenged the music recording industry, and Public Enemy became the first multi-million-selling band who put their album online for free. Public Enemy's music thus functioned as a form of resistance to both racist and capitalist hegemonic structures. Expressions of black nationalism in the West celebate hip hop as something positive that can open people's minds, and at the same time reflect efforts toward "cultural linkages and unity throughout the diaspora, alongside demands for a more prominent place within the nation" (Connell and Gibson 2003: 137). In doing so, black nationalist hip hop has given a voice to the minority inner-city African American community that enables and celebrates black ethnic pride, even within the constraints and implications of a global capitalist music market. According to Tricia Rose,

> [Public Enemy's] ability to retain the mass-mediated spot light on the popular culture stage and at the same time function as a voice of social critique and criticism [is what makes them] prophets of rage with a difference (Rose 1994: 100).

Since its conception, political issues were thus at the heart of much hip hop, including raps about the denigration of black history, and the current exploitation of black people. Indeed, "hip hop theoretically served to distribute the critical narratives of an isolated working class and underclass youth culture across the disjointed African-American diaspora via the marketplace" (Neal 1999: 160). Black expressive culture thereby conveys black nationalist political signifiers in its role to resist the hegemonic cultural order, while articulating numerous anti-capitalist and anti-racist aspects (Gilroy 1987, 1993), including a critique of productivism, work, the labour process, and the division of labour under capitalism; a critique of the state revolving around a plea for the disassociation of law from domination, which denounces state brutality, militarism and exterminism; [and] a passionate belief in the importance of history and the historical process which is presented as an antidote to the suppression of historical and temporal perception under late capitalism (Longhurst 2007: 122).

Their anti-capitalist resistance occurred particularly through the creative mixing, cutting, and scratching by DJs, and toasting by MCs, where commodities of the music industry (e.g. Led Zeppelin, Kraftwerk) were "hijacked", reused, and appropriated into social spaces of pleasure and expression. Rap and hip hop have thereby reinterpreted existing cultural forms in radical ways. It is an example of popular music through which cultural identities surrounding blackness are modelled, reflected, and negotiated, raising not only questions of ethnicity, but also political orientations, gendered discourses, class thinking, and nationalism.

Resistance to Global Capitalism, White Nationalism, and Popular Music

In addition to multicultural and cosmopolitan, feminist and anti-racist expressions of active democratic citizenship, social identities in response to postdemocracy are also mobilized by groups engaged in violent animal rights campaigns, no-global anti-capitalism campaigns, racist organizations, and others. Some of these movements do, of course, raise concerns and questions as regards their compatibility with democracy. Yet they do share with other social movements a discontent with globalization, postdemocracy, internationalism, and the consequences of uncontrolled global capitalism. In the present-day construction of global hegemony, there have been various periodic and undoubtedly troubling outbreaks of neoconservative atavism that are close to and bear resemblance to fascism. Fascism is a form of conservative, nationalist, right-wing socialism associated with anti-bourgeois, anti-democratic, anti-liberal, and anti-Marxist views. Some right-wing movements have used right-wing socialism to describe support for social solidarity as opposed to individualism, commercialism, and laissez-faire economics. These movements seek to maintain the white status quo by preventing free-market entrepreneurship and "creativity" from disrupting the pre-established framework of social organization within global capitalism. In contemporary youth cultures, popular music is a powerful means to negotiate, express, and model ethnocentric political identities. When aligned politically with the "right", such popular music is often most directly concerned with right-wing socialism and white nationalism.

The political terms "right" and "left" emerged in late eighteenth-century Europe and referred to two sides in the French parliament, where politicians sitting on the right were broadly supportive of traditional conservatives, monarchists, and reactionaries and the ones sitting on the left being supporters of the French revolution (1789) and "innovators". In English-speaking countries, "right" and "left" politics emerged in the twentieth century following the general economic shift toward capitalism, with center-right movements, such as the British Conservative Party, becoming supportive of capitalism. By contrast, in the United States the "right" is an integral part of the conservative movement, notably in American politics in the age of Reagan since 1980. Generally, the right considers some forms of hierarchy and social inequality as inevitable, even desirable, on the basis of biology, economics, or tradition. Nowadays, the right also includes neo-conservatives, authoritarians, nationalists, fascists, racial supremacists, Christian democrats, religious fundamentalists, and classical liberals. For instance, some writers differentiate between the "mainstream right" and "extremist right", where mainstream right is used to define more established conservative forces, which became increasingly powerful and present internationally since the late seventies/early eighties, the years in which Thatcher first became British premier and Reagan US president. Interestingly, during the 1980s the National Front in Britain declined following the election of the harshly conservative Thatcher government in 1979, which simply meant that National Front activists switched to or re-joined the Conservative Party. Thus, party allegiance may change without it signifying a change of mind (Downing and Husband 2005: 72). It is important, here, to recognize that there is no major firewall between the extremist right and the mainstream right.[4] Consequently, an analogous mentality of ambiguous tolerance for the extremist right most certainly exists within the more mainstream right. When defining the "extremist right", we must note that academics and researchers often define the term differently, as typologies are nationally specific and change in different contexts and time periods. Even so, a useful typology of right-wing extremism is offered in the tri-partite categorization by Downing and Husband (2005: 61–62).

The "typical" right music fan is white, masculine, and under thirty years of age, who listens to rock and other music for political, musical, and other reasons (Farin 1995: 3). Skinheads are only one part of the right rock scene; right rock is also the music of death metal fans, goths, dark wave fans, as well as "normal" youth. For example, right bands such as Landser and Zillertaler Türkenjäger are often well-known among ordinary school children in Germany (Schmidt 2002), who may identify with the band members who come from the same living conditions as their fans, and admire them as idols and stars. There is even a trend among youths to turn to right-wing extremism as a form of rebellion, and thereby absorb neo-Nazi fashion, music, and ideology as an ever important part of youth culture (Cziesche *et al.* 2005).

The desire for youth rebellion is clearly recognized by the producers of white power music:

> Young people love anything that is seen as rebellious—so when the social workers and the teachers and the parents go "that's taboo", the hope is that young people always rebel, and in our opinion if they are going to rebel, we would like them to do it our way and to listen to our music (David Hannam, Managing Director of the BNP-owned label Great White Records; in Mackay 2006).

In Britain, new groups of far-right extremists deliberately target children and teenagers online, seeking to recruit a new, younger generation of members who are invited to take part in day excursions, while posing with right-wing groups' banners and neo-Nazi emblems (Griffith 2015). Meanwhile, key players on the far-right scene such as Steve Cartwright, former member of the ultra-extremist group Combat 18 and co-organizer of white power gigs in Britain under the banner of Blood and Honour, is

> partly responsible for bringing a concept called "Project Schoolyard" to Britain, which involves activists handing out free CDs of white power music to children outside schools. In the USA, Project Schoolyard was kick-started by the white power label Panzerfaust—named after the anti-tank bazooka used by the Wehrmacht in the Second World War (Mackay 2006; Manson and Mackay 2006).

In both Europe and the United States, music has since the 1990s become one of the most important means to distribute extremist right ideologies among young people, made possible through the internet that enables (often) illegal music production and distribution, and through mobile phones that help the surreptitious organization of illegal concerts (Mackay 2006; Manson and Mackay 2006). Since the early 1990s the right-wing music scene has become subject to strict state control and censorship of bands, distribution of music recordings and merchandise, and skinzines in numerous European countries. Notably, Germany and Italy, with their experience of fascism in the past seventy years, are particularly attuned to the question of "free speech" and "action" among rightist extremists. Germany, for instance, has in place explicit laws banning Holocaust denial, the formation of explicitly Nazi parties, and other extremist-right activities (Bundesamt für Verfassungsschutz 2015a). The increased state censorship of right rock was particularly effective in the area of concert organization (Farin 1995: 4–5). Indeed, "for two years, [British band] Whitelaw tried to get to Germany to play—each time, they were banned" (Mackay 2006). Even so, the popularity of right rock is little affected by such bans, and bands like Whitelaw and Nemesis bring out music with clearly radical lyrics, which can still be purchased by fans in Germany and elsewhere. For instance, recent journalistic discourse reported that

> Neo-Nazis ... are on the rise across Europe and in the United States. In Britain, the British National Party won more than 800,000 votes at the last European elections. In Germany, they have seats in state parliaments and are doing better, electorally, than at any time since the Second World War. Italy is also seeing a marked upswing in votes for the far right. Increasingly central to the political success of parties such as the German NPD—the political grandchild of Hitler's National Socialist German Workers Party—and the BNP is white power music. Bands include Whitelaw, Strike Force 28 and Grinded Nig (whose album *Freezer Full of Nigger Heads* features songs such as 'Jackhammered Nigger Pussy'). Their records are available from most neo-Nazi record distributors online (Mackay 2006).[5]

By contrast, in the US the freedom of speech legislation enables and ensures communication liberties, which is similar in Canada, so that the free speech provisions of section 2 of the Charter of Rights and Freedoms and of the First Amendment are of pressing importance. It is often the left that pursues these principles of freedom of speech, yet in turn this means to plug for the rights of fascists to speak. The commercial hub of white power music is based on West Virginia, USA, in the armed compound of the National Alliance, an organization linked to the BNP and the Ku Klux Klan, from where music CDs, clothes, flags, computer games, as well as other merchandise, are sold. The base also houses Resistance Records, the world's leading white power music label, which specializes in white power music and computer games, such as *Ethnic Cleansing*. Meanwhile,

> The best-known act on the far-right label Resistance Records is Prussian Blue: 13-year-old twins Lamb and Lynx Gaede from Bakersfield, California ... [who] have been performing songs about Rudolf Hess *et al.* to appreciative crowds of white neo-Nazis since they were nine. "We are proud of being white", Lynx has said, "We want our people to be white ... we don't want to just be, you know, a big muddle." Having been nursed in racist doctrine from the teat ... their mother, April, taught them the alphabet this way: "A is for

Aryan, B is blood…" and so on. Grandfather Gaede brands his cattle with swastikas (Mackay 2006).

While record sales by Resistance Records remain in the thousands, the internet "gives such groups an extended reach and generates an outsize sense of power in their audiences [which] should not be dismissed" (Freemuse 2002). There is thus great concern by anti-white power music lobby groups in the US (and, of course, elsewhere) that this music could break into the mainstream music charts.

Many right white power bands in Europe have recognized that the celebration of violence is damaging to them, and have increasingly distanced themselves from the skinhead image and changed their music. So besides heavy metal influences, more recent right rock bands also absorb the sounds of mainstream-rock, pop, techno, singer-songwriter, and ballads. In Germany, the lyrics no longer demand to expel foreigners, but to tackle drug addiction, while the ideology is more German-national, instead of national socialist, and instead of targeting asylum seekers, "lefties" have become the enemy in such lyrics. Right music has as a result become less offensive and racist than right rock of the 1980s, and as such has gained more public consent. In Britain, for instance, Great White Records, the BNP's own record label, also adopts English folk music, while steering clear of inciting racial hatred and instead emphasizing the "plight" of the white man becoming victim to race attack "because he did walk through the wrong part of town" (Mackay 2006; Manson and Mackay 2006). Meanwhile in Italy, white power singer Viking, a dark-haired young woman self-accompanied on acoustic guitar is known in right extremist circles as "Italy's first lady of fascist music". She sings in singer-songwriter fashion, 'Don't Go Round with the Jews', and is a regular chart-topper in the "Nazi Top Ten" (Mackay 2006; Manson and Mackay 2006). In Sweden, another racialist singer is Saga, the "Swedish Madonna of the far right", who has deliberately adopted a mainstream look, despite her celebrity status in the white power underground.

Racism as a naturalized ideology is clearly reinforced through the musical practices of the far right, which more overtly shows the connotations of whiteness as the hegemonic norm in extreme situations of racism which purport that white people "are not of a certain race; they're just the human race" (Huq 2006: 137). Whiteness is an ideal that cannot be achieved as it has connotations of "nothing", helping to construct it as neutral or the norm. Racist and populist movements in the US and Western European countries, particularly, have acquired a new role and respectability by speaking directly from and to "the people" and promoting hostility to immigrants and ethnic minorities. Racist and populist movements do share with the anti-globalization movement a discontent with new forms of democracy, internationalism, and the consequences of uncontrolled global capitalism. Yet, while the far right speaks of the problems of globalization, it focuses these problems on immigrants who are themselves globalization's biggest victims.

Multiculturalism and cosmopolitanism, feminism and anti-racism, populism and right-wing nationalism all reflect in different ways the early twenty-first-century phenomenon variously labelled anti-capitalism, anti-corporatism, anti-globalization, or social justice movement, in which social justice is regarded as a positive, context-specific designation. Some of these currents, such as the alter-globalization movement, are not anti-capitalist per se, but reject the excesses of neoliberalism and negative effects of economic globalization (Pleyers 2010). Perhaps the solution lies with an ideological notion such as corporate social responsibility, a kind of "nice new, fluffy sort of capitalism that … we may all grow to love" (McGuigan 2009: 227). In the age of global capitalist hegemony, postdemocracy is seeing unprecedented opportunities and challenges for humanity, which require us to learn from the tragic mistakes of the past. Postdemocracy renders significant a belief in proactive means of justice delivery. As a global community, if it indeed exists, we need to place renewed emphasis on the ties that bind humanity together and on the need for international cooperation to meet the challenges that humanity faces in order to fulfil humanity's potential. This can only be made possible if all sectors of society, including those whose rights are denied, can meaningfully participate in cooperation, while addressing the plight of those whose rights are most acutely denied. The challenge in global capitalist hegemony is to generate greater understanding and awareness of humanity and human rights, and to transcend toward social forms of democracy globally. Such a commitment would be an integral component of postdemocratic ideology.

Notes

1. It is problematic to generalize; however Colin Crouch, whose work on postdemocracy serves as the key to this chapter, does consider the capitalist conditions in numerous countries, including the UK, Australia, Scandinavia, Baltic Scandinavia, North America, the Netherlands, France, Italy, Spain, Portugal, Greece, West Germany, Austria, and Japan (2004: 5–11).

2. See https://www.youtube.com/watch?v=0sN4hxvuArA&feature=youtu.be (accessed 15 May 2017).

3. The documentary entitled *Chuck D: Pop and Politics* (Morley and Evans 2004) is narrated by Paul Morley and was screened on BBC4 on 15 October 2004. At the time of writing, it could not be located on the BBC4 archive or elsewhere online.

4. E.g. American Republican Party, British Conservative Party, German Christian Democrats, French RPR and UDF, Alleanza Nazionale and Lega Nord (Italy), and similar parties elsewhere.

5. In contrast, the German government reports that "since 2006 the number of subculture-oriented right-wing extremists has constantly been on the decrease. This trend continued in 2014, too, when the potential of subculture-oriented right-wing extremists fell by 200 individuals to approximately 7,200 adherents ... In addition, there are right-wing extremist bands and their environment: individuals issuing relevant publications, operating websites, organising concerts, distributing relevant music or making up the largest share of the subculture-oriented scene as visitors of right-wing extremist concerts" (Bundesamt für Verfassungsschutz 2015b).

After Globalization

Musical globalization is generally understood to be about transformations in economics, culture, and ideology.[1] This book has traced the trajectories of musical globalization since the late nineteenth century, and considered hegemonic cultural beliefs and practices during the various phases of the history of capitalism as these were shaped by Europeanization since the earliest beginnings of globalization. Since the late nineteenth century, popular music emerged around the world as a result of modernization or westernization as part of an historical development that had a certain degree of inevitability. Indeed, the world has gradually become somewhat indifferent to westernization because western modes of being and behaving have been successful. The world was made modern, including popular culture and music, because many non-westerners were eager to learn the ways of the West. Pop-rock music has become universal because of the rise of a mass public, empowered by capitalism and liberal democracy. US domination post-World War II meant that popular culture and music around the world looked American because America, which accelerated global mass capitalism and consumerism, established world dominance (Zakaria 2008: 78). Alongside an emerging advertising industry (late nineteenth and early twentieth centuries) developed the various industries that are now collectively known as "culture industry", "cultural industries", and "creative industries", terms that signify the move away from culture and toward economy in contemporary thought, in which music celebrities have become the heroes and heroines of individualization and the enterprising self, and where the most prominent feature is that of a logoscape of cool brands.

These musical developments were shaped by two major moments of economic crisis in 1929 and 1973, and the evolution of organized and neoliberal capitalism as the solutions to these crises. In the 1930s, Fordism—as both a system of mass production and as a principle of civilization with its quasi-socialist features—triggered the modern phenomenon of mass consumerism and became the model in the US, the advanced capitalist world, and the Soviet bloc (McGuigan 2009: 102). Since the 1970s, economic neoliberalism has become the latest strategy of a project of western-dominated world order. Marked by the deregulation of markets as the condition for speeding and diffusing economic growth, neoliberal globalization claimed culture as a means for communities around the world to adapt and endure. Neoliberalism inspired the "take-off" phase of globalization and helped to cement the western-centric world order with American corporations as the main economic actors. A key effort was to create a consumerist mentality that turns consumption into a sign of distinction (in terms of status and class) and an end in itself. Commodities are thus used to express social identity, rendering consumption both economic and cultural. Neoliberalism, once successful in the US, was gradually adopted by other countries and, on pressure from the US, informed economic governance and fiscal policy at supra-national level. Neoliberalism is now global in reach, and its elements appeal to societies around the world.

And while capitalism is now everywhere, its history has been one borne out of racism and masculine hegemony. Early Europeanization and globalization have had a major impact upon western race/gender/sexuality/capitalist hegemony, while nascent technologies of capital have led to a renewed reification and exploitation of racialized, sexualized, and classed populations, which this book approached critically to offer a critique of the relationship between emergent capitalist formations and culture over the past hundred years. Capitalism, in its various forms, has been instrumental to the maintenance of imperialist white supremacist capitalist patriarchy during the twentieth century and multi-racial white supremacist patriarchy during the early twenty-first century. The history of global capitalist hegemony has had a major impact on the production, distribution, marketing, and dissemination of world popular music globally. Indeed, the concentration of music ownership has been crucial to corporate economic and political power, and, most critically, ideological hegemony. The book explored the way that world popular music has mediated economic, cultural, and ideological conditions, through which capitalism has been created in multiple and heterogeneous ways, understanding world popular music as the production of meaning through language and representation. The present critique of ideology has shown how power relates to representation, and thus how ideological power is constructed in the hegemony of (world) popular music market values in contemporary culture and society.

The following table sums up the trajectories and themes in world popular music explored in this book, while contextualizing these along the timeline of (musical) globalization and capitalism. The various dimensions considered in the book are the work of critical social science—a critique of capitalism's impact upon popular music in historical and world perspective.

Table 1: Trajectories and themes in the development of world popular music: historical, economic and musical dimensions

Historical and economic dimensions		Musical dimensions
"Early" globalization: European expansionism, imperialism, and superiority	Ca. 1500	Spread of European culture and religious music
British Empire and first mass-consumer society Market capitalism	Ca. 1700–1850	
Modernism Liberal (monopoly) capitalism Urbanization	1850–1945	New recording and broadcasting technologies, early mass media Commodification of classical music in Europe and elsewhere, and recordings of local vernacular musics Spread of musical modernization (westernization) Beginnings of US-dominated music recording industry (1920s) "Race music" in the US (1920s)
Take-off phase of globalization Golden Age of (organized) capitalism Advertising New electronic technologies	1945–1975	"Official" beginning of western popular music Consolidation of the US music recording industry Electronic music revolution Youth as a new market for rock 'n' roll (1950s) and rock (1960s) Spread of pop-rock music worldwide Remnants of fascism in European popular music (1960s) Masculine hegemony
New technologies (satellite, cable, digital) Neoliberal capitalism = cool capitalism Global capitalist hegemony The Global Firm Postdemocracy	1975–2008	Consolidation of global music industry and branding Cultural imperialism/musical homogenization MTV and the male gaze Subtle racisms and orientalism Expressive isomorphism/aesthetic cosmopolitanism Multiculturalism and the "birth" of World Music Social (democratic) citizenship and musical activism
After globalization: post-American, post-western age	2008	

What has been called "globalization" is in reality an extreme concentration of a US-European empire, which has become undermined by the 2008 financial crisis and the emergence of new global players in the global capitalist economy. As I finish this book in 2017, economic neoliberalism has failed dramatically and western centrality, US dominance in particular, in the global capitalist economy has declined vis-à-vis non-western countries since the unexpected financial meltdown in 2008. Globalization, as we knew it, that is, globalization qua US dominance of the post-Cold War world, has come to an end, also described as a post-American world (Cazdyn and Szeman 2011: 28). We have entered something like a third stage of globalization discourse. Sergio Fabbrini (2010) talks about a new epoch and describes the new world order as a "post-western world" that is less western than in the past. Even though its component elements have not ended, the ideological undercurrents of globalization have. The new epoch—after globalization—is being born out of uncertainty. What will shape the post-western world is unclear, and so is the way that world popular music will be produced, ideologically manipulated, distributed, and consumed in the future.

Recently, hip hop by musician and Djuki Mala dancer "Baker Boy" (a.k.a. Danzel Baker) from the Arnhem Land, who is a young Aboriginal artist to rap in his indigenous language Yolnu Matha, makes us—once again—see the opportunities of a re-narrated discourse of globalization with new eyes. Baker hails from the Milingimbi community in north-eastern Arnhem Land in the Northern Territory, home to major Australian artists Yothu Yindi and Gurrumul. His song 'Cloud 9' is about nature and the life of young people in remote Aboriginal communities, which spreads the message of a healthy life and an anti-drug, anti-alcohol, anti-crime lifestyle. Baker's quest is to help young people to navigate between cultures and understand the connections between both worlds—the traditional Aboriginal and western one (Vanovac 2017). Baker's rapping in his own language helps to communicate difficult issues, instils in Aboriginal youths pride and hope, and gives a voice to the disempowered who are severely affected by lack of opportunities in communication and education (Margetson 2017).

In the same week in May 2017, during a pop concert by the American singer Ariana Grande in Manchester, whose music is popular with children and teenagers, a 22-year-old Manchester-born resident of Libyan parents, Salman Abedi, carried out a suicide bomb attack, described as the most deadly attack in Britain in a decade. In response, the Dangerous Woman tour was suspended with concerts cancelled in London, Antwerp, Lodz, Frankfurt, and Zurich, and tickets refunded by tour promoter Live Nation. The event sparked emotional reactions from around the music world, including Rihanna, The

Rolling Stones, One Direction, Johnny Marr, Miley Cyrus, Justin Timberlake, Christina Aguilera, Nicki Minaj, and others (Geoghegan and Glynn 2017). Two weeks later, Grande performed a charity "One Love Manchester" concert, featuring Katy Perry, Miley Cyrus, Coldplay, Justin Bieber, Take That, and Liam Gallagher. Katy Perry apparently provided the most defiant moment with her performance of 'Roar', Hillary Clinton's theme song (Pidd and Halliday 2017). Sparking fear and concern for future events, the German police decided to suspend Germany's biggest music festival, Rock am Ring 2017, affecting some 87,000 festival-goers, on the basis of, what turned out to be, misspelled names of two employees of a Frankfurt-based company sub-contracted to set up the festival concert stages, which had "phonetic similarity" to actual IS suspects (Local DE 2017). The ideological forces behind musical events like "Cloud 9", the Manchester concerts, and Rock am Ring, even if lost in the short spaces and ephemeral nature of the daily news, do point to their larger significance, offering a view of how the world works today and how it should work, instilling in young people ideas to address the challenges faced collectively in a way that will produce a better civic future.

This book has sought to make sense of the past and present of capitalism, articulating economic, technological, and cultural globalization and its particular ideological force upon world popular music since the late nineteenth century until the end of globalization. Much of the discussions focused on the way in which consent is produced, managed, and reproduced in the production and circulation of world popular music. Music provides a lens through which to see the way that social life is structured to legitimize a social system that benefits certain social interests over others, or, in short, to understand hegemony. Music reflects deep social assumptions that structure privilege and generate disadvantage. It helps us to truly understand "where power takes on the innocence of tradition" (Cazdyn and Szeman 2011: 36). While globalization, as we know it, is finished, its component elements live on, notably capitalism, even if mutating into a different form. Globalization was a process that reproduced similar processes and structures, yet it also offered opportunities for substantive change in the world. The new epoch after globalization has begun, and perhaps we are seeing already a shift in the way that world popular music is engendered and regenerated, produced and reproduced. Young people today are truly the product of the era of globalization, the first global population, who likely believe in the fact that culture and politics now operate on a global level, with serious implications for how they live and act locally and globally.

The discourse of globalization today is often overshadowed by blunt economic terms and concepts, which have become part of quotidian narrative and the measure for the success or failure of collectives. What is at stake here, however, is to consider an "after globalization" in terms of freedom, democracy, individualism, liberty, safety, and other political categories. Today's global capitalism is not a mere economic dispensation; it has a political logic too. In the current third stage of globalization, the neoliberal shift toward the more practical economic ideologies of capitalism must be reversed—through education, moralism, politics, media, and so forth—toward understanding the way that equality, peace, justice, environmental health, and quality of life can be attained via economic practices and transactions. So, while capitalism is the operating system of the planet, it is precisely this shift in attentiveness to the more romantic political ideologies of capitalism that will produce a better future after globalization.

Note

1. Globalization is also understood to be about transformations in politics, but this is less often considered in studies of (world) popular music.

Bibliography

Achacoso, D. 2014. "Brand Identity for New Artists in the Music Industry". Unpublished thesis. California Polytechnic State University. Online: https://tinyurl.com/calpoly-1130 (accessed 7 December 2016).
Acharts. 2013. Katy Perry. Online: http://acharts.us/performer/katy_perry (accessed 10 January 2014).
Adorno, Theodor. 2001. *The Culture Industry: Selected Essays on Mass Culture*, edited by J. M. Bernstein. New York: Routledge.
Adorno, Theodor, and Max Horkheimer. 1979 [1944]. *Dialectic of Enlightenment*. London: New Left Books/Verso.
Amico, Marta. 2014. "The Staged Desert: Tourist and Nomad Encounters at the Festival au Désert". In *The Globalization of Musics in Transit: Music Migration and Tourism*, edited by Simone Krüger and Ruxandra Trandafoiu, 86–100. New York: Routledge.
Anderson, Benedict. 1983. *Imagined Communities: Reflections on the Origin and Spread of Nationalism*. London: Verso.
Anderson, Ian. 2000. "World Music History". Online: http://www.frootsmag.com/content/features/world_music_history/ (accessed 30 March 2015).
Andsager, Julie, and Kimberly Roe. 2003. "'What's Your Definition of Dirty, Baby?': Sex in Music Video". *Sexuality and Culture* 7(3): 79–97.
Aoyama, Yuko. 2007. "The Role of Consumption and Globalization in a Cultural Industry: The Case of Flamenco". *Geoforum* 38: 103–13.
Appiah, Kwame Anthony. 2012. "Racisms". In *Introduction to Philosophy: Classical and Contemporary Readings*, 6th edn, edited by John Perry, Michael Bratman, and John Martin Fischer, 390–96. Oxford: Oxford University Press.
Armbrust, Walter. 2002. "The Impact of the Mass Media on Egyptian Music". In *The Garland Encyclopedia of World Music, Volume 6*, edited by Virginia Danielson and Dwight Reynolds, 233–41. New York: Routledge.
Arsenault, Amelia H., and Manuel Castells. 2008. "The Structure and Dynamics of Global Multi-Media Business Networks". *International Journal of Communication* 2: 707–48.
Arts Council England. 2005. *World Music in England*. London, UK. Online: http://webarchive.nationalarchives.gov.uk/20160204123549/http://www.artscouncil.org.uk/advice-and-guidance/browse-advice-and-guidance/world-music-in-england (accessed 1 December 2017).
Aubrey, Jennifer, and Cynthia M. Frisby. 2011. "Sexual Objectification in Music Videos: A Content Analysis Comparing Gender and Genre". *Mass Communication and Society* 14(4): 475–501.
Aufderheide, Pat. 1986. "Music Videos: The Look of the Sound". *Journal of Communication* 36(1): 57–78.
Averill, Gage. 1998. "Popular Music: An Introduction". In *The Garlands Encyclopedia of World*

Music, Volume 2, edited by Dale A. Olsen and Daniel E. Sheehy, 92–94. New York: Routledge.
Baker, Houston A. 1993. *Black Studies, Rap and the Academy.* Chicago: Chicago University Press.
Balaji, Murali. 2012. "The Construction of 'Street Credibility' in Atlanta's Hip-Hop Music Scene: Analyzing the Role of Cultural Gatekeepers". *Critical Studies in Media Communication* 29(4): 313–30.
Bartlett, Anne Clark. 2002. "Defining the Terms: Postfeminism as an Ideology of Cool". *Medieval Feminist Forum* 34(1): 25–30.
Battersby, Christine. 1989. *Gender and Genius: Toward a Feminist Aesthetics.* London: The Women's Press.
Baudrillard, Jean. 1983. *Simulations.* Cambridge, MA: MIT Press.
—1994. *Simulacra and Simulation*, reprinted edn. Ann Arbor, MI: University of Michigan.
BBC. 2004. "Indie Labels Unhappy with Merger". Online: http://news.bbc.co.uk/1/hi/entertainment/music/3911491.stm (accessed 20 October 2015).
—2016. "Singer Bjork Denounces Sexism in Pop Music Industry". *BBC*, 22 December. Online: http://www.bbc.co.uk/news/world-europe-38408266 (accessed 15 May 2017).
BBC Newsbeat. 2017. "Rihanna Overtakes Michael Jackson's Top 10 Record in America". *BBC*, 22 February. Online: https://tinyurl.com/newsbeat-39050828 (accessed 15 May 2017).
Beck, Ulrich. 2000. *What is Globalization?* Somerset: Wiley.
Beck, Ulrich, and Edgar Grande. 2010. "Varieties of Second Modernity: The Cosmopolitan Turn in Social and Political Theory and Research". *British Journal of Sociology* 61(3): 409–43.
Belk, Russell W., Kelly Tian, and Heli Paavola. 2010. "Consuming Cool: Behind the Unemotional Mask". *Consumer Behavior* 12(1): 183–208.
Belle, Crystal. 2014. "From Jay-Z to Dead Prez: Examining Representations of Black Masculinity in Mainstream versus Underground Hip-Hop Music". *Journal of Black Studies* 45(4): 287–300.
Bennett, Andy. 2000. *Popular Music and Youth Culture: Music, Identity and Place.* Basingstoke: Palgrave Macmillan.
—2001. *Cultures of Popular Music.* Buckingham: Open University Press.
Bennett, Andy, and Kevin Dawe, eds. 2001. *Guitar Cultures.* Bloomsbury: Berg.
Bennett, Mary Josephine. 2017. "Phoenix Rising: Freddie Mercury's Legacy and the Fight Against AIDS". In *Becoming Brands: Celebrity, Activism and Politics*, edited by Jackie Raphael and Celia Lam, 123–36. Toronto: WaterHill Publishing.
Benson, Phil. 2013. "English and Identity in East Asian Popular Music". *Popular Music* 32(1): 23–33.
Berumen, Gwen. n.d. "Breaking Down Cultural Appropriation in Pop Music and More". *BUST*. Online: http://bust.com/general/12778-breaking-down-cultural-appropriation-in-pop-music-and-more.html (accessed 11 May 2017).
Beynon, John, and David Dunkerley. 2000. *Globalization: The Reader.* London: Athlone Press.
Bhabha, Homi K. 1990. "DissemiNation: Time, Narrative, and the Margins of the Modern Nation". In *Nation and Narration*, edited by Homi K. Bhabha, 291–322. New York: Routledge.

Big Blue Ball [CD]. 2008. Online: http://bigblueball.realworldrecords.com/ (accessed 17 February 2014).
Billboard. 2012. "Katy Perry and Coty Announce Fragrance Partnership". Online: https://tinyurl.com/473942-katy-coty (accessed 10 January 2014).
Bloechl, Olivia. 2005. "Orientalism and Hyperreality in 'Desert Rose'". *Journal of Popular Music Studies* 17(2): 133–61.
Bock, Jannika. 2008. *Riot Grrrl: A Feminist Re-Interpretation of the Punk Narrative*. Saarbrücken: VDM Verlag.
Bogle, Donald. 2001. *Toms, Coons, Mulattoes, Mammies, and Bucks: An Interpretive History of Blacks in American Films, Updated and Expanded*, 4th edn. London: Bloomsbury.
Bohlman, Philip V. 2002. *World Music: A Very Short Introduction*. New York: Oxford University Press.
Borucka, Magdalena. 2013. "Merchandising and Brand Extension in the Music Industry". *Manchester Student Law Review* 190(2): 190–223.
Botz-Bornstein, Thorsten. 2010. "What Does It Mean to Be Cool?". *Philosophy Now* (80). Online: https://tinyurl.com/gtjjmpr (accessed 7 December 2016).
Bourdieu, Pierre. 1984. *Distinction: A Social Critique of the Judgement of Taste*. (*La Distinction: Critique Sociale du Judgement* [1979]). London: Routledge.
Bouton, Doug. 2010. "The Music Industry in Flux: Are 360 Record Deals the Saving Grace or the Coup de Grace". *Virginia Sports and Entertainment Law Journal* 9(2): 312–22.
Bradby, Barbara. 2016. "Phallic Girls of Pop: Nicki Minaj's Sampled Anaconda and the Semiotics of Contradiction". In *PopScriptum, Volume 12: Sound, Sex und Sexismus*, edited by L. J. Müller. Schriftenreihe herausgegeben vom Forschungszentrum Populäre Musik. Berlin: Humboldt-Universität.
Bradley, Regina N. 2012. "Contextualizing Hip Hop Sonic Cool Pose in Late Twentieth and Twenty-first Century Rap Music". *Current Musicology* 93(1): 57–68.
Brinkhurst-Cuff, Charlie. 2017. "'The Album is a Love Letter to Men': Meet Feminist Supergroup Les Amazones d'Afrique". *The Guardian*, 10 February. Online: https://tinyurl.com/2017-feb-20-les-amazones (accessed 15 May 2017).
British Music Experience. 2016. "About the BME". Online: http://www.britishmusicexperience.com/about/ (accessed 10 November 2016).
Broughton, Simon, and Mark Ellingham, eds. 2000. *Rough Guide to World Music, Volume 2: Latin and North America, the Caribbean, Asia & the Pacific*. London: Rough Guides.
Broughton, Simon, Mark Ellingham, and Richard Trillo, eds. 1994. *Rough Guide to World Music* (Rough Guides Reference Titles). London: Rough Guides.
—1999. *World Music: The Rough Guide, Volume 1: Europe, Africa and the Middle East*. London: Rough Guides.
Brown, Timothy S. 2004. "Subcultures, Pop Music and Politics: Skinheads and 'Nazi Rock' in England and Germany". *Journal of Social History* 38(1): 157–78.
Brunner, Anja. 2010. *Die Anfänge des Mbalax: Zur Entstehung einer senegalesichen Popularmusik* [*The Beginnings of Mbalax: About the Emergence of a Senegalese Popular Music*] (Vienna Series in Ethnomusicology). Vienna: University of Vienna.
—In press. *Bikutsi: A Beti Dance Music on the Rise, 1970–1990*. Sheffield, UK: Equinox.
Brusila, Johannes. 2001. "Musical Otherness and the Bhundu Boys: The Construction of the 'West' and the 'Rest' in the Discourse of 'World Music'". In *Same and Other: Nego-*

tiating African Identity in Cultural Production, edited by Mai Eriksson and Maria Eriksson Baaz, 39–58. Stockholm: Nordic Africa Institute.

Bundesamt für Verfassungsschutz. 2015a. "What is Right-wing Extremism?" Online: https://tinyurl.com/verfassungsschutz-de-036213653 (accessed 15 December 2015).

—2015b. "Right-wing Extremist Scene of a Subculture Character". Online: https://www.verfassungsschutz.de/en/fields-of-work/right-wing-extremism/figures-and-facts-right-wing-extremism/subculture-oriented-right-wing-extremist-scene-2015 (accessed 1 December 2017).

Burgess, Richard James. 2014. *The History of Music Production*. New York: Oxford University Press.

Burton, Graeme. 2005. *Media and Society: Critical Perspectives*. Maidenhead: Open University Press.

Calcutt, Lyn, Ian Woodward, and Zlatko Skrbis. 2009. "Conceptualising Otherness: An Exploration of the Cosmopolitan Schema". *Journal of Sociology* 45(2): 169–86.

Calhoun, Craig. 2009. "Cosmopolitan Europe and European Studies". In *The Sage Handbook of European Studies*, edited by Chris Rumford, 637–54. London: Sage.

Campbell, Sean. 2013. "From 'Boys' to 'Lads': Masculinity and Irish Rock Culture". *Popular Musicology Online* 2. Online: http://www.popular-musicology-online.com/issues/02/campbell.html (accessed 14 January 2016).

Castells, Manuel. 2000. *The Rise of the Network Society*. Oxford: Blackwell.

Cazdyn, Eric, and Imre Szeman. 2011. *After Globalization*. Chichester, UK: Wiley-Blackwell.

Chalcraft, Jasper, Paolo Magaudda, Marco Solaroli, and Marco Santoro. 2011. "Music Festivals as Cosmopolitan Spaces". In *European Arts Festivals: Strengthening Cultural Diversity*, edited by the Euro-Festival Consortium, 25–35. European Commission: Directorate-General for Research and Innovation Socio-economic Sciences and Humanities. Online: https://ec.europa.eu/research/social-sciences/pdf/policy_reviews/euro-festival-report_en.pdf (accessed 16 June 2015).

Chalmers, Robert. 2005. "The Bhundu Boys: Lost Boys". Online: http://www.independent.co.uk/arts-entertainment/music/features/the-bhundu-boys-lost-boys-529008.html (accessed 1 December 2017).

Chapple, Steve, and Reebee Garofalo. 1977. *Rock 'n' Roll is Here to Pay: The History and Politics of the Music Industry*. Chicago: Nelson-Hall.

Cherry, Jim. 2015. "November 15, 1967: Jim Morrison Appears in *Vogue* Magazine". Online: http://doorsexaminer.com/doors-history-november-15-1967-jim-morrison-appears-in-vogue-magazine/ (accessed 16 January 2018).

Chesler, Phyllis. 1997 [1972]. *Women and Madness: The Critical Phallacy* (1st edn publ. by Doubleday & Co., 1972). New York: Four Walls Eight Windows.

Clancy, Ronald M. 2008. *Sacred Christmas Music: The Stories behind the Most Beloved Songs of Devotion*. New York: Sterling.

Clifton, Derrick. 2014. "5 Reasons Katy Perry is Pop Music's Worst Cultural Appropriator". *MIC*, 1 August. Online: https://mic.com/articles/95444/5-reasons-katy-perry-is-pop-music-s-worst-cultural-appropriator#.YNr7l4wcP (accessed 11 May 2017).

Coates, Norma. 1997. "(R)evolution Now? Rock and the Political Potential of Gender". In *Sexing the Groove: Popular Music and Gender*, edited by Sheila Whiteley, 50–64. London: Routledge.

Cohen, Sara, and Marion Leonard. 2003. "Feminism". In *The Continuum Encyclopedia of Popu-*

lar Music of the World, Volume 1: Media, Industry and Society, edited by John Shepherd, 74–76. London: Continuum.

Connell, John, and Chris Gibson. 2003. *Sound Tracks: Popular Music, Identity and Place*. London: Routledge.

—2014. "Mobilizing Music Festivals for Rural Transformation". In *The Globalization of Musics in Transit: Music Migration and Tourism*, edited by Simone Krüger and Ruxandra Trandafoiu, 115–34. New York: Routledge.

Cook, Susan C., and Judy S. Tsou (foreword by Susan McClary), eds. 1994. *Cecilia Reclaimed: Feminist Perspectives on Gender and Music*. Urbana, IL: University of Illinois Press.

Cooper, Mark (exec. producer), Ellen Hobson (producer), and Ellen Hobson (dir.). 2013. *How to Be a World Music Star: Buena Vista, Bhundu Boys and Beyond*. Documentary. BBC Four Production.

Coplan, David. B. 2002. "Popular Music in South Africa". In *The Garlands Encyclopedia of World Music*, Volume 1, edited by Ruth M. Stone, 759–80. New York: Garland Press.

Corn, Aaron. 2009. *Reflections and Voices: Exploring the Music of Yothu Yindi with Mandawuy Yunupingu*. Sydney: Sydney University Press.

Crazy About One Direction. 2013. Documentary. Channel Four.

Creative Industries Task Force. 1998. *Creative Industries Mapping Document*. London: Department for Culture, Media and Sport.

Crook, S., John Pakulski, and M. Aters. 1992. *Postmodernization*. London: Sage.

Cross, Brian. 1993. *It's Not about Salary: Rap, Race and Resistance in Los Angeles*. New York: Verso.

Crouch, Colin. 2004. *Post-Democracy*. Cambridge: Polity.

Crouse, Timothy. 1971. "Blue". *Rolling Stone*. Online: http://jonimitchell.com/library/view.cfm?id=252 (accessed 11 December 2015).

Cuvier, Baron Georges. 2012 [1890]. *History of the Natural Sciences: Twenty-four Lessons from Antiquity to the Renaissance*, edited and annotated by Theodore W. Pietsch, translated by Abby S. Simpson, foreword by Philippe Taquet. Paris: Publications scientifiques du Muséum national d'Histoire naturelle.

Cziesche, Dominik, Conny Neumann, Barbara Schmid, Caroline Schmidt, Markus Verbeet, and Steffen Winter (translated from the German by Christopher Sultan). 2005. "Right Wing Extremism in Germany: Shock Mom and Dad: Become a Neo-Nazi". *Der Spiegel* 21/2005. Online: https://tinyurl.com/spiegel-357628 (accessed 15 December 2015).

Danielson, Virginia. 1988. "The Arab Middle East". In *Popular Musics of the Non-Western World: An Introductory Survey*, by Peter Manuel, 141–60. New York: Oxford University Press.

—2002. "Stardom in Egyptian Music: Four Case Studies". In *The Garland Encyclopedia of World Music, Volume 6*, edited by Virginia Danielson and Dwight Reynolds, 597–601. New York: Routledge.

Dann, Stephen, and Elisabeth-Bird Jensen. 2014. "Brand Personalities with Real Personality: Strategies for Individual Brands and Branded Individuals in the Entertainment Industry". Unpublished conference paper. Australian National University. Online: http://citeseerx.ist.psu.edu/viewdoc/citations;jsessionid=1835DBBB79109EF1C8847B46791694 05?doi=10.1.1.596.8434 (accessed 1 December 2017).

David, M. D. 2013. "Deep Racism: The Forgotten History of Human Zoos". Online: https://

www.popularresistance.org/deep-racism-the-forgotten-history-of-human-zoos/ (accessed 16 December 2015).

Davis, Kathy. 2003. "Surgical Passing: Or Why Michael Jackson's Nose Makes 'Us' Uneasy". *Feminist Theory* 4(1): 73–92.

Dawson, Abigail. 2017. "'New 'Women in Pop' Magazine Set to Launch Next Month". *Mumbrella*, 18 April. Online: https://mumbrella.com.au/new-women-pop-magazine-set-launch-next-month-438270 (accessed 1 December 2017).

Day, Jonathan. 2008. *The Politics of Navigation: Globalisation, Music and Composition: An Adventure*. Saarbrucken: VDM Verlag.

DeBeavoir, Simone. 2010. *The Second Sex* (A New Translation by Constance Borde and Sheila Malovaney-Chevallier). London: Vintage.

Delanty, Gerard. 2006. "The Cosmopolitan Imagination: Critical Cosmopolitanism and Social Theory". *British Journal of Sociology* 57(1): 25–47.

Deliovsky, Kathy. 2008. "Normative White Femininity: Race, Gender and the Politics of Beauty". *Atlantis* 33(1): 49–59.

DeNora, Tia. 1997. *Beethoven and the Construction of Genius: Musical Politics in Vienna, 1792–1803*. Oakland, CA: University of California Press.

Denselow, Robin. 2007a. "Rise and Demise of the Bhundu Boys". Online: http://news.bbc.co.uk/1/hi/world/africa/7022752.stm (accessed 31 March 2015).

—2007b. *Brasil, Brasil. A Tale of Four Cities* (Episode 3). BBC Four. Online: http://www.bbc.co.uk/musictv/brasilbrasil/episodes/3/ (accessed 15 December 2015).

—2014. "Tinariwen: Emmaar – Review". *The Guardian*, 6 February. Online: http://www.theguardian.com/music/2014/feb/06/tinariwen-emmaar-review (accessed 11 June 2015).

Desk, Trends. 2017. "WATCH: This Viral Song, 'God, Rid Us of Men!' from Saudi Arabia is the New Feminist Anthem". *Indianexpress*, 5 January. Online: https://tinyurl.com/article-4460318 (accessed 15 May 2017).

DiFranco, Ani. 1998. "Court and Spark". *Los Angeles Times Magazine*, 20 September. Online: http://articles.latimes.com/1998/sep/20/magazine/tm-24504/2 (accessed 15 September 2015).

Dinerstein, Joel. 2017. *The Origins of Cool in Postwar America*. Chicago: University of Chicago Press.

Downing, John, and Charles Husband. 2005. "Racism and the Media of the Extremist Right". In *Representing "Race": Racisms, Ethnicities and Media*, 60–85. London: Sage.

Dubois, Diane. 2001. "'Seeing the Female Body Differently': Gender Issues in *The Silence of the Lambs*". *Journal of Gender Studies* 10(3): 297–310.

Duggins, Alexi. 2017a. "'Stop saying he's unelectable!' Grime4Corbyn Movement Moshes for Jeremy". *The Guardian*, 5 June. Online: https://tinyurl.com/music-2017-jun-05 (accessed 8 June 2017).

—2017b. "#grime4Corbyn – why British MCs are uniting behind the Labour leader". *The Guardian*, 17 May. Online: https://tinyurl.com/politics-2017-may-17 (accessed 8 June 2017).

Durán, Lucy. 2014. "Our Stories, From Us, The 'They': Nick Gold Talks to Lucy Durán about the Making of *Buena Vista Social Club*". *Journal of World Popular Music* 1(1): 133–51.

Edwards, Leigh H. 2012. "Transmedia Storytelling, Corporate Synergy and Audience

Expression". *Global Media Journal* 12(20). Online: http://www.globalmediajournal.com/abstract.php?abstract_id=35333 (accessed 1 December 2017).

Elan, Priya. 2014a. "What Does the Return of the Celebrity Bindi Mean?". *The Guardian*, 15 April. Online: https://www.theguardian.com/fashion/fashion-blog/2014/apr/15/return-of-celebrity-bindi-what-does-it-mean (accessed 11 May 2017.

—2014b. "From Katy Perry to Avril Lavigne, Pop Culture is Peddling Racism". *The Guardian*, 4 August. Online: https://www.theguardian.com/commentisfree/2014/aug/04/katy-perry-avril-lavigne-pop-culture-peddling-racism (accessed 11 May 2017).

Elders, The. 2014. Online: http://theelders.org/ (accessed 17 February 2014).

Elizabeth, De. 2017. "Saudi Arabian Women Release Feminist Music Video for 'Hwages'". *TeenVogue*, 5 January. Online: http://www.teenvogue.com/story/saudi-arabian-women-release-feminist-music-video-for-hwages (accessed 15 May 2017).

EMI Canada. 2003. Sarah Brightman Biography. Online: http://josvg.home.xs4all.nl/cits/sb/sb12-art.html (accessed 12 December 2015).

Fabbrini, Sergio. 2010. "After Globalization: Western Power in a Post-Western World". *Global Policy* (18 September 2010). Online: http://www.globalpolicyjournal.com/articles/global-governance/after-globalization-western-power-post-western-world (accessed 25 May 2017).

Farin, Klaus. 1995. "Rechtsrock – Eine Bestadsaufnahme". *PopScriptum 4 – Rechte Musik*: 6–15. Online: https://www2.hu-berlin.de/fpm/popscrip/themen/pst04/pst04_farin.htm (accessed 15 December 2015).

Feld, Steven. 2000. "Anxiety and Celebration: Mapping the Discourses of 'World Music'". In *Changing Sounds: New Directions and Configurations in Popular Music* (IASPM 1999 International Conference Proceedings), edited by Tony Mitchell and Peter Doyle, with Bruce Johnson, 9–14. Sydney: University of Technology.

—2001. "A Sweet Lullaby for World Music". Online: https://read.dukeupress.edu/public-culture/article-abstract/12/1/145/31579/A-Sweet-Lullaby-for-World-Music (accessed 1 December 2017).

Fenster, Mark, and Thomas Swiss. 1999. "Business". In *Key Terms in Popular Music and Culture*, edited by Bruce Horner and Thomas Swiss, 225–38. Malden, MA: Blackwell.

Fenton, Natalie. 2001. "Feminism and Popular Culture". In *The Routledge Companion to Feminism and Postfeminism*, edited by Sarah Gamble, 84–93. London: Routledge.

Ferguson, Niall. 2003. *Empire: How Britain Made the Modern World*. London: Allen Lane/Penguin Books.

Ferguson, Shelagh. 2011. "A Global Culture of Cool? Generation Y and their Perception of Coolness". *Young Consumers* 12(3): 265–75.

Fields, Brandi R. 2014. "Selling the Beat: Hip-Hop Culture and Product Branding Among Young Adults". Research Papers. Paper 517. Online: http://opensiuc.lib.siu.edu/gs_rp/517 (accessed 29 November 2017).

Finlay, Ellen, and Louise St Guillaume. 2017. "The Silent DisCo: Celebrity, Disability and 'Rights Not Charity'". In *Becoming Brands: Celebrity, Activism and Politics*, edited by Jackie Raphael and Celia Lam, 32–43. Toronto: WaterHill Publishing.

Fiske, John. 1986. "MTV: Post-Structural Post-Modern". *Journal of Communication Inquiry* 10(1): 74–79.

Forgacs, David, ed. 2000. *The Antonio Gramsci Reader: Selected Writings 1916–1935*. New York: New York University Press.

Forman, Murray. 2002. *The 'Hood Comes First: Race, Space, and Place in Rap and Hip Hop.* Middletown, CT: Wesleyan University Press.
Forman, Murray, and Mark Anthony Neal, eds. 2004. *That's the Joint! The Hip-Hop Studies Reader.* London: Routledge.
Foucault, Michel. 2000 [1970]. "The Discourse on Language". In *The Routledge Language and Cultural Theory Reader*, edited by L. Burke, T. Crowley, and A. Girvin, 231–40. London: Routledge.
Fournier, Susan. 2010. "Taking Stock in Martha Stewart: A Cultural Critique of the Marketing Practice of Building Person-Brands". *Association for Consumer Research* 37(3): 37–40.
Fraiman, Susan. 2003. *Cool Men and the Second Sex.* New York: Columbia University Press.
Frank, Thomas. 1997. *The Conquest of Cool: Business Culture, Counterculture, and the Rise of Hip Consumerism.* Chicago: University of Chicago Press.
Freemuse. 2001. "Wal-Mart: Market Censors and Market Mechanisms". Online: http://freemuse.org/freemuseArchives/freerip/freemuse.org/sw6859.html (accessed 2 December 2017).
—2002. "Hate Music: Music with a Heart Full of Hatred". Online: https://freemuse.org/news/hate-music-music-with-a-heart-full-of-hatred/ (accessed 2 December 2017).
Freud, Sigmund. 1964. *New Introductory Lectures on Psychoanalysis.* New York: W.W. Norton.
Friedan, Betty. 2010 [1963]. *The Feminine Mystique.* London: Penguin.
Frith, Simon. 1981. *Sound Effects: Youth, Leisure, and the Politics of Rock 'n' Roll.* New York: Pantheon.
—1988. *Music for Pleasure: Essays in the Sociology of Pop.* Cambridge: Polity.
—2000. "The Discourse of World Music". In *Western Musics and Its Others: Difference, Representation, and Appropriation in Music*, edited by Georgina Born and David Hesmondhalgh, 305–322. Berkeley: University of California Press.
Frith, Simon, and Angela McRobbie. 1990. "Rock and Sexuality". In *On Record: Rock, Pop and the Written Word*, edited by Simon Frith and Andrew Goodwin, 371–89 (reprinted from *Screen Education* 29, 1978). New York: Pantheon Books.
Frith, Simon, Will Straw, and John Street. 2001. *The Cambridge Companion to Pop and Rock.* Cambridge: Cambridge University Press.
Frontline. 2014. "Media Giants". Online: http://www.pbs.org/wgbh/pages/frontline/shows/cool/giants/ (accessed 10 January 2014).
fRoots. 2000. "Minutes of Meeting between the Various 'World Music' Record Companies and Interested Parties, Monday 29th June 1987". Online: http://www.frootsmag.com/content/features/world_music_history/minutes/ (accessed 2 December 2017).
Funkeson, Kristina. 2005. "The Music Industry from the Perspective of Women". Online: https://freemuse.org/news/the-music-industry-from-the-perspective-of-women/ (accessed 2 December 2017).
Gamble, Sarah. 2001a. "Postfeminism". In *The Routledge Companion to Feminism and Postfeminism*, edited by Sarah Gamble, 36–45. London: Routledge.
Gamble, Sarah, ed. 2001b. *The Routledge Companion to Feminism and Postfeminism.* London: Routledge.
Garofalo, Reebee. 1993. "Black Popular Music: Crossing over or Going under?" In *Rock and Popular Music: Politics, Policies, Institutions*, edited by Tony Bennett, 231–48. London: Routledge.

Garrison, Edni Kaeh. 2004. "Contests for the Meaning of Third Wave Feminism: Feminism and Popular Consciousness". In *Third Wave Feminism: A Critical Exploration*, edited by Stacy Gillis, Gillian Howie, and Rebecca Munford, 185–97. Basingstoke: Palgrave Macmillan.

Gebesmair, Andreas, and Alfred Smudits, eds. 2001. *Global Repertoires: Popular Music within and beyond the Transnational Music Industry*. Aldershot: Ashgate.

Geoghegan, Kev, and Paul Glynn. 2017. "Music News LIVE: Reaction to Manchester Arena Attack". *BBC Music*, 23 May. Online: https://www.bbc.co.uk/events/evfwhn/live/cg6g9r (accessed 25 May 2017).

George, Brian. 2007. "Rapping the Margins: Musical Constructions of Identities in Contemporary France". In *Music, National Identity and the Politics of Location*, edited by Ian Biddle and Vanessa Knights, 93–114. Aldershot: Ashgate.

Gervais, Daniel J., Kent M. Marcus, and Lauren E. Kilgore. 2011. "The Rise of 360 Deals in the Music Industry". *Landslide* 3(4): 40–45.

Giddens, Anthony. 1990. *The Consequences of Modernity*. Redwood City, CA: Stanford University Press.

Gill, John. 1995. *Queer Noises: Male and Female Homosexuality in Twentieth Century Music*. London: Cassell.

Gill, Rosalind. 2007. "Postfeminist Media Culture: Elements of a Sensibility". *European Journal of Cultural Studies* 10(2): 147–66.

Gilroy, Paul. 1987. *'There Ain't no Black in the Union Jack': The Cultural Politics of Race and Nation*. Chicago: University of Chicago Press.

—1993. *The Black Atlantic: Modernity and Double Consciousness*. London: Verso.

Godden, Maryse. 2017. "SAUDI SEXISM SCANDAL: Female Pop Band Spark Outrage in Saudi Arabia with Music Video Mocking Donald Trump and Condemning Oppression of Women". *The Sun*, 4 January. Online: https://tinyurl.com/y759h62p (accessed 15 May 2017).

Goffman, Erving. 1979. *Gender Advertisements*. New York: Harper & Row.

Goodman, Barak, dir. 2001. *The Merchants of Cool* (documentary). USA: PBS/Frontline. Available at https://www.pbs.org/wgbh/pages/frontline/shows/cool/ (accessed 10 January 2018).

Goodwin, Andrew. 1992. *Dancing in the Distraction Factory: Music Television and Popular Culture*. London: Routledge.

Griffith, Hywel. 2015. "Far Right 'Targeting New, Younger Generation'". *BBC News*, 17 June. Online: http://www.bbc.com/news/uk-wales-33167441 (accessed 15 December 2015).

Gronow, Pekka, and Ilpo Saunio. 1998. *An International History of the Recording History*, translated by Christopher Moseley. London: Cassell.

Guardian Music. 2017. "Michigan Republicans Consider Kid Rock as Candidate for US Senate". *The Guardian*, 16 February. Online: https://www.theguardian.com/music/2017/feb/16/michigan-republicans-consider-kid-rock-as-candidate-for-us-senate (accessed 11 May 2017).

Guardian, The. 2016. "Björk on Sexism: 'Women in Music are Allowed to Sing about their Boyfriends'". *The Guardian*, 21 December. Online: https://www.theguardian.com/music/2016/dec/21/bjork-sexism-open-letter-music-industry-facebook (accessed 15 May 2017).

Guilbault, Jocelyne. 1997. "Interpreting World Music: A Challenge in Theory and Practice". *Popular Music* 16(1): 31–44.
Hall, Stuart. 1995. "The Whites of Their Eyes: Racist Ideologies and the Media". In *Gender, Race and Class in Media: A Text Reader*, edited by Gail Dines and Jean M. Humez, 89–93. London: Sage.
—1997a. "Race, the Floating Signifier" [Transcript]. *Media Education Foundation*. Online: http://www.mediaed.org/transcripts/Stuart-Hall-Race-the-Floating-Signifier-Transcript.pdf (accessed 2 October 2015).
—1997b. "The Work of Representation". In *Representation: Cultural Representations and Signifying Practices* (Culture, Media and Identities Series), edited by Stuart Hall, 13–74. London: Sage.
—2010. "New Ethnicities". In *Media Studies: A Reader*, 3rd edn, edited by Sue Thornham, Caroline Bassett, and Paul Marris, 269–76. New York: New York University Press.
Hann, Michael. 2017. "From Aretha to Beyoncé: The Black Artists Snubbed by the Grammys". *The Guardian*, 16 February. Online: https://www.theguardian.com/music/2017/feb/16/from-aretha-to-beyonce-the-black-artists-snubbed-by-the-grammys (accessed 11 May 2017).
Harvey, David. 1989. *The Condition of Postmodernity: An Enquiry into the Origins of Cultural Change*. Cambridge: Blackwell.
Hawkins, Stan. 1997. "The Pet Shop Boys: Musicology, Masculinity and Banality". In *Sexing the Groove: Popular Music and Gender*, edited by Sheila Whiteley, 118–34. London: Routledge.
—2006. "On Male Queering in Mainstream Pop". In *Queering the Popular Pitch*, edited by Sheila Whiteley and Jennifer Rycenga, 279–93. New York: Routledge.
Hawkins, Stan, and John Richardson. 2007. "Remodeling Britney Spears: Matters of Intoxication and Mediation". *Popular Music and Society* 30(5): 605–629.
Haynes, Jo. 2013. *Music Difference and the Residue of Race*. New York: Routledge.
Hesmondhalgh, David. 2013. *The Cultural Industries*, 3rd edn. London: Sage.
Hesmondhalgh, David, and Sarah Baker. 2010. "'A Very Complicated Version of Freedom': Conditions and Experiences of Creative Labour in Three Cultural Industries". *Poetics* 38(1): 4–20.
Hesmondhalgh, David, and Leslie M. Meier. 2015. "Popular Music, Independence and the Concept of the Alternative in Contemporary Capitalism". In *Media Independence: Working with Freedom or Working for Free?*, edited by James Bennett and Nicki Strange, 94–116. New York: Routledge.
Heung, Marina. 1997. "The Family Romance of Orientalism: From Madame Butterfly to Indochine". In *Visions of the East: Orientalism in Film*, edited by Matthew Bernstein and Gaylyn Studlar, 158–83. New Jersey: Rutgers University Press.
Hilburn, Robert. 1996. "Khan Demonstrates Why He's World Music Leader of Mid-'90s". Online: http://articles.latimes.com/1996-08-16/entertainment/ca-34650_1_world-music (accessed 15 June 2015).
Hill Collins, Patricia. 2000. *Black Feminist Thought: Knowledge, Consciousness, and the Politics of Empowerment*. New York: Routledge.
Hinton, Brian. 2000. *Joni Mitchell: Both Sides Now*. London: Sanctuary Publishing.
Hirschman, Elizabeth C., and Priscilla A. LaBarbera. 1989. "The Meaning of Christmas". *SV-*

Interpretive Consumer Research: 136–47. Online: http://www.acrwebsite.org/search/view-conference-proceedings.aspx?Id=12181 (accessed 13 February 2014).

Hollows, Joanne. 2000. *Feminism, Femininity and Popular Culture*. Manchester: Manchester University Press.

Hollywood Life. 2013. "Katy Perry Killer Queen 'Own the Throne' Ad Released". *Hollywood Life*. Online: http://hollywoodlife.com/2013/07/24/katy-perry-kill-queen-perfume-ad-own-the-throne-pics/ (accessed 10 January 2014).

Holmes, Su, and Diane Negra, eds. 2011. *In the Limelight and Under the Microscope: Forms and Functions of Female Celebrity*. London: Continuum.

hooks, bell. 2004. *The Will to Change: Men, Masculinity, and Love*. New York: Washington Square Press.

—2015 [1990]. *Yearning: Race, Gender and Cultural Politics* (1st edn publ. by South End Press, 1990). New York: Routledge.

Hopkins, Susan. 2002. *Girl Heroes: The New Force in Popular Culture*. Sydney: Pluto Press.

Hoskyns, Barney. 1994. "Joni Mitchell: Our Lady of Sorrows". *Mojo*. Online: http://www.rocksbackpages.com/Library/Article/joni-mitchell-our-lady-of-sorrows/ (accessed 11 December 2015).

—2005. *Hotel California: Singer-Songwriters and Cocaine Cowboys in the LA Canyons, 1967–1976*. London: Perennial.

Howard, Keith. 2009. "Live Music vs Audio Tourism: World Music and the Changing Music Industry". Inaugural lecture given on 11 November 2008. SOAS, University of London. Online: http://eprints.soas.ac.uk/7151/1/howard_inaugural_formatted_140109.pdf (accessed 18 February 2014).

Huq, Rupa. 2006. *Beyond Subculture: Pop, Youth and Identity in a Postcolonial World*. New York: Routledge.

Huggan, Graham. 2001. *The Post-Colonial Exotic: Marketing the Margins*. New York: Routledge.

Hughes, Diane, Mark Evans, Guy Morrow, and Sarah Keith. 2016. *The New Music Industries: Disruption and Discovery*. Cham, Switzerland: Springer/Palgrave Macmillan.

Hughes, Pascale. 2017. "Storm over Hwages Pop Video Featuring Skateboarding Saudi Women in Islamic Veils". *Evening Standard*, 4 January. Online: http://www.standard.co.uk/news/world/men-make-us-mentally-ill-sing-saudi-women-in-viral-pop-video-a3432221.html (accessed 15 May 2017).

Humm, Maggie. 2003. *The Dictionary of Feminist Theory*, 2nd edn. Edinburgh: Edinburgh University Press.

Hunter, Margaret L. 2007. "The Persistent Problem of Colorism: Skin Tone, Status, and Inequality". *Sociology Compass* 1(1): 237–54.

—2011. "Buying Racial Capital: Skin-Bleaching and Cosmetic Surgery in a Globalized World". *Journal of Pan African Studies* 4(4): 142–64.

Hutnyk, John. 1998. "Adorno at Womad: South Asian Crossovers and the Limits of 'Hybridity Talk'". *Postcolonial Studies* 1(3): 401–426.

Huyssen, Andreas. 1986. *After the Great Divide: Modernism, Mass Culture, Postmodernism*. London: Macmillan Press.

Ibrahim, Magda. 2013. "Lessons Marketers Can Learn from the One Direction Brand Phenomenon". Online: http://www.marketingmagazine.co.uk/article/1208304/lessons-marketers-learn-one-direction-brand-phenomenon (accessed 18 February 2014).

iChance. 2009. "K.I.Z. über ihre Schulzeit, Ausbildung, Lesen und Schreiben". Online: https://www.youtube.com/watch?v=3R4RAJ4WYsU (accessed 16 December 2015).
IFPI. 2005. "Digital Music Report". Online: http://www.ifpi.org/content/library/digital-music-report-2005.pdf (accessed 17 December 2015).
—2016. "Investing in Music: The Value of Record Companies". Online: http://investinginmusic.ifpi.org/ (accessed 17 March 2017).
Impey, Angela. 2000. "Popular Music in Africa". In *The Garlands Encyclopedia of World Music, Volume 1*, edited by Ruth M. Stone, 113–35. New York: Garland Press.
Ivaldi, Antonia, and Susana O'Neill. 2008. "Adolescents' Musical Role Models: Whom Do They Admire and Why?" *Psychology of Music* 36(4): 395–415.
Jackson, Daniel, Richard Jankovich, and Eric Sheinkop. 2013. *Hit Brands: How Music Builds Value for the World's Smartest Brands.* New York: Palgrave Macmillan.
Jackson, Dianne. 1982. *The Snowman* [feature film]. UK Channel Four Films.
James, Robin. 2015. *Resilience and Melancholy: Pop Music, Feminism, Neoliberalism.* Winchester, UK: Zero Books.
Jameson, Frederic. 1991. *Postmodernism, or, The Cultural Logic of Late Capitalism.* London: Verso.
Jamieson, Amber. 2016. "Pop for Politics: How Candidates Brand Themselves with Music". *The Guardian*, 1 March. Online: https://www.theguardian.com/music/2016/mar/01/rock-and-folk-tunes-on-the-campaign-trail (accessed 11 May 2017).
Jhally, Sut (prod. and dir.), Susan Ericsson, Sanjay Talreja (prod.), Sut Jhally, Susan Ericsson, Sanjay Talreja, Jeremy Smith (eds), Jackson Katz, Jeremy Earp (writers). 1999. *Tough Guise: Violence, Media and the Crisis in Masculinity*. Documentary. Northampton, MA: Media Education Foundation.
Jhally, Sut (exec. prod.), Loretta Alper (prod.), Margo Robb (prod.), and Jeremy Smith (ed.). 2003. *Rich Media, Poor Democracy*, featuring Robert McChesney and Mark Crispin Miller. Documentary. Northampton, MA: Media Education Foundation.
Jhally, Sut (exec. prod. and dir.), Sanjay Talreja (prod. and ed.), and Jeremy Smith (assist. ed.). 2005a. *Edward Said: On "Orientalism"* (introduced by Sut Jhally). Documentary, featuring an interview with Edward Said. Northampton, MA: Media Education Foundation.
Jhally, Sut (exec. prod.), Kembrew McLeod (prod.), Thom Monahan (ass. prod.), Jeremy Smith (assist. prod.), and Jeremy Smith (ed.). 2005b. *Money for Nothing: Behind the Business of Pop Music.* Documentary. Northampton, MA: Media Education Foundation.
Jhally, Sut (writer, narr., ed.), Andrew Killoy (add. ed.), Jeremy Earp and Andrew Killoy (post-prod.), Jason Young and John Seely (prod. ass.), Peter Acker and Armadillo Audio Group (sound), Joe Bartone (music), Sweet and Fizzy and Andrew Killoy (graphics). 2007. *Dreamworlds 3: Desire, Sex & Power in Music Video*. Documentary. Northampton, MA: Media Education Foundation.
Johnston, Maura. 2016. "Sexism on Repeat: How the Music Industry Can Break the Cycle". *The Guardian*, 22 March. Online: https://www.theguardian.com/music/2016/mar/11/music-industry-sexism-kesha-dr-luke-miles-kane (accessed 15 May 2017).
Johnston, Nick. 2003. All Times Classics. *Uncut.* Online: http://jonimitchell.com/news/newsitem.cfm?id=979 (accessed 2 December 2017).

Jones, Liz. 1998. *Slave to the Rhythm*. London: Little, Brown Book Group.
July, Miranda. 2015. "A Very Revealing Conversation with Rihanna". *New York Times*, 12 October. Online: https://tinyurl.com/2015-10-12-rihanna-miranda (accessed 11 May 2017).
Kabbini, Rana. 1986. *Europe's Myths of the Orient: Devise and Rule*. London: Macmillan.
Kassabian, Annahid. 2004. "Would You Like Some World Music with Your Latte? Starbucks, Putumayo, and Distributed Tourism". *Twentieth Century Music* 2(1): 209–23.
Katy Perry The Movie. 2012. "Katy Perry Part of Me". Online: http://www.imdb.com/title/tt2215719/ (accessed 4 December 2017).
Katz, Jackson, and Jeremy Earp. 1999. *Tough Guise: Violence, Media, and the Crisis in Masculinity* [Transcript]. Media Education Foundation. Online: http://www.mediaed.org/cgi-bin/commerce.cgi?preadd=action&key=211 (accessed 11 December 2015).
Kearney, Mary Celeste. 2006. *Girls Make Media*. New York: Routledge.
Keel, Astrid, and Rajan Nataraajan. 2012. "Celebrity Endorsements and Beyond: New Avenues for Celebrity Branding". *Psychology & Marketing* 29(9): 690–703.
Khan, Riz. 2011. "Arab Feminism". *Al Jazeera*, 2 March. Online: http://www.aljazeera.com/programmes/rizkhan/2011/03/2011318326616845.html (accessed 15 May 2017).
Kheshti, Roshanak. 2015. *Modernity's Ear: Listening to Race and Gender in World Music*. New York: New York University Press.
Killick, Andrew. 2014. "Should World Music Teachers Teach World Music?: Popular Music and the World Music Survey Course". *Journal of World Popular Music* 1(1): 156–82.
Kim, Susanna. 2013. "8 Celebrity Creative Directors: What They Really Do". *ABC News* (February). Online: http://abcnews.go.com/Business/top-recent-celebrity-creative-directors-brand-ambassadors/story?id=18492843 (accessed 7 December 2016).
Klein, Bethany, Leslie M. Meier, and Devon Powers. 2016. "Selling Out: Musicians, Autonomy, and Compromise in the Digital Age". *Popular Music and Society* [online]. https://doi.org/10.1080/03007766.2015.1120101
Klein, Naomi. 2007. *The Shock Doctrine: The Rise of Disaster Capitalism*. London: Penguin Books.
—2010. *No Logo*, 3rd edn. New York: Picador.
Kleinschmidt, Jessica. 2017. "Nike to Sell Performance Hijab for Muslim Women Athletes". Online: https://tinyurl.com/ybdwwcbo (accessed 31 March 2017).
Knopper, Steve. 2009. *Appetite for Self-Destruction: The Spectacular Crash of the Record Industry in the Digital Age*. New York: Free Press.
Krims, Adam. 2003. *Rap Music and Poetics of Identity*. Cambridge: Cambridge University Press.
Krüger, Simone. 2015. "World Music, World Circuit: In Conversation with Nick Gold". *Journal of World Popular Music* 2(2): 186–210.
—2016. "In Conversation with Steve Levine". *Journal of Popular Music Studies* 28(1): 101–125.
Kurien, C. T. 1999. "Globalisation: A Cautionary Note". *Economic and Political Weekly* 34(52): 3653–54.
Lamb, Peter. 2015. *Marx and Engels' "Communist Manifesto": A Reader's Guide*. London: Bloomsbury.
Lamb, Sharon, Kelly Graling, and Emily E. Wheeler. 2013. "'Pole-arized' Discourse: An

Analysis of Responses to Miley Cyrus' Teen Choice Awards Pole Dance". *Feminism & Psychology* 23(2): 163–83.
Lamere, Paul. 2009. "The Coolness Index". Online: https://musicmachinery.com/2009/07/01/the-coolness-index/ (accessed 7 January 2017).
Langlois, Tony. 2011. "Introduction". In *Non-Western Popular Music*, edited by Tony Langlois, xi–xxvii. Farnham: Ashgate.
Langlois, Tony, ed. 2011. *Non-Western Popular Music*. Farnham: Ashgate.
Lash, Scott, and John Urry. 1987. *The End of Organized Capitalism*. Madison, WI: University of Wisconsin Press.
—1994. *Economies of Signs and Space*. London: Sage.
Lechner, Frank J., and John Boli, eds. 2004. *The Globalization Reader*. Oxford: Blackwell.
—2005. *World Culture: Origins and Its Consequences*. Malden, MA: Blackwell.
Lecocq, Baz. 2005. "Unemployed Intellectuals in the Sahara: The *Teshumara* Nationalist Movement and the Revolutions in Tuareg Society". In *Popular Intellectuals in Social Movement: Framing Protest in Asia, Africa and Latin America*, edited by Michiel Baud and Rosanne Rutten, 87–110. Cambridge: Cambridge University Press.
León, Javier F. ed. 2014. Special Issue: "Music, Music Making and Neoliberalism". *Culture, Theory and Critique* 55(2): 129–271.
Leonard, Marion. 1997. "'Rebel girl you are the queen of my world': Feminism, 'Subculture' and Grrrl Power". In *Sexing the Groove: Popular Music and Gender*, edited by Sheila Whiteley, 230–56. London: Routledge.
—2007. *Gender in the Music Industry: Rock, Discourse and Girl Power*. Aldershot: Ashgate.
Leonard, Marion, and Rob Strachan. 2003. "Authenticity". In *The Encyclopaedia of Popular Music of the World, Volume 1: Media, Industry and Society*, edited by John Shepherd, David Horn, Dave Laing, Paul Oliver, and Peter Wicke, 164–66. London: Continuum.
Lester, Paul. 2015. "Meat is Murder? Rockers Go Head to Head over Animal Rights". *The Guardian*, 10 July. Online: https://www.theguardian.com/music/2015/jul/10/meat-is-rockers-go-head-to-head-over-animal-rights (accessed 11 May 2017).
Levenson, Michael. 2011. *Modernism*. New Haven, CT: Yale University Press.
Levitt, Theodore. 1983. "The Globalization of Markets". *Harvard Business Review* 61(3): 92–102.
Lewis, Lisa A. 1990. *Gender Politics and MTV: Voicing the Difference*. Philadelphia, PA: Temple University Press.
Lewis, Reina. 1996. *Gendering Orientalism: Race, Femininity and Representation*. New York: Routledge.
—2004. *Rethinking Orientalism: Women, Travel and the Ottoman Harem*. London: I.B. Tauris.
Li, Eric P. H., Hyun Jeong Min, Russell W. Belk, Junko Kimura, and Shalini Bahl. 2008. "Skin Lightening and Beauty in Four Asian Cultures". In *Advances in Consumer Research* Vol. 35, edited by Angela Y. Lee and Dilip Soman, 444–49. Duluth, MN: Association for Consumer Research.
Lieb, Kristin. 2007. "Pop Tarts and Body Parts: An Exploration of the Imaging and Brand Management of Female Popular Music Stars". Unpublished PhD thesis. Syracuse University.
—2013. *Gender, Branding, and the Modern Music Industry: The Social Construction of Female Popular Music Stars*. New York: Routledge.

Linnaeus, Carl. 1758. *Systema Naturae per regna tria naturae*. 10th edn. Stockholm: Laurentius Salvius.

Liu, Juliana. 2017. "G.E.M. and the Rise of 'China's Taylor Swift'". *BBC*, 14 May. Online: http://www.bbc.co.uk/news/av/world-asia-china-39894630/the-rise-of-chinas-taylor-swift (accessed 15 May 2017).

Local DE, The. 2017. "Spelling Mistake Triggered Terror Alarm at Germany's Biggest Music Festival". *The Local DE*, 14 June. Online: https://www.thelocal.de/20170614/spelling-mistake-triggered-terror-alarm-at-germanys-biggest-music-festival (accessed on 14 June 2017).

Locke, Ralph P. 2000. "On Music and Orientalism". In *Music, Culture and Society: A Reader*, edited by Derek B. Scott, 103–109. Oxford: Oxford University Press.

Longhurst, Brian. 2007. *Popular Music and Society*, 2nd edn. Cambridge: Polity.

Love, Nancy S. 2006. *Musical Democracy*. Albany, NY: SUNY Press.

Lutz, Ashley, 2012. "These 6 Corporations Control 90% of the Media in America". *Business Insider*, 14 June. Online: http://uk.businessinsider.com/these-6-corporations-control-90-of-the-media-in-america-2012-6?r=US&IR=T (accessed 26 May 2017).

Lynskey, Dorian. 2014. "This Means War: Why the Fashion Headdress Must be Stopped". *The Guardian*, 30 July. Online: https://www.theguardian.com/fashion/2014/jul/30/why-the-fashion-headdress-must-be-stopped (accessed 11 May 2017).

Maas, Georg, and Dieter Zeppenfeld. 2009. *The Real World of Peter Gabriel*. Documentary. Germany: Zinnober Film- und Fernsehproduktion.

Mackay, Neil. 2006. "White off the Scale". *The Guardian*. Online: http://www.theguardian.com/music/2006/jan/22/thefarright.popandrock (accessed 15 December 2015).

MacKenzie, John M. 1995. *Orientalism: History, Theory and the Arts*. Manchester: Manchester University Press.

Madonna. 2016. Madonna's Full Acceptance Speech at *Billboard* Women In Music 2016. 13 December 2016. Online: https://tinyurl.com/2016-7624369 (accessed 6 January 2017).

Magaudda, Paolo, Marco Solaroli, Jasper Chalcraft, and Marco Santoro. 2011. "Music Festivals and Local Identities". In *European Arts Festivals: Strengthening Cultural Diversity*, edited by the Euro-Festival Consortium, 57–67. European Commission: Directorate-General for Research and Innovation Socio-economic Sciences and Humanities. Online: https://ec.europa.eu/research/social-sciences/pdf/policy_reviews/euro-festival-report_en.pdf (accessed 28 November 2017.

Mahdi, Ali Akbar, ed. 2003. *Teen Life in the Middle East*. Connecticut, CT: Greenwood Press.

Making of The Snowman, The. 2002. DVD [unknown director] UK: Universal Pictures.

Manson, Jim, and Neil Mackay. 2006. *Nazi Hate Rock: A MacIntyre Investigation* [DVD]. SMG Television Productions.

Manuel, Peter. 1988. *Popular Musics of the Non-Western World: An Introductory Survey*. New York: Oxford University Press.

Marcus, Sara. 2010. *Girls to the Front: The True Story of the Riot Grrrl Revolution*. New York: HarperCollins.

Margetson, Richard. 2017. "Arnhem Land Artist Raps in Native Language". *Radio Darwin Breakfast*, broadcast 22 May. Online: http://www.abc.net.au/radio/darwin/programs/breakfast/baker-boy-rapper/8546232 (accessed 25 May 2017).

Marglin, Stephen A., and Juliet B. Schor. 1992. *The Golden Age of Capitalism: Reinterpreting the Postwar Experience*. Oxford: Oxford University Press.

Marre, Jeremy, and Hannah Charlton. 1985a. *Beats of the Heart: Popular Music of the World*. London: Plato Press.

—1985b. "Rhythm of Resistance: The Black Music of South Africa". In *Beats of the Heart: Popular Music of the World*, 34–50. London: Plato Press in association with Channel Four Television Company Ltd.

—1985c. "Spirit of Samba". In *Beats of the Heart: Popular Music of the World*, 215–28. London: Plato Press in association with Channel Four Television Company Ltd.

—1985d. "The Romany Trail: Gypsy Music". In *Beats of the Heart: Popular Music of the World*, 167–97. London: Plato Press in association with Channel Four Television Company Ltd.

—1985e. "There'll Always be Stars in the Sky: The Indian Film Music Phenomenon". In *Beats of the Heart: Popular Music of the World*, 137–54. London: Plato Press in association with Channel Four Television Company Ltd.

Marsh, Calum. 2015. "Osheaga's Headdress Ban Shows Festival's Zero Tolerance for Cultural Appropriation". *The Guardian*, 17 July. Online: https://www.theguardian.com/culture/2015/jul/17/osheaga-music-festival-headdress-cultural-appropriation (accessed 11 May 2017).

Marshall, P. David. 2016. *The Celebrity Persona Pandemic*. Minneapolis, MN: University of Minnesota Press.

—2017. "Foreword: The Bridge of the Human Brand". In *Becoming Brands: Celebrity, Activism and Politics*, edited by Jackie Raphael and Celia Lam, 1–4. Toronto: WaterHill Publishing.

Mayhew, Emma. 2004. "Positioning the Producer: Gender Divisions in Creative Labour and Value". In *Music, Space and Place: Popular Music and Cultural Identity*, edited by Sheila Whiteley, Andy Bennett, and Stan Hawkins, 49–162. Aldershot: Ashgate.

McDonald, Marci. 1974. "Joni Mitchell Emerges from her Retreat". *Toronto Star*. Online: http://jonimitchell.com/library/print.cfm?id=600 (accessed 11 December 2015).

McGuigan, Jim. 2009. *Cool Capitalism*. London: Pluto.

—2012. "The Coolness of Capitalism Today". *triple* 10(2): 425–38.

—2016. *Neoliberal Culture*. Basingstoke: Palgrave Macmillan.

McKenna Ward, Anthony. 2010. "Agustín Barrios Mangoré: A Study in the Articulation of Cultural Identity". Unpublished MA thesis. Australia: University of Adelaide.

McLuhan, Marshall. 1964. *Understanding Media: The Extensions of Man*. Canada: McGraw Hill.

McRobbie, Angela. 2004. "Post-feminism and Popular Culture". *Feminist Media Studies* 4(3): 255–64.

—2009. *The Aftermath of Feminism: Gender, Culture and Social Change*. London: Sage.

—2016. *Be Creative: Making a Living in the New Culture Industries*. Cambridge: Polity.

Meier, Leslie M. 2011. "Promotional Ubiquitous Musics: Recording Artists, Brands, and 'Rendering Authenticity'". *Popular Music and Society* 34(4): 399–415.

Meyer, Thomas. 1995. "'Unser Leben heißt Kämpfen bis zum Tod': Rechtsrock als Message-Rock". PopScriptum 4 – Rechte Musik: 46–69. Online: https://www2.hu-berlin.de/fpm/popscrip/themen/pst04/pst04_meyer.htm (accessed 15 December 2015).

Miege, Bernard. 1989. *The Capitalization of Cultural Production*. New York: International General.
Miles, Elizabeth J., and Loren Chuse. 2000. "Spain". In *The Garlands Encyclopedia of World Music, Volume 8*, edited by Timothy Rice and James Porter, 588–603. New York: Routledge.
Mills, Sara. 1995. *Feminist Stylistics*. London: Routledge.
Milner, M. 2004. *Freaks, Geeks and Cool Kids*. New York: Routledge.
Mirza, Taqi Ali. 1986. "The Qawwali". *Journal of Popular Culture* 20(2): 189–92.
Mitchell, Tony. 2005. "Doin' Damage in My Native Language: The Use of 'Resistance Vernaculars' in Hip Hop in Europe and Aotearoa/Zew Zealand". In *Music, Space and Place: Popular Music and Cultural Identity*, edited by Sheila Whiteley, Andy Bennett, and Stan Hawkins, 108–23. Aldershot: Ashgate.
Modleski, Tania. 1988. *The Women That Knew Too Much: Hitchcock and Feminist Theory*. London: Methuen.
Montoya, Peter, and Tim Vandehey. 2002. *The Personal Branding Phenomenon: Realize Greater Influence, Explosive Income Growth and Rapid Career Advancement by Applying the Branding Techniques of Michael, Martha and Oprah*. US: Peter Montaya/Independent Publishing Platform.
Moore, Allan F. 2011. "Series Preface". In *Non-Western Popular Music*, edited by Tony Langlois, ix–x. Farnham: Ashgate.
Morley, Paul. 2010. "Paul Morley's Showing Off… World Music". *The Guardian*, 23 July. Online: http://www.theguardian.com/music/interactive/2010/jul/23/paul-morley-world-music-showing-off (accessed 15 June 2015).
Morley, Paul, and Guy Evans. 2004. *Chuck D: Pop and Politics*. BBC4 documentary, screened on 15 October 2004.
Moy, Ron. 2007. *Kate Bush and Hounds of Love*. Aldershot: Ashgate.
Muchitsch, Veronika. 2016. "Neoliberal Sounds? The Politics of Beyoncé's Voice on 'Run The World (Girls)'". *PopScriptum*, Volume 12: *Sound, Sex und Sexismus*, edited by L. J. Müller: 1–14. Schriftenreihe herausgegeben vom Forschungszentrum Populäre Musik. Berlin: Humboldt-Universität.
Mulvey, Laura. 1975. "Visual Pleasure and Narrative Cinema". In *A Critical and Cultural Theory Reader*, edited by Anthony Easthope and Kate McGowan, 158–66. Buckingham: Open University Press.
Mundy, S. 2001. *Music and Globalisation: A Guide to the Issues*. Paris: International Music Council.
Murphy, David. 2007. "Where Does World Music Come From? Globalization, Afropop and the Question of Cultural Identity". In *Music, National Identity and the Politics of Location between the Global and the Local*, edited by Ian Biddle and Vanessa Knights, 39–64. Aldershot: Ashgate.
Mwesigire, Bwesigye bwa. 2014. "Norway to Restage 1914 'Human Zoo' that Exhibited Africans as Inmates". *The Guardian*, 29 April. Online: http://www.theguardian.com/world/2014/apr/29/norway-human-zoo-africans-as-inmates (accessed 19 January 2016).
Nakano Glenn, Evelyn. 2008. "Yearning for Lightness: Transnational Circuits in the Marketing and Consumption of Skin Lighteners". *Gender and Society* 22(3): 281–302.
Nancarrow, Clive, Pamela Nancarrow, and Julie Page. 2001. "An Analysis of the Concept of Cool and Its Marketing Implications". *Journal of Consumer Behavior* 1(4): 311–22.

Neal, Mark Anthony. 1999. *What the Music Said: Black Popular Music and Black Public Culture*. London: Routledge.

Needham, Alex. 2012. "One Direction Make Transatlantic Pop History with US No 1 Album". *The Guardian*, 21 March. Online: https://www.theguardian.com/music/2012/mar/21/one-direction-us-no1-album (accessed 28 November 2017).

Negus, Keith. 1992. *Producing Pop: Culture and Conflict in the Popular Music Industry*. London: Edward Arnold.

—1996. *Popular Music Theory: An Introduction*. Cambridge: Polity.

—1999. "The Music Business and Rap: Between the Street and the Executive Suite". *Cultural Studies* 13(3): 488–508.

Nettl, Bruno. 1983. "Cultural Grey-Out". In *The Study of Ethnomusicology: Twenty-Nine Issues and Concepts*, 345–61. Urbana, IL: University of Illinois Press.

—2005. "The New Era: The 1990s and Beyond". In *The Study of Ethnomusicology: Thirty-one Issues and Concepts*, new edn. Urbana, IL: University of Illinois Press.

Newell, James Richard. 2007. "Experiencing *Qawwali*: Sounds as Spiritual Power in Sufi India". PhD thesis. Vanderbilt University, Amsterdam. Online: http://etd.library.vanderbilt.edu/available/etd-09262007-151811/unrestricted/newelldissertation.pdf (accessed 15 June 2015).

Nicholson, Linda, ed. 1997. *The Second Wave: A Reader in Feminist Theory*. New York: Routledge.

NME News Desk. 2015. "Rihanna on Racism in the Music Industry: 'It Never Ends'". *NME*, 12 October. Online: http://www.nme.com/news/music/rihanna-64-1209853 (accessed 11 May 2017).

Oakley, Kate, and Dave O'Brien. 2016. "Learning to Labour Unequally: Understanding the Relationship between Cultural Production, Cultural Consumption and Inequality". *Social Identities* 22(5): 471–86. https://doi.org/10.1080/13504630.2015.1128800

Oakes, Jason Lee. 2006. "Queering the Witch: Stevie Nicks and the Forging of Femininity at the Night of a Thousand Stevies". In *Queering the Popular Pitch*, edited by Sheila Whiteley and Jennifer Rycenga, 41–54. New York: Routledge.

O'Brien, Dave, Daniel Laurison, Andrew Miles, and Sam Friedman. 2016. "Are the Creative Industries Meritocratic? An Analysis of the 2014 British Labour Force Survey". *Cultural Trends* 25(2): 116–31. https://doi.org/10.1080/09548963.2016.1170943

O'Brien, Karen. 1995. *Hymn to Her: Women Musical Talk*. London: Virago Press.

—2001. *Shadows and Light: Joni Mitchell, the Definite Biography*. London: Virgin.

O'Brien, Lucy. 1995. *The Definite History of Women in Rock, Pop and Soul*. London: Penguin.

—2002. *She-Bop II: The Definite History of Women in Rock, Pop and Soul*. London: Continuum.

Observers, The. 2016. "The 'Barbs', the Saudi Dance Trend Sweeping the Arab World". *The Observers*, 21 April. Online: http://observers.france24.com/en/20160421-barbs-saudi-dance-trend-sweeping-arab-world (accessed 15 May 2017).

O'Donnell Kathleen A., and Daniel L. Wardlow. 2000. "A Theory on the Origins of Coolness". *Advances in Consumer Research* 27(1): 13–18.

O'Donnell, Kelly M. 2017. "Celebrities and Conflicting Notions of Modern Feminist Embodiment". In *Becoming Brands: Celebrity, Activism and Politics*, edited by Jackie Raphael and Celia Lam, 110–21. Toronto: WaterHill Publishing.

OECD. 2005. "OECD Report on Digital Music: Opportunities and Challenges". Online: https://tinyurl.com/ieconomy-paper100 (accessed 16 December 2015).

Olczyk, Tomasz, and Jacek Wasilewski. 2017. "Rebel with a Cause: Celebrity, Authenticity and Political Capital". In *Becoming Brands: Celebrity, Activism and Politics*, edited by Jackie Raphael and Celia Lam, 83–96. Toronto: WaterHill Publishing.

Oliver, Richard W., and Tim Leffel. 2006. *Hip-Hop, Inc.: Success Strategies of the Rap Moguls*. New York: Thunders' Mouth Press.

O'Malley, Karie. 2017. "The Saudi Arabian Music Video Featuring Skateboarding Women that's Changing Perceptions". *Elle UK*, 4 January. Online: https://tinyurl.com/y7ok-m2fd (accessed 15 May 2017).

O'Neill, Susan. 2002. "Crossing the Divide: Feminist Perspectives on Gender and Music". *Feminism and Psychology* 12(2): 133–36.

Ortner, Sherry B. 2011. "On Neoliberalism". *Anthropology of this Century*, 1 May. London. Online: http://aotcpress.com/articles/neoliberalism/ (accessed 24 February 2017).

Panzacchi, Cornelia. 1994. "The Livelihoods of Traditional Griots in Modern Senegal". *Africa* 64(2): 190–210.

Paris, Mica. 2015. "Why DO So Many of My Fellow Black Stars Want Whiter Skin? MICA PARIS Poses Question as Beyonce Reveals Her Palest Shade Yet". *Mail Online*, 23 October. Online: https://tinyurl.com/tvshowbiz-3286969 (accessed 12 May 2017).

Park, Bae-Gyoon, Richard Child Hill, and Asato Saito. 2012. *Locating Neoliberalism in East Asia: Neoliberalizing Spaces in Developmental States*. Chichester, UK: Blackwell.

Patience, Allan. 1998. "Warming to a Global Society". *AQ: Australian Quarterly* 70(5): 6–13.

Perrone, Charles A. 1998. "Popular Music of Brazil". In *The Garlands Encyclopedia of World Music, Volume 2*, edited by Dale A. Olsen and Daniel E. Sheehy, 107–111. New York: Routledge.

Pidd, Helen, and Josh Halliday. 2017. "'Let's not be afraid': Ariana Grande Returns to Manchester in Show of Unity". *The Guardian*, 5 June. Online: https://tinyurl.com/2017-jun-04-grande-return (accessed 8 June 2017).

Pleyers, Geoffrey. 2010. *Alter-Globalization: Becoming Actors in the Global Age*. Cambridge: Polity.

Pountain, Dick, and David Robins. 2000. *Cool Rules: Anatomy of an Attitude (FOCI)*. London: Reaktion.

Press Release 01 – World Music. 2000. fRoots Feature. Online: http://www.frootsmag.com/content/features/world_music_history/minutes/page04.html (accessed 30 March 2015).

PRS for Music. 2010. "Most Used Music in Commercials Revealed". Online: https://tinyurl.com/aboutus-press-92984309 (accessed 6 January 2017).

Prügl, Elisabeth. 2015. "Neoliberalising Feminism". *New Political Economy* 20(4): 614–31.

Qureshi, Regula Burckhardt. 1986. *Sufi Music of India and Pakistan: Sound, Context, and Meaning in Qawwali*. New York: Cambridge University Press.

Railton, Diane, and Paul Watson. 2005. "Naughty Girls and Red Blooded Women: Representations of Female Heterosexuality in Music Video". *Feminist Media Studies* 5(1): 51–63.

Ralph, Michael. 2006. "'Flirt[ing] with Death' but 'Still Alive': The Sexual Dimension of Surplus Time in Hip Hop Fantasy". *Cultural Dynamics* 18(1): 61–88.

Ramsey, Guthrie P., Jr. 2003. *Race Music: Black Cultures from Bebop to Hip-Hop*. Berkeley: University of California Press.

Raphael, Jackie, and Celia Lam, eds. 2017. *Becoming Brands: Celebrity, Activism and Politics*. Foreword by P. David Marshall. Toronto: WaterHill Publishing.
Real World Records. 2017a. "About Us". Online: https://realworldrecords.com/world-music/ (accessed 1 December 2017).
—2017b. "République Amazone. Les Amazones d'Afrique". Online: https://realworld records.com/release/669/republique-amazone/ (accessed 15 May 2017).
Regan, Nicholas. 2010. "Agustín Barrios Mangoré: Paraguay's Pre-eminent Guitarist-Composer". In *Paraguay: 200 Years of Independence in the Heart of South America*, edited by Robert Munro, 73–76. London: Published and commissioned by Robert Munro.
Regev, Motti. 2013. *Pop-rock Music: Aesthetic Cosmopolitanism in Late Modernity*. Cambridge: Polity.
Renold, Emma. 1997. "'All They've Got on Their Brains is Football'. Sport, Masculinity and the Gendered Practices of Playground Relations". *Sport, Education and Society* 2(1): 5–23.
Reynolds, Simon, and Joy Press. 1995. *The Sex Revolts: Gender, Rebellion and Rock 'n' Roll*. London: Serpent's Tail.
RFI Musique. 2014. Youssou N'Dour. Biography. Online: http://www.rfimusic.com/artist/world-music/youssou-ndour/biography (accessed 12 January 2016).
Rhodes, Jane. 1993. "Race and Cultural Production: Responses to the Birth of a Nation: The Visibility of Race and Media History" (Review and Criticism). *Critical Studies in Mass Communication* 10(2): 184–90.
Ritzer, George. 2011. *The McDonaldization of Society 6*. London: Sage.
Roberts, Soraya. 2013. "Drake: I Didn't Have it Easy Growing up in a Wealthy Toronto Neighborhood". *Yahoo! News*, 17 October. Online: https://tinyurl.com/toronto-1654 46063 (accessed 7 December 2016).
Rocavert, Carla. 2017. "Offstage Humanitarianism: Reality, Drama and 'Successful Misunderstanding'". In *Becoming Brands: Celebrity, Activism and Politics*, edited by Jackie Raphael and Celia Lam, 9–20. Toronto: WaterHill Publishing.
Rose, Tricia. 1994. *Black Noise: Rap Music and Black Culture in Contemporary America*. Hanover, NH: Wesleyan University Press.
Said, Edward W. 1978. *Orientalism: Western Conceptions of the Orient*. New York: Routledge.
—1991. "Performance as an Extreme Occasion". In Said, *Musical Elaborations*, 1–34. New York: Columbia University Press.
—2003. *Orientalism*, 5th edn. London: Penguin Books.
Samson, Jum. 2003. *Virtuosity and the Musical Work: The Transcendental Studies of Liszt*. Cambridge: Cambridge University Press.
Sandercock, Leonie. 2003. *Cosmopolis II. Mongrel Cities of the 21st Century*. London: Continuum.
Savage, Mark. 2017. "We Break Down Katy Perry's Video for Chained to the Rhythm". Online: http://www.bbc.co.uk/news/entertainment-arts-39042467 (accessed 28 February 2017).
Sawhney, Nitin. 2006. "No Barriers. Interview by Maya Jaggi". Online: http://www.guardian.co.uk/music/2006/apr/01/popandrock (accessed 31 March 2015).
Schafer, Murray R. 2004. "The Music of the Environment". In *Audio Cultures: Readings in*

Modern Music, edited by Christoph Cox and Daniel Warner, 29–39. London: Bloomsbury.

Scheibel, Saskia. 2012. "Against all Odds: Evidence for the 'True' Cosmopolitan Consumer. A Cross-Disciplinary Approach to Investigating the Cosmopolitan Condition". Masters dissertation. London: University of London.

Schlachthofbronx GbR. 2018. http://www.schlachthofbronx.com/. Germany: München.

Schmidt, Katharina. 2002. "Rechte Rockmusik". Unpublished report. Online: https://www2.hu-berlin.de/fpm/wip/schmidt_01.htm (accessed 15 December 2015).

Schumann, Anne. 2010. *Danse philosophique! The Social and Political Dynamics of Zouglou Music in Abidjan, Côte d'Ivoire, 1990–2008*. PhD thesis. SOAS, University of London.

Sengupta, Chandan. 2001. "Conceptualising Globalisation: Issues and Implications". *Economic and Political Weekly* 36(33): 3137–143.

Sheehan, Rebecca. 2017. "Why We Should Celebrate Bessie Smith and the Women who Created Pop Music". *ABC News*, 15 May. Online: https://tinyurl.com/news-8526442 (accessed 26 May 2017).

Shelemay, Kay Kaufman. 2001. *Soundscapes: Exploring Music in a Changing World*. New York: W.W. Norton.

Shepherd, John. 1991. *Music as Social Text*. Cambridge: Polity.

Shohat, Ella. 1997. "Gender and Culture of Empire". In *Visions of the East: Orientalism in Film*, edited by Matthew Bernstein and Gaylyn Studlar, 19–67. New Jersey: Rutgers University Press.

Shuker, Roy. 2016. *Understanding Popular Music Culture*, 5th edn. Abingdon, Oxon: Routledge.

Siddiqi, Ayesha A. n.d. "Lily Allen's Anti Black Feminism". *Noisey*. Online: https://noisey.vice.com/en_us/article/lily-allen-hard-out-here-ayesha-a-siddiqi (accessed 10 May 2017).

Silverman, Carol. 2000. "Rom (Gypsy) Music". In *The Garlands Encyclopedia of World Music, Volume 8*, edited by Timothy Rice and James Porter, 270–92. New York: Routledge.

Singh, Fran. 2017. "Girls Rock: The All-Female Music Camp Taking a Stand Against Sexism". *The Guardian*, 3 January. Online: https://www.theguardian.com/music/2017/jan/03/girl-rock-camp-music-industry-sexism (accessed 15 May 2017).

Sisario, Ben. 2006. "Nick Gold, the Musical Matchmaker who Gave Mali the Blues". *New York Times*, 23 July. Online: http://www.nytimes.com/2006/07/23/arts/music/23sisa.html?pagewanted=all&_r=0 (accessed 14 January 2016).

—2010. "Looking to a Sneaker for a Band's Big Break". *New York Times*, 10 October. Online: https://tinyurl.com/25q3dvy (accessed 17 March 2017).

Sittner, Heike (dir. and writer). 2017. *AMIGA: Der Sound der DDR*. Documentary, 1 May. Germany: Mitteldeutscher Rundfunk (MDR).

Smithsonian. 2014a. "American Cool". *National Portrait Gallery*. Exhibition. 7 February–7 September 2014. Online: http://npg.si.edu/exhibit/Cool/index.html (accessed 7 June 2017).

—2014b. "American Cool Exhibition List". Online: https://tinyurl.com/exhibit-cool-PDF (accessed 7 June 2017).

Software Top 100. 2010. "Top 25 Gaming Companies 2010". Online: http://www.softwaretop100.org/top-gaming-companies-2010 (accessed 10 January 2014).

Sorce Keller, Marcello. 2000. "Popular Music in Europe". In *The Garlands Encyclopedia of World Music, Volume 8*, edited by Timothy Rice and James Porter, 204–213. New York: Routledge.
Steger, Manfred B. 2017. *Globalization: A Very Short Introduction*, 4th edn. New York: Oxford University Press.
Steger, Manfred B., and Ravi K. Roy. 2010. *Neoliberalism: A Very Short Introduction*. New York: Oxford University Press.
Steinberg, Shirley, Michael Kehler, and Lindsay Cornish, eds. 2010. *Boy Culture: An Encyclopedia*. Santa Barbara, CA: Greenwood.
Stokes, Martin. 1994. "Introduction: Ethnicity, Identity and Music". In *Ethnicity, Identity and Music: The Musical Construction of Place*, edited by Martin Stokes, 1–29. Oxford: Berg.
—2004. "Music and the Global Order". *Annual Review of Anthropology* 33(1): 47–72.
—2007. "On Musical Cosmopolitanism". *The Macalester International Roundtable*, Institute for Global Citizenship 2007. Paper 3. Online: http://digitalcommons.macalester.edu/intlrdtable/3 (accessed 6 March 2014).
—2012. "Globalization and the Politics of World Music". In *The Cultural Study of Music: A Critical Introduction*, 2nd edn, edited by Martin Clayton, Trevor Herbert, and Richard Middleton, 107–116. New York: Routledge.
Stone, Christopher. 2007. *Popular Culture and Nationalism in Lebanon: The Fairouz and Rahbani Nation*. New York: Routledge.
Stover, Richard D., in collaboration with Carlos Salcedo Centurión and Odalis C. Lepel. 2012. *Six Silver Moonbeams: The Life and Times of Agustín Barrios Mangoré*. 2nd Paraguay edn. Asunción, Paraguay: Barrios Mangoré Project Center and Guitars from the Heart Association.
Sturken, Marita, and Lisa Cartwright. 2001. *Practices of Looking: An Introduction to Visual Culture*. Oxford: Oxford University Press.
Suárez-Orozco, Marcello, and Desiree B. Qin-Hilliard, eds. 2004. *Globalization: Culture and Education in the New Millennium*. Berkeley: University of California Press.
Sweeney, Phillip. 1992. *The Virgin Directory of World Music*. New York: Henry Holt & Co.
Szarán, Luis. 1999. "Agustín Pío Barrios [Nitsuga Mangoré]". In *Diccionario de la Música Hispano Americana*, edited by Emilio Casares Rodicio, 266. Madrid: Sociedad de Autores y Editores.
—2009. "Rock Nacional". In *Diccionario de la Música en el Paraguay* (1st edn 1997). Asunción, Paraguay: Szarán la Gráfica. Online: http://www.luisszaran.org/DiccionarioDetalle.php?lang=es&DiccID=613 (accessed 27 November 2017).
Tagg, Philip. 1990. "Music in Mass Media Studies: Reading Sounds for Example". In *Popular Music Research*, edited by Keith Roe and U. Karlsson, 103–114. Gothenburg: NORDICOM.
Tasker, Yvonne, and Diane Negra, eds. 2007. *Interrogating Postfeminism: Gender and the Politics of Popular Culture*. Durham, NC: Duke University Press.
Tate, Shirley Anne. 2016. *Skin Bleaching in Black Atlantic Zones: Shade Shifters*. Basingstoke: Palgrave Macmillan (Pivot).
Taylor, Timothy D. 1997. *Global Pop: World Music, World Markets*. London: Routledge.
—2004. "Bad World Music". In *Bad Music: The Music We Love to Hate*, edited by Christopher J. Washburne and Maiken Derno, 83–103. New York: Routledge.

—2014. "Thirty Years of World Music". *Journal of World Popular Music* 1(2): 192–200.

—2016. *Music and Capitalism: A History of the Present.* Chicago: University of Chicago Press.

Thomson, Graeme. 2006. "Jinxed: The Curse of the Bhundu Boys". Online: http://www.theguardian.com/music/2006/sep/17/worldmusic (accessed 31 March 2015).

Titon, Jeff Todd (general editor), with Timothy J. Cooley, David Locke, Anne K. Rasmussen, David B. Reck, Christopher A. Scales, John M. Schechter, Jonathan P. J. Stock, and R. Anderson Sutton. 2018. *Worlds of Music: An Introduction to the Music of the World's Peoples, Shorter Version*, 4th edn. Boston, MA: Cengage Learning.

Tomlinson, John. 1991. *Cultural Imperialism: A Critical Introduction.* London: Continuum.

—1999. *Globalization and Culture.* Cambridge: Polity.

Truss, Lynn. 2008. "Great Lyricists: A Case of Blue". *The Guardian.* Online: http://www.theguardian.com/music/2008/jun/24/popandrock.culture2 (accessed 11 December 2015).

Tuchman, Gaye. 1978. "The Symbolic Annihilation of Women by the Mass Media". In *Culture and Politics: A Reader*, edited by Lane Crothers and Charles Lockhart, 154–72. New York: St Martin's Press.

Turino, Thomas. 2000. *Nationalists, Cosmopolitans, and Popular Music in Zimbabwe.* Chicago: University of Chicago Press.

—2001. "The Music of Sub-Saharan Africa". In *Excursions in World Music*, edited by Bruno Nettl, Charles Capwell, Isabel Wong, Thomas Turino, and Philip V. Bohlman, 167–96. New Jersey: Prentice Hall.

Turner, Camilla. 2015. "Sexism is Worse in the Music Industry Now Than It Was in the 1960s, Says Lulu". *The Telegraph*, 1 March. Online: https://tinyurl.com/yanzw5h6 (accessed 15 May 2017).

Urry, John. 1995. *Consuming Places.* London: Routledge.

—2003. *Global Complexity.* Cambridge: Polity.

Usher, Sebastian. 2007. "Arab Youth Revel in Pop Revolution". Online: http://news.bbc.co.uk/1/hi/world/europe/6666725.stm (accessed 14 December 2015).

Ussher, Jane. 1991. *Women's Madness: Misogyny or Mental Illness?* London: Harvester Wheatsheaf.

Van Leeuwen, Theo. 1999. *Speech, Music, Sound.* Basingstoke, Hampshire: Macmillan.

Van Zoonen, Liesbet. 1994a. *Feminist Media Studies.* London: Sage.

—1994b. "Spectatorship and the Gaze". In Van Zonen, *Feminist Media Studies*, 87–104. London: Sage.

Vanovac, Neda. 2017. "Arnhem Land Performer Inspiring Kids with Goal to be First to Rap in Indigenous Language". *ABC News*, 24 May. Online: http://www.abc.net.au/news/2017-05-21/arnhem-land-musician-wants-to-be-first-to-rap-in-language/8543752 (accessed 25 May 2017).

Verlan, Sascha, and Hannes Loh. 2006. *25 Jahre Hip Hop in Deutschland.* Höfen, Austria: Hannibal Verlag.

Vesey, Alyxandra. 2015. "Putting Her on the Shelf". *Feminist Media Studies* 15(6): 992–1008.

Wagner, Tom. 2014. "Review of *Songlines*, ed. Simon Broughton". *Journal of World Popular Music* 1(2): 201–206.

Walser, Robert. 1993. *Running with the Devil: Power, Gender, and Madness in Heavy Metal Music.* Middletown, CT: Wesleyan University Press.

Warren, Caleb, and Margaret C. Campbell. 2014. "What Makes Things Cool? How Autonomy Influences Perceived Coolness". *Journal for Consumer Research* 41(2): 543–63.
Waterman, Christopher A. 1990. *Jùjú: A Social History and Ethnography of an African Popular Music* (Chicago Studies in Ethnomusicology). Chicago: University of Chicago Press.
Werner, Craig. 1999. *A Change is Gonna Come: Music, Race and the Soul of America*. Ann Arbor, MI: University of Michigan Press.
White, Bob W., ed. 2012. *Music and Globalization: Critical Encounters*. Bloomington, IN: Indiana University Press.
Whiteley, Sheila. 2000. *Women and Popular Music: Sexuality, Identity and Subjectivity*. New York: Routledge.
—2005. *Too Much Too Young: Popular Music, Age and Gender*. Oxon: Routledge.
Whiteley, Sheila, ed. 1997. *Sexing the Groove: Popular Music and Gender*. London: Routledge.
—2008. *Christmas, Ideology and Popular Culture*. Edinburgh: Edinburgh University Press.
Wicke, Peter. 2005. "Fascism". In *Continuum Encyclopedia of Popular Music of the World Part 1 Media, Industry, Society* (Volume 1), edited by David Horn, Dave Laing, Paul Oliver, Peter Wicke, and John Shepherd, 228–29. London: Continuum.
Williams, Linda. 1984. "When the Woman Looks". In *Re-vision: Essays in Feminist Film Criticism*, edited by Mary Anne Doane, Patricia Mellencamp, and Linda Williams, 83–99. Los Angeles: University Publications of America.
Wilson, Pamela. 1995. "Mountains of Contradictions: Gender, Class and Region in the Star Image of Dolly Parton". *South Atlantic Quarterly* 94(1): 109–134.
Witness Org. 2014. Online: https://witness.org/ (accessed 4 December 2017).
Wolf, Naomi. 1991. *The Beauty Myth: How Images of Beauty Are Used Against Women*. London: Vintage.
Women in Pop. 2017. http://www.womeninpop.com/ (accessed 26 May 2017).
Zakaria, Fareed. 2008. *The Post-American World*. New York: W. W. Norton.
Zuberi, Nabeel. 2002. "India Song: Popular Music Genres since Economic Liberalization". In *Popular Music Studies*, edited by David Hesmondhalgh and Keith Negus, 238–50. London: Arnold.

Index

360 deal 186, 192

Aboriginal 119, 129–30, 133–34, 155, 265
activism 229–31, 239, 241, 248–49, 254, 264
Adele 116
advertising 5, 21, 42–43, 47–48, 88–89, 91, 99, 104–106, 117, 155, 174–75, 180–85, 188, 222, 225–27, 262, 264
Africa 4, 18–19, 33–39, 51, 56–57, 132, 135, 145, 152, 169–70, 172, 204, 207, 231, 235, 239, 251
  East 150
  South 34–38, 55, 82n, 134, 148n, 247
  West 34, 36, 39, 57, 175, 250–51
Afropop 34–38, 55–57, 172, 250–51
age 12, 68, 81, 107, 109, 160, 168, 186, 201, 207, 248, 256
ageism 69, 112
Allen, Lily 212
America 4, 14n, 63–64, 72, 153, 158, 197, 204, 262 (*see also* US)
  Latin 23–24, 33, 38–41, 58, 82n, 117
  North 5, 117, 145, 237, 260n
  South 18, 39, 51
AMIGA 49–50
androgyny 199–200
anthropology 63, 120
anti-globalization 13, 259–60
anti-racism 13, 135, 232, 260
Apple 89, 178–79, 183, 223, 226
appropriation 97, 118–20, 150, 175, 177, 204, 219, 233–34, 236
Arabic music 25–26, 123 (*see also* Arabpop)
Arabpop 28, 112–14, 249–50
Asia 4, 9, 18, 43, 50–51, 164
  East 18, 121
  South 145 (*see also* India)
  Southeast 145
audience 30, 32, 38, 47, 52, 70, 73, 80, 94, 105, 107, 109, 112, 123, 129, 132, 134, 136, 144–45, 147, 157–58, 162–63, 165, 168, 172, 176, 182–84, 186, 188, 193, 200, 203, 206–208, 215, 222, 224, 231
Australia 16, 18–20, 63, 129, 134, 260n
authenticity 2, 11–12, 70–71, 78, 107, 138–39, 147, 158–65, 167–69, 172, 173n, 179, 187, 191–93, 197, 205–206, 210, 228, 234, 243
authorship 75

Barrios Mangoré, Agustín 23–24
beauty 71–72, 95, 117, 186, 211–14, 245–46
Beyoncé 116–17, 148n, 179, 187, 192, 217–20
Bhundu Boys 161–64, 233
Big Three 46, 93, 97, 103–104, 106, 126, 192 (*see also* TNC)
Billboard 58, 62, 67, 96, 103, 156, 167, 214, 254
black
  community 139, 142, 253
  cool 191
  identity 141–42, 197
  music 7, 19, 34, 44–45, 47, 60–61, 115, 117, 132, 134, 143
  nationalism 140, 251–54
  separatism 132, 254
  women 11, 109–10, 117–18, 194–96, 243
blackness 115, 135–38, 141–43, 148n, 171, 188–89, 196, 219–20, 251, 255
blues 44, 46–47, 53, 57, 60–62, 119, 153, 177, 184, 204–205, 208, 243
body (human) 72, 74, 108, 110–14, 116–17, 186, 194, 201, 214–17, 220, 227n, 235
Bollywood 117, 132, 143–47, 164
bourgeois 196, 209, 218–20, 255
brand 12, 88, 95–96, 126, 142, 148n, 157–58, 178–87, 192–94, 210–12, 220, 231, 245, 247
  endorsement 185
  extension 185, 192, 214
  music brand 160, 184
  persona/lity 180–81, 184–85, 193, 221
  star-as-brand 89
  warehouse 156
branding 11–12, 50, 88–91, 105, 147n, 148n, 156–57, 160, 179–81, 191–92, 197, 211, 214, 221, 250, 264
  music branding 181–88
Brazil 39–40, 82n, 133
Brightman, Sarah 123–24
Britain, 4, 14n, 20, 22, 34, 42, 45, 63–64, 86,

101, 150–51, 153, 161, 232, 243, 245, 256–59, 265 (*see also* UK)
Buena Vista Social Club 41, 155, 157, 235, 237

camp 198–200 (*see also* queer)
canon 62, 69–70, 77, 80, 158
capital (financial) 1, 6, 85, 117–18, 135, 226, 263
    cultural 90, 174, 221
    human 190, 217–18
capitalism
    anti- 179, 255, 260
    cool 12, 131, 178–81, 191, 226–27, 264
    early 6, 15
    global 2, 4, 13, 59, 90, 224, 228–29, 255, 260, 267
    late 5, 13, 91, 255
    liberal 8, 16–17, 81, 84
    market 5, 16, 221, 225, 264
    monopoly 5, 16, 264
    neoliberal 5, 8, 10–12, 84, 86–88, 90, 126, 162, 172, 174, 178–80, 190–91, 209, 226–27, 262, 264
    organized 5, 8–10, 41–42, 81, 84, 264
    the Golden Age of 9, 41, 43, 83n
    unrestrained 229
cassette 17, 27, 50–51, 59, 85, 144, 154–55, 161, 171, 204–206
CBS 45, 50–51, 93
celebrity 12, 88–90, 92, 105, 117–18, 179–80, 184–85, 187, 227–28, 231, 259
    celebrity persona 12, 89, 116, 180–81, 184
censorship 37, 41, 58, 61, 145, 257
Chess Records 46
Christianity 4, 16, 66
Christmas culture 99–100
Chuck D 253–54, 260n
citizen 225, 229–30, 238
citizenship 2–3, 13, 226–27, 229–33, 236, 249, 255, 264
civil rights 13, 44, 83n, 197, 232, 253
civilization 24, 42, 87, 121, 228, 262
class (social) 9, 13, 16–17, 22, 29, 33, 43, 54, 63, 73, 84, 107, 109, 128, 138–40, 142–43, 146–47, 160, 188–89, 229, 246, 255, 263
    middle 38, 139–41, 196–97, 211, 218, 242, 247
    new 174, 209
    upper 146, 193
    working 135, 139, 176, 196–97, 218, 229, 254
cock rock 73

collaboration 38, 155, 167, 170, 192, 233, 236, 238–39
colonialism 1, 4–5, 60, 63–64, 67, 115, 121, 142, 171, 236
colonization 4, 37, 82n, 100
Columbia (label) 18–20, 26, 44, 46, 96, 119
commercialization 1, 6, 29–31, 38, 105, 229, 233–34
commodity 7, 16–17, 21, 31, 81, 86, 98, 127, 180, 225, 233
    fetishism 12, 175, 178, 225–27
Communism 42, 84
conglomerate 93, 185
consumer culture 23–24, 28, 33, 62, 89–90, 98, 105, 157, 175, 178, 226
controlling images 11, 109–10, 190
cool
    conquest of 91, 189, 197, 207
    façade 179
    hunting 174
    seduction 12, 175, 178, 226–27
    technologies 12, 227
coolness 12, 146, 172, 174–79, 189, 191, 193–94, 197–98, 200, 202, 208, 211–14, 220–21
corporation 37, 86, 88, 93–95, 97, 103, 106
    music 2, 11, 92–93, 96, 102–103, 162, 193, 210, 223
    transnational 6, 97, 225
cosmopolitanism 2, 128, 148n, 202, 234–35, 240, 260, 264
    aesthetic 11, 127–30, 132, 143, 147
counterculture 44, 72, 83n, 177, 197, 242
country (genre) 19, 44, 52, 92
creative industries 21, 86, 105, 148n, 174–75, 209, 236, 262
creativity 16–17, 33–34, 71, 73, 75, 77, 79–80, 86, 100, 107, 116, 175, 197, 221, 232, 234, 255
credibility 139, 192–93, 197
cross-media marketing 94–95, 98, 165, 185, 187
Cuba 18, 35, 39
cultural imperialism 2, 11, 97–102, 125–26, 131, 143, 147, 234, 264
cultural industries 21, 69, 87, 91, 102, 174, 262
culture
    global 1, 3, 32, 98, 137, 142
    high 16, 22, 71, 90, 126, 131
    industry 21, 98, 106, 126, 262
    music 15, 23, 49, 58, 109, 162, 210
    online 89, 226

popular 10–12, 20, 25, 27, 60, 62–63, 67, 80–81, 88, 90–91, 97–99, 106, 109, 111, 114, 116, 124, 126, 131, 136, 142–43, 147, 172, 174–75, 178–79, 186, 191, 196, 198, 209–10, 213, 220–21, 224, 227–28, 233, 243, 254, 262
western 2–3, 5, 9, 13, 33, 56, 59, 67, 71, 90, 113, 120, 125, 161, 165, 232–33
Cyrus, Miley 94, 110–11, 212, 220, 266

damage 189–91, 193, 196, 217–21, 227n
dance 19, 21, 28–30, 35, 40, 45, 51, 54, 57, 92, 103, 111, 114, 123–24, 130, 145–46, 155–56, 158, 164, 166, 168–69, 172, 175, 194, 200, 202, 214, 218–20, 238, 244, 249–50
Decca 34, 46, 49, 51–52, 150
democracy 2–3, 13, 43, 64, 87, 125–26, 129, 228–33, 236, 239, 255, 259–60, 262, 267
democratization 1, 3, 128, 222, 224, 231
de-territorialization 2, 127
Deutsche Grammophon 18, 20, 22, 26, 34, 44, 49
deviance 79
deviant 81, 115, 200–201
diaspora 7, 132, 134–35, 144–45, 147, 254
DiFranco, Ani 241, 248–49
digital 92, 104, 127, 182–83, 186, 222–25, 264 (*see also* technologies, digital)
digitization 6, 89, 128, 186, 223–24
disability 109, 188–89, 231
disaffection 175–79, 191, 251
disco 54, 83n, 144
discrimination 3, 37, 175, 242, 253
distinction (status/class) 33, 131, 158–59, 174, 263
downloading 222–24, 254
Drake 103, 111, 116, 192–93

East 18, 49–50, 82, 113, 115, 119–23, 136, 148
egalitarianism 87, 227–28, 231
Egypt 24–28, 118, 123
electric
    amplifier 10
    guitar 28, 34–35, 43, 52–53, 57, 130, 144, 204
    instrument 9, 43, 52, 59, 206
electronic 9, 38, 43, 52, 54, 58, 92, 112, 119, 130–32, 219, 222, 245, 264
EMI 20, 34–35, 49–51, 93, 96, 104, 123
endorsement 117–18, 185
England 18, 51, 53, 135, 146, 152, 244
entrepreneur 87, 96, 186–87, 218, 221

entrepreneurialism 86, 147n, 213
entrepreneurship 86, 187, 192–93, 217, 255
eroticism 111, 122, 144–45, 214, 216
ethnicity 37, 44, 63, 81, 134–39, 143, 160, 186, 201, 252, 255
ethnocentric 13, 255
ethnomusicology 14n, 153, 165, 235
eurocentric 5, 124
Europe 4–5, 9, 14n, 15–16, 18–19, 21–23, 26, 28, 39, 42–45, 47–54, 58–60, 64–65, 83n, 117, 120, 137, 140, 143, 145, 150, 158, 161, 164, 208, 237, 252, 256–59, 264
Europeanization 16, 262–63
exoticism 30, 113, 120, 123, 157, 202, 217
expressive isomorphism 11, 130–32, 264

Fascism 44, 64–65, 255, 257, 264
fashion 12, 17, 65, 71, 77, 88, 90, 92, 100, 102–103, 105, 119, 124, 126, 174–75, 177–79, 185, 187, 192, 198–99, 201, 211–12, 214, 219, 222, 245, 257, 259
feminism 13, 53, 67–68, 77, 179, 200, 208–13, 220, 228, 240–51, 260
    black 112, 208, 212
    first-wave (*see* Suffragette)
    fourth-wave 208, 212
    Gaga 220
    second-wave 108, 208, 241–42
    third-wave 208, 244
femme fatale 75, 121, 215
festival 30–31, 53, 119, 151–52, 166, 181, 206–207, 238, 244, 247, 266
file-sharing 222, 224
film 21, 25, 27–28, 39, 43, 45–46, 54, 86, 94–95, 99, 108, 121, 130, 143–47, 157, 165, 175–77, 186, 196–97, 223, 246
    music 27, 143–46
    noir 177, 214–15
flamenco 28–32, 158
folk 15, 19, 24, 28–29, 46, 50, 145–46, 152, 156, 159, 184
    music 14n, 24, 30, 36, 38, 46–47, 52, 78, 153, 169, 244, 259
    rock 53, 77
    songs 23, 25, 65
Folkways 46–47
Fordism 5, 9, 42, 262
France 18, 31, 34, 42, 52–53, 83n, 93, 132–33, 135, 150, 260n

Gabriel, Peter 155, 167, 170, 234–36, 238–40
gadget 226
gaming 95–96

Index

gangsta rap 92, 137–40, 142, 149n, 194–95
gay 194, 198, 228, 249
gaze
    female 112
    homosocial 198
    male 11, 78–79, 81, 105, 107–14, 190, 199, 215, 217–20, 242, 264
genius 16–17, 22–23, 32, 71, 89, 107, 165–66, 198
genre
    music 11, 50, 73, 78, 82n, 132, 142, 243
    pseudo- 11, 147, 150
Germany 18, 21–22, 31, 34, 42, 49–50, 52–53, 64, 66, 93, 132–33, 135–37, 140–41, 256–59, 260n
girl power 210–11, 241, 246
glam 179, 199
glamour 14, 29, 151, 199, 213
global firm 180, 229–30, 264 (*see also* corporation)
globalization
    after 3, 8, 262–64
    alter- 260
    cultural 2, 11, 97, 126–27, 266
    economic 6, 59, 98, 100, 126, 260
    modern 1–2, 4–8
    musical 3, 8, 60, 126, 262–63
glocalization 135, 137
goth 219
gramophone 17, 22, 25
Greece 18, 28, 83n, 260n
guitar 23–24, 30, 32, 56–57, 62, 77, 153, 161, 167, 198, 201, 204–206, 259 (*see also* electric guitar)

Haza, Ofra 122, 124
heavy metal 59, 65–66, 74, 92, 179, 197–200, 259
hegemony 2, 7–9, 77, 81–82, 84, 86–87, 91, 97, 136, 179, 189, 227n, 230, 251, 255, 260, 263–64, 266
    masculine 67–72, 107, 251, 263–64
heterogeneity 125, 238
high art 16–17, 91, 112, 175
hip hop 32, 92, 96, 111, 115–16, 130, 132, 177, 179, 185, 188–89, 191, 197, 218, 244, 265
    cool 191–97
    German 135–43
    global 132–35
    political 251–55
Hollywood 18, 21, 28, 43, 61, 64, 85, 89, 109, 143, 147, 176, 185, 196, 213, 215

homogenization 1–2, 11, 30, 97, 102–205, 224, 264
homophobia 65, 194, 196
homosexual 196, 199–200
homosexuality 199
human rights 38, 236, 239–40, 260
hybrid 2, 25, 29, 32, 125, 144–46, 151, 161, 172, 222
    identity/ies 2, 9, 32, 56, 59, 143
    music/s/al forms 10, 38–39, 97, 127, 158, 236
hybridity 7, 12–13, 36, 125, 127, 130, 132, 134, 147, 159, 172, 236, 252
hybridization 1–2, 11, 32, 55, 125–26, 128, 130, 168, 238–39

image industry 88, 90, 126
incorporation (musical) 168, 191, 236–37
India 4, 18, 21, 24, 118–19, 143–44, 148n
indie 54, 151, 161, 207–208, 211–12, 245–47
Indipop 143
individualism 12, 23–24, 81, 87, 89, 166, 191, 195, 209, 211–12, 222, 227–28, 255, 267
individualization 209, 217, 225
    hyper- 225
industrialization 1, 9, 15–17, 19, 33, 38, 81
inequality 2–3, 13, 37, 59–60, 86–87, 101, 110, 115, 193, 210, 228, 250–51, 256
internet 1, 67, 85, 88, 94, 104, 113, 132, 144, 150, 156, 165, 177, 183, 221–24, 227, 250, 257, 259
Islam 72, 254
iTunes 183, 223

Japan 5, 18, 24, 42, 44, 50, 52, 83n, 93, 99, 117, 135, 148n, 223, 231, 260n
Jay-Z 178, 185, 187, 192
jazz 19, 21, 25, 32, 36, 44–45, 47, 49–50, 52–53, 57, 60–62, 120, 151, 164, 175–78, 195, 244
journalism 69–70, 75, 97, 174, 177, 243
justice 232–33, 260, 267
    social 3, 13, 230, 232–33, 260

Khan, Nusrath Fateh Ali 155–56, 164–68, 238
Kulthum, Umm 26–28, 112

label (music) 13, 47, 186, 188, 248, 258
    independent 161, 248
    major 105 (*see also* Big Three)
Lady Gaga 179, 200, 211–12, 219–20
language 57, 59, 61, 67, 76, 79–80, 88, 99, 111, 129, 131–32, 134–36, 138–39, 144–

45, 158, 160–61, 167, 169–70, 175–76, 181, 184, 186, 193, 205, 253, 263, 265
Latin America 23, 33, 39, 41, 58, 82n, 117
Latin pop/popular music 18, 41
Lebanon 24
left-wing 83n, 141, 179, 230, 241
license 48, 182
licensing 18, 182–83, 186
LP 17, 24, 43, 45, 50, 52, 58, 83n, 144

Madonna 67–68, 92, 103, 130, 177–78, 185, 200–201, 259
magazine 58, 68, 78, 94, 153, 156, 198, 201, 205, 227n, 244, 247 (*see also* zine)
Mapfumo, Thomas 55–57, 130
masculine 69–73, 77–78, 81, 107, 109, 117, 176–77, 192–93, 196, 198–201, 209, 215, 241, 243–44, 251, 256, 263–64
masculinity 67, 70, 73–74, 80–81, 146, 179, 188, 191, 193–200, 221
  hyper- 179, 191, 194, 197–98
mass media 7, 9, 14n, 17, 25, 28, 35, 38–41, 55, 59, 97, 131, 210, 264
mbalax 35, 57, 169–70
mbira 55–57
microphone 19, 23, 198
Middle East 4, 21, 24–26, 113, 120, 122–24, 145, 204, 249
migrant 2, 132–33, 135, 137–40, 164
migration 1, 7, 31–32, 125, 132–33, 135–36, 150, 225, 237
Minaj, Nicki 111, 117, 185, 212, 266
minstrelsy 60, 176
misogyny 67, 72, 74, 77, 109, 111, 190, 194–96, 218–19, 249
Mitchell, Joni 77–82
modernism 126, 264
modernity 15, 25, 33, 56, 62, 91, 125, 127–28, 130, 171–72
modernization 1, 8, 15–16, 25, 29, 31, 33, 38, 81, 125, 171, 262
  musical 8–9, 15–17, 30, 33–34, 59, 236, 264
Motown 47
movement
  civil rights 253
  feminist 210, 241–42, 246, 248
  liberation 38, 56, 72, 241
  nationalist 38
  of people 1–2, 145, 222
  political 64
  punk 75, 151, 244
  riot grrrl 12, 244–48

rock 58
social 241
women's 76, 208
MTV 6, 11, 43, 88, 96, 103–104, 107, 110–12, 137, 144–45, 177, 184, 212, 254, 264
multiculturalism 14, 151, 164, 232, 238, 240, 260, 264
music
  art 7, 21–28, 33–34, 38, 52, 120, 145
  black (*see* black music)
  business 10, 13, 45, 59, 68–69, 126, 150, 179, 202, 209, 237, 241–43, 246, 248
  classical 21–24, 28, 35, 39, 45, 47, 49–50, 61, 92, 119, 147, 153, 158, 165, 264
  contemporary 83n, 187, 244, 249
  fascist 64, 259
  folk 36, 46–47, 52, 169, 259
  traditional 7, 14n, 15, 18, 35–36, 39, 55–57, 125, 159, 168
  white power 44, 257–59

Napster 182, 222–23
narcissism 71, 176, 198
nationalism 44, 55, 134, 252, 255, 260
  black 140, 251–54
  musical 23, 56
  white 13, 255
Nazi 21, 44, 64–67, 257–59
N'Dour, Youssou 57, 168–72, 233, 239
neoliberalism 3, 8, 10, 13, 15, 84, 86–88, 91, 114, 127, 132, 147n, 148n, 180, 188–89, 220, 225, 227n, 228, 231, 240, 243, 260, 262–63, 265
New Zealand 16, 19, 54, 103, 244
Nicks, Stevie 75–77
nostalgia 44, 135, 157, 208

objectification 48, 107, 109–10, 194, 200
OECD 6, 85, 223
oligopoly 45, 106, 167, 202
omnivorousness 131, 200
opera 22, 26, 30, 49, 61, 121, 244
Orient 120–22
Orientalism 29–30, 113, 120–22, 124, 234, 264
other (the) 2, 24, 59, 68, 71, 80–81, 119–21, 123, 159, 202, 232–33, 243
  gendered 81
  racialized 3, 13
othering 3, 8, 10–11, 59–60, 67, 82, 91, 112, 115, 120–21, 233
otherness 10–12, 59, 67, 110, 114–16, 119, 121, 124, 128, 132, 137, 196

pan-African 135, 252
Paraguay 23–24, 57–59, 82n, 83n
patriarchal 76–81, 101, 108–11, 199–200, 209–10, 217–20, 242
patriarchy 11–12, 71, 77, 81, 109, 112, 190, 194, 196, 200–202, 218–19, 227, 245, 249–51, 263
    imperialist white supremacist capitalist 6, 10, 188–89, 196–97, 241, 263
    multi-racial white supremacist 6, 188–89, 193, 196, 211, 218, 227n, 230, 263
Perry, Katy 44, 94–96, 100–102, 118–19, 212, 220, 266
phonograph 17, 26–27, 43, 61
piracy 34, 104, 150, 186, 223
player piano 17
PolyGram 50–51, 54, 96
pop-rock
    aesthetic 10, 34, 57, 92, 129–30, 204
    music 9–10, 34, 43, 55–56, 125, 131, 148n, 150, 189–90, 231, 262, 264
postdemocracy 3, 8, 13, 148n, 227, 229–30, 240, 255, 260, 264
postfeminism 12, 179, 188, 191, 208–10, 212–14, 217, 220, 241–42
post-Fordism 5, 84, 86
post-identity 196–97
postmodern 12, 28, 91, 98, 126, 178, 196, 202
postmodernism 90–91
postracialism 188
Prince 177–78, 200–202
privatization 86–87, 103, 145, 225–27
production
    musical 7, 15, 33, 97, 150, 158
pseudo-genre 11, 147, 150 (*see also* genre)
punk 54, 65–66, 75, 130, 141, 151, 166, 184, 206, 208, 210–12, 244–48

queer 189, 198, 200, 220, 231, 243, 246

race records 19, 44, 60–62
racialization 60, 63, 67, 115, 189
racism 6, 12, 61–62, 64–65, 102, 112, 114–16, 118–19, 134–35, 140, 151, 188, 193, 196, 218–19, 227, 234, 242, 245, 252–53, 259, 263 (*see also* anti-racism)
ragtime 19, 36, 38
Rammstein 99–100
rap music 132, 134, 141–42, 184, 251–52
RCA 45–46, 51, 94
Real World 13, 155, 167, 236, 238–40
rebel 73, 176–78, 205, 208, 257
reggae 32, 38, 41, 57, 65

representation 11, 42, 64, 73, 75, 91, 107–109, 120, 122–24, 158, 162, 200, 202, 235, 263
resilience 12, 188–91, 193, 211, 218, 220–21, 227n
resilient looking 190, 217–20
right-wing 13, 41, 65–66, 86, 230, 253, 255–57, 260, 261n
Rihanna 103, 116–17, 148n, 220, 265
riot grrrl 208, 210, 244–49
rock 9, 11, 28, 32, 35, 37–38, 40, 43–44, 46, 48, 50, 52–56, 70, 75, 77–78, 80, 83n, 92, 99, 107, 112, 119–20, 130, 136, 141, 144, 148, 161, 166, 170–72, 179, 197–99, 204, 206–208, 231, 234, 242–47, 256–57, 259, 264, 266
    and gender 72–75
    in Paraguay 57–59
    Nazi 65–67
rock 'n' roll 9, 43, 46–47, 49, 53, 59, 62, 72, 177, 191, 197, 207, 242, 264
Romanticism 23–24, 71
Ruby 112–14
Russia 18, 21, 153

samba 39–41, 82, 133–34
Saudi Arabia 249–50
Sawhney, Nitin 164–65
secular 7, 26, 28, 57, 146, 166
self
    enterprising 186, 282
    neoliberal 87–88
    public 12, 89, 184, 226–28
selfhood 157, 166
Senegal 57, 71–72, 133, 168–69, 172, 173n
sexism 6, 12, 67, 69, 71–72, 102, 110–12, 140, 188, 194–96, 218, 227, 247, 249
sexualization 111–12, 114, 212, 215
Shankar, Ravi 119–20, 150, 153
shock 65, 190–91, 212, 245
singer-songwriter 77–81, 103, 184, 250, 259
sitar 119–20, 150, 153, 164
skin bleaching 116–18
skinhead 65–66, 259
slave 61, 63–64, 82n
slavery 16, 63–64, 82n, 148n, 175, 253
social media 100–101, 185–86, 208, 211, 218, 226
socialism 13, 42, 49–50, 66, 84, 255
solidarity 37–38, 66, 76, 139, 160, 236, 253, 255
Sony 50, 93–94, 96, 170, 186, 225
soul (genre) 60, 62, 153, 177, 207

Soviet Union 48–49, 51
Spain 23, 28–29, 31, 39, 82n, 83n, 133, 140, 260n
Spears, Britney 105, 110, 179, 186, 212, 214–17
spectacle 74, 102, 108–109, 118, 166, 168, 191, 199–200, 221, 233
standardization 5, 10, 84, 92, 100, 104–106, 126, 131, 152, 224–25
stereotype 41, 63, 77, 138, 193
Sting 122–23, 169–70, 234–35
stratification 3, 62
subordination 63, 81, 108, 148n, 194
Suffragette 241
sunglasses 177
supremacy 114, 116–17, 183, 196–97
Swift, Taylor 103, 190, 231
syncretic 9, 25, 36–41, 59, 124, 134, 143, 145–47
synergy 90, 94–96, 103, 185

talent 18, 46, 62, 75, 79, 102, 161, 166–67, 225, 243
taste 16, 22, 47, 92, 131, 147, 160–62, 174, 181, 188, 216, 224
    omnivore 131
    univore 22
technology/ies
    broadcasting 9, 15, 59, 264
    communication 5, 84–85, 143, 179, 224
    cool 227
    digital 8, 84–86, 132, 144
    information 85, 180
    mobile 222
    new 9–10, 15, 17, 45, 53, 176, 182–83, 264
    recording 7, 20, 23, 34, 81, 92, 94, 150
television 25, 28, 43, 52, 85–86, 88, 90, 93–95, 99, 103–104, 107, 112, 127, 130, 145, 156, 165, 175, 182, 186, 211
Tinariwen 202–208
TNC 6, 51
tourism 18, 29, 31, 157, 160, 200, 237
tradition 12, 15–17, 19, 24, 52, 55, 70, 72, 78, 100, 121–22, 129, 147, 159, 161, 168, 171–72, 175, 244, 251, 256, 266
transnational 2, 6, 11, 84, 91, 97–98, 102, 104, 127, 134–35, 143, 145, 150, 162, 179, 185, 225, 252

transnationalism 86, 125, 135
travel 1–2, 121, 127, 157, 237

UK 34, 83n, 93, 95, 104, 114, 148n, 152–53, 156, 161, 168, 207, 223, 231, 235, 238, 244, 260n
Universal (label) 93–96, 192
urbanization 1, 7, 9, 15, 22, 29, 31, 33, 37–39, 41, 55, 264
US (United States) 2, 8–10, 14n, 15–16, 18–22, 26, 34, 37, 39, 42–48, 51–54, 58–61, 64, 73, 82n, 83n, 85–86, 88, 92–93, 99–101, 103–104, 106–107, 109–10, 114, 117, 120, 125–26, 132, 134, 136, 138–40, 142, 153, 170, 175–76, 184, 207–208, 223, 242–45, 247, 253–54, 256, 258–59, 262–65

vernacular 28, 48–49, 53, 88, 136, 147, 179, 264
Victor (company) 18–19, 46, 51, 61
violence 61, 65–67, 109, 115, 133, 139–40, 144, 191, 193–96, 200–201, 243, 245, 251, 259
virtuosity 74, 166, 198–99
virtuoso 22–24, 32, 120, 124, 166
voyeurism 110, 114, 194, 197

Warner (label) 51, 79, 93, 95–96, 107, 162, 201
Wehbe, Haifa 112–14
welfare state 86, 228–30
westernization 1, 15–16, 25–26, 28, 38, 81, 100, 125, 162–63, 169, 262, 264
whiteness 16, 117, 143, 259
witch 68, 77
WOMAD 151–53, 155, 166, 168, 207, 238
World Circuit (label) 41, 152–53, 155

xenophobia 140
xenophobic 65

youth 9, 35, 43, 47, 52, 64–66, 88, 95, 107–108, 131, 134–36, 140, 142, 157, 174–77, 186, 232, 244, 248, 251, 254–57, 264

Zimbabwe 55, 56, 161
zine 245, 247 (*see also* magazine)

www.ingramcontent.com/pod-product-compliance
Lightning Source LLC
Chambersburg PA
CBHW050323020526
44117CB00031B/1611